THE GRAMMAR OF EMPIRE IN EIGHTEENTH-CENTURY BRITISH WRITING

This study examines the complex role of language as an instrument of empire in eighteenth-century British writing. Focusing in particular on the relationship between England and Scotland and strategies of national and imperial consolidation, Janet Sorensen explores the tensions which arose during a period when the formation of a national standard English coincided with the need to negotiate ever widening imperial linguistic contacts. Close readings of poems, novels, dictionaries, grammars and records of colonial English instruction reveal the deeply conflicting relationship between British national and imperial ideologies. Moving from Scots Gaelic poet Alexander MacDonald to writers such as Adam Smith, Hugh Blair, and Tobias Smollett, Sorensen analyses British linguistic practices of imperial domination, including the enforcement of English language usage. The book also engages with the work of Samuel Johnson and Jane Austen to offer a wider understanding of the ambivalent nature of English linguistic identities.

JANET SORENSEN is Assistant Professor of English at Indiana University, Bloomington. She has written a number of articles on eighteenth-century topics.

THE GRAMMAR OF EMPIRE IN EIGHTEENTH-CENTURY BRITISH WRITING

JANET SORENSEN

PUBLISHED BY THE PRESS SYNDICATE OF THE UNIVERSITY OF CAMBRIDGE
The Pitt Building, Trumpington Street, Cambridge CB2 1RP, United Kingdom

CAMBRIDGE UNIVERSITY PRESS
The Edinburgh Building, Cambridge, CB2 2RU, UK   http://www.cup.cam.ac.uk
40 West 20th Street, New York, NY 10011-4211, USA   http://www/cup.org
10 Stamford Road, Oakleigh, Melbourne 3166, Australia
Ruiz de Alarcón 13, 28014 Madrid, Spain

© Janet Sorensen 2000

This book is in copyright. Subject to statutory exception and to the provisions of relevant collective licensing agreements, no reproduction of any part may take place without the written permission of Cambridge University Press.

First published 2000

Printed in the United Kingdom at the University Press, Cambridge

Typeset in Baskerville 11/12.5pt [VN]

A catologue record for this book is available from the British Library

Library of Congress Cataloguing in Publication data
Sorensen, Janet.
The grammar of empire in eighteenth-century British writing/Janet Sorensen.
p. cm.
Includes bibliographical references and index.
ISBN 0 521 65327 4 (hardback)
1. English literature – Great Britain – History – 18th century.
2. Imperialism in literature.   3. Politics and literature – Great Britain –
History – 18th century.   4. Literature and history – Great Britain – History –
18th century.   5. Great Britain – Colonies – History – 18th century.
6. English language – 18th century – Rhetoric.   7.Colonies in literature.   I. Title.
PR448.I52 S65 2000
820.9'358 – dc21

ISBN 0 521 65327 4 hardback

For my parents, Donald and Beverly Sorensen

Contents

List of illustrations	*page* viii
Acknowledgments	ix
Introduction	1
1 Scripting identity? English language and literacy instruction in the Highlands and the strange case of Alexander MacDonald	28
2 "A grammarian's regard to the genius of our tongue": Johnson's *Dictionary*, imperial grammar, and the customary national language	63
3 Women, Celts, and hollow voices: Tobias Smollett's brokering of Anglo-British linguistic identities	104
4 The figure of the nation: polite language and its originary other in Adam Smith's and Hugh Blair's *Lectures on Rhetoric and Belles Lettres*	138
5 "A Translator without Originals": William Shaw's Scots Gaelic and the dialectic of (linguistic) empire	172
Epilogue. Jane Austen's language and the strangeness at home in the center	197
Notes	224
Bibliography	283
Index	303

Illustrations

1. Title page to Alexander MacDonald, *A Gaelic/English Vocable*, Edinburgh, 1741. By permission of the Newberry Library. *page* 30
2. From Alexander MacDonald, *A Gaelic/English Vocable*, Edinburgh, 1741. By permission of the Newberry Library. 45
3. From Robert Cawdrey, *A Table Alphabeticall*, London, 1604. Reproduced from the facsimile edition, Scholars' facsimiles and Reprints, Gainseville, Florida, 1966. 70
4. From Samuel Johnson, *A Dictionary of the English Language*, London, 1755. By permission of the Lilly Library. 83
5. From William Shaw, *An Analysis of the Gaelic Language*, London, 1778. By permission of the Lilly Library. 182

Acknowledgments

Writing this book has taught me, again, that it is collaboration and exchange that produce the meaning and value of even the seemingly most autonomous of work. Like language itself, this book makes no sense, would not in fact be possible, without the social interactions that have formed it.

I am deeply indebted to a wide number of teachers, students, interlocutors, friends, and family. The fluidity they have allowed between those relationships is among the gifts for which I thank them. Early conversations with my graduate teachers put this project in motion. Jim Bunn sparked my initial interest in eighteenth-century studies and offered readings of the period's discourses which I continue to find fascinating and fantastically useful; Deidre Lynch inspired me to read creatively and closely, was unstintingly supportive, and provided a model of scholarship at once intellectually imaginative and politically committed; and Bill Warner introduced me to key conversations in the field and helped me to see the relevance of eighteenth-century cultural debates to the questions and contests of our own historical moment.

Friends from graduate school, including Stephanie Foote, Simon Joyce, Anne McGrail, Annie Fergerson, Ron Ehmke, and Marten Clibbens, all sustained me in ways that ranged from the ethereal, in the wit and brilliance of their company, to the prosaic, in their careful eye as readers and attentive ear as listeners.

Colleagues at Indiana University, including Judith Anderson, Purnima Bose, Patrick Brantlinger, Eva Cherniavsky, Jonathan Elmer, David Elton Gay, Mary Favret, Kathryn Flannery, Tom Foster, Susan Gubar, H. James Jensen, Ken Johnston, Andrew Miller, Eugene Kintgen, Richard Nash, Joan Pong Linton, Michael Rosenblum, Lee Sterrenburg, Nick and Julia Williams, and graduate students in my spring 1996 and spring 1999 courses have both challenged and nourished my work in ways in which they might and might not be aware.

Fellow scholars Elizabeth Bohls, Toni Bowers, Leith Davis, Ian Duncan, Susan Fitzmaurice-Wright, Shalini Puri, Joel Reed, Richard Sher, Clifford Siskin, Zoreh Sullivan, and Kathy Temple have asked the questions and provided the details and references that helped make this book what it is. Its shortcomings are mine alone.

Family members, including David and Sarah Sorensen, Susan and Bob Holt, Joan and Emil Sorensen, and George and Barbara Sorensen, have encouraged me in the many steps that preceded and comprised this project.

Benjamin Hoz, polyglot and polysemous, faced the final hours of this book's production alongside me. My gratitude for his sweetness, sanity, and steadfast support remains beyond words.

Linda Bree at Cambridge University Press was all one could hope for in an editor – patient, advocative, insightful.

This book would not have been possible without the generous institutional support of the English Department and the Research and the University Graduate School at Indiana University, the Center for Humanities at Oregon State University, particularly its driving force, Peter Copek, and the Folger Library Grant-in-Aid program. I hope future young scholars will be as fortunate as I have been in receiving support for their research in the Humanities in the coming years.

Introduction

"If I could rightly be said to be either, it was only because I was radically both."
"Henry Jekyll's Full Statement of the Case," *Dr. Jekyll and Mr. Hyde*

Robert Louis Stevenson's monstrously doubled figure points back towards a long lineage of self-divided Scottish literary heroes – and authors. If one literary antecedent is James Hogg's Robert Wringhim, whose murderous doppelgänger betokens the duality of a Calvinist worldview in a modernizing Scotland, the extended cultural ancestry includes a wide range of Scottish figures similarly marked by a "combination of opposites."[1] Frequently, the fault line of their vexed multiplicity is most recognizable in language, a point not lost on Stevenson, whose own text represents speech and writing as alternately capable of producing and concealing distinct identities. Jekyll supplies his "deformed" and "displeasing" double with a differentiating signature "by sloping my own hand backward," from which we might intuit the strange inversion of identities suggested by this same yet opposite graphic presentation of self – when the handwriting of Jekyll and Hyde are compared, there remains "a rather singular resemblance; the two hands are in many points identical."[2] If Jekyll can be traced through his writing, he can also alter that writing for other, "detestable," selves. Alternatively, Hyde is able to cash a check drawn on Jekyll's account because his handwriting is identical, yet Jekyll's second self is marked as essentially different by a shrunken, hunched body *and* a "husky, whispering and somewhat broken voice" (18) with uncontrollable "hissing" (16). Reminiscent of the dilemma of the eighteenth-century Scottish – they might "pass" as English through their writing, but their voiced accent would remain a telltale sign, revealing non-English status – Hyde's distinguishing orality naturalizes his difference as if mapped onto the body itself. Then again, Hyde's marked body disappears in the moment of writing, and Jekyll conceals it in his polite, metropolitan conversations.

If questions of language, writing, and cultural identity are different today – and, as I shall argue, the "combination of opposites" model misrecognizes those questions even as eighteenth-century contexts posed them – the complex position of the Scots continues to haunt British culture today. Nearly three hundred years after Union with England, Scots have voted overwhelmingly to re-establish a Scottish parliament. The opening of the Scottish parliament in 1999 marks only the latest in an ongoing series of transformations of a British constitution, whose legitimacy has, nonetheless, been staked on its longstanding continuity with an immemorial past. Viewed as a bold move into the future – two Scottish reporters write of the vote for a separate parliament: "Scotland reached to the millennium . . . as the people embraced home rule" – this vote has had as much, if not more, to do with perceptions of Scotland's past.[3] In this book I pursue one important aspect of those perceptions of the past, the cherished myth that an ages-old national language – once pure, if now corrupted through international contact or imperial dominance – could bespeak a single culture and people for whom it forms the very basis of national identity. My argument is that the relationships between England and Scotland did not challenge so much as produce the idea that languages conform to national borders. The notion that such an ages-old national language could underwrite Great Britain's national unity is, of course, untenable in the face of its historically checkered linguistic geographies. Yet the notion of an English national tongue consonant with England's national borders, or a Scots national tongue, consonant with Scotland's, remains equally untenable. Not only is the Scots Gaelic language of the Highlands distinct from the Scots language of the Lowlands and the English of England, but each of these discrete languages is internally divided in ways that have made them, at times, incomprehensible to fellow speakers of Scots Gaelic, Scots, and English. It was not only transformations in print technology that fostered the understanding of these languages as singular, unified, and national. It was also the historical and political context that represented and codified linguistic differences in order to incorporate them into a larger British nation.

Difficulty in terminology here signals the complexity of the case of language and national identity in Britain. Is Britain a nation? Or is it merely a state composed of the four nations of Wales, England, Scotland, and Ireland? To what extent does it make sense to group the three non-English nations as a "Celtic periphery" of England?[4] And further, in what ways might we characterize the relationship of England to those Celtic peripheral nations as colonial, making England the imperial nation reigning over those internal colonies? While I show the ways in which a focus on linguistic theories and practices illuminates the uses and limitations of the internal colonialism model below, I want to explain here, briefly, my navigation of this semantic terrain. Great Britain existed as a state formation before the existence of any collective consciousness of a common British national culture. Yet powerful incentives, in the form of international wars, extra-territorial imperialism, and British commercial interests, made a specifically British national consciousness an imperative. I track the contradictions of the attempts to legitimate the idea of a British national culture in the face of the diverse cultures that composed the geo-political entity of Great Britain – and the specific forms of resistant nationalisms articulated in relation to those attempts. At points, Anglo-British efforts at consolidation resemble colonial practices. I spotlight Scotland, in fact, because at times it functioned as a training ground for linguistic practices of imperial domination, including in the Highlands the enforcement of English language usage. Like Leith Davis in her book *Acts of Union: Scotland and the Literary Negotiation of the British Nation 1707–1830*, however, I also point to the ways in which the "nation" of Scotland is itself self-divided.[5] I extend her analysis to argue that Scotland's relation to the Union has been the crucible in which modern notions of the Scottish and British nations as predicated on respective shared language practices have been formed.

The elite of the Lowlands of Scotland have functioned as junior partners in Britain's global imperial project, and so, as I argue below, any sweeping characterization of Scotland as a "colonial" space makes little sense. Yet, as I also demonstrate below, in the eighteenth century the theories and practices of cultural, specifically linguistic, domination of the Highlands come close to those deployed in more distant colonial contexts. At the same time in the Lowlands, privileged Lowlanders consciously mimicked the language of cultural capital, the standard English that printers, teachers, and writers – at times those very Lowlanders – were working to establish. If they never experienced the kinds of economic and political domination that took place in the Highlands, a rampant Scoto-phobia in mid-eighteenth-century England, with its ruthless assertion of the inferiority of all things Scottish, particularly the Scots language, put aspiring Lowlanders on cultural and linguistic tenterhooks. The simultaneous mimicry and standardization of English in which they engaged might offer important revisions to our understanding of the relationship between colonialism, nationalism, and language.

The complex negotiations between Scotland and England, particularly in the dilemma of Scotland's status as both peripheral zone of otherness and central participant in Britain's extra-territorial empire, helped shape and complicate the language-nation connection. The reciprocal yet contradictory pressures that the ideological demands of imperialism and nationalism place on all "national" languages in imperial contexts are dramatically instanced in the case of Scotland. Yet Scotland and all of the countries of the "Celtic periphery" occupy a position similar to, but distinct, from Britain's other colonial spaces. For instance, Britain sought not only to bring the Highlands under the rule of empire but also to integrate them into the British nation.[6] Scotland, then, represents a limit case of the ambivalence between sameness and difference which characterizes imperial English culture in all of Britain's colonial relationships.

Forced to negotiate between a devalued, native "peripheral" Scots or Scots Gaelic and a newly official, recently standardized "central" English, eighteenth-century Scottish writers, more than a few critics have argued, existed in a condition understood as a kind of cultural schizophrenia.[7] Although I will argue that the model is more complex than that description allows, this divided state, between convincing imitation and menacing difference, would appear to be borne out in any number of fascinatingly elaborate cases which instantiate the full repertoire of ambivalency we have come to associate with colonial discourse.[8] Gaelic-speaking Highlander Alexander MacDonald, for instance, sang the praises of English language instruction and taught English to poor children in the remote Hebridean islands. Yet his own publishing history is strikingly ambivalent: he produced the first Gaelic/English glossary (1741), announcing that he hoped it would cause English to "spread more quickly" *and* published the first print edition of Gaelic poems (*Aiseirigh Na Seann Chanain Albannaich* [*The Resurrection of the Ancient Scottish Language*], 1751). The first secular book to be published in Scots Gaelic, MacDonald's collection featured militantly Jacobite poems celebrating Scots Gaelic culture and language. Better known to English audiences, Tobias Smollett was one of the most important arbitrators of English literary taste in mid-century Britain; his *Critical Review* and now-canonical novels founded standards of belletristic judgment and

English usage, the political resonances of which extended far beyond the confines of private discrimination.[9] Yet Smollett's resistance to understanding language as primarily regionally divided – as he saw it, both Celts and Londoners might speak a corrupt "outsider" language or a flawless "insider's" English – renders a singular judgment of his cultural location impossible. Like Smollett, Lowlanders Adam Smith and Hugh Blair confidently adjudicated proper English usage. Yet if the powerful impact they had on consolidating standard English and instituting its canonical literary representatives has been documented, their less-often noted critique of a refined print English and their nostalgia for an oral Gaelic are equally significant.[10] Finally, not long after MacDonald's fearless ventures into print Gaelic, its "Celtomaniac" codifiers, such as William Shaw, exhibit, like Blair, a sentimental feeling for Gaelic's "living" quality at precisely the moment they codify it in accord with "universal" structures found in English and Latin.

This book, then, is about what linguistic practices, representations, and theories produced in particular imperial, colonial, and national configurations of eighteenth-century Britain tell us about the interdependent relationship between those configurations. Eighteenth-century Britain witnessed the solidification of the modern nation state and the cultural appendages we now associate with it. The constellation of political, economic, and social conditions of that period increasingly organized capital and culture into a centralized national block. Much, of course, has already been said about the rise of British cultural nationalism and about its close connections to the consolidation of British empire.[11] Of late, a number of cultural and literary studies have begun to emphasize the shaping influence not only, or even primarily, of Englishness on its colonies near and far, but also of imperial experience and colonial culture on national identity itself, and this is a relationship I elaborate in the course of this work.[12] Another grouping of eighteenth-century studies examines that period's obsession with language – its origins, structures, improvements, and literary representations. Another still has pursued the connections between print, participation in a public sphere, and national consciousness.[13] Few scholars have put together these developments, particularly the centrality of empire to imperial national linguistic and literacy developments. That is what this book does in its analysis of the gendered figurations of the complex linguistic interactions between England and Scotland. I show how the mutually constitutive yet deeply conflicting relationships between national and imperial ideologies are nowhere more apparent than in linguistic use and theorization – the very site upon which so much of nationalism's naturalizing rhetoric and empire's claims to superiority are based.

While the term "cultural schizophrenia" might appear so loaded as to provide infinite readings of the conditions and actions of the writers I study, it is in fact too limited to describe fully the context or import of their cultural work. For the "split [*schiz*] mind [*phrene*]" that the term denotes suggests a failed reconciliation between two pre-existing identities. To understands the, by turns, lithe and maladroit mediations of these writers as ambivalent responses to pre-given English ("foreign") and Scottish ("native") cultures leaves the most interesting questions unasked. It is like interpreting Jekyll/Hyde's tortured response to the dilemma of "good" versus "evil" or "culture" versus "nature" without investigating the ways in which the text constructs, characterizes, and genders those very concepts. Alternatively, it is like analyzing the text's construction of good and evil or nature and culture without considering the ways in which the one is figured through an Anglo-Saxon type, smooth-faced, tall, and decorous, the "pink of proprieties," while the other is represented through a conventional Celtic type, hirsute, dwarfish, "troglodytic," "ape-like," and deformed to the point of being "hardly human" (18).[14] The question to ask is not simply how these Scottish writers actively negotiate their own cleft cultural identity through English, Scots, and Scots Gaelic languages, but how, as they write themselves through those languages, they also simultaneously construct an understanding of the social meaning of those languages and the character of the cultures that have produced them. As they position themselves through language, these writers help develop notions of orality and literacy, dialect and standard, linguistic particularity and universality, femininity and masculinity, and their distribution between colonial, imperial, and national languages. My interest in these writers, then, is more in terms of how their writings can be seen to work both with and against an internally expanding British empire. If, for instance, Adam Smith's notion of the "impartial spectator" resident in all subjects' psyches figures the self-estrangement of the assimilating Scot, the aesthetics of polite language that he develops naturalizes and evades the foreignness of a standard language beyond Scottish borders.[15] Further, as its Scottish writers move between an externally imposed fixed standard and an internally derived vernacular, they illuminate the condition of all Britons.[16] "Core" writers such as Samuel Johnson and the "heir" to his authoritative English style, Jane Austen, do not escape this doubledness, though it is of a quite different sort, and are responding to, as often as they are dictating, the terms of these cultural linguistic productions. The writings of the center turn out to be as ambivalent as those of a supposedly "schizophrenic" periphery.

In her discussion of the formation of British identity, Linda Colley has rightly noted that British nationalism is not merely a homogenizing compound of multiple identities:

> Britishness [does not] supplant and obliterate other loyalties. . . . Identities are not like hats. Human beings can and do put on several at a time. Great Britain did not emerge by way of a 'blending' of the different regional or older national cultures contained within its boundaries . . . nor is its genesis to be explained . . . in terms of an English 'core' imposing its . . . hegemony on a helpless and defrauded Celtic periphery. (6)

This model of Britishness, however, is fairly static. While the "hats" metaphor implies active switching, as the person wearing the hats assumes a different identity with each new hat, the peaceful coexistence of identities that can be "put on several at a time" is not always born out in the linguistic evidence. And not only the notion of oscillation between but also fabrication of identities is key to an understanding of Scottish and British linguistic deployments in this period. Whatever it is that human beings are putting on "several at a time" when they construct their identities, those qualities actually change in these relationships. Presenting a more complex conceptualization of British national identity than most, Colley is still open to the criticism that her historiography underestimates the messy and open-ended inventions of British identity as well as the incompatible antagonism between some of those identities, such as allegiance to the Hanover regime versus a resistant Jacobitism.[17] In language the fluid mediations between and constructions of affiliations, which sometimes remain unavoidably contradictory, are most obvious, for these produce multiple senses of what it means to be English, Scottish, Celtic, and British. If the writers I examine can be said to be any of these, it is because – to rephrase Jekyll's statement – they have played a central role in concurrently defining them all.

GRAMMAR UNIVERSAL: EMPIRE AND THE GRAMMAR OF MIND OUT OF TIME

In titling this work "The Grammar of Empire", I shift the object of study from the subject's pathologized response to an intrusive dominating culture to, instead, mutually informing British linguistic cultures. The use of linguistic criteria also reorients post-colonial studies away from a strictly visual criteria focused on the imperial gaze. As I locate particular writers within imperial/national linguistic cultures, I urge an acknowledgment of their agency in producing those cultures. In this way, I hasten to add, I am not arguing either that language and the discourse of linguistics finally determine world views or social conditions or that imperial linguistic discourse always follows a fixed, universal structure, as static conceptions of "grammar" would suggest. Thus, I take issue with Ferdinand De Saussure's notion of language as "a self-contained whole and principle of classification," a notion which V. N. Volosinov has critiqued as "the idea of language as a system of conventional, arbitrary signs of a fundamentally rational nature" that arose in "the Age of the Enlightenment."[18] In contrast to the understanding of language and its principles as self contained, Volosinov argues that "language acquires life and historically evolves precisely in concrete verbal communication, and not in the abstract linguistic system of language forms, nor in the individual psyche of speakers" (95) and that "the laws of language generation are sociological laws."

In using "grammar," then, I invoke a figural sense of "grammar" as a characteristic system and view the relationship between imperial, national, and colonial linguistic cultures as a syntax wherein all elements contribute to the overall meaning through their relationships to each other. My metaphorical use of the term points to the ways in which this study turns to questions of language, without itself being a work of historical linguistics. I am not a linguist, and, for better or worse, I do not bring formal and quantitative linguistic methodologies to bear on my analysis. I hope, however, to point students of cultural studies toward the important work of historical linguistics. A focus on writings about, representations of, and evidence of language practices can tender a more nuanced reading of the internal differences within those amorphous entities of Gael, Scot, and Briton. For that work reveals that there is no way to predict, via post-colonial theories, the lexical and syntactical accommodations speakers and writers will make in specific circumstances. Study of those accommodations often reveals more complex and supple responses to cultural domination than we might have anticipated. One case in point is the work of Charles Jones, who in his studies of eighteenth-century grammars and pronouncing dictionaries published in Scotland shows that they "were not holding up for emulation some version of London society English, but rather a Scottish standard of the type spoken by members of the clergy, the universities and the legal profession."[9] Thus Jones's statistical work discovers an important modification to a formula of colonial mimicry. In highlighting the contradictions in the cultural productions of the British nation and empire and the identities of the men and women who lived in and under them, linguistic criteria move analysis beyond a structuralist binary of self/other.

As a literary critic making use of the methods loosely and perhaps clumsily grouped under the rubric of "cultural studies," I incorporate Marxist, feminist, and post-colonial approaches to texts ranging from linguistic archival material, including dictionaries, documents regarding colonial English instruction, grammar books, to poems, novels, and rhetoric and elocution lectures. If these are, obviously, not the only ways of approaching these texts, they are inarguably essential to a better understanding of them. As I redirect post-colonial and cultural studies toward the complexities disclosed in the linguistic density of cross-cultural linguistic practices, I aim for a revaluation of such historical linguistic research. While the research of my own study is markedly distinct from its methods, I aim to reveal the adjacency of historical linguistics to the questions cultural studies and post-colonial studies ask. Both historical linguists and students of cultural and post-colonial studies need to address that adjacency, ideally bridging it through research. Such interdisciplinary studies, more difficult than they initially seem, offer a valuable means of deeper understanding of inter-cultural social relationships.

Since each chapter discusses a particular interactive linguistic site and the interventions of specific writers, here I want to trace the movement of the "characteristic principles," so to speak, that a reading of those specific histories together reveals. As I examine the principles, rules, and structures that an adoption of grammar simply as a figure for empire's rhetoric and workings might leave unhistoricized, I do so by historicizing the concept and connotations of grammar itself. More than merely metaphorical, my use of the term "grammar" is also literal, and a brief review of its multiple historical meanings might suggest several of the project's key concerns and even the trajectory of its central argument. A telling reflection of relationships of the first British empire and a weighty intervention in the rise of the second, the *Oxford English Dictionary (OED)*, nonetheless, illuminates a subterranean history of closely related cultural and linguistic relationships in its dutiful recording of "grammar's" sedimentary meanings. Once "pertaining to letters [and] literature," the *OED*'s gloss of "grammar's" Greek "*grammatike*" and Latin "*grammatica*" roots tells us, the term's meaning "came to be restricted to the linguistic portion of this discipline." That more narrow designation arose, we should not be surprised to find, in the context of pedagogy, specifically, perhaps surprisingly, in the context of colonial pedagogy, as instruction in an official version of Latin took place in Rome's colonies.[20] No longer anyone's "native" tongue, Latin became a language in which meaning was produced not through daily interaction but through books and in classrooms, and "grammar" contracted into its sense as "rules" and "principles" necessary for training generations into a language that was not their own. This restrictive understanding of language – that it can be reduced to and known through a set of fixed rules – points to an important observation resonating in this project: the pressures of translation and bilingual instruction, in the context of imperial power relationships, shape the ways in which language itself will be understood. Similarly, attending to linguistic practices, from the pedagogical methods of English instruction in the Highlands to the linguistic choices different Scottish subjects make in their writing and speaking, reveals the ways in which the experience of empire changed the way eighteenth-century British writers thought about how language works.[21] As Alexander MacDonald and William Shaw translate and codify Gaelic, for instance, they borrow from and augment a universalist view of linguistic structure. The view of language fostered by such systematizing projects, a view Volosinov names "abstract objectivist" (*Marxism*, 45), would, in turn, influence the vision of language in the center, in England.

The conceptualization of language and its structure that arose in the pedagogical, philological relationship to "foreign" languages can be mapped with greater specificity. In the eighteenth century, as the *OED* informs us in its first listing of the term's meaning, "grammar" came to be understood as "general, philosophical, or universal grammar, the science which analyzes those distinctions in thought which it is the purpose of grammar to render in expression." The theory of universal grammar promoted early on by the highly influential Port-Royal Grammar (*Grammaire générale et raisonnée* 1660, English translation, 1753) held that there existed a uniform structure of language behind surface distinctions of particular languages, that "the general features of grammatical structure are common to all languages."[22] Noam Chomsky details the assumptions of the "philosophical grammarians," as he calls subscribers to the theory of universal grammar, regarding case. He approvingly describes how for these grammarians "the use of the names of classical cases for languages with no inflections implies only a belief in the uniformity of the grammatical relations involved, a belief that deep structures are fundamentally the same across languages, although the means of their expression might be diverse" (45). While Chomsky's acquittal of the philosophical grammarians sounds harmless enough, my point is to place their vision of language within an historical context, noting the ways in which such ideas facilitated less innocuous imperial ideologies.[23] The assumption of "a uniform set of relations into which words can enter, in any language" and the assumption which accompanies it, that "these correspond to exigencies of thought" (45), are particularly troubling when we remind ourselves that for the philosophical grammarians, Western European languages, primarily Latin, provided the basic grid of those "uniform sets of relations" into which were plugged "colonial" languages such as Gaelic, and rarely vice versa.

In the eighteenth century, the most widely recognized exposition of universal grammar was James Harris's *Hermes, or a Philosophical Inquiry Concerning Universal Grammar* (1751), from which the *OED* takes its illustrative citation. Harris, following, in his way, the basic tenets of universal grammar, twinned grammatical structures with corresponding universal structures of human thought. Lauded throughout the eighteenth century, Harris's text delineates the "universal" parts of speech, explaining their purpose and their links to the universal human thought patterns they represent. Believing that there is "one truth, like one sun, that has entered human intelligence through every dark age" (x–xi), Harris suggests that a universal truth and reason have existed across time and space. Neither the universal grammar that reflects universal human thought processes nor the truth such thought structures discover and announce, then, represents an understanding or knowledge that has developed across time, nor do these thought structures and knowledges vary across space. Basing his thought on "one of the great commonplaces of the eighteenth century: the doctrine of the uniformity of human nature in all ages and climes" (Aarsleff, *From Locke*, 159), Harris argues, "As far as Human Nature, and the primary genera both of substance and accident are the same in all places ... so far all languages share one common Identity" (11).

Seventeenth- and eighteenth-century theories of languages were formed in relationship to a wide variety of social and political world views, and I certainly do not want to be amiss in failing to acknowledge, for instance, the theological discourses at work in theories regarding linguistic diversity, in which Babel represents humans' fall from grace, or regarding the possibility of universal language, in which the assembly of a universally understood language might signify redemption. My point is merely to add another dimension to our understanding of these linguistic theories, specifically the historical exigencies of empire and translation, for these have been underexplored in discussions of eighteenth-century linguistics. Harris's understanding of thought structures, and the grammatical categories that rendered them, as universal is related, I want to argue, to colonial linguistic encounters.[24] Britain moved across spaces such as the Highlands of Scotland, constructing and assimilating cultural and linguistic differences. The work of translators and missionaries in these locations depended upon a view of language as transparent, based upon universal principles of reason and language's ability to "mirror" the world around it. The *Encyclopaedia Britannica* entry for "grammar as a science," for instance, explains that it "examines the analogy and relation between words and thing; and thus furnishes a certain standard by which different languages may be compared."[25] Embedded in this understanding of "grammar as science" are linguistic negotiations of imperial encounters and the belief that the "disorder" of the languages Europeans confronted in their voyages of discovery and relations of commerce and war could be "reduced" to universal thought patterns and their grammatical expression.

Part of what allows thought and its communication to "share one common identity" and to move across times and places without modification in theories of universal grammar is their detachment from material embodiment. Harris writes, "SOME things the MIND performs thro' the BODY . . . Others it performs without such medium; as for example when it thinks, and reasons, and concludes." While Harris acknowledges particular differences between the material expression of languages, his primary interest is in language as a dematerialized reflection of those idealist, universal powers of mind, a focus made obvious in his figuration of Hermes, the god of language and namesake of Harris's text. The frontispiece to his work depicts Hermes as a head wearing a winged helmet. As Roy Harris has noted, this image implies that "no other part of the human figure but the Head . . . was deemed requisite to rational communication."[26] As it courses through time and space, a "winged" language incurs no shift in meaning in this graphic display of language as incorporeal.[27] Questions of embodiment are also linked to a complex vector of competing rhetorics of gender, and I shall consider these as I show how a disembodied Latin, and then English, gets contrasted to an embodied – and feminized – Gaelic. Similarly, the calls for "linguistic austerity" or plain language of the earlier part of the century also invoke gendered concepts of language and identity.[28] National and imperial concepts of language engage highly gendered tropes which I explore throughout this work.[29]

THE GRAMMAR OF BOOKS AND SCHOOLS: COLONIAL AND NATIONAL PEDAGOGY

The "imperial grammar" understanding of language had much to do with the demands of pedagogy, and it is important that a further listed definition of "grammar" is as a shorthand for both "grammar book" and "grammar school." Both assumed a learned distributor and ignorant receiver of knowledge; as institutionalized bodies assembled pedagogical subjects for instruction, they also instituted relations of power. In its early post-classical sense "grammar" meant not simply the study of Latin or of linguistic structure, but also "knowledge peculiar to the learned class." It is here that we find, as etymologists rightly delight in observing, the etymological origins of our present-day "glamour" – a Scots corruption of "grammar" – a linguistic factoid introduced to English speakers and readers by none other than Walter Scott. Although the occult (and now feminized) learning to which "glamour/grammar" refers is today clearly distinct from the prosaic knowledge of linguistic rules, the synonymy is not accidental, especially in the Scottish context. The provenance of the "learned class," "grammar" inevitably claims to mirror but, in fact, establishes power relationships between speakers of various regional, classed, and gendered languages.

An additional, related strand of this project is an analysis of those pedagogical relationships and the parallels between colonial and imperial national linguistic instruction. Enabled by the rise of print and by monumental shifts from religious to secular consciousness, the standard language constructed throughout the eighteenth century figured centrally in the national subject's ability to imagine him or herself as a member of a national community.[30] The grammar books which transmitted that standard were more often to be found in the hands of English children (primarily boys), women, and middle-class aspirants to a higher status than in the hands of, say, Highland students. Their position in relation to the "official" language was not dissimilar.[31] The model of language that a universal grammar theory made possible was equally useful for construction of an official national and imperial language and aligned the position of Scottish pedagogical subjects and the "vulgar," women, and children of England. Yet the technologies of linguistic codification deployed in the Highlands, the Lowlander methods of linguistic and literary transmission, and the colonial tropes circulated to describe the project of linguistic standardization in England – a matrix of practices and theories I refer to as "imperial grammar" – worked both with and against the building of a national language.

Not only were the "marginal" members of the national community and/or empire in a position to "learn" the meaning and terms of their membership, but middle- and ruling-class members of society were also learning these terms, in ways less obvious than the rote instruction of the classroom and grammar book. Interestingly, as we trace further meanings of "grammar" we find that, in a way we ourselves might recognize today, grammar also came to mean a term of derision, a meaning also emerging, as James Harris's use of "universal grammar" did, in the eighteenth century. The *OED* cites Tobias Smollett's *Humphry Clinker*'s protagonist, Matthew Bramble, cranky but tender-hearted patriarch of the Bramble clan. Bramble describes his pedantically articulated observation that "exceptions . . . confirm and prove a general canon" as a "grammarian's phrase." Here the grammatical is associated with an older, male character who is, however, becoming outmoded. If the association with Matthew suggests the "masculine" authority of grammar as a disciplinary force, his awkwardly phrased maxim also connotes the overly formal, unnecessarily wordy phrasings of grammatically correct statements. The association with Matthew, then, also makes "grammar" less than glamorous.

NATIONS AND LINGUISTIC DIVERSITY: THE GRAMMAR OF TIME OUT OF MIND

With evidence for the decline in regard for Matthew's type of grammar, a merely logical, overtly prescriptive grammar, I trace a cultural national counter-movement ostensibly positioned against imperial grammar. While imperial grammar codified "timeless" principles of linguistic structure and a static national lexicon, it was also seen to empty language of its immediate impact and to undermine the notion that the nation's best speakers spoke the best language "naturally." Immediacy, particularity, and aesthetic discrimination were becoming increasingly important factors in the rhetoric that linked nation and language.

In *Hermes*, Harris attempts to address the discrepancy between universal grammar and discrete national languages. An idea of language thoroughly saturated in an Enlightenment world view, Harris's theory of universal grammar negotiates as it reinforces the homologous universal/particular and synchronic/diachronic binaries he believes operate in language. While the "grammar universal" that underlies language "respects principles essential to all languages" (11), national differences accent language in practice. Harris relegated the linguistic diversity evident in material language – particular words and ways of saying things, as opposed to their underlying universal structures – to national essences and institutions. Just after the declaration that all languages "share one common identity," Harris goes on to explain that

As far as peculiar species of substance occur in different regions; and much more as far as the positive institutions of religious and civil policies are every where different; so far each language has its peculiar diversity. To the causes of diversity here mentioned, may be added the distinguishing character and genius of every nation. (11)

Specific distinctions between languages arise from historical ("religious and civil politics") and essential ("the character and genius of every nation") causes, both of which distinguish between diverse languages on a national basis. In one stroke Harris connects the particular to the national and insists on the "essential" character of national difference, posing a contradiction not as easily circumvented as his theory maintains.

It is at this juncture that the pressures of imperial and national ideology begin to work, not with each other, both codifying and systematizing a stable grammar, but against each other. The British, in their imperial expansion – which entailed a claim to move righteously through a widening compass of space – needed to negotiate, as more than a few writers have shown, a complicated relationship between difference from and similarity to their colonized subjects.[32] An emerging nationalist rhetoric first adopted and then rejected the "universal" model of language that would make them the same. What imperial technologies gave the standardizers of national languages in promising a means of fixing and stabilizing the language, they took away in the implication that language is both highly mediated through static structures and not particular to a unique community of people. Such a model of language worked against the nation's claim to an unassimilable identity stretching across time, and the limitations of that model led both English and Scottish writers to develop an alternative model of language as unique and particular customary practices through time – ancient and untranslatable, culturally specific and material – and capable of eliciting deeply felt bodily responses, and in these senses ungrammatical.[33] This gave rise both to a rejection of earlier, disembodied visions of language in general and English in particular and to a symbolic reclamation of Gaelic, which had already been figured as embodied and historied (and gendered female) in ways that English had not. In their nostalgia for an oral Gaelic, for instance, Blair and Shaw believed Gaelic had a capacity to motivate a physically sensed national affiliation in a way that print English could not. Similarly, Robert Fergusson responded to Johnson's Latinate and abstract English lexicon by representing a Scots vernacular of a particular and material nature.

To sum up the movement of my argument, I rethink two main theories of language of the eighteenth century in terms of the divergent ideologies of the British empire and nation, referring to them as the "imperial grammar" and "cultural nationalist" models respectively.[34] Whereas the British nation claimed – and still claims – to speak across distance in time, eradicating difference over generations in that particular nation, the British empire claimed to speak across distance in space, universalizing experience over the miles of its new territories. Despite my critique of the "plain" rational, space-transcending language in the imperial grammar context, and the figurative, culturally specific, time-transcending language in the cultural nationalist context, however, I do not mean to critique either of these concepts of language *per se*. My point is to explore the claims that colonial and national discourses make about these conceptions of language within a particular historical location and to critique them *in that context*.[35] I aim to trace a dialectic through which, in specific historical contexts, these views of language produce each other; the synthesis of this dialectic suggests an alternative, transnational model of language which I shall outline below.

REVISING THE INTERNAL COLONIALISM MODEL

In this study I interrogate the use and limits of one of the more influential models of the Scottish/English relationship, Michael Hechter's concept of internal colonialism, which he defines as "the political incorporation of culturally distinct groups by the core."[36] Hechter asserts the colonial economic status of Wales, Ireland, and Scotland, yet the emphasis of his model is on colonial cultural and geographical relationships.[37] The internal colonial relationship consists of:

two collectivities or objectively distinct cultural groups: (1) the *core*, or dominant cultural group which occupies territory extending from the political center of the society . . . out-ward to those territories largely occupied by the subordinate, or (2) [the] *peripheral* cultural group. The model therefore assumes that these respective cultural groups are to a large extent regionally concentrated (emphasis in original). (18)[38]

In his understanding of hierarchies as spatially organized, a concept which he borrows from Immanuel Wallerstein, Hechter perceives a parallel cultural hierarchization. In time the geographically/culturally peripheral group might well "reactively assert its own culture as equal or superior to that of the relatively advantaged core" (10). Thus, for Hechter, not only are inequitable power structures arranged along the lines of culture and geography, so too are the possibilities of resistance.

However, Hechter's analysis is in some need of refinement. Linda Colley has argued that his characterization of the diverse cultures of the "Celtic periphery" as homogeneous maintains a core/periphery dichotomy not subtle enough to express the intricate relationships operating between these spaces (12).[39] As a binary, the internal colonial schema leaves undisturbed notions of a dominant homogeneous English culture and an equally homogeneous – "authentic" – subordinate Celtic culture. This understanding of the Scottish/English relationship, which is, for Hechter, an instance where "separate groups remain culturally intact" (48), is precisely the model I critiqued at the opening of this introduction, for it implies separate, essential, homogeneous English and Celtic cultures – a separateness and internal homogeneity that I countered with Jekyll's formulation. Thus, despite much evidence to the contrary, the internal colonial model forces Hechter to argue that post-1688 England was marked by "great political stability" and to echo H. J. Hanham's assertion that "there was in England no social or religious barrier between landlord and tenant . . . such as there was in . . . Scotland" (118). In addition, Hechter argues that the Celts remained "culturally intact": their "ancient culture and 'ethnicity'" persisted, despite multiple external contacts (48).

The spoils of empire lured a great number of Scots to London and to the assimilation of a standard "English" (which they also helped construct), and this movement did divide the "literati" from their less well-placed and less socially mobile compatriots. It does not follow that the England to which they assimilated was homogeneous, in which class and gender divisions were not profound, or that their influx into the "core" left no mark on a consistently singular English culture. Further, while early in the eighteenth century, and prior to the Hanoverian victory at Culloden, the English did "disparage the indigenous culture of their peripheral group" (64), the Celtic revival of the later part of the century rebuts the notion that they insisted upon a pure English language and culture free of Celtic influence. Nor, consequently, does it follow that the Celtic culture of those "left behind" was left unchanged by the imperial relationship to England. Lowlanders who assimilated English culture and language, such as James Macpherson, Hugh Blair, and William Shaw, were notoriously ambivalent about the Scots Gaelic language of the Highlanders and, in fact, helped to shape it, and attitudes towards it, in ways which were taken up repeatedly in the next century. The version of their "own culture" which they "reactively asserted" in the face of English cultural domination could never be an "untainted" version of pre-Anglo-contact culture.

My point in arguing against the notion of an "authentic" Scottish culture that could be asserted to challenge Anglo dominance and against the habit of viewing linguistic dualism as merely a Scottish phenomenon is not to expose an "invented tradition" of Scotland.[40] Rather, I counter its informing logic which, when followed through to the English context, naturalizes "native" English; if Scottish writers are conflicted merely because of an imposed "foreign" language, then the English language of English speakers, readers, and writers must be somehow free of alienating hierarchies. My overriding goal is to contest those characterizations of English (and "Celtic") national languages, and the consciousnesses they would consolidate, as homogenous and stable, characterizations made even by otherwise perceptive critics.[41] The notion of a homogeneous national language papers over the distinct hierarchies of national social structures within both Scotland and England.[42]

Part of the problem with the internal colonial model – a problem which has already been addressed in much post-colonial theory, but has yet to be fully taken up by theorists of the internal colonial relationship – is its dependence on notions of spatial hierarchization. Convinced that capital relations establish hierarchies that ultimately supplant spatial borders, Manuel Castells has described the breakdown of traditional place-based structures of social and political control by the "placeless logic of an international economy" in the late twentieth century as "a space of flows superseding a space of places."[43] Over two hundred years earlier, Lowland and English investors who stood to gain from the free flow of capital between the Highlands and the rest of Britain made every effort to facilitate the movement of capital by destroying the localizing forces that hindered it.[44] In attempting to abolish the "regional" languages of the Highlands, the British state and capital interests aimed to overcome the particular cultural practices that tied them to distinct territorial affiliations. As Tom Nairn writes, "Modernization and all its concomitants (industrialization, political democracy, general literacy, etc.) notoriously tend towards uniformity and the standardization of many aspects of existence" (*Break-up*, 134). The resulting "space of flows" depends upon

> historically established mechanisms of social, economic, and political control by the power-holding organizations. Since most of these mechanisms of control depend upon territorially based institutions of society, escaping from the social logic embedded in any particular locale becomes the means of achieving freedom in a space of flows connected only to other power holders. (Castells, *Informational*, 349)

What emerges from the destruction of regional cultures, however, is not pure uniformity or standardization. Finally, Castells writes, "The process of uneven restructuring within regions and cities also increases disparity within regions rather than among regions" (346).

I want to make use of Castells's model to propose a transnational explanation of the multiple, layered senses of what it means to be English, Scottish, Celtic, and British. In one of the more helpful summaries of the formation of nation-states, Robert J. Foster uses the terms "central" and "peripheral" not to describe imperial/colonial relationships, but to name the internal hierarchical relationships catalyzed through the installation of an official national culture. He writes, "Nation-state formation thus entails a (hegemonic) struggle for homogenization that constructs a (contested) border between the central 'mainstream' and peripheral, heterogeneous units of the nation-as-community."[45] The divisions perpetrated by the imposition of Standard English in England and Scotland, then, were not necessarily regional alone. Mary Louise Pratt has argued that the heterogeneity submerged in the linguistic construct of "linguistic community" is the figure in the carpet of all such communities.[46] Rather than consolidating the superiority of English and of all English speakers, no matter the class or gender, over Scots, the imposition of English on Scotland constructed a transnational dominant language against which the lower classes and marginalized populations of both countries might (but rarely did) respond together. Not only severing and hierarchizing populations along geographical lines, a common dominant language also divides populations into linguistic "haves and have nots" across geocultural borders. As the linguistic prescriptivism of the age rewrote "the heterogeneities of actual usage" into "binary oppositions of right and wrong," as Lynda Mugglestone notes, and as the use of right and wrong language increasingly announced not regional location but class position, "not 'the place of a man's birth' . . . but instead his social level," the focus on region alone remains untenable.[47]

In contrast to a core/periphery model of internal colonialism, the transnational model stresses the increasing economic and linguistic stratification not only between empire and colony but also *within* the regional "core" and "periphery." Just as displaced languages, such as a feminized Scots Gaelic, are reified in the transnational cultural marketplace as folk cultures, the hierarchies – of gender, of class – within the regional "official" national language become rigidified. The tropes of syncretism and hybridity used to describe the resulting societies are not in themselves inherently progressive. What remains necessary is a retention of Hechter's notion of the unevenness of economic and power relationships in relation to the "pluralism" embraced by Britain's constructions of itself. If the linguistic Anglicization of eighteenth-century Scotland represents an early attempt to transcend the "space of places," then we might begin to situate these processes at an earlier historical moment. Importantly, we might perceive the productive contradictions within and resistance to these phenomena not as recent developments but as inhering in the very logic of imperial cultural and economic exchange.

THE LINGUISTIC DIALECTIC OF EMPIRE: RE-READING COLONIAL AMBIVALENCE

Of vital importance to our understanding of British cultures, the linguistic productions I study are not simply highly sensitive barometers of cultural interaction and power relationships, but are also key arenas of negotiation and struggle. In the linguistic dialectic I track, the universalizing impetus of imperial grammar enables and then gives way to a nationalist particularism, and the possibility of transnational exchanges of language emerge from this productive opposition. This first chapter, in which I rehearse the theory and practice of "imperial grammar" and a later Gaelic "cultural nationalist" response, consists of two parts. First, I analyze the records of the Society in Scotland for the Propagation of Christian Knowledge (SSPCK), a charity group which administered the education of poor Highland children into Protestantism and English literacy. I discuss Highland SSPCK instructor Alexander MacDonald's

Gaelic/English Vocable (1741) as a representative moment of "imperial grammar," characterized, as it is, by a naive and telling belief in the transparent relationship between word and thing and, consequently, between languages. Yet the rhetoric and strategies of the SSPCK were impossibly doubled: as they made use of such glossaries to enforce a print literacy on Highland populations, the SSPCK also created Gaelic literate subjects. Second, therefore, I consider the ways in which the Society's dual address redirected its goals, examining further the case of MacDonald, a Highland Jekyll and Hyde, as he initially assimilated and then rebelled against an imposed Anglo-British linguistic culture.[48] In his militant Gaelic poetry MacDonald called for the insurgence of the Gaelic-speaking people and their language, manipulating, and not manipulated by, the linguistic identities he performed.

While Samuel Johnson's "partitioned" identity has been much remarked, in Chapter 2 I re-read one aspect of that "self-division," his ambivalence between a prescriptivist stance and a resigned descriptivist stance as he compiled his *Dictionary* (1755).[49] I argue that this ambivalence was a function of Johnson's pivotal role in the shift in England to a cultural nationalist view of language. Although his *Dictionary* bears many of the traces of forms and assumptions of "imperial grammar," including a gendering of language as female in its chaotic reproduction, he also attempts to incorporate – and in the process reifies – the prosaic language of the people. A core figure who is himself divided, Johnson's case asks us to rethink the relegation of cultural ambivalence solely to the periphery. In his attempt to incorporate both the "imperial grammar" vision of language and a newly emerging view of language which privileges customary usage, Johnson constructs a national language which is ostensibly inclusive and yet implicitly exclusive of the language of most British subjects – a "nobody's language," in a sense. The reader of his *Dictionary* recognizes his or her gendered, classed place in the nation at the very moment of recognizing the national language. I close the chapter with the Scots protests to his lexicon as they assert a material Scottish culture in the face of Johnson's at-once incorporating and alienating language.

Lamenting the fate of the Jacobites at Culloden while at the same time playing a leading role in the politicized literary culture of London, Tobias Smollett also exhibits the contradictions we have come to associate with "colonial ambivalence." Yet the distinctions between his case and MacDonald's forcefully iterate the multiplicity of positions suggested by such ambivalence. Clearly, not all colonial ambivalencies are alike. In Chapter 3 I show how in the impeccable style of his novels and reviews, Smollett helped establish the standard English consolidated in the eighteenth century. In emphasizing the central role of Lowlanders such as Smollett in producing London's print culture, I revise a critical tradition which foregrounds Smollett's Scottish identity and decries the "cultural dissociation" by which Smollett's "creative talent . . . suffered enforced dislocation from its cultural roots . . . severed by the Union from its cultural traditions."[50] The language of "severed roots" naturalizes the old dualism, in which an imposed artificial English weakens or "severs" a Scottish literary and linguistic national culture shared by all Scots. I am interested in stressing in Smollett, as in MacDonald, his active borrowing from and re-making of both English and Scottish literary and linguistic cultures and in relating his class status to the role he played in shaping notions of "Britishness." In the scatological "Celtic" dialect depicted in his novels and political periodicals – and spoken primarily by women – Smollett institutes the insider/outsider distinction used to determine true British status. His women and working-class English speakers use a language which is at once physically disgusting – "grace" becomes "grease" for example – and "embodied" to the extent that their mispronunciation highlights the oral dialect of these outsider characters. Spatial dichotomy gets rewritten in social terms, where a chain of associations between Celtic outsider/women/working-class English is no longer underwritten by geography.

The role of Lowlanders in establishing institutions of English studies has been most widely discussed in analyses of the rhetoric lectures of Adam Smith and Hugh Blair.[51] These Scots have long been acknowledged as central to the founding of "the new rhetoric," yet it is only in the last several years that scholars have begun to situate their important contributions to rhetoric studies, the institutionalization of literary studies, and the understanding of the relationship between literacy practices and modern subject formation within the "peripheral" space of Britain. If the contributions of these peripheral writers remind us, once again, that the center of imperial culture is endlessly displaced, they should also prompt us to recognize the ways in which the specific needs and ideological contours of place shape the character of those contributions. In Chapter 4 my interest in the respective *Lectures on Rhetoric and Belles Lettres* of Smith and Blair has less to do with their much remarked role in founding the rules of English vernacular and installing a canon of British writers than in their awkwardly naturalizing nationalist rhetoric connecting "native" language to feeling. They deploy aesthetic discourse to locate themselves and their students within a British nation through class-based critical perception. Attempting to map national identity onto the privileged body itself, they are, however, frustrated by their logocentric belief in the power of oral language.

Embodied, historied, affective, Gaelic promised the suturing linguistic powers that English lacked. In Chapter 5 I re-evaluate the late-eighteenth-century "Celtomania" in both England and Scotland that forwarded this belief. While the symbolic reclamation of Gaelic is often explored through the Ossian controversy, I examine the related writings of William Shaw and "Celtomaniac" poets and philologists such as John Clark, who "edited" *Works of the Caledonian Bards* (1778), to show how a transnationalism which initially eradicated the local now constructs a new version of it for sale in the cultural marketplace. In his *Analysis of the Gaelic Language* (1778), the first Scots Gaelic grammar to be published, Shaw mourns the loss of oral Gaelic while systematizing it through "universal" Latin/English structures. A local Gaelic – now feminized as a pale ghost to a thriving English – is thus produced alongside a global English. The idea of language as culturally specific discredits the view of language as rational and capable of the infinite translation empire demands. At the same time, this idea of language as culturally specific also disqualifies the much translated, much "corrupted" language of English from true national language status. While many have commented on the "pluralist" or "multicultural" sense of Britain that emerged out of the Celtic revival, few have insisted on the uneven relationships that dictated the terms of that synthetic culture. I end with the far-fetched claims of Gaelic philologists who argued that Gaelic was the originary language, in which sound and sense mapped onto each other perfectly; it, and not English, was, thus, the once-universal language. These Celtic writers adopt the universalizing claims which had been made, tracing the circle back, around English, in response to imperial confrontations with Gaelic. While the imitation of imperial rhetoric in the work of these Gaelic writers troubles imperial discourse, it also remains stranded in its fictions.

I argue that these cases illuminate the condition of British national linguistic identity itself, and I look at two archetypically "English" writers – Samuel Johnson and Jane Austen – to make that argument. In the Epilogue I return to England's "center," the lush green home counties and tony language depicted in Austen's novels. While Austen's novels have come to signal to generations of readers the Englishness of England, particularly through their language, I consider the ways in which "central" linguistic discourse is as doubled as that of "peripheral" assimilated spaces. The relative flexibility at the upper strata of British class structure put many middle class English subjects in the same position as assimilating middle-class Scots making their way into the elite, in part through decorous linguistic practice. Austen's novels proffer a domestic linguistic tourism, showcasing high-end use of the language unfamiliar to many outside the pages of her books. As I trace efforts to characterize Austen as shadow to or daughter of Johnson, I argue that as a necessarily doubled figure as a woman writer in this period, Austen estranges the "native English" language and its transmission, particularly through the formal method of free indirect discourse. Faulty cultural transmissions and linguistic misrepresentation function as "repetitions" that are never the same.

THE LIMITS OF CULTURAL NATIONALISM

It follows from my critique of the internal colonial model and my emphasis on the ways in which appeals to an "essential" linguistic culture internalize center/periphery models of power, that I am suspicious of the claims of Gaelic, Scots, and English cultural nationalisms; I am especially interested in exploring the ways in which linguistic practices and theories augment and problematize those claims. As Partha Chatterjee and David Lloyd argue, the shortfalls of resistant nationalisms lie in their dependence upon the rhetoric of imperial discourse.[52] This does not mean, however, that I perceive the political character and significance of all nationalisms as the same. To understand all nationalisms as contradictory, symbiotic constructions does not mean that the judgment of them ends in the same place. Instead, I want to retain the important distinction between oppressor and oppressed nations theorized by V. I. Lenin, which recognizes the qualitative differences between nationalisms which work with and against the prerogatives of empire.[53] Impossible to judge outside of specific global contexts, all nationalisms are not alike. Too many academic scholars, as Alok Yadav has pointed out, suspend the distinctions between oppressed and oppressor nations in a self-serving denunciation of both. Worse yet, if they do draw distinctions, these often work in favor of a "sound" European nationalism against a "dangerous" resistant nationalism.[54] The claims of particular nationalisms must be evaluated within a larger global system, and while we cannot expect to find a thoroughly effective opposition mounted on the claims of national culture difference, the nationalism of oppressed nations can represent a limited form of resistance within a larger context of imperialism.

However – and this is a significant however – just as we cannot characterize all nationalisms in the same way, we cannot characterize all efforts at critique of nationalism in the same way. If Hans Kohn, Anthony Smith, and the other "Western" writers on nationalism whom Yadav cites repudiate nationalism in order to "obscure . . . a more pressing distinction between 'official' nationalism . . . and 'insurgent' nationalisms" (200), this critique does not hold true for all critics of nationalism.[55] One might recognize and support the insurgent character in the nationalism of oppressed nations without giving uncritical support to the nationalist form that that insurgence takes. Thus, I want to reserve the right to criticize nationalisms of all stripes because their rhetoric and practice obscure the pressing distinctions of class and gender in the claims of a culture (and language) shared by all its members. While I applaud the ends of strategic essentialism that certain forms of linguistic nationalism offer, I am not convinced it is the most effective strategy for achieving liberatory ends. The negotiations of linguistic identities point to more complex and striated relationships than that strategy can address.

Much as we can relate the ongoing standardization of language to the movement of imperial capital and its tendency to eradicate difference, leaving dead languages, marginalized cultures, and reified cultural products in its wake, the appeal of alternative "national" histories is understandably strong. They have an enduring appeal because we are surrounded by linguistic standardizing processes, such as those of the composition classroom, when, for instance, the still popular *Elements of Style*, like its eighteenth-century predecessors, commands its students to "use orthodox spelling," "do not use dialect," "use figures of speech sparingly," and "prefer the standard to the offbeat."[56] The politics of such imperatives will not be lost on anyone who has followed the volatile discussions around English-only legislation or on anyone who has assimilated or educated students into a standard English and has remained sensitive to the cultural differences forsaken in that process.

The response to this scenario, however, must be something other than the charged linguistic relativism of the cultural nationalist model. That way of thinking about language – as the stable, unique product of hoary linguistic customs – is equally problematic. As Guillory has shown, the attempt to revalue particular cultural productions in the absence of considerations of relations of production leaves the logic of cultural nationalism in place. It is that logic, with its appeal to venerable tradition, which we must, ultimately, dismantle. Its dangers are recognizable in Britain's subordination of its national Arts Councils to the Department of Heritage. Such a shift in conceptualizations of cultural and even linguistic productions is chilling, as it suggests that they are what has been produced in the past, their value predicated on temporal remoteness. While cultural nationalism announces itself as a turn towards history, it is the multiple and alternative histories of languages, and not a single constructed history of English and its origins, which we must explore.

In insisting on the reciprocal relationships between English and Scottish languages and cultures, I extend and slightly trouble the contributions of my own forerunners, to whom my work is clearly indebted. Robert Crawford's groundbreaking study demonstrates the Scottish influences informing the most canonically "English" of literary and cultural traditions, and Katie Trumpener's subtly rendered and impressively historicized work on Celticism and British empire proposes the "centrality, interconnection, and international influence" of Anglo-Celtic literary cultures and identifies some of the key literary innovations of the late eighteenth century as having their "origins in the cultural nationalism of the peripheries."[57] It is, however, just such identification of origins, influences, and traditions that, one might argue, reproduce rather than abnegate the imperatives of national rhetoric formalized in a national canon, a cultural formation which, as Guillory shows, is closely tied to linguistic and literacy pedagogy. Such canon revision might be exactly the point if "insurgency" along Gaelic nationalist lines is the end of such cultural work. Yet it has been my argument that that nationalism and the conceptions of language on which it depends are a product of imperial relationships more effectively addressed through transnational responses.

Trumpener makes a compelling case for the "systematic underdevelopment of Englishness" that British empire wrought, an underdevelopment which leaves London not the center of Englishness but the "blind spot of a patched-together empire" (15). Yet what is the basis of unity, we might ask, for the "distinct, national, and non-English character" (16) that that empire precipitates in the peripheries? Where are their blindspots, so to speak? To counterpose a "cultural memory," somehow shared equally by all of the nation's members, to an Enlightenment imperialism, which relies upon a universalizing rationalization, might be posing the opposition in choices starker than they need be, and in terms perilously close to the national dualism long ascribed to the Scots.

The friction of difference in *all* cultures and languages is one of my abiding points. If my study of the language models and representations in evidence in the writing between England and Scotland in the eighteenth century begins with their critique – as I commence it here – it ends with a recognition of struggle and competing views of language as existing, not between nations, but between all language users, some of whom might come together briefly, contingently, but repeatedly to contest the powers that would make their languages the same. I stress the inventive transcodings of imperial messages of power, but not simply to celebrate a resistant nationalism. Instead, the creative borrowings of alternative linguistic communities demonstrate the limits of official languages and "national" literary cultures, hinting at progressive transnational links yet to be fully realized.

CHAPTER I

Scripting identity? English language and literacy instruction in the Highlands and the strange case of Alexander MacDonald

Nothing can be more effectual for reducing these countries to order, and making them usefull [sic] to the Commonwealth than teaching them their duty to God, their King and country and rooting out their Irish language.

An Account of the Society in Scotland for Propagating Christian Knowledge (1716)[1]

Mhair i fòs,	She [Gaelic] still endured,
'S cha téid a glòir air chall,	Her glory shall not fade,
Dhaindeoin gò	Despite the strangers' hate
Is mì-run mòr nan Gall.	She's not dismayed.
. . .	. . .
'S i labhair Calum	Famed Malcolm Canmore
Allail a' chinn mhòir;	Talked in Gaelic speech,
Gach mith is maith	And all on Alba's soil
Bha 'n Alba, beag is mòr.	Both poor and rich
'S i labhair Gaill is Gàidheil,	Both Gall and Gaidheal,
Neo-chléirich is cléir,	Clerical and lay,
Gach fear is bean,	All who could speak
A ghluaiseadh teanga 'm beul.	Did talk it in his day.
Alasdair Mac Mhaighstir Alasdair,	Alexander MacDonald, *The*
Aiseirigh Na Seann Chanain Albannaich	*Resurrection of the Ancient Scottish*
(1751)	*Language* (1751)[2]

Translator and schoolmaster for the missionary society which aimed to eradicate Gaelic from the Scottish Highlands, but also – and better known as – a famous Gaelic poet for the Jacobite cause, Alexander MacDonald (Alasdair Mac Mhaighstir Alasdair) straddled a nexus of conflicting intercultural contacts in the eighteenth-century Highlands. His critics have long celebrated him as one of the greatest Gaelic poets, not least for his ability both to preserve Gaelic literary traditions and to innovate a poetics that mixed Gaelic, English, Lowland Scots, and classical forms as evidenced in his 1751 collection of militant Jacobite poems *Aiseirigh Na Seann Chanain Albannaich* (*The Resurrection of the Ancient Scottish Language*).[3] Recent moves towards understanding British literature as not simply the literature of England in English, but also as inclusive of the literatures of the diverse languages and cultures of the British Isles might foreground this collection – the first secular book printed in Scots Gaelic – and its endlessly fascinating, chameleonic producer.[4] Yet considering MacDonald's "case" also revises our notions of Britishness and the relationship between the socio-cultural entities which constitute it. For MacDonald's work forcefully highlights the ways in which those linguistic and literary cultures are best understood not as a series of separate indigenous traditions, some supplanted by others, but as products of colonial and national discourses and resistant responses to their inconsistencies.[5] Not simply a matter of literary borrowings, MacDonald's work signals the adoption of Anglo-British notions of a single standard language and an affiliated cultural identity in the production of notions of Gaelic and British identities.

My aim in this chapter is neither to trace the multiple literary influences MacDonald reworks in his poetry, nor to demonstrate the intimate connection between his poetry and the general social context of the mid-century Highlands: that work has been executed comprehensively in the studies of Derick Thomson and Murray Pittock, among others.[6] Rather, I situate MacDonald's poetics in relation to his dismaying participation in the missionary group which sought to equate Gaelic language with ignorance and barbarism and to replace it with English and, it was hoped, a resulting political quietude. It was with that goal in mind, MacDonald averred, that he produced the first published Scots Gaelic/English glossary in 1741, ten years before the publication of his collection of incendiary Gaelic poems.[7] Yet MacDonald's complex response to the Anglicizing rhetoric around language and literacy reveals the ways in which the imperial forces that worked to root out the Gaelic tongue could not ultimately contain the ends to which that instruction would be put. The material that forms the basis of this chapter – records of English language and literacy instruction in the Highlands, the glossaries and translations produced for that instruction, and MacDonald's Gaelic verse – provide some of the richest, and most neglected, evidence of the intricacies of British imperial and nationalist cultural strategies.[8] Analyzing the conjunction of MacDonald's literary and literacy practices shows how the English literacy instruction, designed to devalue Gaelic, provided the theoretical and practical underpinnings for its revaluation.

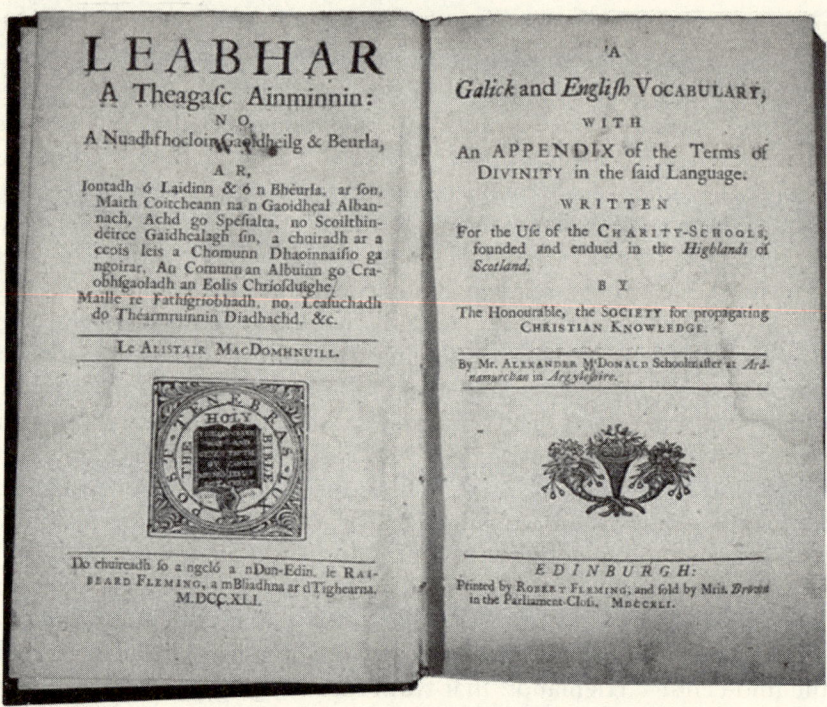

Figure 1. Title page to Alexander MacDonald, *A Gaelic/English Vocable*, Edinburgh, 1741. Photo courtesy of the Newberry Library, Chicago.

MacDonald's case thus disrupts an older model of British imperial practices and colonial responses, in which the British state sought to eradicate the threateningly different social organization of the Highlands in part through extinguishing the language and culture of the people it conquered. Further, as a kind of addendum to that model, a resistant nationalism is seen to reassert the value of its now-fading language and culture in the face of the imperial forces that imperil them – a resistance model seemingly encapsulated in the move and counter-move in the two passages that serve as epigraphs to this chapter. But it is not that simple. In demanding that Highland subjects translate their languages into an English idiom, the British summoned all of the ambiguities accompanying bilingual literacy and the enforced performance of national identity. Thus, if the logic of what Manuel Castells calls the "space of flows" demands that subjects transcode language and experience, such transcoding is notoriously "noisy"; neither message nor medium survives this transit intact.9 Newly literate populations and their defiant agendas occasionally interfere.

In this scenario, MacDonald does not merely recover suppressed indigenous language and poetry. Rather, he appropriates the very terms in which the British language converters couched their efforts to assimilate Highlanders. While Anglo-British administrators hoped to spread English in the Highlands and connect the English language to British authority and cultural identity, MacDonald's involvement in that process allowed him to help standardize Gaelic and link it to a new Gaelic national identity. The mutual relationship between British colonial discourse and the content and form of MacDonald's response suggests that MacDonald's writing was what Mary Louise Pratt has called autoethnographic – constructed "in response to or in dialogue with metropolitan representations."[10] It is fair to say, then, that MacDonald's verse exceeds the category of "Gaelic," thus problematizing Gaelic nationalist claims made around him by writers such as Thomson and Pittock. As Malcolm Chapman argues, Scottish literary critics have been too quick to adopt a seamless nationalist vision of MacDonald's poetry, attributing both a legitimating ancientness to its sensibilities and an impossibly proleptic quality to its politics as they trace an unbroken thread of pristine Gaelic culture from Jacobitism (and before) to twentieth-century Scottish nationalism.[11] However, if Chapman's analysis is salutary in its insistence on MacDonald's ambivalent character – and he points to Thomson's failure to mention MacDonald's Scots Gaelic/English glossary as evidence of Thomson's simplification of this complex character – he, like those he assails, stops short of mapping the relationship between the poetry and the literacy work. For Chapman, MacDonald's compliant preface to the glossary represents a "wholehearted acceptance of a status quo" (59), his later Jacobite poetry a function of a "failed career" and an attempt to escape the illiterate company of Highlanders (62). These approaches have placed limits on a complete understanding of MacDonald and the workings of cultural and linguistic interaction in the Highlands. Alternatively, a fuller consideration of MacDonald in relation to institutionalized literacy instruction in the Highlands reveals transcultural interaction and resistance in a place and time rarely credited with such achievements.

In the first half of this chapter I examine the social history and (contradictory) ideological assumptions behind Anglo-British efforts to integrate the Highlands through language and literacy, the project in which MacDonald participated for over a decade. The first of the opening quotations articulates the aims and brutality of the project, revealing the violence behind the formation of a single "British" identity, to be sure. Undoubtedly, English instruction, tied to a Whig and Protestant worldview, helped "foster a British, rather than a local or even Scottish loyalty."[12] Yet the more closely we examine linguistic and literacy theory and practice in this context, the more readily we perceive the complexities that make clear-cut binaries – particularly the spatial hierarchy of "core" and "periphery" – impossible. Antithetical rhetorical positions and methods gave rise to contradictions available for MacDonald's appropriation.

To explore the resulting doubled character of translating colonial subjects and their resistant literacies, in the second half of this chapter I consider MacDonald's case; his highly politicized "distortions" of the message of English linguistic superiority draw both from that message's assumptions about cultural identity and literacy and from adapted Gaelic literary traditions to forge an alternative identity. In tracking the "migrancy" of English language and literacy in the colonial Highlands, I hope to reiterate the validity of Sara Suleri's formulation that "the migrant moment of dislocation is far more formative, far more emplotting, than the subsequent acquisition of either postcolonial nation or colonial territory."[13] In the "carrying across" that translation entails, English literacy displays a surprising volatility, while the ends to which the technology of literacy gets put cannot be completely determined by the imperial grammarians. This phenomenon reminds us of Tom Nairn's important qualification that standardization takes place only through "prolonged struggle against (and forced compromise with) social diversity."[14] In fact, the notion of linguistic standardization, so important for the building of the British nation, itself informed the move toward a Gaelic standard with its own cultural national importance. Contemporaneous with a hegemonic (instrumental) Enlightenment discourse, adjacent to the center of the thriving British empire of the eighteenth century, the imperial grammar operating in the Highlands and MacDonald's wily response to it demonstrate that we need not cross oceans or centuries to discover the contradictions of that imperial grammar.

DOUBLED TALK: THE COMPETING DEMANDS OF HIGHLAND ENGLISH INSTRUCTION

The "daunting" of the Gaelic-speaking Highlanders, the ruthless suppression of their linguistic diversity, in which MacDonald found himself involved, began at least as early as the 1609 Statutes of Iona which called for the extirpation of Gaelic. In 1616 the Scottish Privy Council issued an Act for erecting schools in Scotland so "that the vulgar Ingleshe toung be universallie planted, and the Irishe language, which is one of the chieff and principall causes of the continuances of barbaritie, and incivilitie, among the inhabitants of the Isles and Heylandis, may be abolished, and removit."[15] These were early moves in a campaign for English language use in the Highlands, an ongoing push for Highland assimilation into the Protestant faith and British rule that lasted throughout the eighteenth century, all the more pressing after 1707. Britain's post-Union absorption of the Highlands was proving particularly difficult because of Jacobitism but was of crucial importance, as Highlanders made up approximately half of the Scottish population in the mid-eighteenth century.[16] Anglo-British authorities linked Highland intractability to their use of Scots Gaelic; as "natural" a defect as their "barren" land, it marked them as distinct and inferior. An early pamphlet detailing the orchestrated work toward linguistic assimilation in the Highlands reads, "The poor people labour under disadvantages peculiar to themselves, arising chiefly from the nature of their country and language."[17] Criminalizing "Irish," administrators attributed Jacobitism to its use; one early document claims, "Ignorance of the Christian religion and the English language is the great occasion of their being in this unhappy dependence and alliance."[18]

The chief organ of the linguistic conversion enterprise was the Society in Scotland for the Propagation of Christian Knowledge (SSPCK), for which MacDonald, a Gaelic-speaking Highlander whose own family had Jacobite sympathies, served as an instructor from roughly 1729 to 1745. Displeased with the failure of the crown to enforce the law that each Highland parish maintain a school, a group of wealthy Edinburgh men assumed the mantle of that project.[19] The Society they formed received its charter from Queen Anne (in 1709, just after a failed invasion by the Old Pretender) and subsequent moneys from membership subscriptions, Church of Scotland collections, British monarchs, and a London corresponding society. The SSPCK established twenty-five schools by 1715, growing to 325 at their height by 1795, chiefly at the borders between Lowlands and Highlands, and educated about three hundred thousand students by the end of the century.[20]

The disbanding of the Scottish parliament created a power vacuum in Scotland that opened spaces to private Lowland gentlemen. The dissolution of parliament, however, also compromised the newly urgent efforts of British domination of the Highlands, for that move fanned the flames of Jacobite indignation. In the Lowlands the lawyers, wealthy merchants, military officials, and landowners who composed the membership of the SSPCK attempted to fill the leadership vacuum. Although they drew from the model of literacy instruction implemented by the SPCK in England, the fact that this "colonizing force" was primarily Scottish underscores the complex nature of relations in eighteenth-century Britain, a complexity we shall be examining throughout this book. It was primarily through their private initiative and not the British state – generally negligent in compliance to its own policies of Highland education – that this project of linguistic assimilation was sustained.[21] If the Society construed British national identity as a kind of performance of which even the most "barbaric" Highlander was capable, the rising Lowlander elite was itself very anxious about its own improvement – and its own "performance" of Britishness.[22] While their efforts were ostensibly dedicated to re-positioning Gaelic-speaking Highlanders within a revamped Britain, the administrators of the SSPCK also attempted to re-situate themselves through that work.[23]

Those new allegiances were formed in part through a shared assertion of the superiority of English culture and language.[24] The SSPCK promoted English and Protestantism as a means to secure Anglo-British hegemony in the fluctuating sociopolitical waters of post-Union Scotland. My use of Antonio Gramsci's term "hegemony" speaks to the new leadership's struggle for the hearts and minds of the Highlanders, specifically through inculcating them with the superiority of English. Gramsci writes that "the supremacy of a social group manifests itself in two ways, as 'domination' and as 'intellectual and moral leadership' . . . there can and indeed must be hegemonic activity even before the rise to power."[25] The crown annexed the estates of those who participated in the rebellion of 1745, and English instruction also took place on the very sites and at the expense of those formerly hostile enclaves, representing a power wavering between the Repressive State Apparatus and the Ideological State Apparatus that Louis Althusser theorized.[26] Thus the overt repression of dismantling the separate administrative infrastructure of the Highlands (annexing leading Jacobites' estates and banning heritable jurisdictions) was directly tied to the ideological strategy of English education. Nancy Dorian explains the significance of such education in the Highlands: "the schools have a more pervasive effect in remote areas than most other national secular institutions, touching far more people directly than, say, the police or the courts, and the schools' impact is greater because it begins so early in the individual's life."[27] The Society's schools' effect was pervasive to the point of policing individual language choice. Monitored by peer censors in the playgrounds, children were severely punished when caught using Gaelic.[28] English language and literacy instruction formed the basis of elite Lowland Scots' venture for moral leadership, particularly exercised on the Highland poor. The author of "Observations about the Improvement and Reformation of the West Highlands in the Year 1754" writes, for instance, that "no punishment inflicted will answer this purpose [the integration of the Highlanders] until they are made acquainted with the social ties and binding nature of every private virtue . . . to answer this purpose [we need] proper schools for instructing the children in the English language."[29] The most disenfranchised Gaels had the least access to English education, and as D. J. Withrington has pointed out the SSPCK's schools attempted to minister to the poorest of the poor, those presumably least invested in the economic benefits of union.[30]

Pierre Bourdieu compares rival languages within a community to forms of cultural capital with widely varying values and argues that the "official language" has the highest value – exchangeable for jobs, prestige, and status. On a small scale, the SSPCK literalized this value by offering to its students material goods – specifically, new shoes and new suits of clothing – in exchange for demonstrated literacy in English.[31] Bourdieu explains the recognition of linguistic value as accessory to an internalization of power structures, writing, "Thus known and recognized throughout the whole jurisdiction of a certain political authority, it [the official language] helps . . . to reinforce authority."[32] If they did not dictate the terms upon which varying languages stood, however, Gaelic speakers did negotiate their way within this revised linguistic economy, revealing an agency often underplayed in analyses of colonial discourse. Although the case of the Highlands reveals a repressive administrative model of forced education into English, colonial subjects who learned English in order to speak the language of value might be described as viewing this instruction as instrumental.[33]

Language and literacy, however, also remained lively battle zones in the ceaseless, if often submerged, cultural wars around class and colonial power in the Highlands. Although barely legible in the official documents that form the basis of our knowledge of the Society and its interaction with the Highlands, faint traces of evidence show signs of resistance to the official language and literacy instruction of the Sassenach.[34] A 1718 report from St. Kilda records that the people "are not forward to send their children to school."³⁵ Schoolmaster John Ewing at Knockbreck suffered the indignity of having his fuel for fire repeatedly stolen – hardly a sign of reverence for literacy instruction.³⁶ As further evidence of irreverence, the Society records, "Kerr's Spelling Book which is sent to the Society's schools is often destroyed by young scholars."³⁷ Also significant, a schoolmaster's wife sent a letter to the Society requesting that they send a letter "giv[ing] her husband all suitable encouragement for strengthening his hand in disciplining," hinting at a less than complacent student body.³⁸ In 1747, in the wake of the open warfare of the Jacobite rebellion and the consequent overt politicization of cultural and linguistic practices, schoolmaster William Grant reported that books sent to his school had been "carried off by the rebels."³⁹ One can only guess why the books were taken. Were the Jacobites attempting to curtail the work of the Hanover-supporting Society? Were the books perceived as valuable? Recorded briefly between the confident claims for the success of the Society's work, these incidents give us only scant information about the reasons for resistance, and I am reluctant to speculate too generally about them. Yet they do suggest that even as some actively sought out instruction from the Society, others were more wary, even hostile. As late as 1800, while Daniel Kerr schoolmaster of Glen Urquhart whipped his students if he heard them speaking Gaelic, "one result was that schoolboys dealt drastically with any of their fellows who had the presumption to speak English out of school hours."⁴⁰

At best, the SSPCK could be said to have embraced an Enlightenment vision of spreading the benefits of rationality and knowledge. In a 1746 anniversary sermon for the SSPCK, for instance, Robert Wallace recoils when he "behold[s] the severe and constant labors of so many of my brethren of mankind, which often deprive them of the opportunities and indispose them too much for the relish of knowledge."⁴¹ He quickly adds, however, that "the children of the rich ought not be trained up in the same way as the children of the poor" (21). More telling is the immediate link Wallace makes between the power of reason he hopes the Society will develop in their Highland students and the acceptance of Hanoverian rule. "Ignorance and superstition," on the other hand, lead to such things as the contemporary "wicked and horrid rebellion" (31).

In their bid for hegemony, the Society's advocates described Highlanders as deprived of knowledge, but this was, of course, not true, even by their definition of knowledge.⁴² Alexander MacDonald's father, for instance, graduated from Glasgow University in 1674 and sent his son there, intending him for the Church or law. Although he did not graduate, MacDonald received a classical education, an image Rev. T. Murchison conjures: "may we not think of him sitting uncomfortably on a hard bench in a dull classroom, while the professor drearily discoursed in Latin about Aristotle?"[43] At the same time, MacDonald revered the waning Gaelic literary culture embodied in the MacMhuirich family of hereditary poet historians who had served the lords of the Isles and the Clanranalds since the thirteenth century.[44] As Black writes, "there is abundant evidence that Alasdair had sat at the feet of the Mac-Mhuirichs" (12). Thus, MacDonald drew from two learned cultural traditions prior to contact with the SSPCK, not lacking in intellectual leadership so much as he was linked to a leadership antagonistic to the state. MacDonald's family's disaffection with the Church and State of Anglo-Britain ran deep. As one anonymous writer put it in 1750, they "idolize the nonjuring clergy and can scarcely keep their temper when speaking of Presbyterians" – in fact Alexander's father's nonjurancy lost him his living.[45]

Donald Meek has shown how the SSPCK functioned as a "missionary" society, bringing a foreign language and religion to the Highlands, and has also discussed the complexities that emerged when the "missionaries" were, like MacDonald, native Highlanders (383).[46] Educated and trilingual, at home in a Jacobite stronghold, MacDonald's ambivalence towards his work with the Society was inevitable. Yet Highland young men who showed intelligence and whose native tongue was Scots Gaelic were prime candidates for the job of SSPCK schoolmaster. The tricky implications of using "native" missionaries suggests one of a series of tensions in the Society's program, and here I want to consider these as a prelude to examining the forms of resistance they helped produce, particularly in MacDonald's writing.

One of the most significant difficulties the Society faced was how to construct and address the Highlanders as a cultural entity, suggesting an ambivalence that would return to haunt them. Geographically near to but culturally remote from England, the Highlanders of Scotland posed the question of identity and difference in particularly thorny ways, and this was complicated further as the Highlands oscillated in the British imagination between colonial and national space. Much as depictions of colonial populations, from native Americans to Africans, had stressed their outlandish differences – in appearance, manners, cuisine, social organization, and language – many descriptions of the Highlanders focused on cultural oddities, manufacturing stereotypes which continue to circulate. I will not rehearse fully those characterizations, as Peter Womack's masterful *Romance and Improvement* already catalogs them exhaustively.[47] Among the lasting caricatures he enumerates are the beggarly Scot, the vicious warrior, the semi-coherent fool – whose language is not different but "substandard" – and the superstitious peasant. Womack's extensive bibliography reveals that there was no shortage of texts – travel narratives, poems, cartoons, published "letters" from the Highlands – fabricating these images in a virtual industry of Highland exoticization. The SSPCK was one of the key producers of such images. Womack cites one representative passage:

There, society still appears in its rudest and most imperfect form; Strangers to industry, averse from labour, inured to rapine; the fierce inhabitants scorn all the arts of peace, and stand ready for every bold and desperate action. Attached to their own customs . . . they have hitherto continued a separate people.[48]

The particularity of the Highlanders was central to the Briton's sense of self, and this process of negative identity formation helped justify the brutality of imperial power.[49] Prosperous gentleman to the impoverished peasant, polite bon vivant to the refractory gladiator, well-spoken reader to the unintelligible illiterate, and rational thinker to the gullible rustic, Anglo-British identity and "superiority" depended to a certain extent upon producing a fixed "other" status for the Highlander. Yet, while on the one hand eighteenth-century travel writers, moral philosophers, and government administrators exoticized Highland culture, on the other they sought to bring the diverse cultures of the Highlands into British allegiance by rendering them somehow the same as their southern neighbors.[50] Although not synonymous, the philosophical gloss of the Highlanders' situation and the benefits of their "improvement" were never far removed from the gambit of expanding capital relations and their pressures towards universalization.[51] "Civilization," as defined by Scottish Enlightenment thinkers such as Adam Ferguson and William Robertson, depended upon the development of industry and commerce characteristic of the most advanced stage of society.

English language would function as the transparent medium of their incorporation. One document describes the Society's hope that "Britons from North to South may speak the same language, live united and loyal under the same sovereign."[52] English instruction and industrialization were mapped directly onto each other when, in 1738, the SSPCK received a second letters patent from King George to open industrial and spinning schools. Linguistic conversion was increasingly tied to the bottom line; the Society asserts, "If the people were reduced to religion, humanity and industry, and the low countrey [sic] language, how much would such a reduction not only save charges and prevent losses, but mightily promote the wealth of the rest of the kingdom."[53] Unlike later educational policies in India, where "the goal of 'civilizing the natives' was far from being the central motivation in official efforts at educational activity," such a goal was precisely the point in the Highlands, particularly in the first half of the eighteenth century.[54] Girded by an Enlightenment vision of stadial social progress, the Society's educational policy became part of a developmental program for jump-starting this "retrograde" population out of an anachronistic barbaric stage.

Thus, if the Highlanders are inequivalent to the Anglo-British, like the distant native Americans and East Indians, they are also equivalent. One sermon promoting the work of the Society illuminates the ideological loop of these conflicting characterizations of the Highlands. The preacher refers first to the oppositional otherness of the Highlanders as indicated by the Jacobite rebellions, stating, "Twice hath the unhappy influence . . . carried some . . . to attempts which, had they been successful, must have ruined us."[55] He goes on to claim the Highlanders as national subjects, however, asserting that unlike more remote colonial subjects, "these are 'our own'." He concludes by arguing that the work of the Society in the national/colonial space of the Highlands will provide a model for future colonial pedagogy in more distant places, writing "After this good society . . . had settled the means of divine instruction in the remote parts of our own country, a voice was heard from afar, saying, 'Help us'."

The author of *The Highland Complaint* (1737), a wealthy Highlander educated in the south, perceptively critiqued these contradictory stances. Arguing that, on the one hand, the Society constructed the Highlands as distant and exotic and, therefore, necessarily removed from decision-making regarding their own fate, he writes, "Tho' our Distance from Edinburgh be not above 140 Miles, yet we find it as sufficient to exclude our Heritors and Ministers, from having any Vote in disposing the pious Funds [of the SSPCK] destin'd for our Welfare, as if we were the t'other Side of the Alps." [56] On the other hand, he notes that the SSPCK assumed a universalizing knowledge of the Highlands because its members had geographical knowledge of them, a means of overcoming space. He observes, derisively, "With great Exactness, they have the chorography, nay the Topography of the Highlands and Isles laid before them." The contradictions this writer protests remind us of Homi Bhabha's characterization of knowledge in a colonial context: "Colonial discourse produces the colonized as a fixed reality which is at once an 'other' and yet entirely knowable and visible."[57] Bhabha theorizes colonial discourse as precipitating an uncanny mimicry, reflecting "the desire for a reformed, recognizable Other, as *a subject of a difference that is almost the same, but not quite.*"[58]

Although Bhabha does not examine colonial linguistic and literacy issues in detail, they offer a prime example – and complicate considerably – the ambivalence he describes: if language marked Highlanders as distinct, it was also a pivotal site of assimilation.[59] This ambivalent slippage between known and unknown/unknowable, between constructed distance and illusory proximity, is inherent in the translation that takes place in an imperial context. In a 1756 document the Society inserts the Gaels into a general linguistic frame, explaining that the SSPCK aims "to introduce among the Highlanders a knowledge of the English language, to fit them for understanding and being understood by the rest of the world."[60] The Society's belief that English language might "civilize" the Highlanders betrays a characteristic faith in a universal structure of language, a faith at once generous in its sense of shared linguistic structures and yet authoritarian in its imposition of English as the universal norm.[61] Eric Cheyfitz describes a similar policy of missionaries in eighteenth-century North America who "instructed" and proselytized in English:

we must recognize a progressive strain in this imperial foreign policy, one that apparently welcomes homogenization, but – and here homogeneity harmonizes itself with hierarchy – only in the terms of the policy maker, who writes a script in which the other, in order to be heard, must say: 'for your sake I have become a civilized man . . . for your sake I will be whatever you will me to be'. (5)

While Cheyfitz's assessment is both compelling and apt, that hierarchized homogeneity is, however, by no means stable, and this instability arises at the very moment when English literacy crosses cultures and languages.

The case of Alexander MacDonald is a revealing example of that instability. In the dedication to the Scots Gaelic/English glossary he prepared for the Society, MacDonald plays to that universalizing rhetoric, explaining how conversion of the Highlanders to English "will make these young Ones more useful the sooner, as Servants at home, and also when they come Abroad to the Lowlands, and be employed in the Navy, or Army, or in any other Service in the Commonwealth" (*Gaelic/English*, v). Even though there is evidence that MacDonald took part in the 1715 rebellion, these sympathies are carefully concealed as he allays the fears of Society members wary of the publication of a print Gaelic necessary for a bilingual glossary.[62] MacDonald, then, deploys a kind of double talk, engaging the Society's own rhetoric of the hopes of homogenizing universality in order to mitigate the profound implications of printing Gaelic and the elaboration of a particular Scots Gaelic identity, which I shall explore below.

In addition, the Society's aim to teach not only English but literacy in English posed the threat of an additional instability. While they maintained a faith in the disciplining powers of literacy, they could not, in the end, control the specific uses to which colonial subjects, such as MacDonald, would put it. Literacy, as I shall show, provided a new technology of liberation. The Society, however, could not avoid the teaching of literacy and celebrated this teaching in fairly unalloyed terms. Protestantism, with its emphasis on the word of God and one's personal relationship to the Bible, necessitated the teaching of literacy.[63] Sue Zemka has discussed the emphasis on reading in reference to another British evangelical body, the British and Foreign Bible Society, saying, "Converting the world to the Bible meant first converting much of it to literacy."[64] This exigency is borne out in the 1774 *Account of the SSPCK* which maintains that full conversion of the Highlanders to Protestantism could only come through reading: "To render any attempts for this valuable purpose successful, something more than mere preaching was necessary. This, though repeated on every Sabbath-day, if not enforced by private admonition, and frequent reading of the scriptures, can have but little effect in convincing and converting mankind."[65]

In teaching literacy, the SSPCK saw itself as fulfilling Enlightenment goals of bringing a tangible, visible word – light – to darkness, powerfully imaged in the Society's logo of a hand holding up an opened Bible, its luminosity reflected in the many rays shooting out of its leaves; the accompanying motto was, significantly, *"Post Tenebras Lux."* The technology of literacy also, of course, facilitated the administration and ideological frame of empire in conveying legal documents, records, accounting tables, and royal proclamations – the written stuff of colonial administration.[66] As Roy Harris suggestively argues, "writing overcomes the limitations of time, place, and memory."[67] In as much as writing functions as a medium of communication operating across space, it enables the physical administration of colonial expansion. And in effacing both spatial and temporal distance, writing can seem free of history. While particular histories might introduce disabling differences into communication, a standard writing practice sublimates such difference.

Thus, while we now have come to see that the distinction between orality and literacy was "fuzzy at every point in the eighteenth century,"[68] the Society invoked ontological powers of literacy: "In the low country of Scotland, even the poorest people . . . are . . . provided with Bibles, catechisms, by reading which they have it much in their power to improve themselves."[69] In his analysis of early-eighteenth-century Kirk Session Minutes from the Isle of Arran, John Crawford concludes that "community leaders linked illiteracy with disorderly behaviour; [and] book use, or at any rate, Bible reading was seen as a means of social control."[70] Like the evangelical Bible Societies after them, the Society attributed almost magical transformations to reading, exhibiting a blind belief in the reformatory powers of the act of reading.[71] They shared this belief with ministers involved in the over three hundred "awakenings" of villagers in Cambuslang, near Glasgow, who marveled not only at their parishioners' spiritual conversions but also at the power of those conversions to move them to seek literacy instruction. One such minister Jo Willison writes that the "thirst after knowledge is particularly remarkable . . . several who cannot read . . . being so desirous to be better acquainted with the word of God are resolved to learn to read."[72] While the primary objective was conversion to Protestantism, this resultant hunger for literacy was most welcome to the Society.

The script they hoped to teach their young pupils to read, however, was in English, and this is a move that has recognizably political ends.[73] For the Highlands of Scotland, as for parts of Ireland and Wales before them, the Anglo-British imposition of an official print English was a subjugation to a hierarchizing force even as the narrative of that imposition was greater participation in British polity. More complicated than a mere "linguacide" of Gaelic, the official use of English in Scotland was meant to convince the Highlanders of the naturalness of their national (public) British, Protestant identity – and, inversely, of their subordinate colonial relation to the native speakers of that language. Most dangerous about this instruction into English literacy would be the way in which it presented the literate subject back to his or herself.

It would be inaccurate to suggest that the Society strategically planned the particular form that literacy instruction took at their schools and, further, to suggest that these political aims had fully crystallized in discussion. Early meeting minutes record no internal discussion about pedagogical policy; the SSPCK simply assumed that moving straight into English literacy would be possible. Teachers distributed English Bibles, expecting children to read them at once. MacDonald's own student Duncan MacKenzie recalled that before a Presbyterial committee of examiners "he . . . was able to read the Scriptures fluently and intelligibly. The reverend gentlemen were well pleased and gave the school a favorable report."[74] It is important to note that this moment, however, is more about the listeners – hearing the words and attributing moral reformation to that scene of reading – than about the student who is reading. The English-only literacy instruction was found to be largely "a rote learning without comprehension."[75] In class, children read aloud the Bible in English, but their level of comprehension was very low – not surprising, given that English was not their native tongue.[76]

When, by the mid-eighteenth century, the simplistic vision of the universal reformative powers of the mere act of reading aloud English began to fray, the SSPCK begrudgingly acknowledged that Gaelic instruction in literacy had to accompany English instruction, and instructors began to teach English literacy via simultaneous translation between Gaelic and English texts.[77] The Society printed *Mother's Catechism* in Gaelic with facing English pages in 1758 and, similarly, the New Testament – discussed as early as 1744 – in 1767, with an initial printing of 10,000 copies. Although teaching Gaelic literacy and printing Gaelic met with opposition, Samuel Johnson, himself no great defender of Gaelic language and culture, supported it, writing:

When the Highlanders read the Bible, they will naturally wish to have its obscurities cleared, and to know the history, collateral or appendant . . . When they once desire to learn, they will naturally have recourse to the nearest language by which that desire can be gratified; and one will tell another that if he would attain knowledge, he must learn English.[78]

The teleological education into literacy, which was to end in a specifically English literacy, had important repercussions as it attempted to conflate learning with English culture.

Forced into teaching literacy in Gaelic before moving onto English literacy instruction, however, had important and unpredictable consequences for newly Gaelic-literate students and the power relationships between Anglo-British forces and Scots-Gaelic-speaking Highlanders. Thus, as I am trying to illustrate, the entwining of language and literacy instruction and Protestant evangelicism presents a dense site of ideological cross currents, and my focus is on the complex meaning of literacy and translation in this context. Consider John Balfour's description of the revival at Nigg (located north of Inverness) parish:

> It is surprising to observe with what industry many, especially of the younger sort, endeavoured to acquire reading. Some read the Psalms in Irish metre, and teach others in the same way. . . . But as the generality are still illiterate, that disadvantage is much made up to them, by the hearing of others read the Scriptures . . . which they translate currently as they read.[79]

Such scenes reassured Balfour, but my point is that both the moments of "endeavouring to acquire reading" and translating seem to open up possibilities for the reading and translating subject, not only in the sense of power that literacy in English might bring, but also in the power of translating English print back into their native Gaelic. In the case of MacDonald, the social act of reading, writing, and translating had, on occasion, the effect not of shoring up Hanoverian Protestant hegemony but undermining it. His case allows us to modify, slightly, Brian Street's important claim that literacy "is a social process in which particularly socially constructed technologies are used within particular institutional frameworks for specific social purposes."[80] We might introduce into Street's passive construction a multiplicity of agents. For the purposes of my argument, the important insertion would be colonial subjects such as MacDonald, who used literacy against hegemonic institutional frameworks.

As the translator who facilitated this transition, MacDonald reveals the shifting significance of the cross-cultural movement of language and literacy.[81] In many ways MacDonald, as glossary compiler, seems to help build the linguistic economy of a rising Anglo-Britain, and I want to examine that position before moving into an exploration of the ways in which the Society's plans for the glossary backfired. The glossary alienates Gaelic as it represents it as isolated words on a page, dependent on their English counterparts next to them for meaning. The vocabulary contains rather awkward transliterations of cultural concepts specific to the English and Lowlanders, such as terms of British nobility and officers of state. More egregious examples include "Sioneral Tigh an Chuinadh *The General of the Mint*" (*Gaelic/English*, 43) and "An tárd chonstabuill *The Lord High Constable*" (42). Such concepts had no exact equivalents in the Highland society of 1741, a fact betrayed by these crude transliterations. They were an unusual selection of terms for a

Literacy in the Highlands: scripting identity?

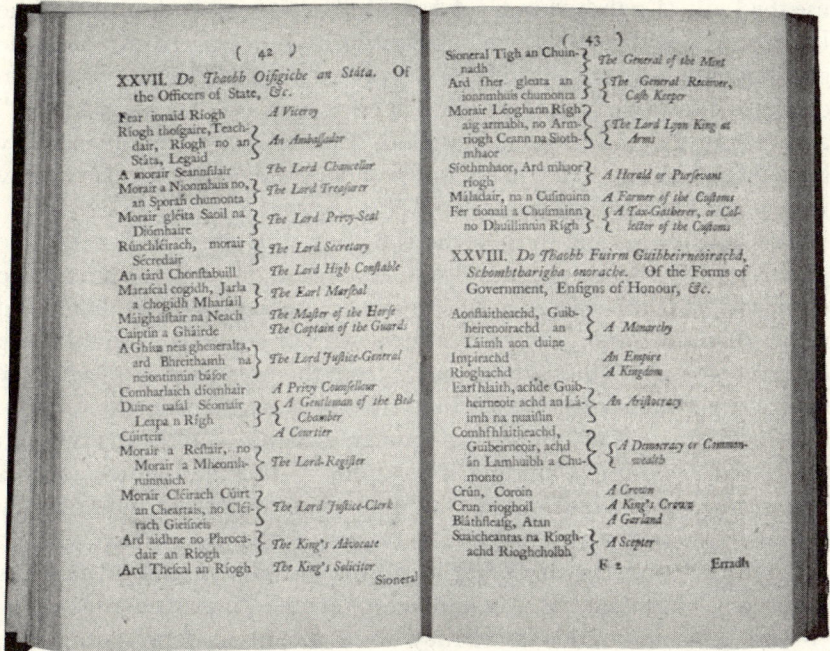

Figure 2. From Alexander MacDonald, *A Gaelic/English Vocable*, Edinburgh, 1741. Photo Courtesy of the Newberry Library, Chicago.

relatively short (161 pages plus appendix), by no means comprehensive, catalogue of English and Gaelic. (Under the category "Of the Fire," for instance, which includes related terms such as "fire-brand," "tinder," and "spark," neither "torch" nor "log" is listed.) In this way the glossary seems designed to give Highlanders a verbal form through which to recognize British power.

Some of the religious terms, too, merely spell out "loan" words, more accurately deemed imposed words, in Gaelic form, as in "Anbaisdich *Anabaptists*" (163), "Aingeal *An Angel*" (2), or "Spiorad *A Spirit*" (2). Clearly conceived with Bible reading in mind, the glossary offers double translations of Biblical terms – retaining Greek or Latin terms, such as "assary" or "talent" but converting those into English, as in "Feoirlin, no *Assarium*, umha cuinnte, 9 Pighinin Alb} *A Farthing or Assary, Halfpenny Farthing*" and "Tallan, 187 Puint 10 Sceall Sasgunich} *A Talent of Silver, 187 Pounds 10 Shillings*." The dual translations suggest that in all cases English or Latin must be the mediating form; when the Society proposed the vocabulary, its leaders suggested that its composer simply use the Latin/English glossary *A New Vocabulary* (1720) and substitute the Latin words with Gaelic – a substitution twice over. Even when the glossary includes terms from everyday life, it translates these quotidian concepts into English-derived terms. Terms such as "Peticota *A petticoat*" and "Ribin *A Ribband*," as luxury goods from the South, might arguably have taken an English form, but one wonders, did Gaelic speakers really have no word for "Na Hemarodain *The Hemerhoids*"?

Not only suggesting that Gaelic is a poor equivalent to English, the glossary also depends upon and shapes a vision of language *per se*. The emphasis – for the sake of easy conversion – is on the individual word rather than on larger grammatical structures or contexts. Ronald Black describes the ambiguities that emerge from the pressures of the glossary form: "e.g. '*Rud a cheangal*, To bind'. *Rud a cheangal* means literally 'to bind a thing.' . . . Lacking such a context, *a cheangal* could equally mean 'to bind it (or him),' 'binding it (or him).'" This ambiguity appears precisely because MacDonald "faithfully translated Latin infinitives by Gaelic infinitives, which are not fundamental to the language" ("Mac Mhaighstir," 29). Downplaying form, the glossary model suggests, as Tejaswini Niranjana has noted, that words could maintain a transparent relationship to the ideas they were meant to represent.[82] The experience of empire, and the efforts to translate between cultures, is a largely unrecognized influence on this early eighteenth-century conception of language, demonstrating a compelling moment of empire's impact on British national culture.[83] A variety of pressures were at work in establishing the "naively representational" concept of language, including the "new science" interested in communicating its discoveries to a wide audience and new styles of preaching dedicated to making the word of God accessible, but we must also consider the experience of empire as influential in shaping those linguistics. The Royal Society's, and particularly Thomas Sprat's, call for plain style – for a "return back to the primitive purity, and shortness, when men deliver'd so many things, almost in an equal number of words" – for instance, was influenced by the interrelated phenomena of the new science and commercial empire as information was made accessible for investors, merchants, and colonial administrators.[84] Like the forces of rising commerce and the new science, the alienating exchange of colonial translation depends on, and thereby promotes, an understanding of language as a series of words, each reducible to an equivalent. Downplaying form, such a model suggests that words could maintain a transparent relationship to the ideas they were meant to represent.[85]

The semiotic economy of emerging Highland commodity exchange and of imperial grammar share a logic of equivalence, as colonizing investor and profiteer seek to transform the diverse objects and languages they encounter into exchangeable forms.[86] Under this system words function as tokens, objects emptied of specific historical social traces, so that they may function as generalized transmitters of value.[87] In order to circulate on the transnational scale that capital and empire demanded, both Gaelic and English were alienated, their value expressed in an equivalent from another language. The invasive movement of capital, however, eventually necessitates a recognized universal equivalent, a signifier of pure value that will facilitate rapid exchange. Behind the scenes, English is the universal equivalent of the many languages of its empire, waiting in the wings to assert its inarguable and abstracting value.

And yet MacDonald was also able to manipulate this logic of equivalence. Word lists like MacDonald's glossary are examples of the vision of language as a collection of tokens which enable the transparent transmission of meaning through simple exchange. While its logic of substitution suggests a transparent, dematerialized word, however, the glossary also materializes or "thing-afies" language in a way that an alternative focus on syntax and grammatical structure might not.[88] This very reification of Gaelic that occurs also gives a new – prized – material, embodied, visible print existence to Gaelic. Unlike the Anglo terms cited above, glossary entries such as "Ubh *An egg*," "An Talamh *The Earth*," and "A Ghrian *The sun*" are clearly not mere transliterations, but are transcriptions of Gaelic. MacDonald suggests the link between the ramifications of this newly standardized print Gaelic and his political agenda when he encrypts none-too-subtle codes of Jacobitism within its pages, including "King Charles Martyrdom, January 30th" in his list of Saints' Days.[89] Further, the glossary fails to translate Gaelic words or concepts for English readers, who would be primarily the Lowland administrators who funded its publication. These readers would have no way of learning such concepts other than by talking to a native Gaelic speaker, which would be a potentially tense, disempowering exchange.[90]

Most important, MacDonald's glossary and the Revd James Stuart's translation of the New Testament from Greek to Gaelic (1767) and, later, the translation of the Old Testament not only gave a material, visible being to Gaelic, but also helped standardize it.[91] One translator of the Old Testament admitted he had sometimes been obliged to use "words which may not be known in every district of the Highlands. To remedy this inconvenience, he has likewise subjoined, in notes, other words which convey nearly the same meaning." Thus, a series of regional Gaelics became mutually comprehensible. In addition, the potential confusions of the classical Gaelic of Irish and Scottish manuscript writing were left behind. Stuart's Gaelic translation of the New Testament omitted all (potentially confusing) quiescent letters, for instance, and in simplifying the language for a wider print readership, helped standardize it. Significantly, as Donald Meek has observed, by 1807 the style of the Scottish Gaelic Bible was "noticeably closer to Scottish Gaelic usage" than the classical Gaelic translations of the seventeenth century; its grammar and syntax, particularly its verb system, was Scottish Gaelic vernacular.[92]

This printing of a distinctively Scots Gaelic vernacular had, in the eighteenth-century context, major implications for the development of a Scots Gaelic cultural identity. In the glossary and Bible translations disparate Gaelic linguistic communities became acquainted with a single print Gaelic standard.[93] While the Society might have wanted the knowledge of Gaelic merely to facilitate the larger project of learning English, nonetheless, its publications both gave a material, print form to the Scots Gaelic language and created a large body of Gaelic readers, and this had an impact beyond the Society's control. One writer has argued, for instance, that the New Testament translation "gave new impetus to Gaelic prose" and that the large-scale Gaelic literacy the Society helped produce was reflected in the long succession of Gaelic periodicals that began to appear early in the nineteenth century.[94]

To transcribe means not only to make a written copy, but also to record for subsequent reproduction – and that is exactly what happened after the "transcription" of Gaelic in MacDonald's glossary as well. In his groundbreaking and frequently cited critique of nationalist discourse, Benedict Anderson rightly draws our attention to the interplay of language, literacy, and print culture in the development of nationalist ideology. He argues that the dispersal of select languages through print formed "unified fields of exchange" that enabled modern nations to think themselves.[95] If Partha Chatterjee is right, however, and Anderson fails to "pursu[e] the varied and often contradictory political possibilities of this process" (*Nation*, 21), there are few cultural formations that better attest to those contradictory political possibilities than language instruction in the eighteenth-century Highlands. For the theory and practice of such instruction betrays a telling ambivalence at work in the universalizing project of linguistic standardization and assimilation attempted there. Its requisite translation and print materialization of Gaelic could maintain neither the seamless, exact equivalence, nor the cultural and political superiority of English that its proponents desired. Once a print Gaelic was introduced into Highland communities, newly literate populations rejected its status as a mere bridge to English literacy. The part of the code conveying the superiority of the English language was altered and challenged.[96]

As a revision of Bhabha's understanding of colonial ambivalence we might also note that this doubling has less to do with the colonialists' desire than with the agency of the colonial subject, such as Alexander MacDonald, transcoding and code-switching an imposed English. Not surprisingly, it is the doubled agenda of British empire – the universalizing movement of capital and English literacy coupled with the continued need for an "other" marked by inferiority – that produces a doubled Highland subject, imitative and yet still distinct from the imposed English culture and language. The glossary, a key technology of transcoding, reveals the transnational regime's inability to sustain one-way exchange and points to a set of critical issues in the process of imperial expansion. Tejaswini Niranjana describes colonial translation as "overdetermined not only because multiple forces act on it, but because it gives rise to multiple practices. The strategies of containment initiated by translation are therefore deployed across a range of discourses, allowing us to name translation as a significant technology of colonial domination."[97] Yet translation is overdetermined not simply in terms of its multiple strategies of containment, but also in terms of its multiple transcodings, which provide openings for resistance. If, in 1719, Society meeting minutes declared, "The Society is resolved to give no encouragement to the teaching to read the Irish language, and therefore they will furnish no books for that purpose," those dreams of one-way translation were dashed by the reality of literacy instruction.[98]

TALKING BACK: THE LANGUAGE OF HIGHLAND RESISTANCE

When we read MacDonald's glossary work in relationship to his poetry, we see that MacDonald was aware of the significance of establishing a print vernacular of Scots Gaelic and, under the cover of the Society, hoped to create a new – Gaelic – "unified field of exchange and communication." In mapping British allegiance and identity to the English language so clearly, the Society provided an easy target for –

and language of – resistance. MacDonald made use of this target when he shifted his allegiances during the Jacobite campaign of 1745. While he had signed a pledge of allegiance to the Hanoverian regime and the Protestant religion when he became a schoolmaster for the SSPCK, four years after the publication of the glossary MacDonald jumped ship, openly converting to Roman Catholicism and accompanying Prince Charles from the moment he landed on Highland shores, eventually taking a Captain's commission in his army. After several unsatisfactory meetings with him in 1745 the Society dismissed MacDonald from his teaching post for "wander[ing] through the country composing Galick songs stuffed with obscene language."[99] The Society's focus on his language is telling, for in 1751 he published his collection of agit-prop Jacobite poems in Gaelic, a move breathtaking in its daring. MacDonald composed poetry and songs in Gaelic, some of it nature poetry, some of it Jacobite poetry, throughout the early eighteenth century, and several of these poems would have circulated in manuscript form. MacDonald treasured Gaelic script, training himself to write it and lamenting that his training was not more systematic and that he was one of the last to have this skill.[100] Publishing these poems was even more significant, however, for in doing so MacDonald adopted the technologies of literacy instruction and print production, along with the ideological intersection of language and identity forwarded by the SSPCK, to subvert their aims. MacDonald, circulating throughout the countryside promoting Jacobite politics in 1745, even found a ready-made social network created by the infrastructure of the Society's organized literacy instruction. Putting this agitational linguistic nationalist spin on MacDonald's glossary helps explain what seems a considerable tension between his initial "assimilationist" position and his later rebel status as an outspoken, eventually fugitive, Jacobite poet writing and publishing in Scots Gaelic.

His lessons on language and cultural identity learned through his work with the SSPCK, MacDonald took that experience to his written interventions in the creation of a Gaelic national linguistic identity. MacDonald locates legitimating traits of the nation – ancientness, cultural superiority, and royal history – in a shared, stable language, and in doing so he borrows from his British enemies the illusion that there is a "single" national language, regardless of the fact that the varieties (some mutually incomprehensible) of Gaelic were legion.[101] The Highland instance of linguistic colonialism, then, could not be said to "involve fairly simple relations of becoming . . . the colonized becoming the

English," but rather, inversely, enabled what we might refer to as the colonized becoming Gaelic.[102] MacDonald reveals the colonized becoming Gaelic, as it were, as he highlights his interactions with the prince regarding Scots Gaelic in his *Journall and Memoirs of P – C – Expedition into Scotland*, in which he boasts:

H.R.H. drunk the grace drinks in English which most of us understood. When it came to my turn I presumed to distinguish myself by saying audibly in Erse (or Highland language) *Deochs laint-an Reogh*. H.R.H. understanding that I had drunk the King's health made me speak the words again in Erse and said he could drink the king's health likewise in that language, repeating my words. (*Lockhart Papers*, vol. ii, 482)

Such an exchange represents an important moment in a developing Gaelic cultural nationalism. Not deriving its authority simply from the divine right claims of the Stuarts, this emerging Gaelic nationalism is also based on the notion of a distinct vernacular language, one which the prince himself must be taught by his underlings. In a turn on his former schoolmaster role, MacDonald became the prince's Gaelic tutor, no longer teaching poor Highland children English, but royalty Gaelic. In promoting a standard Gaelic vernacular, MacDonald helped constitute a new national figure of the "Gael" as a native speaker of the "ancient language of Scotland." I say he called this figure into its modern being, for the last semi-autonomous Gaelic polity – and this not the whole of Gaelic-speaking Scotland, but only the western region – had ended in the late fifteenth century. Further, the twinned traditional bases of Gaelic identity, described by Donald MacAulay as "*dùthcas* . . . native place" (referring to a specific region much smaller than the whole of the Highlands) and "*dualchas* . . . people and kin" (41), make the notion of an ancient Gaelic general *national* identity an anachronism, as all claims of ancient national identity are.[103] We see MacDonald calling this new national figure of the Gael into being in his heritage-asserting use of a "*brosnachadh*" in his poem "Incitement to the Highland Clans in the Year 1745" ("*Brosnachadh Nam Fineachan Gaidhealach 'S 'A Bhliadhna 1745*"). Deploying a form used traditionally to impel a particular clan to battle, MacDonald replaces the clan name with the general term "the Gael."

He establishes this new national figure in modern terms that would make little sense in an earlier political context, namely by pointing to shared cultural, particularly linguistic, artifacts. Like the Anglo-British, who were themselves in the process of developing their own culturally based sense of national identity, MacDonald points to cultural vestiges, such as clothing, as signs of national identity. He insists, for instance, that the plaid peculiar to the Highlands serves as material evidence of a unique, noble nation. He praises the outlawed clothing of the Highlanders in a poem called "The Proud Plaid" (*"Am Breacan Uallach)."* In the national vestment he is "readier in my equipment far/Than redcoats with their clumsy gun" (*"Na b' ullaimhe air m' armachd/Na dearganach 's musgaid ghlagach"*). Arguably, this link of culture and identity had been imposed upon the Highlanders by the British state, which had made wearing plaid illegal, and "The Proud Plaid's" subtitle in translation is "Being a song composed in praise of the kilt and plaid after the Unclothing Act." Yet, like the Anglo-British attempt to eradicate Gaelic use, these repressive efforts on the sartorial front met with an inverting resistance in MacDonald's writing.

As the British sought to destroy clan affinities and as they unwittingly helped create a standardized "national" Gaelic language in the course of converting Highlanders to English, they put in place the possibilities for a subversive Gaelic nationalism that MacDonald predicates on a national, standardized Gaelic language. MacDonald associates Gaelic language with a Gaelic cultural nationalism in the title poem of his collection, *The Resurrection of the Ancient Scottish Language*. In it MacDonald limns Gaelic as a powerful agent and his figurative use of language in the poem directly challenges the stultifying, anti-metaphorical language of catechisms and glossaries. Gaelic words "flow" and "enslave" as MacDonald claims for this language the power officially associated with English; demoting English as he revalues Gaelic he demonstrates the modular status of linguistic nationalism. In asserting of Gaelic that "she needs no loan" (*"Cha 'n fheum i iasad"*), MacDonald argues that Gaelic, not English, is the language of value – "Words in profusion/Are her stores of wealth" (*"A tighean-taisge,/Dh' fhoclaibh gasda làn"*). He thereby contests the Society's devaluing of the symbolic capital of Gaelic, to use Bourdieu's conceptual frame.

If the ideologies informing and enabling British conquest of the Highlands had relegated the Gaelic-speaking populations of the Highlands to a primordial status, here MacDonald appropriatively reclaims that status in order to assert Gaelic's preeminence based on that very ancientness. As Gaelic antedates Latin, Greek, and French, those languages are all "slaves" "to Gaelic's noble tongue" (*"I do 'n Ghàilig chòir"*). Like other European writers on language, MacDonald posits an originary, pristine, singular language. For him, Gaelic is that universal, superior language, and he ends the poem by claiming, "Of every nation's grammar/She's [Gaelic's] the golden root" (" 'S i 's freumhach òir/'S ceud ghràmar glòir gach sluaigh").[104] There is no mention of English (presumably a mere heterogeneous upstart), but the poem abounds in references to the days when all – including the "nobles, princes, and dukes" ("Ar flaith 's ar prionnsan") of Alba, the Gaelic name for the Island of Britain and then Scotland – spoke Gaelic. Gaelic was once, and clearly MacDonald hopes it will be again, the language of a united Scotland. Of all the tongues that "came down" from Babel's time, the speaker of the poem insists, "'Twas Gaelic won renown" ("'S i Ghàidhlig a thug buaidh"), and its origins are located even further back in time, as "its accents swift/from Eve's fair lips did flow!" ("'S bu shiùblhlach Gàilig/Bho bheul àluinn Eubh!").

In locating a unitary Gaelic nation in a remote past, MacDonald anticipates the bardic revival of the latter half of the century that Katie Trumpener has so ingeniously critiqued in *Bardic Nationalism*.[105] The opening poem of Macpherson's *Poems of Ossian*, "Cath-Loda" begins and ends with the reminder that it is "A tale of the times of old!" and a footnote argues that in the events represented in the poem,

. . . we have a very probable account given us, of the origin of monarchy in Caledonia. The *Cael* or Gauls, who possessed the counties to the north of the Frith of Edinburgh, were, originally, a number of distinct tribes, or clans . . . Trenmor was the first who represented to the chiefs the bad consequences of carrying on their wars in this irregular manner . . . Tramor . . . totally defeated the enemy [the Romans] by his superior valour and conduct, which gained him such an interest among the tribes, that he, and his family after him, were regarded as kings.[106]

Significant because it identifies the unifying force of a single Gaelic monarchy as early as the second century, Macpherson's text, like MacDonald's poems, projects back into the past a cultural formation which was in fact relatively recent. Yet, unlike Macpherson, Mac-Donald aims not only to represent but also to recover defunct bardic relations of literary production of the past in the present. For Mac-Donald as for later antiquaries, the figure of the bard is produced out of the cultural relationships experienced at the "Celtic periphery" and is "the mouthpiece for a whole society, articulating its values, chronicling its history, and mourning the inconsolable tragedy of its collapse" (Trumpener, *Bardic*, 6). MacDonald, like Macpherson, sought out and revered the written stuff of ancient times – one old Gaelic manuscript is said to have passed through his hands before making its way to Macpherson, providing a literal link between them.[107] Like Macpherson, he also ties Gaelic to classical culture to "outflank English" cultural authority.[108] Unlike the nationalist antiquaries behind the later revival in the 1760s Trumpener describes, however, MacDonald does not simply position himself as the diligent but distant student of a culture long vanished, but instead as the bard himself. We know that after reading Martin Martin's description of the bards writing on their backs, stones on their belly, for instance, MacDonald went so far as to replicate this physical posture.[109] Writing earlier than Macpherson, much closer to the immediate scene of linguistic and literacy battles, in a period when the outcome of those battles had not yet been determined, MacDonald had a more active sense of his own ability to participate directly in those struggles, urging armies on in 1745 and mourning their lost battles, just as bards had done centuries earlier. Examples of MacDonald's activist stance are abundant and reflect a temporal relationship to the scene of action not centuries later but four years after the loss at Culloden. Spurring the Highlanders to battle, the speaker of "Incitement to the Highland Clans in the Year 1745" ("*Brosnachadh Nam Fineachan Gaidhealach 'S 'A Bhliadhna 1745*") celebrates their bravery and shared hatred of their foe, in the form of King George and his "red coats." This more direct engagement is also apparent in his overt imagery of violence, imagery often literally "clouded over" in Macpherson's accounts. "Be swift to smite the foe" ("*'S bithibh guineach, deònach*"), the poem's speaker urges, as he describes weapons at the ready and revels in the grim violence of blades: "Keen edge to hack and slay" ("*Geur gu sracadh shròn aig'* ") and "whistling cleaving blows/ That heads and bodies sever" ("*bhuillean, sgoltadh mhullach/Sios gu bun an rùmpaill*") – images that make clear the violence the poems presented to the British state: "when ye draw the ribbed blades O'er fields ye'll marrow scatter;/With gore and brain like drifted dust/Ye'll mountain wastes be-spatter." This difference in levels of engagement is also figured in the very distinct temporality of each writer's poetics. If Macpherson's tales of "times of old!" allows for a nostalgic joy in grief, MacDonald's poems, set in the present, ruminate on recent defeats and fantasize about Jacobite victories in the near future. He might occupy the anachronistic position of the bard in a Highland world subject to English instruction and increasingly oriented toward print productions, but he also directly intervenes in, responds to, and exploits those new technologies.

Thus there are important parallels, but even more important distinctions between MacDonald and the writers of a later bardic nationalism. In focusing on MacDonald, then, I am also revising Trumpener's perspective, which emphasizes Celtic influences on "English" literature. MacDonald also helps us see how the influence of British technologies and articulations of cultural power were taken up by Scottish writers.[110] My emphasis also argues with those writers who have understood MacDonald's work as "indigenous," who are no doubt right to point to the ways in which this poetry moves beyond the classical Gaelic literary traditions once shared by Ireland and Scotland. MacDonald's innovation of organically Scottish forms is evidenced, for instance, in his attempt to use the *ceolmor*, the traditional meter for bagpipe compositions, as the meter for his poem "Praise of Morag."[111] Yet in insisting on a purely Scottish character of MacDonald's literature, these writers miss out on the transnational influences that MacDonald's literacy work illuminates, not only in his adoption of diverse literary forms, but also in his seizure of Anglo-British estimations of the cultural importance of language. Thus, while Pittock writes of MacDonald's poems as "mediated texts," that is, "A takeover of traditional format . . . [a] process, whereby high culture speaks in the folk voice in the cause of an outlaws' alliance," they mediated not simply across time and class intranationally but also across emergent international cultures (*Poetry*, 4). They were a product, as Thomson puts it, "of the detritus of an old system and the stimulus of external contacts, together with the break up of the old system and the painful building of a new one."[112] MacDonald moved between and manipulated a variety of linguistic and poetic conventions comprising his interactions within Lowland Scottish university circles, an English-allied SSPCK, and rural Highland communities.[113] In the *brosnachadh*, "Incitement to the Highland Clans" the speaker promises, "Up in the sky fierce warlike Mars/Will guide you when you smite," ("*'S bidh* Mars *creuchdach, cogach, reubach,/Anns an speur 'g ur seòladh*"), and the reference to a Roman god reminds us that MacDonald's poems seldom fail to incorporate allusions to and the language of a variety of poetic traditions. To observe that MacDonald also appropriated elements of an Anglo-British program for cultural hegemony is not to argue that MacDonald's gestures were merely derivative, but rather to understand the mutual influence of these social bodies and to illuminate the very limits of the British efforts.

My reading of MacDonald's alternating positions and myriad literary borrowings also differs from the "cultural schizophrenia" that David Daiches and others have attributed to eighteenth-century Scottish writers, for I am stressing MacDonald's active participation in the creation of what is now seen as a national Gaelic literary tradition.[114] If his literacy work was tactical, as I have been arguing it might have been, and the form and content of his poetry a composite of traditions learned through contact with other cultures, his activities might appear less a "schizophrenia" and more the "intentional hybridity" Robert Young has described as "contestatory activity, a politicized setting of cultural differences against each other dialogically."[115] Thus, although I have referred to MacDonald's as a "strange case," alluding to Stevenson's *The Strange Case of Dr. Jekyll and Mr. Hyde,* I mean to revise the conventional understanding of the Jekyll/Hyde figure as applied to Scottish writers. MacDonald was not merely prey to competing, imposed literary and literacy traditions; he also manipulated them for his own cultural program. While it is true that seemingly assimilated Scots such as MacDonald could – and were often forced to – "pass," the Hyde-like MacDonald forces us to rethink this assimilation. His Jacobite poetry is merely the material evidence for what had been true all along: the constraining demands that he mimic English literacy and identity produced neither a homogeneous British subject, nor a passively doubled Highlander, but an actively recoding border crosser.

If this is a type of colonial mimicry, the indeterminacy of mimicry that Bhabha describes as "at once both resemblance and menace" is certainly apposite in this case. MacDonald and Hyde both represent menaces, particularly because of the close resemblance they are capable of bearing to those they imitate and the ways in which they take up their technologies in order to destroy them. We see this dangerous mimicry at work in, again, the title poem. As Ronald Black observes, in this poem MacDonald enmeshes the form of Presbyterian catechism – which he would have taught in his capacity as a Society instructor and catechist – into his revolutionary verse. Black writes:

The preliminary arguments of his ode to Gaelic reflect Question 1 of the Shorter Catechism, *Creud is crìoch àraid do'n duine?* 'What is man's chief end?'
    Gur h-ì as crìoch àraid
    Do gach cainnt fo'n ghréin . . .
(The chief end/Of every speech under the sun is . . .) communication, he says, self-expression, improvement, and (quoting Hosea xiv:2)
    . . . gu laoigh ar beòil
    Dh'ìobradh do Dhia nan dùl –
    Is i h-àrd chrìoch mhór
    Gu bhith toirt dò-san cliú.

(... to render the calves of our lips/To God of the elements – /Its great high end is/To be giving Him praise.). This reflects the answer to Question 1, *Is crìoch àraid do'n duine, Dia a ghlòrachadh, agus a mhealtainn gu suthain*. 'Man's chief end is to glorify God, and to enjoy him forever.' (17)

I quote Black's research at length because it demonstrates, in startling terms, the ways in which MacDonald makes use of the literacy forms with which his newly literate audience would have been familiar in order to remake the message inscribed in those forms. As Pratt would put it, this is not an "autochthonous form of self representation" but a "collaboration and appropriation of idioms of the conqueror" (*Imperial*, 7). The rote bluntness of the catechism structure inculcates a habitual sense of self as powerless mimic – the mimicry is structured into the incorporated repetition of the questioner's language in the respondent's answer. The image of Highland students who, like their Lowland and English counterparts, echo in English the very words of the English-speaking instructor presents an imperious scene of enforced impersonation. MacDonald's redirection of the catechist's line of questioning, however, is extraordinary both for its practical appeal to a form with which his students would have been familiar and for its radical implications in wielding that form to cut at the very heart of colonialist rhetoric. Resembling Hyde's alternating performance and abomination of Jekyll's identity, MacDonald assimilates not only the use of English, but also, and more importantly, the association of language and cultural identity; yet his performance of that identity redounded with the threat of a code gone awry. Recall that Jekyll describes the "ape-like tricks that he [Hyde] would play me, scrawling in my own hand blasphemies on the pages of my books, burning the letters and destroying the portrait of my father."[116] The Anglo-British authorities perceived MacDonald as a "monster" as he scrawled the "blasphemies" of Gaelic Jacobite poetry, now understood by a newly literate readership. The town's hangman set a copy of his poems ablaze in the center of Edinburgh, renouncing the profound threat to authority that the poems represented.

MacDonald, then, is perhaps best characterized as a transvestite figure to the extent that he performs acceptable and oppositional national (linguistic) identities in an equally convincing fashion; his successful practice of each makes obvious the scaffolding of their construction. My use of the provocative figure of "transvestism" intentionally invokes the complex gendering of language and linguistic practices at work in the Highlands, a gendering I have only been able to touch on briefly thus far. On a figurative level, I use this term to get at what Lori

Chamberlain describes as gendered "metaphorics of translation."[117] If, as Chamberlain has shown, print culture, with its emphasis on the original, has figured translation as a secondary, reproductive activity, then critical interpretations of MacDonald's oeuvre that overlook his glossary translating work in favor of his poetry might be said to fall into this understanding of the productive, primary powers of "original" poetry. But even on the level of his poetics, in his embrace of a bardic tradition which eschews notions of originality and his conscious borrowing from a range of cultural codes, MacDonald could be said to inhabit the "overcoded" realm of translation, rejecting, or at least playing with the dominant associations of poetry with masculine, originary power. The overcoding of translation threatens, as Chamberlain writes, "to erase the difference between production and reproduction which is essential to the establishment of power . . . Translations can, in short, masquerade as originals, thereby short-circuiting the system" (460). It is this masquerading that I want to accentuate in MacDonald, and not his supposed "original" contribution to an indigenous literature. If, as Chamberlain also points out, the gendered quality of "fidelity" is central to the metaphorics of translation, MacDonald's transvestite status, his infidelity to either tradition per se, poses a seditious challenge to the terms and values of linguistic translation and cultural transmission.

If the term "transvestite" is useful in terms of these metaphorics of translation, interrogating notions of "originality" and authentic identity prior to performance or outside of the logic and complications of reproduction, it is also useful in the more literal social history of gender construction in the Society's work in the Highlands. The SSPCK hoped to import, along with Anglo-British economic and linguistic relationships, more fixed gender roles. Until 1738 only boys attended the schools, and even after girls were allowed in, they always remained in the minority. When the Society admitted girls in 1738, they calmed members' misgivings about introducing girls to the "masculine" sphere of English by introducing weaving and housewifery instruction, thus hoping to impose a gendered division of labor.

Language also functioned as a means of distinguishing and gendering public and private spheres. The use of Gaelic remained "acceptable" in the home and in the church, but not in arenas of British state control – schools, legislative bodies, etc. Unable to control language use in the home, and unwilling to change the format of Gaelic sermons – the Church of Scotland allowed sermons to be preached in the native tongue of a parish (sermons were, however, written in English) – the SSPCK was most interested in marking English as the official language and getting Highlanders to understand it and associate it with political authority. This public/private divide was also mapped onto the literate/oral distinction: written language was associated with those in power, such as teachers, ministers, and some Lowlanders; the oral was associated with the marginalized, such as older people, women, and those without the means to send their children to any school.

The SSPCK's distinction between public and private language use functions as another discursive ambivalence which MacDonald exploits, for the division between public/English and private/Gaelic space and culture produced doubled Highland subjects. The gendering of Gaelic speaking as female and private was open to a resistant politicization when the Society described its work in the "public" English instruction of boys as an effort to make the Highlanders more "tame and gentle," "to direct their morals, and to train them up in the social virtues," and to "increase . . . piety and virtue" (*Present State* 36, 39, 41). As Gaelic continued to be spoken in the home and church, these were also the spaces where the direct "taming" through state intervention would not occur.[118] MacDonald makes use of the "female" space not subject to such "taming" as he reclaims Scots Gaelic personified as a combative woman. Throughout his poem "The Resurrection of the Ancient Scottish Language," MacDonald genders Scots Gaelic as female, apostrophizing, "O splendid granddam" ("*O 'n t-seann mhathair chiatach*"), and emphasizing both conventional Anglo-British eighteenth-century feminine gender qualities, such as reproductive capacity (he describes a personified Scots Gaelic as "yet bearing varied fruit" ["*Lìonmhor's mìle buaidh*"]) and unconventional ones, such as martial characteristics (she is also "fit to destroy" ["*An labhairt shìolmhor*"]). In this understanding of gender, distinct from a later feminized nostalgic vision of Celtic language and culture, the "feminine" ancient Gaelic is "In style, both hard and keen" (" '*Na glòir fìor ghuineach, cruaidh*"), "strong," "wise," and "vehement" and is also imbued with agency; she "urges men to slay" ("*Bhrosnachadh an t-sluaigh*") and has "loosened every knot" ("*Dh' fhuasgladh snaoim gach cùis'*"). If MacDonald had earlier celebrated written English as that language best suited for British military presence throughout the empire, he seems to have made use of prevailing notions of gender and respective English/Celtic identities to "resurrect" a powerful feminine Celtic position in this later poetry.

Although MacDonald's open resistance through the appropriation of imperial grammar's rhetoric of linguistic superiority and universality highlights the colonial subject's ability to act as linguistic agent, the consequences are mixed. His work powerfully exemplifies resistant nationalism's turn to what Partha Chatterjee might call an "inner domain of cultural identity."[119] For Chatterjee, resistant nationalism turns not to the outer, material culture of official bureaucratic nationalism but to "an inner domain bearing the 'essential' marks of cultural identity." As MacDonald invokes the linguistic and cultural uniqueness or "essence" of the Gaels, as he reanimates their now "private" and feminine language, he revalues an inner domain of cultural identity. Chatterjee reads such resistant nationalism as something more than a modular nationalism simply imitating dominant European predecessors, and his caveat that resistant nationalism is neccessarily more than the "consumption" of prior European models is an important revision to our understanding of its distinct mode. Yet we might want to stop short of Chatterjee's full endorsement of this form of nationalism, not because it is somehow more dangerous than official nationalism, but because it is imperial relations which have rendered that "inner" space as the only one available for such feelings. Further, the aspects of the turn to an inner cultural domain that Chatterjee believes to be its greatest strengths are those that are to my mind its most profound limitations. Chatterjee insists that the public/private divide is less significant than an inner, spiritual/outer, material divide, for this makes possible the notion of community in what had previously been understood as a private, individual realm. This "community," in turn, and the inner, spiritual domain of cultural identity on which it is predicated, neutralize class difference in the interest of community building. In this inner realm of community, elite and subaltern are no longer understood as acting " in opposition" to each other but instead "negotiate" "for the purposes of producing consent" (13). This, I would argue, is indeed intrinsic to MacDonald's, or any, cultural nationalist politics. In the Scottish context, in particular, Pittock has argued that Jacobitism and its mixing of high and low culture reflected and helped produce "crossclass links."[120] But this is a far less progressive phenomenon than either Chatterjee or Pittock believe it to be. In an era in which those class distinctions were increasingly profound, and the recognition of those class dynamics all the more crucial, both in the Highlands and in the rest of Britain, Chatterjee's claim that sovereignty could already exist, and continue to thrive, within the spiritual realm of a resistant nationalism seems pyrrhic indeed.

MacDonald reveals the reversals and complexities of colonial literacy instruction, and in trying to assess the significance of his case I have tried to bear in mind Laura Murray's perceptive observation that we must "come up with complex readings" that move beyond "celebratory readings of resistance and bleaker readings of total subjection to the ideology of the colonizer."[121] The way in which MacDonald fabricates a linguistic cultural identity in resistance to Anglo-Britain's imperial grammar has much to tell us about the status of all nationalist claims. Yet when MacDonald is enlisted in narratives of Scottish nationalism, it is not because he illuminates the recoding and appropriation of a dominant set of ideas and technologies.[122] Instead, he has been incorporated into an "indigenous" national tradition which undervalues his transcultural gestures. Hugh MacDiarmid, for instance, a central figure of modern Scottish nationalism, has edited volumes of MacDonald's texts, yet these have for the most part failed to highlight the international and cross-cultural borrowings and re-codings of MacDonald's writings.[123] Given MacDiarmid's own "intentional hybridity," his invented languages, and his playing of languages against each other, we might imagine the Scots' embrace of MacDonald to revolve around his own "intentional hybridity," but that has not been the case. This neglect of what I see as a key aspect of MacDonald's important work has happened, in part, because while we can point to MacDonald's multiple and inventive cultural appropriations, it was not to the fluidity of cultural borders that he overtly pointed. Instead, like his English nationalist contemporaries, he projects the standardization and stability of a newly printed language back into a misty, unified (national) culture of Alba.[124]

Despite the way he positioned his poetry, MacDonald's work, particularly in the combination of glossary and poetry, comes closest to a dialogic hybridity, what Alfred Arteaga defines as a discourse, "asserting dialogue by articulating an alternate discourse and by organizing itself in internal dialogue."[125] MacDonald demonstrates for us the interdependence of imperial grammar and national language and the performative quality of all national identities. This observation closely resembles the point with which we began: as a decreed language and literacy move across space, transcoded by colonial peoples, the social meaning of language use and literacy changes. Finally, the fluctuating, transnational significance of the language and literacy instruction is most compellingly figured not in any stable British or Gaelic national moment but in the literal movement – the mass emigration – it enabled. M. G. Jones writes that the SSPCK "shares the responsibility, with the changing economic conditions of the second half of the century, in inciting adventurous spirits to leave the country . . . a slow and steady trickle of Highlanders into the Lowlands persisted throughout the century, and . . . the stream of Highlanders who left the country to find homes across the seas seldom dried up" (*Charity*, 211). We might recall MacDonald's glossary dedication promise that such a glossary will help make young Highlanders useful not only at home but also as they move into the Lowlands and throughout the commonwealth. If MacDonald's reworkings of the Society's ambivalent methods and ideologies overturned the core/periphery relationship it hoped to maintain, the Society's own institutional literacy instruction blurred that relationship on a geographical level, as Highlanders moved both south, into the Lowlands, closer to England, and throughout the outposts of the British empire.[126] In also blurring the boundaries between universal and particular and between public and private so central to the Enlightenment discourse that informed it, MacDonald's manipulation of imperial grammar disrupted the center/margin binary integral to eighteenth-century Britain's understanding of itself. The case of MacDonald points to the need to reorient literary and cultural studies of eighteenth-century Britain away from the notion of indigenous national traditions and towards the intersections and global movement which produced the linguistic cultures we now call "Gaelic," "English," and "British." The neglected cultures of émigré Highlander communities would be one important place to start such work. Meanwhile, in the center of Britain, the response to the threat of the migration of English literacy was a move away from the spatialized continuous present of an imperial linguistic economy to an emphasis of the temporal "age old" character of the English nation and its language, a move to which we turn in the next chapter.

CHAPTER 2

"A grammarian's regard to the genius of our tongue": Johnson's Dictionary, *imperial grammar, and the customary national language*

At the same time as British administrators sought to convert Highlanders to English, British lexicographers and grammarians were reappraising the value of English itself, converting the British themselves to using, or at least recognizing as authoritative, a newly standardized version of the language.[1] Central to this national linguistic conversion was Samuel Johnson's *Dictionary of the English Language* (1755). My use of the concept of "conversion" to describe this education process points toward my contention that the *Dictionary*, along with the steadily increasing number of grammar books, alienated English from its contemporary speakers in ways not dissimilar to colonial linguistic practices. If, as Luke Gibbons writes, "those cultures on the receiving end of colonialism have had little choice but to fashion their identities in the presence of others," English subjects on the receiving end of standardized English now fashioned their linguistic identities in the presence of this newly official language.[2] As the *Dictionary* establishes a supraregional national standard, it refigures class and gender linguistic distinctions as cultural, ethnic, and, importantly, spatial differences, borrowing from the conventional markers of colonial difference. According to Johnson's stipulations in the Preface to his *Dictionary*, those cultural differences render their speakers' languages too particular to be properly national. Yet the disinterested, "general" position from which Johnson believes standard English could be produced is the position of nobody, making this standard in several senses "nobody's language."[3]

To claim that the lexicon of the *Dictionary* represents a language foreign to many English speakers works against notions of a national linguistic patrimony that have accrued around the *Dictionary*. Few printed works in English have made as forceful or lasting a case for the idea of a single vernacular and its status as national cultural heritage.

As a hefty printed tome, the folio, two-volume first edition of the *Dictionary* offered the weighty authority of the complete record of a self-contained language as large and significant as the Bible.[4] Johnson suggests this language was produced by and mirrored an equally contained nation, referring to the "genius of our tongue," to "characteristical difference(s) of tongues" between nations (*Plan*, 32) – he defines "nation" as "a people distinguished from another people; generally by their language" – and to a "fabric of the tongue" unique to each nation (Preface, 9).[5] In such phrases he naturalizes the language-nation connection. Benedict Anderson and Marshall McLuhan before him have identified print technology as the key catalyst in the connection of a single language to a single nation, arguing that print capitalism's standardization of vernacular languages helped readers conceive a stable national identity as material and concrete as the black and white of the printed page.[6] If, however, the central argument of this project is valid, if language theories and practices reveal empire's influence on national cultural formations, then these influences must also be at work in even its most "nationalist" print productions. As we saw in Chapter 1, an Anglo-British agenda around language and cultural identity influenced a Scots Gaelic nationalist poetics. But it is also true that the cultural perceptions and accompanying technologies that a rising Anglo-British administration used to negotiate colonial linguistic relationships also helped shape the construction of a standard English.

The resulting tension between colonial and more obviously national ways of thinking about language is related to long-standing debates, over which so much ink has been spilled, about whether Johnson hoped to fix English or merely to record it.[7] John Barrell has noted the eighteenth-century shift to a more clearly national understanding of language with a model of linguistic authority derived from the customary practices of "the people" (itself a vexed term, as Barrell points out) moving away from analogical principles. While he links this new model to arguments about the political authority of an ancient English constitution marshaled to defend the ousting of the Stuarts, the alternative "rational analogy" model extends beyond the defense of absolutism he perceives.[8] In posing universal laws against customary practices, the rational analogy model accords with the dictates of colonial linguistic pedagogy, posing as it does a set of fixed trans-temporal and trans-spatial laws.[9] In his popular *Short Introduction to English Grammar* (1762) Robert Lowth, for instance, appeals to this grammar when he writes, "English as it is spoken in polite society offends grammar" and aims to teach pupils the "main principles of grammar in general."[10] Many earlier grammarians celebrated English, yet urged its improvement in accordance with the rules of a universal grammar, thereby effacing, in a sense, the particularity of that vernacular.[11] "General grammar" was, Johnson claimed, the only assistance he had in arbitrating English lexicography in his *Dictionary*.[12] Fixing the language according to universal, external principles corresponds with the imperatives of imperial translation and codification, while describing the customs of common usage internal to Britain coincides with a nationalist rhetoric.[13] In making use of both models, Johnson's *Dictionary* awkwardly pivots between them.

While many writers have commented on the production of the *Dictionary* in relation to other European vernacular dictionaries, few have sought connections between it and the cultural matrices of an expanding empire.[14] It is not by accident that Johnson's mammoth *Dictionary* appeared in a period dominated by wars over and with colonial sites, also an "intensely creative period in terms of patriotic initiatives and discussion of national identity in Great Britain and Europe."[15] Johnson's *Dictionary* must surely be reckoned as one of those initiatives, most infamously in its Franco-phobia.[16] The universal coin of the realm, circulating throughout Britain's expanding empire, English could also reflect the superiority of its imperial national culture.[17] A. Archibald Lane foregrounds this possibility, invoking former imperial powers when he asks, "were we as industrious in . . . cultivating our language, as the Greeks and Romans . . . we might have as learned Leaders . . . as they had who by their Learning, Civility and Eloquence in their mother tongue, enlarged their Dominions. . . . [Since] these learned languages are now dead, ought not the British . . . to polish . . . their living language?"[18] Close to our focus on internal colonization, J. C. D. Clark links the final triumph of English vernacular over classical learning to the defeat of Jacobitism. Johnson began his *Dictionary* "in spring of 1746, as the Stuart cause was going down to final and crushing defeat," signaling the last blow to a once-thriving Scottish classical humanist tradition with which Johnson had identified.[19] While the lingering influence of Latin is apparent throughout the *Dictionary*, Johnson's interest in English, "so far as it is our own," reflects the revaluation of English in relation to Latin that had been taking place throughout the Renaissance.[20] Clark's perhaps overstated claim that Johnson was a Jacobite need not undermine his larger point: that an Anglo-British dominance over Scotland figures in Johnson's retreat from a purely classical tradition and in his contribution to the development of an official vernacular English.

In the first section of this chapter, I examine how imperial contexts influenced the particular model of language promoted by English grammarians and lexicographers in the eighteenth century, but here I want to pause briefly to consider one important difference between language models in colonial and national contexts: their distinct claims of spatial and temporal continuity. Anglo-British administrators legitimated British expansion into the Highlands as a civilizing movement through space, demanding a "general" or "universal" model of language capable of endless translation. English nationalists, however, validated the claims of the nation by invoking the movement of a unique English culture through time, tracing its roots to a distant past.[21] The claims of the two are nonetheless connected. In both the colonial and national cases, those attempting to implement the recognition of a standard language articulate their efforts as a means of overcoming foreignness — either the foreignness produced by spatial or by temporal borders. In his *Proposal* for correcting English, for instance, Jonathan Swift warns, "genius for History . . . will be read with Pleasure but a very few Years, and in an Age or two shall hardly be understood without an interpreter."[22] Johnson also laments that in the absence of a "grammatical and settled" English, "Homer has fewer passages unintelligible than Chaucer," and Shakespeare's language has become "obsolete . . . his sentiments obscure . . . by accident and time."[23] The impenetrability of writing from as recent as the sixteenth-century Johnson "hope[s] to remove by my book."[24] The specter of a receding and thus increasingly "foreign" national literature horrifies Johnson. It was in the very language of that literature that, in his optimistic moods, he hoped to site, tautologically, an eternal English vernacular and a superior Anglo-British learning.[25]

The construction of a standard aimed at overcoming the estrangement of time depends upon the exclusion of the language of many English speakers. In the first half of the eighteenth century, for instance, dramatic class and regional differences were legible in a written English whose "standard" version grammarians and lexicographers were still determining. Consider the language of this sentence, written by William Perfed, a steward, in 1730: "Hee tould mee hee would bee oute a boute May day next and desiread of mee to aquant you with it and that hee would cale of mee for an aser at that time," next to the Earl of Chesterfield's language in a sentence written in 1729: "When I had the honor of seeing his majesty, I had not time to beg permission to pay my duty in England, where not only my own inclinations call me . . . but where also my own private affairs render my presence necessary."[26] While Johnson would write off much of Perfed's language as at best "dialect," it is important to remember that behind the naming of a particular usage as "dialect" or nonstandard is a social struggle.[27] Thus, in constructing national subjects in their relationship to hearing, speaking, reading, and writing one particular version of the language, the "standard" language also constitutes them as belonging to the nation on differing terms.[28] These hierarchized terms construct certain members as "outsiders" and inferior at precisely the point at which they recognize the national language.[29] Registering an uncomfortable awareness of that struggle, Johnson's *Dictionary* oscillates between the rhetoric of inclusion and exclusion and between the languages of the general and particular, of everybody and nobody, and of the public and private.[30]

The resulting instability of the divide between "native" and "outsider" denaturalizes, like a ghostly colonial presence, the "homogeneous" language of general national identity that dictionaries and grammar books profess. This link between colonial and national "outsiders" is not surprising. The crucible of standard English formation was not British society itself so much as it was the "other" spaces of colonial linguistic and literacy instruction. As Wechselblatt writes, "to colonize – to reproduce English culture in others – is to (retroactively) produce a national 'common language' at home. Englishness . . . depend[s] for its exemplarity upon the prior production of itself abroad" ("Pathos," 393). The rhetoric around an imperially facilitated national standard enabled not simply an "us/them" binary but also gradations of "Englishness" within English society. Many, notably Robert DeMaria, have pointed to Johnson's ironic stance regarding the ultimate impossibility of this work, yet Johnson's acknowledgment of the futility of fixing English points not simply to a failed ideal. It also invites us to reimagine a series of multiple, contingent language communities for whom day-to-day language experience consistently challenges the notion of a single, shared "ideal" language. The idea of a standard language that speaks and writes a single national community is resisted both within the text itself and by its many readers; such an idea, then, must be continuously remade and reasserted in the *Dictionary* and in the rhetoric of nationalist linguistic community in general.

I. IMPERIAL LEXICOGRAPHIES

English and the "alien word"

Not only did the rhetoric of British empire help motivate the construction of a standard English, but the very technologies and models of language produced in the colonial context, what I have been calling "imperial grammar," also helped organize the structure of that standard, and in this section I trace that connection. The earliest word guides in English featured clusters of words organized around a specific object, such as a "ship," arranged in a quasi-narrative format.[31] The alphabetical dictionaries from the Renaissance on mark a change in structure, and while fragmenting those earlier conceptual frames, seem to ratify the possibility of total knowledge, containing everything "from A to Z." In their arbitrary but highly effective alphabetical organization, they endorse a classificatory system which would render knowledge transparent and are thus recognizable as a product of what Foucault called the episteme of the "Classical Age" of the Enlightenment, distinguished by its "taxonomy" and "'general grammar' that was quite alien to . . . historical analyses and works of exegesis."[32] While forces cut against these structures, both within the *Dictionary*'s text, and externally, through its readers, it is important to bear in mind the ways in which the alphabetical dictionary connotes an ordered control of language and the world it would represent. If, as DeMaria argues, following Umberto Eco, "We might dispense[ ] with the fictions of definitions and leave[ ] the dictionary in the condition of a passive tool" (*Johnson's Dictionary*, ix), we come to this point despite, and not because of, the dictionary's structure.

If we are to avoid a formal determinism, however, overarching claims about the structural and cultural significance of dictionaries must be nuanced in terms of the historical circumstances in which specific readers make use of dictionaries. The alphabetical dictionary, for example, appeared in the context of imperial commerce, in the form of polyglot glossaries. Designed for merchants widening their scope of trade, some of the first glossaries consisted of lists of foreign words encountered in exchange with new populations.[33] Produced out of the exigencies of negotiation, it is not surprising that these quick-and-ready guides to key words in foreign tongues worked on the principle of a one-to-one equivalence between terms, limiting their lists of linguistic counterparts to the barest of essential information and establishing a truncated conception of language in the process.

The most significant predecessors to the English vernacular dictionaries, however, would be Latin and Latin/English dictionaries, and these, too, often reflect the structure of those word books produced in imperial contexts. Judith Anderson suggests that many of these alphabetized print collections instill an understanding of language as a fixed system of individual words, and not as an infinitely generating system responding to myriad contingencies.[34] The structural hermeticism of these Latin/English dictionaries facilitates the revaluing of the vernacular itself. Anderson argues that the print dictionaries of the Renaissance became "a kind of cultural touchstone" and adds, "there comes to be something reassuring, reliable, 'scriptural' about an authoritative book that contains the meaning of words" (92). The at times abbreviated understanding of language in these Latin/English dictionaries is undoubtedly related to their status as pedagogical tools, and the "hard word" dictionaries that followed them in the seventeenth century, guiding less-educated readerships through the rocky terrain of difficult and foreign words that they might encounter in their reading, exaggerate the alienating features of these earlier dictionaries. Robert Cawdrey's *A Table Alphabeticall* (1604), for instance, containing "the true writing, and understanding of hard usuall English wordes, borrowed from the Hebrew, Greeke, Latine, or French, &c." is a spare, utilitarian word list (Fig. 3).[35] Although they feature words a reader would find in English texts, these dictionaries read much like bilingual dictionaries, taking translation of foreign terms as their premise. The concentration on the single word recalls the one-to-one relationship between word and thing – a logic of equivalence – discussed in relation to the glossary form in Chapter 1. With no distinction in the typeface between the "foreign"-derived words and their "English" definitions, a logic of synonymy suggests that one word is the exact equivalent of another, without a sense of the variety of possible meanings available to that defined word. The readers of these "hard word" dictionaries, one suspects, would not be in much of a position to question their closed frame of linguistic meaning.

This static understanding of language suggests V. N. Volosinov's concept of the alien word, the priestly foreign language encountered by a conquering army or the agents of an infiltrating commerce.[36] More broadly, the "alien word" suggests a way of looking at language shaped by an exclusive consideration of languages in imperial relationships, a

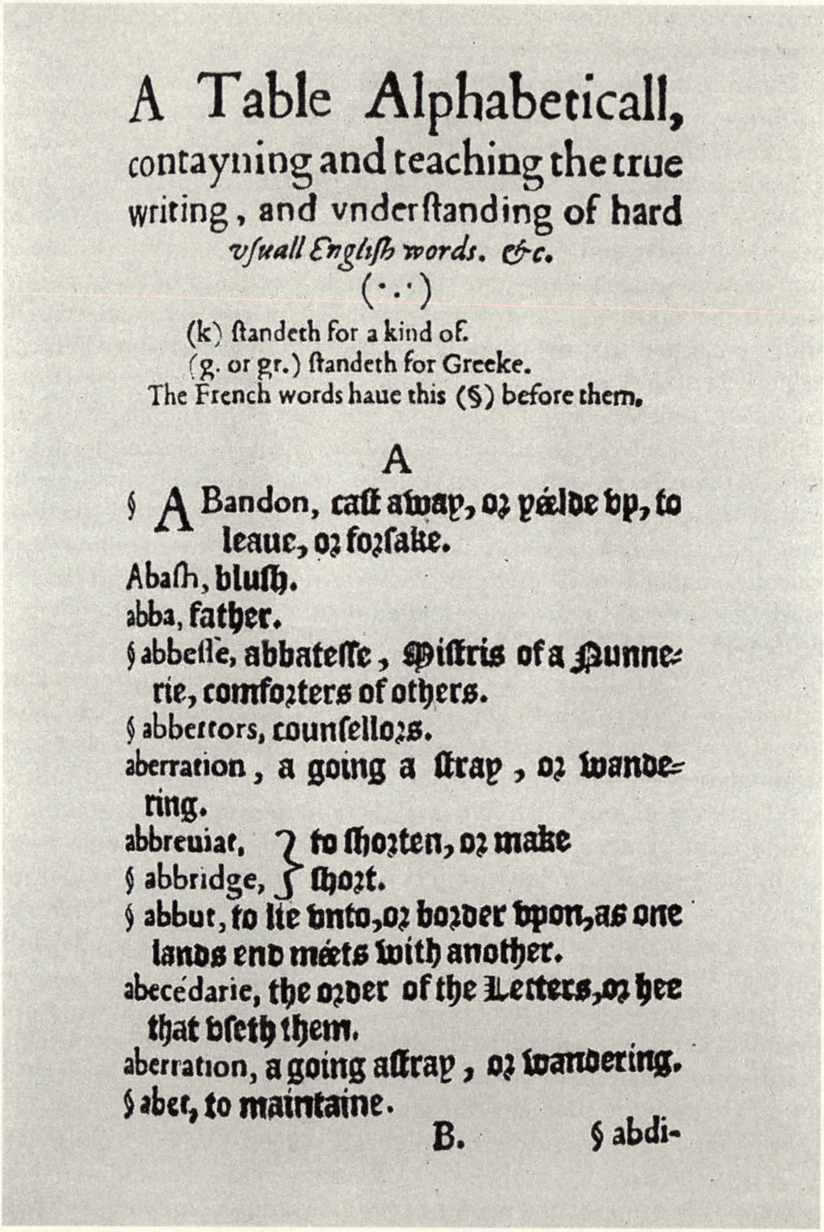

A Table Alphabeticall,

contayning and teaching the true writing, and vnderstanding of hard *vsuall English words. &c.*

(∴)

(k) standeth for a kind of.
(g. or gr.) standeth for Greeke.
The French words haue this (§) before them.

A

§ A Bandon, cast away, or yælde vp, to leaue, or forsake.
Abash, blush.
abba, father.
§ abbesse, abbatesse, Mistris of a Nunnerie, comforters of others.
§ abbettors, counsellors.
aberration, a going a stray, or wandering.
abbreuiat, } to shorten, or make
§ abbridge, } short.
§ abbut, to lie vnto, or border vpon, as one lands end meets with another.
abecédarie, the order of the Letters, or hee that vseth them.
aberration, a going astray, or wandering.
§ abet, to maintaine.

B.   § abdi-

Figure 3. From Robert Cawdrey, *A Table Alphabeticall*, London, 1604.

filter emphasizing foreignness and domination. Because the philologist focuses on the "monumental" language of another culture (Volosinov argues that the imperial philologist "tears the monument out of the generative process of that particular ideological domain" [73]), the resulting philology perceives a passive *language* rather than active *languages*. Written from a perspective of alterity to the particular culture and language they define, these glossaries and grammars conceal the multivalent nature of the foreign language they order. Like Volosinov, Raymond Williams traces the "advance in empirical knowledge of languages" and the "wholly remarkable analysis and classification of this knowledge" to "its political history, within the dynamic development of Western societies in a period of extending colonialism."[37] He also asserts that "the privileged situation of the observer" constitutes the linguistic object of knowledge as "in texts, the records of a *past* history; in speech, the activity of an alien people in subordinate (colonialist) relations."

Although both Williams and Edward Said after him locate this colonial philology in the nineteenth century, their analyses are applicable to earlier periods of linguistic study, as evidenced in the glossary structure we discussed in Chapter 1.[38] Volosinov argues that this perception of language organizes not only the way linguists look at foreign languages, but ultimately the way they will view their own, "dictat[ing] that notions about the word be preeminently oriented toward the alien word" (75). When, for instance, in 1702, the *New English Dictionary* includes "native" English words from daily speech, they, too, are arranged on the model of the dictionaries of foreign, difficult words. An alienating model, this systematization of the native language initiates and later reinforces a view of English as stable, even as its systematization is predicated on interlanguage translation. The emergence of interest in the establishment of a standard vernacular is well known – John Dryden, Joseph Addison, Jonathan Swift, Alexander Pope, and Daniel Defoe all argued for the establishment of a language academy to "fix" the English language – but its contemporaneity to British imperial grammarians' reduction of colonial languages to a "stable" authoritative print version in glossaries of the languages of North America and the Highlands is less often remarked.[39] It is not mere coincidence, then, that we find in Johnson's *Plan* allegories of imperial conquest describing the "taming" of English and its speakers. Nor, then, is it only the Gaelic-speaking Highlanders who experienced an alienating codification of their tongue in the eighteenth century.

At odds: "primitive signification" and the figurative language of the nation

It would be far too simplistic – and inaccurate – to argue that Johnson merely borrowed from the methods of imperial grammar to construct a standard lexicon, for we shall soon observe how competing nationalist imperatives worked against those methods. Also, I am not accusing Johnson of imperialist sympathies – far from it. Johnson denounced imperialist expansion on many occasions, writing at one point, "I do not wish well to discoveries, for I am always afraid they will end in conquest and robbery."[40] Yet in maintaining that literate societies were more advanced than "oral" ones, and that English literacy could lead to colonial "improvement," Johnson helped develop an imperialist ideology that founded Britain's right to expansion on its supposed superiority in language use and literacy, particularly in the Highlands.[41] The image of language's stable relation to the world offers a consoling sense that newly discovered languages, formidable ancient languages, and even the English language itself could be mastered along a universal arrangement of correspondence anchoring prolific language to an objective material world. In this section we shall see how Johnson, while he despairs of the possibility of a seamless word/world mapping, frequently attempts to return to that comforting vision of language in the "philosophic" language and material "primitive" terms he privileges. Making use of a logic of equivalence we have identified with imperial grammar, many entries take the form of synonyms, as in "TO FOB, 1. to cheat; to trick; to defraud" or antonyms, as in "STANDING . . . 3. not running." Similar to the bilingual glossary, the native word dictionary translates one word for another, and in both cases that translation often takes place through a structural principle of substitution based on a binary of identity or difference. We can observe the appeal to a stable word/world relationship most clearly in the number of "philosophic" words, W. K. Wimsatt's name for the scientific, descriptive terms that Johnson's often includes.[42] Johnson remained committed to "philosophic" words, which – because they registered a quantifiable and systematic universe and because they were often based on Greek and Latin, dead languages – promised stability across space and time. No longer common to anyone, the Latin that students learned in their grammars and dictionaries was beyond the "corruption" of daily usage, lofty in its authority and fixedness.[43] The *Monthly Magazine* quotes Johnson as having said, in defense of his Latinisms, "Every language must be servilely formed after the model of some one of the ancient, if we wish to give durability to our works" (Leonard, *Doctrine*, 50). Included Latinate words such as "BUCCELLATION" meaning "in some chymical authors... a dividing into large pieces" or "CICATRIZATION"... [the] act of healing a wound" might circulate with ease across cultures – understood by Latin-reading natural philosophers as part of a universal scientific language – but would be unlikely to circulate in general society, and so their meaning might remain relatively set. Further, their illustration from passages from such works as *Sharp's Surgery* and *Harvey on Consumption* drew from a scientific, seemingly transparent discourse.

Johnson's was one of the earliest native word dictionaries, however, to reckon with multiple meanings (with the exception of Benjamin Martin's *Lingua Britannica Reformata* [1749], which is said to have borrowed the technique from Johnson's *Plan*). To control those multifarious meanings, he assembles definitions in order from "radical primitives", root words or etymons, to their contemporary, and as Johnson sees it, corrupt, meanings. For instance, Johnson defines "capital":

CAPITAL
1. Relating to the head.
2. Criminal in the highest degree, so as to touch life.

Privileging the "natural and primitive signification," Johnson locates it first in the sequential rankings of his numbered definitions. Turning to the assumed certainty of the term's "etymology" – a word whose own etymon derives from "truth" – Johnson offers the originary Latin equation (from *capitus*, meaning head) to substantiate the solidity of the word's "first" meaning through an appeal to the authority of an ancient language and the material world. The "metaphorical" sense comes after, even if it is more familiar, and is admitted only when there are sufficient examples from polite writers. He separates the literal from the metaphorical as in

LUMINARY
1. Any body which gives light.
2. Any thing which gives intelligence.
3. Any one that instructs mankind.

and

CANDID
1. White. This sense is very rare.
2. Free from malice; not desirous of finding faults; fair open; ingenuous.

TO WEATHER
1. To expose to the air.
2. To pass with difficulty.
3. ... to accomplish against opposition.
4. To endure.

All of these definitions begin with reference to the material world, a "referent," appealing especially, in the case of "luminary" and "weather" to the natural world and to a vaguely scientific discourse. While candid comes from the Latin *candidus*, which translates as white, listing the first definition of "candid" as "white" is a stretch, which even Johnson admits.⁴⁴ Johnson demotes metaphorical meaning to third position in his line-up of multiple definitions, even if the metaphorical is the more well-known meaning of a word. His *Dictionary* definition of the word "metaphor" gets at the lawlessness it portends: "The application of a word to an use to which, in its original import, it cannot be put."⁴⁵ Johnson's ordering of definitions proposes that associative, random, creative aspects of metaphor, in contrast to the stability of "philosophic" meanings, are corrupting ephemera. The implicitly chronological rankings of definitions, from "primitive" and philosophical to recent and metaphorical, might pose a Utopic past of word/world correspondence, but they also document a fall from such linguistic grace. We find this even in non-metaphorical usages, as in the word "calamanco":

CALAMANCO. n.s. [a word derived, probably by some accident from *calamancus*, Lat. which, in the Middle Ages, signified a hat.] A kind of woollen stuff.

He was of a bulk and stature larger than ordinary, had a red coat, flung open to shew a calamanco waistcoat. *Tatler*, No. 96.

A word which meant "hat" in the Middle Ages has slipped into meaning a type of fabric; in this entry "calamanco" literally travels from the head to the torso. The word of everyday contemporary usage does not point back to its own continuity in time, but to difference through time, and the *Dictionary* becomes, as Johnson wryly admitted, a document of its own impossibility.

Johnson cannot maintain a regulatory ranking which would subordinate lawless metaphorical usage to the systematic coherence of "philosophic" discourse, not only because his attempt to order multiple meanings points, unavoidably, to shifts in meanings, but also because in promoting the uniqueness and value of the English language and British nation through time, Johnson draws from literature in English to illustrate a word's meaning. Like the compilers of earlier dictionaries,

Johnson envisions his *Dictionary* as assisting not only scholars but also new readers and even foreigners. Yet its price of 4 pounds 10 shillings put it out of the reach of such folks until it was later sold in a serial or abridged edition, making it initially more a handsome acquisition for the libraries of the well-heeled. For these readers the *Dictionary* would be a purchasable piece of English linguistic and literary patrimony. Increasingly understood as the means of transmitting a specifically national culture into the future, literature, even as it appears in fragmentary form in the *Dictionary*, conveys English national particularity, superiority, and continuity. These literary quotations, however, undermine the promised stability of those structures borrowed from imperial grammar. In quoting literature, Johnson continually encounters figurative language. Oddly he uses it to exemplify the "natural and primitive" meanings of words. Consider, for instance, his entry for the word "gem":

GEM.
1. a jewel, a precious stone of whatever kind
   I saw his bleeding rings,
their precious *gems* new lost, became his guide
   Led him, begg'd for him, sav'd him from despair. *Shakespeare*
Love his fancy drew;
   and so to take the *gem* Urania sought. *Sydney*

Categories of literal and figural blur as "a precious stone" is personified. The *Dictionary* teems with examples of this merging of figural and literal. The first definition of "flock" (the noun), for instance, links it again to a material reference from the natural world, as "a company; usually a company of birds and beasts." Yet the illustrative quote is figural, "How will she love when the rich golden shaft/Hath kill'd the *flock* of all affections else/That live in her. *Shakesp. Twelfth Night.*" In associating plural affections with "a company, usually a company of birds or beasts," this quotation strangely animates "affections."

This is one of several ways that the "national" language, materialized through illustrations from the nation's "finest writers," challenges the simple codification and transparent view of language of imperial grammar. The same slippage is evident in the exemplary quotation for "capital." He cites Milton, recording, "Needs must the serpent now his capital bruise/Expect with mortal pain. *Paradise Lost. b. xii.l.383.*" Milton is, like Shakespeare, well known for his nimble puns, and these lines ask us to associate the serpent with a bruise "criminal in the highest degree" as well as "relating to the head." Such linguistic agility is one of the very aspects canon-makers celebrate in Milton, and yet the word-play of his writing also compromises the stabilizing efforts of the *Dictionary*. I am inclined to disagree, then, with DeMaria and others who adopt Johnson's claims that the lists of quotations help readers understand even further shades of meanings. While they do present hues of meaning, such quotations also sacrifice clear meaning for the sake of displaying the maximum number of quotations from British authors whom the *Dictionary* affirms as canonical, and, by the same turn, from whom the *Dictionary* derives its authority. Their metaphorical examples unmoor word from material world, working against the promise of the philosophic word. The very fragmentariness of the quotations speaks to a particular readership – one familiar enough with the authors cited to recognize the quotation and its context. Alternatively, such quotations might precipitate a desire in the *Dictionary*'s less-well-read readers to acquire such knowledge, thereby consolidating a national identity around a collection of canonized national authors, thus simultaneously limiting and constructing a national reading community. But such citations cannot help stabilize the language.

Legions of scholars have commented on how Johnson elegizes his defeated hopes of fixing the language. Johnson writes, "Kindred senses may be so interwoven, that the perplexity cannot be disentangled, nor any reason be assigned why one should be ranged before the other" (Preface, 4). In this dramatic image of infinite regress, we might be tempted, as many Johnson scholars have been, to identify the source of Johnson's dilemma in the heroic, if overly ambitious, goals he had set out for himself. According to this reading, we are struck, as we are meant to be, by his humility in the face of this challenging project, one of the high-water marks of the Enlightenment. The *Dictionary*'s massive scale, its aim to control through ordering and categorization, and its logic of equivalence demonstrate its indebtedness to Enlightenment thought, and yet the literal/figural blur points towards Enlightenment's very limits. Johnson's "failure," however, is more accurately understood as an ideological breakdown, namely the incompatibility of an Enlightenment-influenced "imperial grammar" and a rising cultural nationalism that imperial expansion had helped precipitate. If the *Dictionary* is a "failure" at living up to the fixed codification of the imperial grammar vision of language, that is in part because of its competing agenda as an artifact of cultural nationalism. As such an artifact, the *Dictionary* does very different work, work to which we shall now turn.

2. TOWARDS A NATIONAL TONGUE

The "wide sea of words": gendering language and its regulation

For Johnson, if language withholds the possibility of word/thing correspondence, that is in part because it is always "increasing" and changing, and he, like other writers of the period, genders the "living" language he confronts female, especially in its tendency towards growth and corruption. We have come to understand the centrality of motifs of reproduction to nationalist rhetoric; each successive generation must believe that it is in some sense performing its own nationhood, reproducing and yet modifying the meaning of national membership.[46] This national rhetoric fits rather effectively with an image of the nation's language as endlessly growing and changing. And yet Johnson and many of his cohorts perceived this quality of language as regrettable. The language, capable of reproduction, does so in excess, and he complains of the "exuberance of signification which many words have obtained, [so] that it is scarcely possible to collect all their meanings" (Preface, 16). In a related and much-cited passage he writes, "Words are the daughters of earth . . . things are the sons of heaven. Language is only the instrument of science, and words are but the signs of ideas: I wish, however, that the instrument might be less apt to decay, and that signs might be permanent, like the things which they denote" (Preface, 2). Strangely characterizing "things" as permanent, Johnson contrasts words as impermanent inasmuch as they are "earth's daughters" and, like all that lives on Earth, capable of growth and decay. It is this living, changing quality that Johnson laments. He positions things, and perhaps the scientific technologies analyzing them, as somehow outside of time and its corrupting force but also betrays an anxiety that even the scientific discourse that sets out to analyze these things depends on the unreliable *terra incognita* of language.

Johnson's gendering of language change corresponds to an Enlightenment image of nature as wild and entangled, fluid and unstable, in need of order and hierarchy. Citing the work of Luce Irigaray and Helene Cixous, Ruth Salvaggio has described the Enlightenment configuration of that "space" of nature, writing, "The Enlightenment mind . . . figured this 'other' space as a fluid realm outside the pristine islands and systems of men. It was the very fluid quality of this space that marked it as distinctly feminine, problematizing Enlightenment boundaries."[47] Explicitly identifying language with such fluidity, William Warburton writes, in 1747, "We have neither grammar nor dictionary, neither chart nor compass, to guide us through this wide sea of words" (Starnes and Noyes, *Dr. Johnson's*, 148), and, anticipating the chaos of language as he prepared to chart it in 1747, Johnson expresses fear of getting lost in this unsystematized terrain and being caught in its clutches. He worries that "in the extent of such variety I shall be often bewildered, and in the mazes of such intricacy, be frequently entangled" (*Plan* 34), for, unlike "every species of English literature," which has been cultivated, language has been "neglected, suffered to spread, under the direction of chance, into wild exuberance" (Preface, 1).

On one level, "Dictionary Johnson" can clearly be aligned with such Enlightenment figures as the encyclopedia writer or scientist, continually asserting an ordering force over a feminized space of the unknown and unordered. Confronted by this "speech copious and without order," Johnson puts himself in the role of order-maker. Yet Johnson perceives violence committed on the growing and living speech when "fixed" by transfer to the lifeless realm of the *Dictionary*, and indeed the "growth" represented by the metaphorical creations of poets form the life's blood of his illustrations. He attempts to preserve examples from living speech but admits they have been "mutilated" in his "hasty detruncations" (Preface, 5). In order for living language to be controlled and systematized, it must go through a process described in terms of brutality, and a movement from life to death – especially troubling as the *Dictionary* is meant to prolong linguistic life. Johnson images the lexicographer's ultimate dream as being able to "embalm his language, and secure it from corruption and decay" (Preface, 8); the ideal form for the object of examination is life-less but life-like, at best a perfectly preserved corpse. In this necrophillic figure is a revealing characterization of the *Dictionary* project. The body of language – gendered female – is open for endless inspection, preserved intact so that a total knowledge is possible. Dead, it is no longer capable of the entangling threat of unregulated growth. It is perhaps predictable, then, that Johnson describes his desire to "pierce deep into every science" (Preface, 7).[48]

On "waking" Johnson describes his dreams of linguistic embalmment as "laughable . . . indulgence" (Preface, 8), and this is in part because this way of thinking about his project is incompatible with the nationalist imperative to represent the language of "the people." He remonstrates in the Preface, "No dictionary of a living tongue ever can be perfect, since while it is hastening to publication, some words are budding, and some falling away" (28). If one – flawed and unattainable – means of ordering the language is through a scientific discourse of calculated collection and protected preservation, which is an approach akin to imperial grammar, another means is more directly sanctioned by a nationalist discourse, which, instead of killing growth, regulates it. Johnson makes use of imputed relationships of reproductive legitimacy, of bloodlines and familial connections, as a means of determining what constitutes acceptable growth.[49] Alluding to etymologies as words' family trees, Johnson only approves of those whose ancestry is "legitimate," enlisting a Utopian vision of a community of kindred native words following a patrilineal model of known descent. The *Plan*, for instance, invokes criteria of "pedigree" (16) and "purity" (4), and the Preface naturalizes English lexical "bloodlines" to an even greater degree, referring to words as having "ancestors" (10) and "genealogies" (6), to derivatives having "mother terms" and to words sharing a "race" (4). The language, in turn, might serve as a model for the ideal nation, where all legitimate members could claim legitimate consanguinity.

Words without pedigrees and traceable family trees comprise bastard words, words traceable only to bad stock. Hoping to regulate such reckless reproduction and bastardy, Johnson announces in the *Plan*, "we shall secure our language from being over-run with cant, from being crouded with low terms, the spawn of folly or affectation, and of which . . . no legitimate derivation can be shewn" (16). "Fugitive cant," the language *most* living because it is "always in a state of increase or decay," is not "durable" enough to appear in the *Dictionary* at all and must be "suffered to perish with other things unworthy of preservation" (23). Attempting to stop illegitimate reproduction and circulation, Johnson disparagingly labels words such as "budge" and "cajole" as "low" and "cant." In addition, the *Dictionary* warns that "bamboozle" is "a cant word not used in pure or grave writings" and that "agog" is "a word of uncertain etymology." Johnson also writes of "bandog" (a mastiff) "the original of this word is very doubtful." He writes of the word "bantling" (a young child) "if it has any etymology, it is corrupted from the old word 'bairn,' a little child, a low word," and, we might add, a Scots word. Such markers are meant to limit or curtail the usage of these suspect words and prevent their further reproduction.

Polite language and the "incontinency of female eloquence"

While Johnson at times figures language as a reproducing body, recall, in contrast, the frontispiece to Harris's *Hermes*, depicting the god of language as a bodiless head, its material transcendence suggested by the winged helmet it dons. If Johnson claims at some points to rely on "general grammar," alternatively, his embodied image of language suggests that his conception of language is quite different from Harris's universal, timeless structure and is instead a more particularly national, culturally specific, and continuously changing entity. The language of a nation, Johnson in fact suggests, could never be learned through a set of universal grammatical laws, for these fail to capture the *je ne sais quois* that makes the language distinct. The quotations he chooses to illustrate the *Dictionary* entry for "GRAMMAR" revealingly assert, "'We make a countryman dumb, whom we will not allow to speak but by the rules of *grammar,*' *Dryden*" and " 'The beauty of virtue still being set before their eyes, and that taught them with far more diligent care than *grammatical* rules,' *Sidney*." In selecting these illustrations, Johnson belittles the instructive power of grammatical rules; they silence fellow citizens (the second listed definition of "countryman") and have little power to instruct effectively.

Against the rote rules of general grammar stand the cultural prerogatives of customary usage and refined conversation over which women, at least in some writers' characterizations of polite society, hold sway. Many eighteenth-century writers, especially David Hume, see women as the initiators and mediators of polite language. Hume believes they "refine and polish human passions and behaviour," in part by "encouraging the exchange of politeness and refinement."[50] He asks, "What better school for manners, than the company of virtuous women; where the mutual endeavour to please must insensibly polish the mind, where the example of the female softness and modesty must communicate itself to their admirers?" (134). The Earl of Chesterfield's advertisement for the *Dictionary* provides one example of the contemporary gendered terms upon which the customary authority for language relies. He writes, "The genteeler part of our language . . . owes its rise and progress to my fair countrywomen, whose natural turn is more to the copiousness, than to the correction, of diction."[51] Chesterfield describes, "The difficulties he [Johnson] would have to encounter, if he attempted to reconcile the polite with the grammatical part of our language," juxtaposing two distinct models of language closely allied to those I am mapping.[52]

Although Johnson certainly had his differences with Chesterfield, in drawing from customary practice and polite letters, he turns to a feminine cultural zone – different from, for instance, a patriarchal divine right model of authority or an authority derived from an Enlightenment model of language operating according to principles of universal reason. Although Johnson and some of his contemporaries characterize living language in its boundless and chaotic disorder as feminine, it is a discourse of politeness and refinement – also gendered female, but for very different reasons – that is capable of bringing that language to order. Quintilian had long ago made "custom" the arbiter of proper usage, although eighteenth-century grammarians often paid mere lip service to this axiom. Johnson demonstrates a greater actual deference to custom, which I am linking to a shifting notion of language in relation to cultural nationalism. He writes, "Speech was not formed by an analogy sent from heaven. It did not descend to us in a state of uniformity and perfection, but was produced by necessity and enlarged by accident" (Preface, 17) and admits, reluctantly, that he has "been often obliged to sacrifice uniformity to custom" (2). Unlike earlier writers, who had confidently called for the public authority of a state-sponsored governing body capable of authoritarian regulation of language, Johnson rejected the rules-driven regulation of the French and Italian academies, identifying instead customary usage as the basis of a "private-sphere" authority of his *Dictionary*.

Johnson is, however, not entirely comfortable with the turn toward a female authority of polite and customary usage, particularly as the language of women is connected, in his mind, to their disconcerting reproductive capacities. Patricia Parker, for instance, has provided a rich elaboration of the history of characterizations of metaphor as threatening and feminized "reproductive" language, as she examines the "linkages between female copia, of body and of word, and the copiousness of texts."[53] This discourse stereotypes women as ceaseless gossips, possessing orifices in need of control, and associates the expansion of meaning with the figure of female dilation. The Earl of Chesterfield draws from this gendering of language's reproductive capabilities in his 1754 "puffs" for the *Dictionary*. He wonders if Johnson will allow into his *Dictionary* "those words and expressions, which, hastily begot, owe their birth to the incontinency of female eloquence" (*The World*, 100). Eloquence, a talent that, when masculine, is a form of control over language, connotes a lack of control in women. The use of the term "incontinency" suggests specifically a lack of control over the body, both a failure to control sexual appetite, or what a woman takes in, as it were, and an inability to control evacuative functions, what a woman lets out. Chesterfield goes on to describe the consequence of such incontinency, the scene of a word's birth. He writes, "I never see a pretty mouth opening to speak, but I expect, and am seldom disappointed, some new improvement of our language. I remember many expressive words coined in that fair mint. I assisted at the birth of that most significant word, 'flirtation'" (*The World*, 100). Such scenes suggest that in appropriating the production of linguistic value, polite women destabilize the "universal" value of English. Like MacDonald's "unfaithful" translation, a feminine linguistic production threatens the status quo of meaning production.

It seems no coincidence that the term coined in this instance – "flirtation" – is also sexualized. The freedom associated with minting words from a pretty mouth is explicitly a license, perhaps for the sexual freedom that might follow verbal flirtation, and it is interesting to recall that for Johnson, it is this orifice that is the source of his lexicographical problems.[54] Johnson refuses to define "FLIRTATION" in its modern "sexual" sense, and instead evasively defines it as, "a quick sprightly motion." The closest he gets to the sexual sense is one definition of "flirt, n. A pert young hussey." He attempts to control the term's usage here, yet the example he cites works against him, as the "sprightly motion" itself flirts with metaphorical tantalization. He quotes Pope who writes that "a muslin flounce, made very full, would give a very agreeable *flirtation* air." Similarly, the illustrative quotations for "TO FLIRT" describe making sprightly motions with a fan. Such motions, clearly, are part of the conventional body language of desire associated with flirtation as we, and his readers, would understand it. Yet this seems to be an association Johnson seeks to suppress. Importantly, Johnson describes flirtation as "a cant word among women." Like Chesterfield, but without his humorous "indulgence," Johnson views women as dangerous creators of new words and often attributes the strain of "fashionable" cant to women, warning against "female phrases and fashionable barbarisms."[55]

Directly preceding the word "to flirt" in the *Dictionary*, and related, is the word "FLIPPANT a word of no great authority, probably derived from *flip-flap*." (Fig. 4) Here the quality of volubility is again female. Johnson, following Addison, links this quality, half jokingly, to a biological cause. While Johnson genders language as excessively reproductive and chaotic, this characterization slips into one of women themselves as responsible for boundless linguistic reproduction. Parker gives account both of the insistence that women's "talkativeness" and their linguistic solecisms and neologisms be controlled, and of the means of doing so,

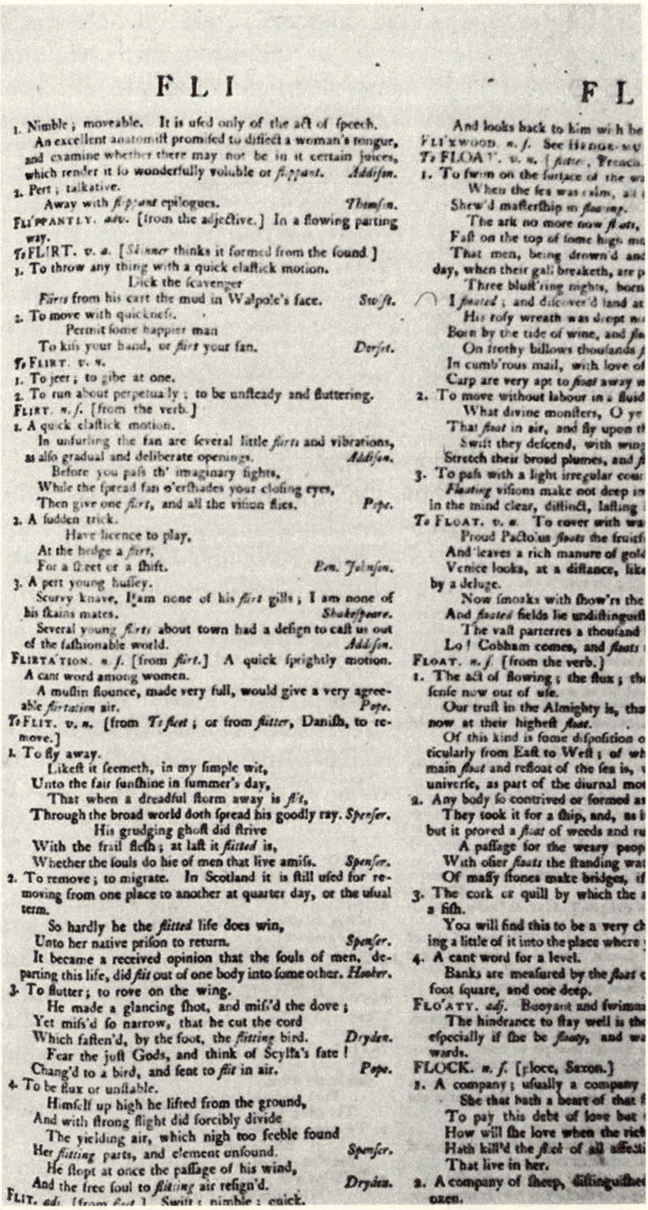

F L I

1. Nimble; moveable. It is ufed only of the act of fpeech.

An excellent anatomift promifed to diffect a woman's tongue, and examine whether there may not be in it certain juices, which render it fo wonderfully voluble or *flippant*. *Addifon.*

2. Pert; talkative.

Away with *flippant* epilogues. *Thomfon.*

Fli'ppantly. *adv.* [from the adjective.] In a flowing parting way.

To FLIRT. *v. a.* [*Skinner* thinks it formed from the found.]

1. To throw any thing with a quick elaftick motion.

Dick the fcavenger
Flirts from his cart the mud in Walpole's face. *Swift.*

2. To move with quicknefs.

Permit fome happier man
To kifs your hand, or *flirt* your fan. *Dorfet.*

To Flirt. *v. n.*

1. To jeer; to gibe at one.

2. To run about perpetually; to be unfteady and fluttering.

Flirt. *n. f.* [from the verb.]

1. A quick elaftick motion.

In unfurling the fan are feveral little *flirts* and vibrations, as alfo gradual and deliberate openings. *Addifon.*

Before you pafs th' imaginary fights,
While the fpread fan o'erfhades your clofing eyes,
Then give one *flirt*, and all the vifion flies. *Pope.*

2. A fudden trick.

Have licence to play,
At the hedge a *flirt*,
For a fheet or a fhift. *Ben. Johnfon.*

3. A pert young huffey.

Scurvy knave, I am none of his *flirt* gills; I am none of his fkains mates. *Shakefpeare.*

Several young *flirts* about town had a defign to caft us out of the fafhionable world. *Addifon.*

Flirta'tion. *n. f.* [from *flirt*.] A quick fprightly motion. A cant word among women.

A muflin flounce, made very full, would give a very agreeable *flirtation* air. *Pope.*

To Flit. *v. n.* [from *To fleet*; or from *flitter*, Danifh, to remove.]

1. To fly away.

Likeft it feemeth, in my fimple wit,
Unto the fair funfhine in fummer's day,
That when a dreadful ftorm away is *flit*,
Through the broad world doth fpread his goodly ray. *Spenfer.*

His grudging ghoft did ftrive
With the frail flefh; at laft it *flitted* is,
Whether the fouls do hie of men that live amifs. *Spenfer.*

2. To remove; to migrate. In Scotland it is ftill ufed for removing from one place to another at quarter day, or the ufual term.

So hardly he the *flitted* life does win,
Unto her native prifon to return. *Spenfer.*

It became a received opinion that the fouls of men, departing this life, did *flit* out of one body into fome other. *Hooker.*

3. To flutter; to rove on the wing.

He made a glancing fhot, and mifs'd the dove;
Yet mifs'd fo narrow, that he cut the cord
Which faften'd, by the foot, the *flitting* bird. *Dryden.*

Fear the juft Gods, and think of Scylla's fate!
Chang'd to a bird, and fent to *flit* in air. *Pope.*

4. To be flux or unftable.

Himfelf up high he lifted from the ground,
And with ftrong flight did forcibly divide
The yielding air, which nigh too feeble found
Her *flitting* parts, and element unfound. *Spenfer.*

He ftopt at once the paffage of his wind,
And the free foul to *flitting* air refign'd. *Dryden.*

Flit. *adj.* [from *fleet*.] Swift; nimble; quick.

F L

And looks back to him with he

Fli'xwood. *n. f.* See Hedge-mu

To FLOAT. *v. n.* [*flotter*, French

1. To fwim on the furface of the wa

When the fea was calm, all
Shew'd mafterfhip in *floating*.

The ark no more now *floats*,
Faft on the top of fome high mo

That men, being drown'd and
day, when their gall breaketh, are p

Three blufl'ring nights, born
I *floated*; and difcover'd land at

His rofy wreath was dropt no
Born by the tide of wine, and *flo*

On frothy billows thoufands *f*
In cumb'rous mail, with love of

Carp are very apt to *float* away w

2. To move without labour in a fluid

What divine monfters, O ye
That *float* in air, and fly upon th

Swift they defcend, with wing
Stretch their broad plumes, and *f*

3. To pafs with a light irregular cour

Floating vifions make not deep im
in the mind clear, diftinct, lafting

To Float. *v. a.* To cover with wa

Proud Pacto'us *floats* the fruitf
And leaves a rich manure of gold

Venice looks, at a diftance, lik
by a deluge.

Now fmoaks with fhow'rs the
And *floated* fields lie undiftinguifh

The vaft parterres a thoufand
Lo! Cobham comes, and *floats*

Float. *n. f.* [from the verb.]

1. The act of flowing; the flux; th
fenfe now out of ufe.

Our truft in the Almighty is, tha
now at their higheft *float*.

Of this kind is fome difpofition o
ticularly from Eaft to Weft; of wh
main *float* and refloat of the fea is,
univerfe, as part of the diurnal mo

2. Any body fo contrived or formed a

They took it for a fhip, and, as i
but it proved a *float* of weeds and ru

A paffage for the weary peop
With ofier *floats* the ftanding wat
Of maffy ftones make bridges, if

3. The cork or quill by which the
a fifh.

You will find this to be a very ch
ing a little of it into the place where

4. A cant word for a level.

Banks are meafured by the *float*
foot fquare, and one deep.

Flo'aty. *adj.* Buoyant and fwimm

The hindrance to ftay well is the
efpecially if fhe be *floaty*, and wa
wards.

FLOCK. *n. f.* [flocc, Saxon.]

1. A company; ufually a company

She that hath a heart of that f
To pay this debt of love but
How will fhe love when the rich
Hath kill'd the *flock* of all affecti
That live in her.

2. A company of fheep, diftinguifhe
oxen.

Figure 4. From Samuel Johnson, *A Dictionary of the English Language*, London, 1755.
Courtesy, The Lilly Library, Indiana University, Bloomington, Indiana.

from the metal "scold's bridal" apparatus, placed over the head of gossips to the "chastening of trope" in Renaissance rhetoric handbooks. Similarly, the *Dictionary* half-heartedly functions as a fetter on meaning, an attempt to lock in signification before it can reproduce any further. Like those devices Parker adduces, it confronts the "specter of endlessness" so dangerous to "legitimate" discourse and aims to control it.

The double identity of linguistic custom

Just as the "imperial grammar" model of language brings its own internal contradictions to Johnson's efforts to establish a national lexicon, the appeal to customary usage poses serious dilemmas for his project. For Johnson the gendered reproductive qualities of the language make its stabilization impossible, and the appeal to polite language poses the threat of the incursion of female "barbarisms." In this section we shall consider how the codification of customary language might also be said to alienate the language from itself. This will mean determining the significance of Johnson's inclusion of such decidedly un-philosophic words, as "BUSKBASKET, the basket in which cloaths are carried to the wash" or "BEAR GARDEN, a place in which bears are kept for sport," tellingly illustrated with a quotation from the *Spectator*, "I could not forbear going to a place of renown for the gallantry of Britons, namely to the bear-garden." The inclusion of such "common," in the sense of "vulgar," words indicates the extent to which Johnson is interested in recording not a potentially universal language, but a regional and particular language, with humorous references to culturally specific, quotidian practices. His "hegemonic theory of language," as Olivia Smith calls it, is thus more complex than a simple appeal to Latinisms, "pure diction" and "general language" (*Politics*, 20). While less prescriptive than his fellow grammarians of the time, he shares with them the alienating impulse towards language as he catalogues (and regulates) minute distinctions in the use of prepositions or sixty-six definitions of "to stand." Could a similar alienation be said to be at work when he records folksy legends such as that associated with the

> SHREWMOUSE ... to which vulgar tradition assigns such malignity, that she is said to lame the foot over which she runs. I am informed that all these reports are calumnious, and that her feet and teeth are equally harmless with those of any little mouse. Our ancestors however looked on her with such terrour, that they are supposed to have given her name to a scolding woman

or colloquialisms such as "SCRAPER . . . 2. a miser; a man intent on getting money; a scrapenny. 3. a vile fiddler" or slang such as "HALF-SEAS OVER" meaning "half drunk"? Allon White argues that all dictionaries reproduce a high and low language, with many entries themselves appearing as "strange hybrids" of low dialect and high philological information.[56] He writes, "Whatever the humble aspiration of its makers, [the dictionary] functions to situate and hierarchize words in such a way that the implicit system actively produces the difference between high and low" (126). His argument that lexicographers maintain this distinction by associating high language with the "serious" and low with humor is certainly borne out in Johnson's treatment of terms such as "bear garden" and "shrewmouse." It is not entirely clear, however, that Johnson can preserve the high/low distinction completely, or that he can as quickly dismiss the low, "including it as excluded" (White, *Carnival*, 133). This is because terms such as "bear garden" are freighted with more ideological baggage than simple "lowness." They also suggest the odd particulars that distinguish national cultures. While the imperial grammar model emphasizes transparent equivalence, the national custom model highlights – and narrates as national – idiosyncratic details that make cross-cultural equivalence impossible. Words such as "ABBEY-LUBBER, a slothful loiterer in a religious house," "FLIPP . . . a cant word [meaning] a liquor much used in ships, made by mixing beer with spirits and sugar," and "COBNUT . . . a boy's game; the conquering nut," for instance, refer to everyday habits and common customs. Part of the warp and woof of daily existence, this language draws from the immediacy of daily experience as it substantiates the authority of "the" nation through its particular, shared customs, especially language.[57] In attempting to naturalize what are in fact arbitrary borders, the national custom model of language posits historical language communities creating and privy to specialized linguistic meaning. It is this shared, communal quality which allows Johnson to include the last of his sixteen definitions for "end," which reads, "An END has a signification in low language not easily explained; as, most an end, commonly: perhaps it is properly on end, at the conclusion; or corrupted from some old word not easily recoverable." Although its signification is obscure, this use of the term refers to a community of "low language" users who *do* understand this use of the phrase and to a past community who did perceive its now-irrecoverable origins. Such "corrupted" words cannot be fully excluded from Johnson's *Dictionary* because they hint at a community with shared habits which influence the shape of the language – even national literary language – through time.

Jerome Christensen, in his study of David Hume, has argued that the ideologizing of the customary was symptomatic of a generalized social crisis in eighteenth-century Britain. He writes, "In the face of drastic social change that affected the habitual life of all classes, it became necessary to ideologize the customary, to theorize about practical knowledge."[58] One of those "drastic social changes" was the realignment of class forces, as landowners shared power with a wealthy merchant class, and the successful resolution of this upheaval depended upon the reorganization of social power into a "national" polity. Thus Christensen's notion of the "ideologization of the customary" might be productively linked to the development of cultural nationalism, and it is this ideologization that imparts an alien quality to the "common" words of the *Dictionary*. The appeal to custom and the consolidation of the nation state also suggest a shift in models of authority. The bald authority suggested by a general grammar and the grammarians who administered its laws was increasingly alien to a rising bourgeoisie who were rejecting the brute repression of feudal society in favor of a more invisible authority of consensual ideology.[59] The external regulation of imperial grammar would be repugnant to a consolidating class of bourgeois subjects. The imperial grammar view of language, therefore, was giving way to an alternative view, one responding to the view of cultures and their languages as unique and "untranslatable," and one deriving its authority from privately organized speakers, readers, and writers through time.[60] Johnson foregrounds this temporal authority when he writes, "Since the rules of stile, like those of law, arise from precedents often repeated, [I shall] collect the testimonies on both sides, and endeavour to discover and promulgate the decrees of custom, who has so long possessed . . .the sovereignty of words" (*Plan*, 25).

The common, customary language the *Dictionary* includes is, however, strangely doubled, and this doubling reflects the contradictory rhetoric of temporality of common law, a discourse which influenced Johnson's linguistic criteria. In ghostwriting the Vinerian lectures (following Blackstone's lectures) for his friend Robert Chambers, Johnson contributed to the formalization of British common law, yet this contribution has been largely neglected. British common law distinguishes nation from empire, for if the nation shares with empire the need to communicate across space, it differs from it in its strict maintenance of borders legitimated, in part, by that region's supposed common identity across time. The nation depends upon precedent for its sense of continuous identity, as eloquently put in this pithy description of English customary law in Sir John Davies' Irish Reports of 1612 "so framed and fitted to the nature and disposition of this people ... it is connatural to the Nation, so as it cannot possibly be ruled by any other Law. This Law therefore doth demonstrate the strength of wit and reason and self-sufficiency which hath been always in the People of this Land, which have made their own Laws out of their wisedome and experience, (like a silk-worm that formeth all her web out of her self onely)."[61] Uniquely appropriate to govern that nation, the nation's laws do not participate in larger, universal principles. The image of the (female) silkworm connotes an organic, elegant process of self production. As Wechselblatt has argued, however, the temporal discontinuity between laws existing from "time immemorial" and the daily instantiations of them creates a slippery position for the national customary language – and the national identity it buttresses.[62] Johnson points to the paradoxical quality of this formulation when he writes of the folly of copying, or attempting to make the same through time, "that which every variation of time or place makes different from itself" (Preface). The authority of the national language's time immemorial status is undermined by the need to point to the continually emerging banal practices of everyday life to substantiate it. In the Vinerian lectures Johnson writes, "Modes of common life, when changed, are forgotten, because no one records what everyone knows."[63] If the *Dictionary* is in fact based on custom, it would be recording "what everyone knows," and its reason for doing so would be precisely to endow those modes of common life (and language) with an uncharacteristic permanence – so that they would not be forgotten. As with any attempt to enshrine distinct cultural practices as *national* culture, however, the shift of linguistic practice from everyday communication to the status of a sign of age-old national identity transforms it, in a sense doubling it.

English, native and foreign

In Chapter 1 we observed how the official language of empire reached ever outward to bring larger numbers of subjects under imperial domination. One compelling figure of this phenomenon in Johnson's England is the pile of slips of paper discovered with quotations for the *Dictionary* on one side and Francis Barber's writing on the other (Reddick, *Making*, 66–7). Johnson's servant Barber, brought back to England from the Caribbean as a slave, was learning English by writing both his English name and the word "England" repeatedly on the reverse side of scrap pages from the *Dictionary* manuscript in the garret where the *Dictionary* was being compiled. Here the colonial subject is inscripted into standard English at the very site of its production. Imperial language is reified to the point of being slips of paper and the repetition of the name "England" and a "proper" English name. The alienation of English from colonial subjects – from Caribbeans to Highlanders and even some Lowland Scots – comes as no surprise. My argument, however, is that the *Dictionary* makes English alien even to many of its "native" speakers, and in this sense the position of colonial subjects and of national provincial, female, and labouring-class subjects would be aligned.

Johnson describes his work in producing the *Dictionary* as a process of collecting (Preface, 3), through which each word in the collection is metonymically linked not simply to an entire, self-enclosed English lexicon but also to the history of English society. Adam Smith, in his review of Johnson's *Dictionary* approvingly noted, "To explain hard words and terms of art seems to have been the chief purpose of all the former compositions which have borne the title of English dictionaries. Mr. Johnson has extended his view much further, and has made a very full collection of all the different meanings of each English word."[64] Yet as Susan Stewart writes, "The point of the collection is forgetting" (152), in as much as the new context, the collection, provides a very different frame for understanding. Words in the *Dictionary* are both emptied of a variety of meanings and filled with the significance of legitimacy through their status as part of a national collection.[65] In the monumental collection of the native word dictionary the language is staged as national, separated, as it were, from its users in order to make them spectators of their own linguistic patrimony.[66] The act of collecting the customary language of the nation is, then, a cultural work far more significant than mere recording. If nationalist rhetoric contrives an image of a unified national people who can be traced backwards and who continue to move forward in time together, it can only do so by forgetting the linguistic evidence of social division. In this way the moment of linguistic preservation is also one of forgetting, a doubled movement that parallels the rhetoric of nationalism itself, which, as Ernest Renan has pointed out, is predicated on forgetting.[67]

The sense of struggle with and within the language is pronounced in the *Dictionary*, relocated, however, from class and other internal social divisions to spatial and ethnic distinctions through familiar, distancing tropes for figuring colonial populations. Although precepts against "foreign" terms were certainly not new in Johnson's time, most interesting for our discussion of the interrelatedness of empire and national formations is Johnson's use of imagery of imperial conquest and colonial contamination as he attempts to displace the differences within language to more manageable terrains than the manifold practices of the "general" English population. If the legion of contexts and meanings of language threaten a kind of cultural pandemonium, Johnson recasts any lack of linguistic "integrity" as a function not of the heteroglossic character of social language intra-nationally but of invasive foreign languages inter-nationally. In this section we shall examine the many groups Johnson tars with the brush of "foreignness," as the speakers of true English shrink to almost nil.

The language Johnson invokes in his effort to say what constitutes the national lexicon is necessarily fictive. This is not only because English itself was an infamously hybrid language, but also because no language exists in the "undefiled" – uncontested and univocal – state which Johnson claimed for the language of Elizabethan England.[68] The myth of a once-pure language, unvaried by internal difference, could only be maintained by contrasting it with languages beyond the nation's borders. Yet in conjuring images of linguistic pollution and of the civilizing conquest of disorder as he describes his approach to contemporary English, Johnson makes native speakers of English foreign enemies within, difficult to differentiate from the colonial subjects without. Consider the much-commented-upon provocative choice of imperial motifs of exploration and conquest Johnson employs to represent the *Dictionary* project. At the end of the *Plan* he explains that "I . . . like the soldiers of Caesar, look on Britain as a new world, which it is almost madness to invade. But I hope that though I should not complete the conquest I shall at least discover the coast, civilize part of the inhabitants, and make it easy for some other adventurer to proceed farther, to reduce them wholly to subjection, and settle them under laws" (33). This is a curious image, for he is colonizing his own nation in this allegory of domination, and the inhabitants he seeks to civilize are the nation's words. Applying imperial figures of discovery and repression to the "refractory" elements of the "native" linguistic terrain suggests that in constructing the national language the *Dictionary* draws from external – alien to the "natives" – forces.

Frequently bandying the terms "omit" and "admit" in the *Plan* and Preface, Johnson puts himself in the role of the efficacious customs official who turns back foreign neologisms. Of all the corrupting influences that might befall a language, Johnson maintains that "the great pest of speech is frequency of translation" (Preface, 9). Not only do loan words result, but the whole "fabrick of the tongue" is altered. Referring to national languages as having their own "fabrick" and falling victim to structural changes precludes a view of language as transparent and interchangeable across nations. In introducing the notion that grammar itself might be relative and discrete between languages, Johnson lends a compelling sense of urgency to the protection and preservation of the nation's language.[69] Reluctant to include foreign words at all, Johnson ropes off foreign-derived words with stigmatizing italics, as in

> CALIPH [*khalifa*, Arab. an heir or successor] A title assumed by the successors of Mahomet among the saracens, who were vested with absolute power
>
> PAGOD [Probably Indian]
> 1. An Indian idol.

The very act of making a very "full collection" of an imperial nation's language mandates the inclusion of such words. Johnson attempts to naturalize the notion of a "national" lexicon by referring to "native" words – the *Dictionary* defines "native" as "produced by nature, not artificial" and "conferred by birth" – and the foreignness of these words, on the other hand, is evident in their reference to exotic political and religious practices. Yet the arbitrarity of inclusion both in a lexicon and nation continues to be undeniable – the Act of Union, for instance, which joined Scotland to England, argues against an essentialist understanding of what it means to be British.

In fact, the first and most obvious case of exclusion is the Scots and their language. Johnson's attitude towards the Scots is apparent not only in his notoriously derisive definition of "oats" but also in illustrative quotes such as "'Scots are like witches; do but whet your pen,/*Scratch* 'till the blood come, they'll not hurt you then.' Cleave."[70] Among deleted Scots words and meanings are "paik," meaning "a strong blow," "pantaloon," the name for "Scots courtiers after the Restoration," and "pand," "a narrow piece of drapery," words one might reasonably expect to see in the *Dictionary*, given that the *OED* documents them as circulating in England in Johnson's age. Further, as Alan Reddick has discovered, Johnson's Scottish assistants often made "ob-

servations on Scottish or regional usage which were written on to slips
... [which] were ignored by Johnson" (*Making*, 99). Johnson did include
some Scots words in his *Dictionary*. At times these words mark Scotland
as both culturally and naturally distinct, as "firecross . . . a token in
Scotland for the nation to take arms: the ends thereof burnt black, and
in some parts smeared with blood" or "plaid . . . an outer loose weed
worn much by the highlanders in Scotland" or the 1774 revision of "roe"
from "a species of deer" to "a species of deer, yet found in the highlands." Any Scots words which he did include receive "warning labels"
such as "confined to Scotland" or "still retained in Scotland."[71] "To
Lout" meaning "to pay obeisance," for instance, is described as obsolete
and used in Scotland; "to flit" is defined "in Scotland it is still used for
removing from one place to another on quarter-day"; and "to scranch,
to grind somewhat crackling between the teeth," is no longer used in
England, but "the Scots retain it." These definitions distance temporally
England from Scotland.[72] Some of these words and meanings, however,
have exhibited the kind of time- (and border-) transcending staying
power Johnson wanted to reserve for "English" alone. Basker notes,
"bambouzle," "giggle," and "sliver . . . in Scotland still denotes a slice
cut off: as, he took a large sliver of beef," continue to have meaning for
contemporary English speakers, reminding us of the inherent flaws of an
attempt to separate the languages of co-existing people.[73] By labeling
Scots words with derogatory phrases, eliminating his assistants' information regarding Scottish usage, and banning most Scots terms,
Johnson both exoticizes and represses Scots.[74]

Johnson's decision to eliminate or warn against Scots words seems
rather capricious, as their genealogical difference from English is not
always clear. "To Lout" for instance, comes from Saxon roots.
"Mickle" meaning "much" (obsolete in England, but apparently still
circulating in Scotland as Johnson includes its pronunciation there –
"muckle") also shares Saxon roots. Similarly, words clearly marked as
Scots, such as "wee" (meaning small) are identified in the *Dictionary* as
having Saxon roots. While some argue that Scots is a separate language
from English, sharing only a common linguistic ancestor, by mid-
century many Scots lived in London, and Johnson's elimination of Scots
terms from acceptable English would have an impact on their status.
Further, the distinction between the "foreign" words of Scotland and
words used in the north of England is often indistinguishable. The north
of England was a liminal space for Johnson; he often lumped it together
with Scotland, and warned *Dictionary* users of the languages of both.

Many words receive a warning label as "BAUBEE . . . a word used in Scotland and the North country." Included Scots terms "HAVER" and "PIGGIN" for "oats" and "a small vessel," respectively, are described as being from the northern counties and provinces, the boundary between the north of England and the south of Scotland no longer clear. Like Scots, words from the north are too "foreign" for the *Dictionary*. We find many examples of the exclusion of northern words by comparing the contents of John Ray's *Collection of English Words not Generally Used* (1674) with Johnson's *Dictionary*.[75] Johnson leaves out Ray's collection's "creem" . . . a word used in Cheshire to mean "put," "donnaught/donnat," a Yorkshire word for "good for nothing," "freelage," a Sheffield word for "privilege," and "cleam," a Lincolnshire word for "glue together," and "braughwham," a Lancashire term for "a dish of cheese." The particularity of these words is Johnson's reason for their exclusion, and even Ray's title explains, "they are not generally used." As such, they sully the waters of uncontaminated general English, as did the languages of particular classes, professions, and, as we have seen, women.

The title of Johnson's work, as it appears on the first page, was "A General Dictionary of the English Language." Consistent with the writings of the legions of grammarians defining and disseminating a "national" language in this period is Johnson's appeal to the "general" as he "sought . . . to codify a non-localized, supra-regional 'standard.'"[76] On these terms it is understandable that he leaves out or warns against slang terms, Scotticisms, the language of particular trades, and even provincial regions. These languages Johnson refers to as "cant," which he defines as "a corrupt dialect used by beggars and vagabonds" and "a particular form of speaking peculiar to some certain class or body of man." In listing the denigrating use of the term first, any "particular" language becomes suspect, and Johnson characterizes them as "outsider" languages, making "foreign" the native language of many, if not the majority of native English speakers – a move perhaps predictable for someone who defines "PROPER" as "not common." According to Johnson, languages of manual workers and tradesmen, as in the excluded "paduasoy" which names a strong-corded or gros-grain silk, are especially prone to particular, "cant" terms. Johnson defines "general" in revealingly contradictory terms: if it means "the whole, the totality; the main, without insisting on particulars," he is quick to warn that the second and third definitions of "general" listed, "The publick; the interest of the whole" and "the vulgar," respectively, are "not in use." In a similarly contradictory move Johnson does not exclude all outdated, particular words from his "general" lexicon. A quick review of almost any page of the *Dictionary* reveals archaic Latinisms not "generally used."[77] And the *Dictionary* includes at least 851 terms labeled "obsolete," and many labeled "no longer used" or "not generally used."[78] In fact, the attribution of "generality" to what is particular is central to the nationalist rhetoric.

Nobody's language?

The divisions between the categories of particular and general become increasingly vague, even inverted. In his *Life of Samuel Johnson*, Boswell describes how words "pretty current," even "universally used," are nonetheless unacceptable to Johnson's representation of the "genuine lexicon." Boswell writes, "He found fault with me for using the phrase to *make* money. 'Don't you see (said he) the impropriety of it? To *make* money is to *coin* it: you should say *get* money.' The phrase, however, is I think, pretty current. But Johnson was at all times jealous of infraction upon the genuine English language, and prompt to repress colloquial barbarisms; such as . . . *line*, for *department* or *branch* . . . He was particularly indignant against the almost universal use of the word *idea* in the sense of *notion* . . . Johnson called this 'modern cant'" (362). The barbarians are no longer at the gate, where they can be held in check by border guards. They are ever-mounting ranks inside society. Working in collusion with corrupting metaphor, the "common people" are not the source of general language but the means of its corruption. Boswell paraphrases Johnson: " 'Sir, it will be much exaggerated in popular talk: . . . they do not mean to lie; but, taking no pains to be exact, they give you very false accounts. A great part of their language is proverbial. If anything rocks at all, they say *it rocks like a cradle*' " (338). It is interesting to consider this critique of metaphor as the proclivity of common people in light of the heavily metaphorical language of the poets in his entries. In "outlawing" vulgar usage, Johnson emphasizes a distinction between the "general" national print/literary language he is claiming to record and an illegitimate popular yet "particular" language, insisting that "the strict and critical meaning ought to be distinguished from that which is loose and popular" (*Plan*, 24). This distinction from the common is a key criteria constituting "official language." Pierre Bourdieu describes the qualities of official language: "the properties which characterize linguistic excellence may be summed up in two words: distinction and correctness ... value always arises from deviation ... with respect to the most widespread usage, 'commonplaces,' 'ordinary sentiments,' and 'vulgar expression.'"[79] If the general and the distinct sound like oppositional categories, they are, yet it is this contradiction that informs the construction of a standard language. Consequently, the native speaker, like the colonial subject, is led to recognize, if not utilize, an official language quite distant from her own.

For Johnson, appearance in the printed text of England's best writers provided the basis of distinction. The "common" language he collects in the *Dictionary* is often not that which is spoken in the "common intercourse of life." It is instead language *represented* as such in various works of literature, always once removed, reified from daily life. Thus, even though a number of "cant" terms make their way into the *Dictionary*, it is on the basis of their appearance in the national literature – the "low" use of "end" described above is one example – Johnson cites Shakespeare in his illustrative quotation.[80] Johnson's self-proclaimed hope for the *Dictionary*, that, since "the chief glory of a nation arises from its authors . . . I shall not think my employment useless or ignoble if . . . distant ages gain access to the propagators of knowledge and understand the teachers of truth," is tautological, for Johnson aims to memorialize the language which he imagines has already been memorialized in the literature of the nation.[81] Similarly, "FUSTILARIAN, a low fellow, a stinkard, a scoundrel, a word used by Shakespeare only" and "SCROYLE (this word I remember only in Shakespeare) a mean fellow; a rascal; a wretch" make their way into a text meant to be representative of common language. They are "particular" as Johnson defines it, "relating to single persons; not general" and "individual; one distinct from others" and it is difficult to imagine how the language of Johnson's *Dictionary* is "national" as he defines it, "public and general, not private and particular." Difficult, that is, unless we revise our understanding of "public and general" language to include only that language which appears in respectable print sources.

This leads us to wonder what a general language is and who might actually speak it. One reference point for the celebration of the general is a neo-classical aesthetic which dictates, as Johnson assents, "Nothing can please many, and please long, but just representations of general nature" (61). Johnson praises Shakespeare's writing in his Preface to Shakespeare (1765) as the epitome of the general language. Based on what we have seen of the *Dictionary*, however, Johnson's famous description of this ideal language seems purely Utopian. He writes

> If there be, what I believe there is, in every nation, a stile which never becomes obsolete, a certain mode of phraseology so consonant and congenial to the analogy and principles of its respective language as to remain settled and unaltered; this stile is probably to be sought in the common intercourse of life, among those who speak only to be understood, without ambition of elegance. The polite are always catching modish innovations, and the learned depart from established forms of speech, in hope of finding or making better; those who wish for distinction forsake the vulgar, when the vulgar is right; but there is a conversation above grossness and below refinement, where propriety resides. (Sherbo, *Yale*, 70)

A spatial metaphor describes how linguistic propriety "resides" in a liminal middle zone, in which case Johnson's task is merely to record it. The position of its speakers is that of the ideal national citizen unencumbered by the demands of politeness or the limits of grossness. Here the "genius" of the national tongue continues on, unmolested. This golden mean of language promises a usage beyond change. Yet if it "never becomes obsolete," Johnson also bemoans the obscurity of Shakespeare's language in his own day. Matching the ever-receding temporal vanishing point of this language – no longer used by living authors it is increasingly in need of "translation" from the works of past authors – the social body speaking this language continually shrinks. If it is not too difficult to imagine the liminal space "above grossness and below refinement" that generates proper language, the task grows harder as Johnson describes it as the space of a language available only to those without occupation or even particular class affiliations, as John Barrell has shown.[82] The material interests of tradesmen, craftsmen, the impoverished, and the polite hinder them and their language with differentiating particularities. The "dialects" of residents of Britain's provincial margins are clearly too particular. Yet even the language of a gentleman in the nation's center, because of the linguistic class markers he must deploy, cannot be said to speak this general national language. As language carries at least a double burden, marking not only national membership but also the status within that nation of its user, it would seem to defeat its ability to signify the general at every moment of actual use.[83]

Perhaps the language Johnson describes here is best understood as "nobody's" in the fascinating historical sense of that term which Catherine Gallagher has outlined. Gallagher writes, "In eighteenth-century England Nobody was not a complete cipher, for the name had come to signify a common person, a person of no social consequence. Henry Fielding, for example, defined 'No Body' as 'All the People in

Great Britain, except about 1200.' Hogarth also seems to have intended his Nobody to stand for the common man, and 'opposed him . . . to the pretentious Somebody.'" What seems especially useful about the eighteenth-century figure of "Nobody" that Gallagher describes is its literal disembodiment, which suggests the transcendent, "common" vision available to, well, nobody. Keeping this figure in mind, we might say that "Nobody" speaks the language Johnson describes, a language at once common but removed from material interests, a language that cannot be located anywhere specific, but is specifically English. Gallagher uses the term "nobody's story" to name verisimilar fiction – a story predicated not on an actual person but on the realistic and probable depiction of a clearly fictional character. In inviting identification outside the limits of proprietary bodies that Hume had identified, this fictional mode enables the motile sympathy necessary in a volatile marriage market (for women) and unpredictable financial markets (for men). Yet I would argue that such transferable sympathies are also an important basis for national affiliation, which demands a sense of affinity to anonymous fellow citizens. The idea of a national "nobody's language," detached as it would be from any group in particular, provides a basis for imagining national fellows. In the standard nationalist formulation, what is common to everyone – the *Dictionary's* language, the literary heritage – must belong, or be seen to belong, to nobody in particular.[84] As Garcia Canclini writes, "goods gathered in history by each society do not really belong to everyone, although they formally appear to belong to everyone" (135).

To return to the link between this vision of language and the imperial context in which we have been considering it, the status of the national subject of literacy is not far removed from that of the colonial subject. It makes sense, oddly, that five out of six of Johnson's assistants on the *Dictionary* were Scottish. For while they were highly literate, English – especially as it was presented in the *Dictionary* – was their second language. Although they were charged mainly with the task of mere transcription, they seem the most suited to the reified English of the *Dictionary*. In an exaggerated way, they shared the position of many English speakers – the language of the *Dictionary* was not their own.[85] And yet their training in letters allowed them to assist in the codification of it. Their labor effaced in the renowned narratives of Johnson's years of "isolated" lexicographic drudgery, they might be said to be the real "nobodies" of the *Dictionary*'s production. Similarly, consider Johnson's remark after reading the Scottish Hugh Blair's collection of sermons. In a letter to Boswell he writes, "Please to return Dr. Blair thanks for his sermons. The Scotch write English wonderfully well" (*Life*, 328). Blair, a lecturer on Rhetoric and staunch supporter of the SSPCK, strove to eliminate Scotticisms from his and his students' speech and writing. In the halls of Edinburgh University he taught students a "legitimate" English language far different from their own language. Once again, this outsider status put him in the position of teaching an English that could be far purer than a native speaker's. As one who spent his life in Edinburgh, Blair would not have had the opportunity to learn the English of the English vulgar, much less find himself using or "corrupting" their language in his everyday interactions. Similarly, his students' exposure to this English was from print sources, the "best writers" in English. One's proximity to the ideal might derive from one's distance from the oral exchanges within a spectrum of English speakers.

In referring to the social analysis of Bourdieu and the shared position of "native" and "colonial" subjects in relationship to standard English and literacy, I am also invoking the literacy institutions "converting" Britons to "proper" English. John Willinsky notes that Johnson (as did *OED* compiler John Murray) "began his career in schoolrooms rather than in the academic study of language," and I want briefly to consider the *Dictionary* as a form of pedagogical address, and the ways in which that address forms, and transforms, its readers' understanding of their place within a national linguistic "community." Here I modify Gallagher's thesis to argue that the relationship of different subjects to "nobody's language" varies, depending where a subject is situated within institutional structures of power. While the ideal general language Johnson aims at might be an unattainable one, the relationship of different speakers to that ideal could be mapped on an asymptotic curve, approaching, if never realizing, that ideal.[86] Reading the *Dictionary* is an educational process that asks its readers, in the words of Garcia Canclini, to "convert yourself into what you are" (*Hybrid*, 135). That is, the same process which brings "vulgar" *Dictionary* readers, and lower tradesmen, women, and Scots into their understandings of themselves as members of a nation also brings them into their understandings of their position within a national hierarchy.[87] We cannot consider an individual's relationship to the "national" language of the *Dictionary* without considering the range of literacies – oral and written – a reader might bring to it. While such an analysis extends the bounds of this chapter, we might briefly map where such a study might begin. As literacy historians have documented, the rise in literacy rates, especially in the final quarter of the century, took place primarily amongst the middle class, the upper levels of which were almost universally literate by this point. Struggling to prove their accomplishments in all realms of cultural poise, many professional men, officials, retail tradesmen, ladies, craftsmen, yeomen, and farmers sought to prove an identification with the language and literacy of their "betters." Positioned at the flexible top strata of a class pyramid, their education into literacy could be a simultaneous entry into a national and bourgeois status.[88] While the "polite" readers' relationship to the language of the *Dictionary* would undoubtedly be alien at points, it could not be as alien as that of the lower classes, largely illiterate in this period. In London the unskilled laboring and servant classes received literacy instruction from charity schools run by the Society for Propagating Christian Knowledge, the work of whose sister organization in Scotland we have encountered in Chapter 1.[89] Coached into print literacy by the same disciplining forces as those used on Highland children, they shared a position with those Highland pedagogical subjects (and, like them, put their new literacy to equally uncontrollable ends, often rejecting religious tracts printed by the SPCK in favor of broadsheets and chap-books). My point in raising what might seem like tangential literacy history issues here is to demonstrate that if we put the relationships of Johnson's *Dictionary* to imperial and national hegemony into conversation with each other, we find important parallels in their ideological work. These parallels are perhaps best brought home in DeMaria's astonishing discovery of Johnson's alteration of Caliban's famous lines, as he quotes it to illustrate "to learn":

> You taught me language, and my profit on't
> Is, I know *not* how to curse: the red plague rid you
> For *learning* me your language. (*Johnson's*, 17, first ital mine)

Much recent criticism has persuasively read Caliban's position as that of colonial subject, for whom learning the colonialist's language has also meant learning to curse, with the multiple meanings that such cursing might have.[90] To illustrate the word "LEARNING" Johnson selects the colonial imagery evoked by *The Tempest*. Aligning Caliban and the literacy-learning subject allots them to the same position, that of the barbaric outsider in need of linguistic "civilizing." In interpolating "not" into this passage ("I know not how to curse"), Johnson seems to anticipate and to attempt to foreclose the potentially dissident character of literacy instruction. Circumventing this subversive possibility, Johnson's Caliban laments the fact that in teaching him language, his master has taught him *not* to curse and robbed him, in one sense, of his ability to protest. Learning is recast as an inherently moralizing and disciplining force capable of fending off all possibilities of resistance.

Instructing Lexiphanes: the Dictionary's *resistant readers*

If the *Dictionary* helped maintain national and imperial hegemony by means of its hierarchized invitation to a "shared" national literacy, it was also subject to resistance.[91] In the case of two Scottish writers, resistance takes the form of a reversal of the roles of student and teacher and a re-appropriation of images of embodiment. Lowlander Robert Fergusson, in his poem "To Dr Samuel Johnson: Food for a new Edition of his Dictionary" poses a material, regional language against Johnson's general language.[92] Like many others, Fergusson ridicules Johnson's penchant for Latinate words, satirizing Johnson's lexicon as a literal "nobody's language" with a series of Latin neologisms such as, "scrutation," "scrutator," "scrutinize," and "scrutinous." Humorously remote from daily life, Johnson's language, particularly his "philosophic words," represents "the whole revolving scientific names that in the alphabetic columns lie" (4–5) but is "far from the knowledge of mortalic shapes" (6). Fergusson's poem's knowledge and language, on the other hand, are close to "mortalic" shapes. As he resists the "verbal potentate and prince" (38) and "Great Pedagogue" (1), whose authoritative *Dictionary* is "speculiz'd by taper blue,/While youth STUDENTIOUS turn thy folio page" (43–4), the speaker reverses the direction of knowledge transmission, fantasizing a confrontation between Johnson and the material particularities of Scotland. He not only imagines "force feeding" Johnson Latinate words of Fergusson's own making, including "salamandrian," (57) "brimstonic," (56) "consignate," (17) and "Lexiphanian" (35) but also aims to bring "indigenous" Scottish products, oats and whiskey, to Johnson's "orifice." The poem constructs an oppositional Scottish identity through material cultural details and their Scots expression and then points to the absurdity of Latinizing – and thereby generalizing? – such particularities with the absurd "Lochlomonidan" (14) and "usquebalian" (60, from the Gaelic usquebae, "whiskey"). Finally, if Johnson's standard is, ideally, a general, unlocatable language, Fergusson's Scots national language is resolutely located within a particular place and (lower) class: oats and whisky counter the imported delicacies that are eaten by the Anglicized middle class he critiques elsewhere.[93]

In re-directing the consumption of learning through control of Johnson's mouth, Fergusson recasts Johnson's – and not women's – mouth(s) as pervious and in need of regulation. Fergusson's fellow Scot Archibald Campbell also turns to Johnson's mouth in his critique of Johnson's language, caricaturing Johnson as the eponymous "word shiner" of his 1767 *Lexiphanes*.[94] Materializing language, comparing it to food as Fergusson had, the grand finale of Campbell's satire is a coaxing of Johnson to ingest an emetic which compels him to vomit up the multisyllabic Latinate "word worms" inside of him. We might pause a moment and consider this scene in relation to Chesterfield's self-described midwifery cited earlier in the chapter.

> SECOND PHYSICIAN
> ... heave again, my friend, put your fingers in your throat, I beseech you, my dear Sir, bring me up all your hard cant words, of two and three, and if you can, of four syllables.
> J——n
> Boax, Boax, Boax. (*Lexiphanes*, 126)

In the nonsensical sounds of vomiting – "boax" – Johnson's own language resembles the nonsensicality attributed to oral Scots and Scots Gaelic.[95] Refiguring Johnson as birthing his own "cant" words, the passive agent of a linguistic reproduction over which he has as little control as one has over esophageal – or birth canal – spasms, a feminized Johnson is instructed (and given "severe lashes" [xv]) on the basics of good writing. Unlike Fergusson, Campbell attacks Johnson on his own terms, turning not to a regional vernacular but to Smollett's more recognizably "general" (according to Campbell) English.

Johnson's language and even his textual production of a *Dictionary* is, alternatively, "unnatural":

> I cannot help thinking a living language stands in small need of a grammar or dictionary. The existence of either is plainly impossible before people have begun both to speak well and to write well. While they continue to do so, they are needless; and after a bad taste is once introduced, they will rather do hurt than service, at least if we are to judge from your writings. (141–3)

The *Dictionary* is no longer the prohibitor but has become the agent of growth without regulation; the "bad taste" it introduces will spread, grow, be reproduced – when indiscriminately consumed and used by lower classes. Campbell compares Johnson's and his impressionable followers' rejection of "the old approved writers" to "a green-sickness girl, gorged with . . . trash, nauseat[ing] the nicest dainties set before her at a regular meal" (165), invoking that sickness associated with reproduction itself. That figuration of linguistic reproduction as a kind of pregnancy returns us to the gendered notions of production and reproduction. If Chesterfield had figured women's linguistic productions as a kind of birth, Johnson, quite taken with the size of his *Dictionary*, invokes a pregnancy motif as he refers to it in a 1755 letter to Thomas Warton as "*vasta mole superbus.*" While Bruce Redford translates this phrase as "proud in its prodigious bulk" (*Letters* vol. I, 100), this neutralizes the sexualized connotations of "mole," which Marie-Helene Huet tells us "describes an inability to fully produce a child and characterizes the generation and delivery of a shapeless body, as if the mother had been incapable of giving birth to a fully formed human being."[96] If Johnson regards his literary production as a kind of reproduction, we might remind ourselves of the ways in which "lesser" cultural activities, such as translation, were feminized as "reproduction" as opposed to the "production" of original work. As in the case of MacDonald, their confusion of "productive" and "reproductive" cultural activities destabilizes the value system dependent on the separation of those spheres. Even the status of that to which Johnson has given birth, however, is puzzling. Is he incapable of the "reproduction" that comes naturally to "flippant" women? According to Fergusson and Campbell, and maybe even Johnson, what has "come out" of Johnson is itself stillborn, removed as it is from life. (Campbell also portrays an aged, barely comprehensible Johnson as literally impotent, unable to reproduce.)

Campbell uses Johnson's own linguistic criteria of purity against him, attacking Johnson's language itself as foreign and impure, "a Babylonish Dialect . . a parti-colour'd Dress, / Of patch'd and py-ball'd Languages" – the very language of his *Rambler* is in need of "translation" into "tolerable good English" (107); it is Johnson who rejects the "language of our ancestors" for a "barbarous new jargon" (xxii). This charge that the *Dictionary* was essentially "un-English" recurs throughout contemporary criticism, anticipating, in some ways, my point that the *Dictionary* represents a language estranged from its users. T. Collinson seizes the ground of high learning, writing "that the *Dictionary* was encumbered with a vast quantity of words not English, and great numbers were left out . . . from the Doctor's being wholly unskill'd in the Northern tongues, from whence our language is derived."[97] H. W. Tytler, another Scot, accuses Johnson, of having, "with impunity, barbarized the same language [English] with innumerable

Greek and Latin compounds" (Sherbo, "Nil," 173). Characterizing the particularity of the *Dictionary*'s lexicon as a "national cheat" George Mason assails Johnson: "purposely to make what should be a register of our allowable words only a partial collection of them, is defrauding the public."[98]

Perhaps because Johnson himself tropes linguistic difference as spatial or ethnic difference, all of these critiques appeal not to an alternative way of thinking about language but simply aim to reflect more accurately ethnic and geographic borders.[99] For these writers, it is not the very alienating act of "collecting" a "native" national language that is the problem. It is simply that the artifice of "conversion" is too apparent – the collection's resulting "foreignness" is literal for them. Reiterating the "foreign" label in a more politicized register, John Horne Tooke writes, "Nearly one third of this dictionary is as much the language of the Hottentots as of the English; and it would be no difficult matter so to translate any one of the plainest and most popular numbers of the *Spectator* into the language of that dictionary, that no Englishman, though well read in his own language, would be able to comprehend one sentence of it."[100] In describing Johnson's lexicon as no more English than that of the "Hottentots," Tooke suggests that the *Dictionary*'s language is not only foreign but also the language of an "inferior" and "degraded" people.[101] Since, in the British imagination, the Hottentots were firmly lodged within the uncivilized stage of a universal schema of human development, the "slavishness" believed to be concomitant with that stage hints that Johnson's standard is the language of an unfree people. Tooke's radical politics lend a progressive sense to his reproach of the "outsider" position of the *Dictionary*'s pedagogical subject, and several critiques have argued that Tooke's *The Diversions of Purley* (1798, and vol. II, 1805) champions a more recognizable vernacular, particularly with its etymologies of Saxon terms.[102] Appealing to Saxon, he calls for a return to the language of a free people before the Norman yoke.[103] However, in distinguishing between the "language of the Hottentots" and his treasured English and locating the language of a free people in a "pure" England, Tooke recuperates an exclusionary nationalist rhetoric – one which John Wilkes deployed in his Scotophobic campaign. It is impossible to think of any language as singular, as "national," without the defining contours of "outsider" languages and without, thereby, borrowing from imperial rhetoric.

Worse, Tooke's vision of a free language leaves in place – even reinforces – the notion of a once-pure national lexicon. In its appeal to a veritable "golden age" of pure Anglo-Saxon English usage, this rhetoric is not unlike MacDonald's own. Both posit a once-homogeneous, anachronistically "national" language. Johnson is, surprisingly, not far from either, as he perceives a present-day corruption of Elizabethan "wells of English undefiled" and attributes the causes of this corruption to outsiders. In moving from the grammar of empire, with its universalizing impetus and atemporal view of language, Johnson claims to record a national, at-once particular – vaguely historical, customary – and general English. His recording of that national language, however, is of course necessarily selective and his model of language has it the wrong way round. It locates linguistic creolization in the forces of rising empire and commercial corruption instead of in the very condition of language, a condition which the *Dictionary* elides.[104] So Johnson – and his critics – get it backwards. But it is nationalism's point to get it backwards: somewhere in the unruly practices of everyday language, nationalist rhetoric will always claim, flickers the reminders of the nation's origins. The *Dictionary* reminds the nation's members that, in speaking one language, they are remembering to forget together.

CHAPTER 3

Women, Celts, and hollow voices: Tobias Smollett's brokering of Anglo-British linguistic identities

As he revels in language's physicality, invoking oral pronunciation and aural reception through alliteration and onomatopoeia with such titles as *Roderick Random, Peregrine Pickle,* and *Humphry Clinker,* Tobias Smollett is the eighteenth-century novelist most interested in representing nonstandard English alongside his measured English prose. His ability to estrange English – a linguistic technique which influenced the droll "Englishified" language of that emblematic figure of Englishness, Charles Dickens – stems in part from his bilingual status as a Scot.[1] The very sound and diction of his novels' titles make the English language strange: in highlighting its harsh, guttural /k/ and /a/ sounds and in alienating terms from their usual meaning by using abstract terms such as "fathom" or "random" or absurdly specific words such as "pickle" and "clinker" for proper names, Smollett gives the language an almost foreign or antiquated ring. The emphasized materiality of the words also points to the English language's checkered history, with its hodgepodge hybrid origins, especially its northern European influences, said to have been neglected in Johnson's *Dictionary*. Sensitive to its ability to indicate a wide range of social strata, as well as its slippery relationship to the world it would name, Smollett's writings frequently represent linguistic multiplicity. Even his novel titles contain subterranean Scots meanings: in eighteenth-century Scots "clink" could mean "money or cash," "rod" could mean "road," and "pickle," "a grain of oats" or "a small particle."[2]

While the complex political and cultural relationships between Scotland and England seem an obvious starting point for discussion of Smollett's use of language, especially his representations of peripheral dialects, few of the critical discussions that have focused on language have considered his efforts to broker an Anglo-British identity.[3] More recent criticism has taken up questions of Smollett's Scottish status and his participation in the production of British national identity, yet these in turn have not given extensive thought to Smollett's critical interventions in or literary representations of language.[4] Language, however, was one of the most important sites of Scottish negotiations of Anglo-British identity – "negotiations" which extended far beyond mere linguistic assimilation.[5] I examine Smollett's non-fiction prose and *The Expedition of Humphry Clinker* (1772) to illustrate the major yet unacknowledged role of Lowland Scots at the center of English print culture, ghosts in the machine of the period's copious literary production. Smollett did not simply assimilate English identity but helped construct it. In concentrating on language I revise recent understandings of Smollett's role in national identity construction, much of which has emphasized his advocation of eradication or toleration of difference. Smollett maligns the manners and values of the aristocracy, Terence Bowers asserts, in order to make a place for a more properly *British* national middle class and to create "cultural homogeneity between the governors and the governed" (*Reconstructing*, 17). While Bowers applies this analysis "upwards," describing Smollett's role in the displacement of European aristocratic for British middle-class cultural practices, I would like to extend that analysis "downwards" to consider the way Smollett positions the uneducated, women, and other speakers of non-standard English outside of the British nation. Thus, while Crawford sees *Humphry Clinker* as "expose[ing]" and "dispel[ing]" (*Devolving*, 75) prejudice, I argue it deflects it from one group to another. I aim to extend Aileen Douglas's analysis of Smollett's castigating figurations of the body and femininity (and the ways in which his novels undercut their own ability to delimit a masculine from feminine sensibility) by showing the work these figurations do towards positioning Smollett within the British nation.

Deeply invested in constructing British identity, Smollett emphasizes the exchange of language as central to its formation. He depicts postal networks as figures of national interconnectedness and represents letter-writing, in his epistolary novel, as the literate practice which could mediate between a public, perhaps national, and a private self. Most crucially, he refines and polices a standard English language that would serve as the medium of British identity. In his final novel Smollett positions himself as recorder of "Celtic" dialects for an English readership. Through his untrustworthy "translations" he establishes the standard-English-using Scot as national insider to linguistic outsiders, be they Celts or lower-class Londoners – a breathtakingly bold move in the face of that era's English jingoism and open animosity to Scots.[6] In this way, he participates in the eighteenth century's standardizing of a national vernacular in which class linguistic difference came to supersede regional linguistic difference. Smollett achieves this shift through a feminizing embodiment of the language of Celtic and English "outsiders" such as laborers and women. In *Humphry Clinker*, the language of Welsh women characters, Tabitha and her maid Win, magnifies the oral and embodied character of a feminized Celtic-inflected language, evident in Win's statement: "I set and cry by myself, and take ass of etida, and smill to burnt fathers, and kindal-snuffs; and I pray constantly for grease."[7]

In contrast to localized, embodied outsider languages, Smollett represents standard English as placeless and dematerialized. The English Smollett praises in others and uses himself is deemed rational precisely because of its disembodied character – consider his language in *The Briton*, a political periodical he edited in support of the Bute ministry: "I have been reproached as an advocate for the present ministry, and as a panegyrist of Lord B – te . . . [T]his however is a task which, I apprehend, any man has a right to decline, without any imputation upon his character."[8] In his writings for this periodical, Smollett maintains a position of "disinterest" and strives to ward off allegations of Scottish bias, and his decorous, controlled language reflects those efforts to portray an impartial judge removed from regional attachments. English stands as the "transparent" language in contrast to a hopelessly opaque, disgustingly "material" Celtic dialect where "grace" becomes "grease." In rewriting spatial dichotomy in social terms, the linguistic borders are not drawn between a fixed Celtic periphery and an English core but instead between those speakers and writers able to adopt – and stabilize – a constructed standard English and those disrupting that standard.

"NON-ENTITIES; OR LIKE THE ECCHO, VOICES AND NOTHING MORE": LITERATE SCOTS AT THE HEART OF LONDON'S PRINT CULTURE

It is easy to understand Smollett's personal stake in a linguistic model of a British nation that inverts and/or dissolves the conventional rubicon between English center and Celtic periphery, for this supercession of region revises Johnson's emphasis on their linguistic differences. Yet it is also worlds apart from Jacobite Alexander MacDonald or Robert Fergusson, both of whom mutinously brandished a regional, peripheral language in the face of a universalizing English.[9] Their contrasting linguistic practices also obviously suggest very different expectations about who their reading audience would be. Writing for an urban Lowland readership, Fergusson, for instance, draws from local imagery of Edinburgh life; with references to "the Nore Loch Brig" in "Auld Reekie," for instance, his poetic descriptions of Edinburgh offer no points of comparison for English readers. In Smollett's *Present State of All Nations* (1768), on the other hand, the comparative sense is obvious. Devoid of any Scots terms, the assumption of an English readership is implicit in his description of the high street buildings of Edinburgh: "every floor or story of this city is a separate tenement, like those of the inns of court of London."[10] The point of view to which Smollett caters is deliberately English; as Crawford points out, even the novel which features the trials and tribulations of a Scottish hero, *Roderick Random*, fails to represent Roderick's differentiating Scots tongue on the page for fear of alienating English readers (*Devolving*, 57).

In his incessant striving for British national status in this period, of which Richard Sher writes, "national prejudice towards Scotland was rampant in England," Smollett turned to various strategies, especially linguistic strategies, that would reorient his position within the British national community.[11] Like the Lowland SSPCK administrators, Smollett distanced himself from the culturally "other" Highlanders, aligning himself with England against the Highlands, in spite of the proximity of his family's estate to the border of the Highlands and their ancestral links to the Highlanders.[12] He protests, "The first and great divide of this country is that of the distinction between the Lowlands and Highlands, which were originally inhabited by two nations that widely differed from each other.... These differences still subsist" (*Present*, 1) and suggests his enmity towards Highlanders in his observation that "if the truth be known, cleanliness is a virtue very rarely found in this part of the world [the Highlands]" (9). Those Highlands could and should be colonized, his semi-autobiographical protagonist in *Humphry Clinker*, Matthew Bramble, argues, as they are a more appropriate area than North America to fulfill the British "strange itch to colonize" (256).

As an aspiring Lowlander of the land-owning class, seeking and gaining his fortunes in London, the distancing of Highlanders from Lowlanders, particularly through mastery of the linguistic standard, offered a basis of national membership much more accessible than a regional or ethnic yardstick to which Smollett could never match up. Yet the question of where to locate Smollett is not an easy one to answer.

His was a fluctuating position within the core/periphery divide that his own case helps destabilize. Is he a peripheral figure merely assimilating the cultural practices of the center? After all, he was a very vocal leader of the resurrection of the movement for a British academy that began in mid-century. We know that Smollett was obsessed with weeding Scotticisms from his language, and his proposed academy would standardize and make available a stable version of the language to all – both native and non-native speakers of English – aiding and abetting his efforts to eliminate all traces of a distinctive Scots language from the English lexicon. If Smollett's calls for an academy seem related to his position as an assimilating outsider hoping more effectively to blend in with the literate London class in which he circulated, that position did not disqualify him from helping to arbitrate what that standard should be. Smollett did not imagine himself, as a Scot, necessarily on the receiving end of "proper" English, merely aping the language of his geo-cultural "betters"; he conceived of himself as being in a position to dictate it. In fact, some of the Scotophobia stemmed from the fact that "since the 1750s the Scottish literati had been vigorously challenging the English assumptions of supremacy" (Sher, "Percy, Shaw," 212). In the absence of an official academy, Smollett and his staff at the *Critical Review* from 1756 to 1763 assumed the role of "protectors of the language and arbiters of usage – a kind of English academy de facto," as both Robert Spector and James Basker have argued.[13] The *Critical Review* devoted large portions of its reviews to a critique of deviations from standard English, as in this attack on an anonymous military treatise, *The Target*: "it were to be wished, however, that the treatise had been translated into English. In its present appearance, we know not to what dialect it belongs."[14] Here Smollett is the linguistic insider, authorized to judge dialect and standard. Such a role aligns Smollett and his heterogeneous editorial staff (consisting of other Scottish, Irish, and English writers) with Johnson himself, who only a year earlier had published his *Dictionary* and forwarded similar claims of authority.[15]

Like Johnson, Smollett, in his model of a linguistically-based nation, suggests that the apperception of (homogeneous) national status that comes with recognition of a standard language simultaneously involves recognition of (heterogeneous) class and gender status. That Smollett and Johnson shared an apparently democratic but, in fact, exclusive understanding of standard English parallels their broader similarity in terms of their social positions and roles. As Michael Rosenblum writes, "Smollett is a younger and somewhat lesser Cham who presides over the institution of literature from his perch in Chelsea.... Like Johnson, he is both Grub Street writer and cultural arbiter."[16] In these dual roles, both make "literature accessible to a broader audience" and yet adjudicate distinctive class taste at the same time. Thus, despite evidence of Smollett's status as an outsider trying to assimilate, it is as difficult to refer to him as it would be to refer to Johnson as a "peripheral" figure. As the editor of *The Briton*, Smollett held an "insider" position; as propagandist for King George III and the ministry of the Scottish Lord Bute he was, as Rosenblum puts it, less the "hireling propagandist" that Walpole deemed him and more a "hegemonic mover and shaker." In addition, as James Basker has pointed out, as editor of the *Critical Review* Smollett, like Johnson, not only helped shape the national language but also the literary values of his contemporaries. Such values clearly had resonance beyond the aesthetic field, as analysts of the role of literary criticism in the formation of the public sphere and the rise of bourgeois hegemony in Britain have pointed out.

Parallels between Johnson and Smollett are nowhere more clear than in their deep commitment to defining standard English. Although Damien Grant contrasts Johnson's "defensive" (*Smollett: A Study*, 74) stance towards language to what he sees as Smollett's often "imaginative, free-associative" (88) use of language, Smollett's attitude towards language is actually very close to Johnson's, both sharing a sense of the importance of establishing a standard English which would be central to the exercise of critical judgment in the exchanges of the public sphere (74). In fact, as Louis Martz has argued, both shared a style distinguished by a "rigid parallelism" and studded with "words of Latin and Greek derivation ... [which] gave the impression that the author had imbibed the spirit of science, spoke with learned authority, and was presenting his materials with scientific accuracy."[17] While Grant celebrates Smollett's elaboration of the "infinite possibilities" of language (*Smollett: A Study*, 78), more often than not those displays of a wildly generative language serve as a reminder of the monstrous capacities of language if not kept at bay – especially as it is mainly his uneducated women characters who use this language – situating him close to Johnson in outlook. In his prose Smollett was the very model of correct, even elegant style. Reviews of his *Complete History of England*, for instance, praised his style as "in general clear, nervous and flowing,"[18] and as the century wore on, Smollett was increasingly commended for his style.[19]

Yet Smollett is also a Scottish cham, and part of the work of this chapter is an analysis of the complexities of Smollett's assertion of cultural authority. The stigmatizing view of the people and culture of Scotland put Smollett in an awkward relationship to what continued to be a regionally biased linguistic standard. In a larger cultural frame, Smollett could only ever be the butt of the popular stereotyping of the period, an activity in which Johnson sometimes indulged, which linked the "lesser" linguistic practices of the Lowland Scots tongue to an equally inferior, "beggarly" and "grasping," peripheral Scottish people.[20] Regardless of his efforts to assimilate, Smollett was continuously attacked on the basis of his Scottishness, and it is interesting to note that some of the most vicious attacks on him as a Scottish outsider centered on the questions of linguistic practices now so often consigned to fairly narrow belletristic study of style. That his opponents would focus their political and cultural vitriol on the flaws of Smollett's style is particularly telling, reminding us that issues of style and language had an unambiguously political valence in this period. Some publications, such as J. Johnson's *New Royal and Universal English Dictionary* (1762), impute all solecisms with the damning label of Scotticisms whether, as Sterling Leonard puts it, "They are as common in England as in Scotland [or are] personal predilections . . . peculiar to J. Johnson."[21] Similarly, Wilkes's *North Briton*, a periodical established to counter the Bute-promoting propaganda of the Smollett-edited *The Briton*, continuously singled out words and phrases that marked Smollett's status (and Bute's) as a Scot and, therefore, an outsider. In one case Smollett's *The Briton* takes up such an accusation, as a "hearty well-wisher to South Briton, altho' a native of Argyle" sympathetically writes to *The Briton*'s editor, insisting that:

The man who calls himself the North Briton, has hinted more than once that you are my countryman, and affirmed that you cannot write English; as a proof of this assertion, he hath twice twitted you in the teeth with the word *glorification* printed in *italics*. Now, although I don't pretend to be a connoisseur in the English language, I will affirm . . . *glorification* is an English word . . . found in all the common dictionaries. . . . On the other hand, I could wish he would settle the authenticity of the word vouchsafements, used as a substantive in the same page; a word which I [haven't] seen in any dictionary.[22]

In this passage, "a native of Argyle" (in fact one of the many personae Smollett adopts in the pages of *The Briton*) demonstrates the stakes involved in one's style and diction: one's right to claim authority within a national community can be determined through the pedigree of the words a writer or speaker uses.[23]

The fact that these contests over linguistic propriety took place in journals staffed by Scots and hacks, who, for all their cultural authority, remained largely faceless cultural workers, reminds us that, as Leonard points out, these battles were "fought most hotly by persons who had had to earn and prove their gentility" (*Doctrine*, 174). Alternatively, the English "patriot" attempting to exclude Scots from the national circle depends upon finding visible, material clues indicating an impostor status. An anonymous pamphlet, *The Battle of the Reviews* (1760), seizes on telltale linguistic signs as it assails the "essentially" Scottish Smollett. Its author refers to Smollett with the anti-Scottish epithet "Sawney" and the self-explanatory "MacSmallhead" and derides Sawney MacSmallhead's language as

sometimes embellished with the gay flowers of figurative thoughts... but that ... often degenerates into what the French call a *Faux brillant*, bearing no remote Resemblance to a Coat edged with Tinsel, instead of Gold or Silver Lace, which, however, may strike at a Distance, but discovers the Cheat when closely examined.[24]

Here the link between an abusive name, which draws attention to Smollett's Scottishness and a long critique of his style, which turns on tropes of counterfeit and dissimulation, gets at the underlying suspicion of Smollett's false relationship to the English language he claims to refine. Superficially, Smollett's command of English, even of its familiar figures, might seem impressive, the passage suggests. Yet at bottom it is a "cheat" – no Scots speaker could ever claim such mastery. A Scot will always be once-removed from the "authentic" value of the golden mean of proper English, an opinion which echoes earlier assertions of the valuelessness of non-English languages and the distant position native Scots necessarily occupy from the creation of real linguistic value.

The pamphlet goes on to vilify the Celtic editorial staff of the *Critical Review* in terms that are particularly striking, at once disembodying and embodying these marginal hacks:

the laqueys ... enjoyed in fair and legible Letters the Names of Duncan Mac Croudy, Archibald Mac Bonacs, Donald Mac Haggess, and Paddy Fitzpatrick ... Being without Characters as I said, I was apt to surmise that they were Non-Entities; or like the Eccho, Voices and Nothing more. (*Critical Heritage*, 166–7)

This fascinatingly imaged assault jokingly disputes the actual physical being of these "peripheral" writers beyond the letters on the page that spell their names. If they are without "characters" of one sort, they are only characters of the printed sort. In Chapter 4 I discuss the ways in which eighteenth-century aesthetic discourse presupposes a landed, white, male body capable of registering tasteful responses and here I anticipate that discussion by noting that these Celts are, alternatively, seen as being without bodies. The writer suggests that their only reality might exist on the level of sound – "Eccho, Voices and Nothing more." On the other hand, these Celt writers might be "nonentities" precisely because of their inability to rise above the lowly physical status of the "voice" – a corporeal, corrupting mode of expression in contrast to an Enlightenment privileging of the abstract written sign as mode of rational discourse. If the male propertied English body provides entry into the "disembodied" realm of the public sphere, the body marked by a Celtic-accented voice prevents such entry.

Whereas the echo figure suggests the "doubled" status of these writers, directly invoking the notion of linguistic mimicry, "Eccho" also suggests an incorporeal presence, and when we consider that a good number of the mid-century's Grub Street hacks and ghostwriters were Scots – recall the Scottish composition of Johnson's *Dictionary* staff, for instance – we might indeed begin to imagine these Celtic cultural workers as "ghosts in the machine" of English print culture. "Smollett," reigning over the lot, was himself a hack writer – his *Complete History of England* was a notoriously hasty production, and he, too, did the "invisible" work of editing and translating – notably *Don Quixote*. In order to do this work, these Scots had to remove the Scots "particularities" from their language, disembodying themselves, in a sense. In *Humphry Clinker*, Jery's description of the Sunday open house held at S–'s (Smollett's) home depicts this class of workers much as spirits who have temporarily taken human form in their time off, only, one suspects, to disappear again during the work week. The pressures of tending to a "general" English demand that they render their linguistic particularities invisible in their work, letting their linguistic differentiae show only amongst each other and when not at the work of print production. Those partaking in the weekly relaxation at Smollett's were

journeymen, to more creditable authors, for whom they translated, collated, and compiled, in the business of book-making. . . . [N]ot only their talents, but also their nations and dialects were so various, that our conversation resembled the confusion of tongues of Babel. We had the Irish brogue, the Scotch accent, and foreign idiom. . . . The most learned philosopher of the whole collection . . . [was a] Scotchman [who] gives lectures on the pronunciation of the English language. (*Humphrey Clinker*, 126–7, London, 10 June).

These Celtic and foreign word workers speak a Babel – outside of the pale of Englishness, their mix of dialects does not even suggest another, lesser, unified nation. The oral Babel audible in their afternoon's leisure entertainment remains undetectable in the print productions they manufacture during the week. Proper style and the highest standard of writing, presumably, can be achieved regardless of one's continuing audible link to a regional dialect – yet in order to achieve it, the Celtic writers must become "nonentities . . . voices and nothing more." The Scottish wordsmith stands in striking contrast, alternatively, to the increasingly embodied pathologized English author in the eighteenth century.[25]

In his *Dictionary* Johnson defines "voice" as "any sound made by breath," invoking a physical presence of an otherwise bodiless point of view. He also defines it, however, as "vote; suffrage; opinion expressed." It would also, then, be important that the polemical *Battle of the Reviews* figures these spectral Celtic figures of Smollett and his co-workers as "voices" because this figuration might speak to the *Battle*'s author's anxieties around an assembled "army" of Celtic perspectives invading the British review world. Later, when Smollett ghostwrites a legion of pro-Scottish, pro-Bute letters as editor of *The Briton*, all of which "voice" ministry-supporting points of view, such fears of voice as vote might be said to come to a fruition of sorts.

Acknowledging that the voice indeed might be the final moment of insurmountable difference, Smollett himself pokes fun at the presumptions of a Scot who would give lectures on the pronunciation of English, much like William Kenrick who had written "there seems indeed a most ridiculous absurdity in the pretensions of a native of Aberdeen or Tipperary to teach the natives of London to speak and read."[26] This Scottish elocutionist is not capable of seamless assimilation. Instead, in pointing to the limits of that assimilation, he will expose such efforts as absurdity. Thus, before we too decisively locate Smollett as a "core" figure, we do well to keep in mind these complex and contradictory contemporary figurations of the Scottish minions to an English print culture – "voices and nothing more," a "confusion of tongues," and ghostly presences. We might also remember that early in his career Smollett had written a lamentation for the fate of the Jacobites at Culloden, "The Tears Of Scotland" (1746). The imagery of this poem adds another layer to the fraught meditations on physicality, embodiment, and particular regional affiliations. In the poem's final stanza Smollett writes, "Whilst the warm blood bedews my veins,/

And unimpair'd remembrance reigns;/Resentment of my country's fate,/Within my filial breast shall beat."[27] Although it is important to note that in these lines Smollett already emphasizes the pastness of Scottish struggle, his sympathies with the defeated Jacobites are unmistakable. He refers to his "sympathizing verse" (line 54) and links the Jacobites cause to himself in the use of the first person, referring to the "resentment of my country's fate," and he conjures images of "ravish'd virgins" (14), perishing infants (16), and "pious mothers doomed to death" (41) – not the stuff of objective distance.[28] He ties pro-Scottish feelings not to "head" and rational analysis but to a separate "heart" and the physicality of "warm blood" and a beat within the breast.

The speaker's own relationship to physicality here seems especially important, since insuperable cultural difference was associated with the physical, speaking body. It is when he is in open sympathy with the Celtic cause that the speaker describes bodily sensations and responses. While the poem is written in standard English, its appeal to physicality – in its imagery, initial musical ballad form, and evocation of sentimental physical response – is a gesture which, on a more exaggerated level, is also one of the distinguishing features of Smollett's fiction. The imagery of a victimized nation turns on the highly gendered tropes of violated motherhood and vitiated reproduction, and the speaker's own response is feminized. Scotland's tears are his tears; its condition elicits sentiment from a native son. We will have a chance to critique this essentialism, but here I want to hold out the possibility that in the context of the hegemony of an abstracting "general" English language, the particularity and corporeality presented in this poem works against an Anglo-British grain. This physicality might suggest a note of resistance, might "interrupt the stories eighteenth-century society chose to tell about itself," as Douglas argues it does in Smollett's fiction.[29] If the appeal to a physical pro-Scottish feeling falls into a developing English/Scottish "head/heart" binary, it also opposes the idea of an omnipotent, uncontested English language and historical narrative and demonstrates one way in which Smollett figured the gap between his core and peripheral positionings.

Indeed, it is the physicality of spoken language, with its audible, unignorable residue of accent, which presented the greatest hindrance to Smollett's attempts at assimilation. Despite moving to London, and notwithstanding his status as "a gentleman by birth, education, and profession," as he liked to put it, Smollett was not comfortably enough distanced from the battles between openly hostile Scots and dominating English that were raging in the North. As Crawford records, "Alexander Carlyle recalled being with Smollett in London at the time of Culloden. The two men had to walk with drawn swords, for fear of attack, and Smollett cautioned Carlyle 'against speaking a word, lest the mob should discover my country and become insolent'" (*Devolving*, 62). Interestingly, Smollett feared that his language, or more precisely its physical "embodiment" in speaking, would be the giveaway sign of Scottish difference. In an episode which pointedly, even violently, reiterated Smollett's peripheral status, he, like his disinherited Scottish character Roderick Random, feared for his life if his Scottish identity were to be discovered in his speech. Silenced, one can neither claim that Smollett's Scottish status never undermined his cultural authority, nor ignore the ways in which Smollett understood that Scottish status as marked on the body. If Scots "difference" was naturalized in the physicality of "voice," the question for Smollett became how to negotiate that line of differentiation in an appeal for Anglo-British credibility.

A conventional analysis might simply read Smollett's later power plays and his ongoing struggle to erase his linguistic differences as a maneuver for position dearly purchased through the suppression of a Scottish identity he more keenly adopted in his youth. As I have been arguing throughout this work, however, both "Scottish" and "English" identities are mutually formed by the relationship between them. It is in the movement between abrogation and assimilation of "Englishness" that Smollett's Scottish identity is best understood, not in the notion of a pristine Scottish culture infiltrated or overwritten by English practices. It is through the relationship to England, and not prior to it, that a body-based, separate linguistic Scots identity emerges – and is exaggerated in Smollett. What is interesting about a Scottish cultural difference, naturalized as it is mapped onto the physicality of the body, is how Smollett manipulates and exaggerates this trope in his own construction of Britishness alongside "Celticness."

IMPERTINENT CONVERSATION: CORE, PERIPHERY, AND DANGEROUS NATIONAL COMMERCE

We have seen the ways in which the regional distinctions at work in Johnson's *Dictionary* break down, yet it remains significant that such regionally based spatial hierarchies often form the *Dictionary*'s criteria for establishing what standard English is and what it is not. Whatever standard English consists of, Johnson proposes in his *Dictionary*, it cannot comprise peripheral dialects. Johnson condemned Scots as the most peripheral dialect – both temporally and spatially – of all. Inversely, the "general" language of the "center" of London is the most worthy of imitation and promotion. I would now like to move into a brief discussion of Smollett's own models of the space of the nation, in evidence in his *Present State of All Nations* and *Humphry Clinker*, in order to determine the ways in which he, by turns, dissolves and leaves intact that binary in his linguistic model. In *Humphry Clinker* Smollett's image of a national linguistic community makes use of the metaphoric spatial relationship of inside/outside, yet he purposefully detaches a regional binary from any particular geographic regions. His image of the nation holds out the possibility of a common – across space if not, certainly, across class or gender – national British community composed of subjects literate in standard English. Further, Smollett ostracizes the language of the Celtic periphery, but he also lauds the purity and moral superiority of that space, juxtaposing it to a tawdry, (linguistically) corrupt English center. His displacement of spatial hierarchies onto class-based linguistic ones remains incomplete as he continues to use and invert core/periphery dichotomies.

Using travel as a thematic and narrative frame not only in his *Present State* and *Travels through France and Italy* but also in his nation- and empire-traversing novels, Smollett clearly exploits literal spatial cognition as one of the dominant means through which to comprehend the nation. Taking the form of a tour, *Humphry Clinker* offers an image of the nation as a seemingly inclusive and enclosing geographic circuit. This symbolic figure of the nation had been explored by many, including Defoe, for whom, as for his contemporaries, Betty Schellenberg observes, "The form of encompassing circuits would seem to be a means of establishing the borders of the nation."[30] Although the tour of *Humphry Clinker* is not a complete circuit of the nation, its trajectory to remote regions of the Highlands hints at the tracing of the British nation to its recently extended perimeter, its far-reaching northwestern Highland boundaries. His representation of travel to remote outposts, however, while it widens the circle of Britain, recuperates a stark contrast between "periphery" and "core." In their imaginings of the British nation in the first half of the eighteenth century, many writers turned to the spatial imagery of a superior central core and subsidiary peripheral regions and depicted the unification of these disparate secondary areas and the center into one nation through centrifugal and homogenizing commerce. Daniel Defoe, for instance, in his 1724–6 *Tour Thro' the Whole Island of Great Britain*, repeatedly describes the "greatness" of the nation of Great Britain as deriving from its trade, specifically the movement of distinct regional commodities, such as oysters, hops, and timber, to the nation's center. This exchange process integrates distinct regions into a unified, if at times incoherent, mis-shapenly growing center. The fears Defoe enunciates regarding London's wild growth are mitigated in his delight in the dynamic circuitry of national trade whose roads all end there. In his description of England and Scotland in *Present State*, Smollett embraces this center/margin spatial national model. Cultural difference is physically located and visible within the respective spaces – core or periphery – which the narrator describes. Bread available in the "core," London, is "light, sweet, white, and easy of digestion" (Vol. II, 220). He describes London as "inferior to few or none in respect of extent, wealth, and populousness ... industry, politeness, learning, and ingenuity" (Vol. III, 160). As a mere "province," Smollett represents Lowland Scotland as a pale imitation of a greater English culture. He writes, "Lowlanders speak an ancient dialect of the English language . . . [T]hey likewise copy their southern neighbours in their houses, equipage, habit, industry, and application to commerce; while the Highlanders . . . retain their original ferocity, sloth, and martial disdain of all lucrative employment" (Vol. II, 3). It is important to note that Smollett's descriptions of Scotland owe more to earlier textual accounts – epistolary tours, travel descriptions – than they do to his own experience.[31] Something of a hack job, the publication also suggests Smollett's efforts to write himself into an Anglo-British position by adopting an Anglo-British textual attitude toward the Highlands, diametrically opposed "other" to both. The circuit he describes defines a central national culture, made great by the traffic of goods and people to it, which then, at best, radiates outwards.

Smollett adopts and describes spatial, core/periphery distinctions within the British nation, but as I have argued, he cannot leave those intact given that he himself is from the "periphery" and hopes to redeem his status within the center. As many before me have noted, Smollett inverts the significance and characterizations of *Present State*'s center and margin in *Humphry Clinker*. In Smollett's period, other loosely Tory-influenced visions of center and periphery, town and country, similarly reversed their value, representing the center, London, and the movement of goods and people towards it, not as the foundation of national identity in its ever-expansive accumulation of people and goods, but instead as the source of national corruption.[32] Recall Walter Shandy's harangue against the continual "overflow" of traffic to the body politic's "head," London, as one example of this view. Similarly, in *Humphry Clinker* Matthew Bramble inveighs against the corruption of London, imaging it as a "dropsical head" (ed. Knapp, 87).

In this spatial model, the unbalanced circulatory movement by which a periphery merely gives to the core is devastating for the nation's periphery and, consequently, the entire nation. *Humphry Clinker*'s key representative Scottish character, Lismahago, upbraids defenders of the Union along these lines, arguing, "There is continual circulation, like that of the blood in the human body, and England is the heart . . . [Scotland] retains neither gold nor silver sufficient for her own circulation" (278). Yet if, as Lismahago suggests, the core/periphery relationship deprives the periphery of its own extensive circulation, Matthew believes that that lack might not be an altogether bad thing. Commerce, which according to Defoe made Britain great, and travel itself, which made that nation knowable, are both horrific in Smollett's final novel. The very movement of goods across distances contributes to their spoilage and deceptive appearance – the Colchester oysters praised in Defoe's *Tour* come in for attack by Matthew who writes, "The green colour, so much admired by the voluptuaries of this metropolis [London], is occasioned by the vitriolic scum, which rises on the surface of the stagnant and stinking water" [in which they are stored] (121).

In referring to London oyster consumers as metropolitan "voluptuaries," Matthew Bramble enlists a polemic against luxury common in the period, as John Sekora has demonstrated.[33] Views on luxury in the eighteenth century were manifold, from Mandeville's ringing endorsement to Smollett's invectives against it, but my point in referencing this discourse is to note luxury's absence, as Smollett depicts it, from the "peripheral" locus of Scotland and to observe his favorable characterization of the impact of that absence on peripheral language. These dual conceptions invert the core/periphery binary he installs elsewhere. Matthew suggests that because London is the site of commerce, which is by nature predicated on deceit and the manipulation of signs, it is also the site of linguistic corruption.[34] A description of London's adulterated bread provides one good example – sophisticated to appear whiter and better (to entice purchase), it is in fact less healthy than its country equivalent, which might not look as good. He complains that "the bread I eat in London, is a deleterious paste, mixed up with chalk, alum, and bone-ashes; insipid to the taste and destructive to the constitution" (120).

If the semiotic system of the center, London, is corrupted – to the point of being literally unpalatable – how can its verbal language be meritorious?

In *Humphry Clinker* one of the most troubling aspects of the excessive "circulation" of goods and people and the slippage of signs that takes place in the nation's center is the way in which it levels social class distinctions. Such leveling is dangerous to a social authority which depends on precisely such hierarchies; the flow of people and goods to the city and the consequent social confusion act like a disease deforming the body politic. The destabilization of class is depicted as anathema, reminding us of Smollett's own investment in a national body that insists on class rather than regional and "ethnic" distinctions. Charlotte Sussman has convincingly linked the anxieties around class leveling to the stomach-churning images of the merging of physical bodies that takes place in the nation's center spaces. Mixing and exchange take on their most repugnant sense in Matthew's description of the coalescing bodies at Bath: "the first object that saluted my eye, was a child full of scrophulous ulcers. . . . I retired immediately with indignation and disgust – Suppose the matter of those ulcers, floating on the water, comes in contact with my skin, when the pores are all open, I would ask you what must be the consequence?" (45, Bath, 28 April).

Matthew rails against the physically revolting character of an analogous class confluence in London as well. He writes:

When I see a man of birth, education, and fortune, put himself on a level with the dregs of the people, mingle with low mechanics . . . expose themselves to the belchings of their beer, the fumes of their tobacco, the grossness of their familiarity, and the impertinence of their conversation, I cannot help despising him, as a man guilty of the vilest prostitution. (104, London, 2 June)

Matthew draws a direct connection between an egregiously physical lower class – they are resolutely embodied as they belch and smoke – and the "impertinence of their conversation." Language of the lower classes is every bit as physical and "gross" as their invasive belchings. Further, once a sign of class place, conversation now taking place between classes becomes one more in a series of sign systems undergoing corruption. The emphasis on the class-blurring character of this impertinent conversation suggests that a dislike for it might be one cultural element Matthew and any English estate-owning counterpart would – and should – hold in common.

While many critics have celebrated the play of signs or the incommensurability between signifier and signified in *Humphry Clinker*, it is important to remember that this linguistic transgression registers disgust with class fluidity, especially as it is figured through repugnantly feminized sexuality.[35] Matthew despises those who violate linguistic class bounds as prostitutes; to use language beneath one's station is an act that both feminizes and degrades the offender. To compare such a man to a prostitute suggests that his use of language devalues proper language, just as prostitution revalues social institutions of reproduction. This linguistic exchange, then, destabilizes value, a value which Smollett might well want to re-appropriate in the face of accusations about the valueless, "tinsel" quality of his language. Thus the most troubling linguistic deception is not that which aims upwards on the social ladder, as his might be said to, but that which works downwards. If their enemies sought to expose the fraudulent language of Scottish wannabees – their language looks fine, but is cheap imitation – here Smollett displaces such suspicions onto lower class subjects: it is they, and not Scots, who disguise themselves. Matthew complains, in London "fashionable figures . . . upon inquiry will be found to be journey men taylors, serving-men, and abigails, disguised like their betters" (88, London, May 29). Although Matthew's tone in these observations is a tad too curmudgeonly for the reader to take him entirely seriously, the force of the inarguably disgusting images associated with class convergence is too dramatic to allow a complete dismissal of his point.

There are two alternatives to which Matthew turns to recuperate the vision of a properly classed, static, and uncorrupted version of the collective body of the nation. First, he presents peripheral regions such as Scotland as the last preserve of uncorrupted social space. Not a cultural backwater with only a few distinct commodities to contribute to the nation's hub, the "Celtic periphery" is a self-sufficient, thriving cultural space. Like Matthew's Celtic estate, Scotland produces everything it needs – its own superior "turnips, cherries, gooseberries, apricots, peaches, grapes," and even "pine-apples" (223), circumventing the need for corrupting commerce. He describes Scotland as the source of wholesome, unadulterated goods, writing, "The beef and mutton are as delicate here as in Wales . . . [T]he bread is remarkably fine" (217). Free of abstracting exchange and potentially dangerous cultural and class incursions, these peripheral spaces leave a stabilizing social stratification and signification intact. In contrast to the center, the insular peripheral regions of the nation, with their regional differences preserved, come to figure as the source of the nation's greatness, delineating spaces of national virtue.[36] At the furthest remove, the Hebridean islands, particularly the remote Isle of Lewis, were "unacquainted with venality, having neither gold nor silver; but bartering the produce of their farms for the little necessities of life" (*Present State*, Vol. I, 478). Similarly, the inhabitants of St. Kilda are "sensible, honest, and chaste and hospitable; very circumspect in traffic . . . they are a model of innocence and simplicity; and perhaps a golden age was never so much realized as at St. Kilda . . . [I]gnorant of luxury and vice[,] . . . they obtain the necessities of nature without money" (*Present State*, Vol. I, 451). As mistaken as these characterizations might be, they envision peripheral societies as inhabiting a semiotic economy outside of the destabilization concomitant with the use of that abstracting sign, money. These spaces offer a preserve of national culture and a stable linguistic system unavailable to "metropolitan" culture.

In his second means of establishing a classed, static, and uncorrupted nation, Smollett rejects such spatial distinctions, however, and instead turns to a linguistic standard that might set the bar high enough to retain distinctions between classes. Soon after Matthew's apoplectic response to a world turned topsy turvy, he appeals to language as the last embattled sign system capable of maintaining the "readability" of class. Finding Humphry Clinker lecturing his fellow servants on the evils of swearing, Matthew exclaims, "But Clinker, if you should have eloquence enough to persuade the vulgar, to resign those tropes and figures of rhetoric, there will be little or nothing left to distinguish their conversation from that of their betters" (100, London, 2 June). At risk here are both the distinguishing "Billingsgate" tropes and figures of the language of the lower classes (an opinion reminiscent of Johnson's) and the distinctive powers of eloquence that should remain, Matthew believes, the provenance of the upper classes. Far from signaling a healthy nation, the social space in which all classes speak the same language endangers the very terms upon which that nation has been set. As Philip Withers would write in 1788, "Purity and politeness of expression is . . . the only external distinction which remains between a Gentleman and a Valet, a Lady and a Mantua-maker."[37] It is that class distinction and not a regional one that Matthew hopes to retain.

KNOWN THROUGH LETTERS: THE EPISTOLARY WRITING OF THE NATION

In Matthew's view the core has become corrupt. Two means to preserve a coherent, virtuous collective society continue to exist: retreat to the periphery or exchange of a proper standard language. The question remains, however, as to the compatibility of these two alternatives. According to the logic which identifies the periphery as an insular sanctuary, for instance, one would imagine its language would be equally free of corruption, an ideal national language. One character in Smollett's final novel, the Scottish Lismahago, makes that case, and his argument is discussed in the final section of this chapter. Smollett vacillates on this question, however. In this section I want to explore the linguistic national model elaborated in *Humphry Clinker*, paying close attention to the models of literacy presented in the novel's epistolary format and to a less favorable characterization of the language of the periphery as it is multiply constructed in those letters.

Whilst the circuits of commodity exchange and even human travel corrupt the sign systems and stable hierarchies of a cohesive body politic, the circuits of the epistolary exchange of language highlight the regional interchange necessary for enabling notions of a greater social/national body. The private, easily intercepted personal networks which distribute the letters of an increasingly literate population help establish this sense of public space and connective networks through textual contact.[38] At the most advanced level of this interchange is the postal network, which itself serves to illuminate the extensive public circuits which bind the nation together. The epistolary novel not only represents but also transmits, so to speak, the notion of social interconnection through the image of postal circuitry. Also, the conventions of the epistolary novel are particularly suited to presenting and dispersing a particular version of the language as national "standard."[39] If we have seen the cultural work that Johnson's *Dictionary* performs around establishing "correct" diction and usage and the reader's relationship to it, we have also noted the awkwardness and limits of national language transmission in the dictionary format. The alienating quality of dictionaries, with their columns of words out of context, is overcome by novelistic fiction, which showcases words in use in the represented exemplary and flawed prosaic speech of admirable and censurable characters, respectively. The eighteenth-century English novel, then, while subtly (and not so subtly) instructing in gendered moral codes and related bourgeois values, also educates its readers in proper language usage and literacy practices.[40] Sympathetic characters in whose intrigues the epistolary form makes us especially interested, *Humphry Clinker*'s educated heroes and heroines invite linguistic imitation of their language, inspiring recognition of a language which the reader shares or understands that she should share with them. Further, the epistolary novel form implies an internalization of print's standard codes in the letters of Matthew, Jery, and Lydia, converting the most "private" aspects of language into publicly monitored expression. Their "plain" and intimate language is immediately linked to each letter-writer in its direct relationship to the writing body of each correspondent, thereby naturalizing the "official" English of their letters. Registering no distinction between the form of their speech, their personal handwritten letters, and the printed page of the book, the novel suggests that standard English is not necessarily an imposed, alienating language, but might be the language of the most intimate expression – of minute details of the body's working (or not working), of highly personal responses to the goings on of daily life, and of deeply felt sentiment.

The epistolary form of the novel also exaggerates the at-once private and public character of language use in general. Language was perhaps the most significant and arguably the most subtle of a variety of nationalist cultural practices enrolled in a rhetoric of national custom in which every instance of language use reflected, or ideally would reflect, both the expression of the private individual and that individual's participation in a larger community marked by its shared linguistic system. Expression through language, with its sense of individual choice combined with the (nationally) publicly set parameters of a speaking public and listening/reading audience, is an especially important enactment of the at-once public and private quality of national consciousness. In highlighting the mediations between private and public the letter form also points to the infractions between these spheres, and the motif of violated borders between public and private figured in the epistolary form runs throughout the book. [41] Through chinks in a wall both Jery and Tabitha furtively peek at Mat and a woman in private conversation; Tabitha's maid Win confesses in the very letter exposing Lydia's secret doings that her "Mistress bid me not speak a word of the matter to any Christian soul" (7); and various bathing and swimming scenes uncomfortably force the issue of the blurry bounds between public and private. These often embarrassing scenes – Win's drawers fall off in a public bath, Matthew's private swimming carriage accidentally expels him into public view – suggest that one should be aware of and moderate one's actions to an omnipresent witnessing public. The form of the epistolary novel – private letter, now publicly viewed – emphasizes that point. Importantly, characters do not experience, view or write about such breaches as total and action-stopping violations; they are unavoidable, part of a given condition, and this condition – that the private might be exposed to public view – it should be remembered, makes the epistolary novel possible in the first place. Yet they do feel embarrassment at moments, a product of the hinge between public and private that letters represent.[42]

The notion of a private language on display to a public is demonstrated in the very diction of the letters.[43] Despite Matthew's and Jery's occasional Latinate aphorisms, the "private" language of the day-to-day interactions and "secret" thoughts that their letters record disposes with the unmistakably "public," stentorian language of classically influenced Augustan satire. Comparatively sympathetic characters, such as Mat, speak in a familiar style, often of feelings, in a style loosely metaphorical, as in "I cannot express the half of which I felt at this casual meeting of three or four companions, who had been so long separated, and so roughly treated by the storms of life" (56, Bath, 5 May). Jery dots his letters with such subjective, amicable phrases as "I must tell you" (72) and self-disclosing declarations as "I must own, to my shame . . . I am afraid of being detected in a weakness" (23). Through their self-revealing letters we know of Mat's bowel problems, of Lydia's secret love, of Jery's possible paternity out of wedlock, of Tabitha's churlish treatment of her servants, and of Win's sexual affairs.

On the other hand, it is a "pedant" who "involved himself in a cloud of Greek and Latin quotations" (116–17 Jery/London, 5 June); the novel reserves hyperbolically "public" language for less sympathetic characters. It is the reprehensible Scot character Micklewhimmen who calls up a bastardized Latin to defend his cowardice, "I'm no accountable in *foro conscientiae*, for what I did, while under the influence of this irresistible pooer." Micklewhimmen deploys a detestable sophistry in run-on sentences to argue against his accusers as he protests, "Instinct never acts but for the preservation of the individual; but your preservation was out of the case – you had already received the damage, and, therefore, the blow must be imputed to revenge, which is a sinful passion, that ill becomes any Christian, especially a Protestant divine; and let me tell you, most reverend doctor, gin I had a-mind to plea, the law would hauld my libel relevant" (177, Scarborough, 1 July). In combining Micklewhimmen's low Scots dialect with his inflated rhetoric, Smollett makes the disreputable status of both clear. His linguistic jumble, an unlovely mix of Scotticisms, Latinisms, and confused and self-important syntax, locate him outside of the circle of the core linguistic community.

Not only do we get a representative sampling of a range of subjective private thoughts, then, but we also get those thoughts in the differing languages of a motley bunch on a sweeping circuit of Britain. As the travelers make the circuit of the hinterland of Britain, their multiple letters, with their alternative perspectives, varying dialects, and reportage of other dialects, such as Micklewhimmen's, suggest (if they don't actually deliver) a comprehensive whole, the plenitude of the nation. The variances of the letter-writers' language and of the recorded language of dialect-speaking characters they encounter, seem to offer a sampling of Britain's linguistic diversity. The book then promises a kind of "linguistic tour" of the nation, presenting manifold language practices much as it catalogs the nation's customary and geographic variety. Like the claims of nationalist rhetoric itself, which boasts the inclusiveness and plurality of the national culture, this linguistic social map has the appearance of comprehensiveness. Further, that this reconstruction takes place through a series of recordings of and responses to the same events encountered in a quasi-national tour is additionally significant. If Benedict Anderson has emphasized the importance of the novel in developing national consciousness because it structures a temporality of simultaneity and imagined shared experience, Smollett's epistolary novel exaggerates that sense. Presenting multiple personal perspectives of the same event, *Humphry Clinker* illumines the simultaneity of actions and perceptions.

Yet Smollett's tours of Britain in *Present State* or *Humphry Clinker*, like those by whom he was influenced, do not, ultimately, encompass a comprehensive whole. This is true for two reasons. First, the letters from various regions do not collect so much as they produce signs of cultural difference. The introduction of the letter into a larger social and spatial network necessitates the regional by-line; their movement in space demands that the characters consciously locate themselves in a particular place, and this image provides an effective figure for my general argument: that the institution of larger social networks *produces* a particular understanding and privileging of local, regional affiliations. Second, the novel divides those produced differences into a binary of an insider and outsider, particularly in the representation of language. In this way the text displaces the "core/periphery" spatial conceptualizations of Britain – which Smollett alternately confirms and inverts – onto linguistic practices.

The effect of the circulating missives of the standard English writers of a "transparent" language is to render the writers bodiless. While it is true that Matthew obsesses about his body and registers his violent physical reactions to various perceived encroachments, my focus is on the language in which he expresses these feelings. In a standard prose which effaces the writers' particular regional location, (supposedly) transcending space and time and distinctive linguistic markers, these letter-writers evade the confines of space and materiality altogether. Thus, while the novel emphasizes the material differences of particular regions, it evaporates those differences in the circulating, transcendent standard English of Mat, Lydia, and Jery. Although they are from the "Celtic periphery," the letters of these writers betray no trace of a dialect. To speak and write the standard language is, ideally, to leave behind the markers of cultural difference. Mat suggests that bodies and objects are best fixed in regional space, yet a standard English language, on the other hand, circulates throughout the nation in the letters of the center-identified writers. Smollett's novel, in its modeling of "good" language as "disembodied" standard English and "bad" language as a lewd corporeal Celtic dialect, maintains and develops the linguistic distinctions that attempt to keep that sign system in place.

If the proper language of the standard English writers is disembodied, the language of Tabitha, Win, Micklewhimmen, and even Humphry Clinker is "materialized" – either by emphasizing their oral pronunciation or by displaying, in their misspelled language, a gross physicality. Inasmuch as their language is outside the pale of polite society (and their characters no less off-putting – Tabitha, for instance, is cheap, ornery, and scheming, Win is untrustworthy, selfish, and sexually profligate) the standard English of the other characters becomes all the more worthy of respect and imitation. The solecisms of these outsider characters quickly become scatological, as in Tabitha's observation, "I wrote to doctor Lews for the same porpuss, but he never had the good manners to take the least notice . . . for which reason, I shall never favour him with another, though he beshits me on his bended knees" (156). The whole of Tabitha's first letter is littered with anal and fecal references: "bumdaffee," "shit," "wind-seller," "rumping," and "commode."[44] Nick Williams's term – "Scotological" – gets at this continuing connection of the Scots vernacular and the corrupt manifest in Smollett's writings.[45] After the bitter debates over linguistic technicalities – such as the question of whether "glorification" is a Scotticism – one imagines a sort of immense release in these forays into absolutely bawdy, culturally marked language. Yet that release is accompanied by images of disgust, all the more forceful for coming from the mouths of women who, as a gender, had to excel even further in their linguistic practices than their male peers to prove gentle standing.[46] So, unlike the linguistic multiplicity of his compatriots Robert Fergusson or Robert Burns, Smollett's at-times exuberantly playful, law-breaking language works in the interest of reaffirming the superior status of standard English; his support of English remains unshaken as he constructs that English against the substandard language of ill-educated women and marked inhabitants of the Celtic periphery. According to Bakhtin, the ambiguity of scatological references of Rabelais's age had been sufficiently disciplined by the eighteenth century and made into a kind of "pornography." Consequently, such scatological language could no longer be claimed as subversively carnivalesque in Smollett's era.[47]

Surprisingly, it is difficult to disagree with John Gibson Lockhart's assessment, when he writes, "The impression it [*Humphry Clinker*] conveys is certainly a painful, a disgusting one. The Scotsmen [of Smollett] are the Jockeys and Archies of farce – Time out of mind the Southrons mirthmakers – the best of them grotesque combinations of simplicity and hypocrisy, pride and meanness."[48] Important, however, is the association of truly grotesque language with women, and we might link this characterization to the period's ideological connection of threatening female sexuality to their equally threatening excessive linguistic generation. Unwittingly humorous, Tabitha's and Win's language signals the dangers of straying outside of standard literacy, cautionary exempla for the novel's readers. Broken, inflected with "vulgarisms," archaisms, malapropisms, and regional "dialects," their miserable written language, which attempts to represent phonologically the sounds of mis-spoken English, reflects their peripheral status. In contrast to the locationless language of standard English, the language of these women is profoundly located, particularly in its inherent orality, an orality which also indicates their peripheral status. Tabitha's and Win's letters are marked by conventions of representing oral language, such as apostrophes and truncated words. Win relates her lover's infidelity and her reaction to it, "I ketched him in the very fect . . . But I have gi'en the dirty slut a siserary" (70, Bath, May 15; a footnote tells us "sisery" is a corruption of "certiorari," meaning a scolding [358]). Their mistaken pronunciation is compounded by their mistaken grammar – "ketched" is used for "caught" – for example.

As a widely circulating novel that so clearly distinguishes between acceptable and unacceptable language use, *Humphry Clinker* would be an important cultural production in the development and spread of standard English. As such, its relationship to the establishment of what

Benedict Anderson would describe as a national linguistic community might seem too obvious to be in much need of analysis. This reading, however, stops short before reaching the true complexities of the cultural work that *representations* of linguistic practices are doing in this text. We need to ask, for instance, what kind of linguistic community *Humphry Clinker* constructs, a question answered in part by looking at how the novel constructs it. Anderson's analysis has come in for some critique, notably by Mary Louise Pratt, who has attacked the notion of "linguistic community" on which he bases his understanding of national community as a linguistic Utopia which ignores the relational, contested, and consequently heterogeneous constitution of language.[49] Less a shared mix of linguistic practices, Pratt argues, the linguistic standard is defined relationally, working "across rather than within lines of social differentiation" (61). In other words, the linguistic value of the standard is not a given, as Anderson suggests it is, and is certainly not inclusive, as the term "community" suggests, but is determined through struggle between social groups.

This is, of course, the paradox of the "national" Standard – it is the language that claims to be "without accent." Yet it derives that "universality" against the multiply "accented" language of others. Never completely stabilized, the standard depends upon an "outsider" language against which it can be defined – but which in turn responds to and resists the dominant language. The resulting heterogeneous character of the language troubles the notion of a homogeneous linguistic community. Pratt follows Noelle Bisseret Moreau in arguing that "linguistic heterogeneity is produced by the homogeneity of the shared social referent (or dominant ideology) . . . From this perspective, the codes, languages and competencies postulated by the linguistics of community are embodiments of this shared social referent with respect to which all messages, parole or performances situate themselves" (59). In other words, embedded in heterogeneous linguistic practices – and what holds them together as alternative linguistic communities – is a response, and struggle against, an imposed "homogeneous" dominant world view and its language. Smollett's novel, however, reverses this picture in a logic resembling nationalism's claims regarding language: a homogeneous normative language is instead produced out of, and supersedes, heterogeneous languages. In that move, neither the indecorous language of "outsiders" nor its speakers is capable of resistant agency. Tabitha and Win, for instance, are merely passive and primordial illiterates whose language is in dire need of regulation. If Smollett's recognition of the national language as not inherent but constructed and performed is one step forward, his understanding of this language as produced out of earlier, primitive linguistic dystopias incapable of responding to it takes two steps back.

That Tabitha and Win are in some sense "literate" – they do read and write, despite their highly imperfect understanding of language and grammar – also prompts a recognition of literacy as not an all-or-nothing proposition. Thus, when Ernest Gellner and his followers posit universal literacy as a precondition for modern nationalism, it is no wonder that their resulting model of the nation is of a culturally homogeneous society.[50] The model of the nation looks quite different when we understand the gradated character of literacies themselves. Tabitha's and Win's language, unlike that of their standard English-using counterparts, continually opens up to double meanings over which they have no control; they do not respond to so much as they misapprehend the dominant language. In their language, strewn with catachrestic expressions, the reader is aware of the absurdity of their meanings while they are not. Using Bisseret's argument about the dominant language as the figure in the carpet of meaning, we might say that the reader's very knowledge of the dominant language these women transgress might help establish a basis of (an exclusive) linguistic community amongst those readers who get the full impact of – and remain comfortably distinct from – the mistaken language and grammar of these women. Even the representation of Lydia, who writes in a correct standard English, suggests that national membership might be gendered to exclude women. Her simplest words imply unintentional irony. We know, for instance, the real reason her head aches when she writes, "I had the happiness to hear the celebrated Mrs. —, whose voice was so loud and so shrill, that it made my head ake through excess of pleasure" (93, London, 31 May). In contrast, one wonders what Humphry Clinker's writing – presumably as uneducated, or even less so, than Tabitha and Win, would look like – he does not even get an epistolary voice. He does intersect with their subliterate world as his speech, as represented on the page, is reproduced as unmistakably oral, "I am so an please your worthy ladyship . . . I ha'n't a shirt in the world" (81, London, 24 May). Yet the sincerity of his use of language is not to be doubted. While neither Tab nor Win nor even Lydia can control the multiple meanings of their language, Humphry takes language too literally. When Win pathetically overstates her hurt at Matthew's brusque skirmish with her dog, Chowder, and announces that Mat can kill the dog if it makes him happy, Humphry reaches for his knife to accommodate her.

It is critical that an unconsciously doubled, mistake-ridden language is used by women, for in this period in British history women's literacy trailed behind that of men by a ratio of roughly three to two, and Smollett's depiction of their failed attempts to mimic literacy both reflects and naturalizes that educational difference.[51] As in Chesterfield's writings, in Smollett's novel women's exclusion is key to a model of national affiliation predicated on literacy. In *Humphry Clinker*, construction of an English/Scottish British nation through language enforces the simultaneous production of uneducated women as outsiders, reminding us of Kathleen Wilson's observation of "women's contingent and subordinate position within the imagined community of the nation."[52] If the work of the SSPCK and even of dictionary makers such as Johnson demonstrates a belief in the abilities of linguistic pedagogy to insure national assimilation, these women seem even beyond the help of language instruction. Both Win, because she is a "sarvant," and Tabitha, perhaps because she came into what little literacy she has in an era prior to the explosion in grammar books for women, fall outside of the corrective powers of literacy instruction.

The literacy of Tabitha and Win, for instance, remains tied to the grossly physical. In their world, an abstract alphabet itself takes a material, consumable form. Win conceives of a mode of literacy instruction for an unfortunate illiterate friend. She writes, "Poor sole! it goes to my hart to think she don't yet know her letters . . . I will bring her the ABC in ginger-bread; and that, you nose, will be learning to her taste" (109). Here, the only way an ill-educated woman will have some relationship to letters is through oral gratification, and the physicality of Tabitha's and Win's language often references what comes out of and goes into their bodies – the image of consuming the alphabet plays neatly into that conceit of uncontrollable female consumption.[53] Nowhere is their absurdity more obvious than in their assumption of the role of literacy instructor. Win assumes this role when she chastises her friend: "O, voman! voman! if thou ad'st but the least consumption of what pleasure we scullers have, when we can cunster the crabbidst buck of hand, and spell the ethnitch vords without lucking at the primmer" (109). No "sculler," Win is at the farthest remove from one, her own spelling in need of "the primmer" indeed. Their most glaring offense is their effort to enter into learned discourse, as in Tabitha's name for engaging in rational discourse "to argufy." It is difficult not to see the linguistic riot of Tabitha's and Win's language as analogous to the material spoilage through movement and putrefying commerce of the core, London. Both suggest inappropriate intermingling and violating of spatial and class bounds. Tab's and Win's language is most objectionable when its affectation marks their transgression beyond their proper station, above their lowly, barely literate status.

PERIPHERAL LANGUAGE: LINGUISTIC NO MAN'S LAND

We cannot, however, simply relegate the language of Tabitha and Win to the periphery, and that of Matthew, Jery, and Lydia to the center, and be done with it. The novel is an uneasy intersection of spatial and linguistic models of the nation. Consider Jery's description of Lismahago's argument about the propriety of the English spoken in Edinburgh. The letters record the language of the emphatically Scottish nationalist Lismahago as a flawless English, as opposed to the previously cited Micklewhimmen. Although it is clear we are meant to take the arguments of this crusty and proud Scottish character with a grain of salt, it is not as clear that we are to dismiss him when he maintains that:

the English language was spoken with greater propriety at Edinburgh than in London . . . Scottish dialect was, in fact, true, genuine old English . . . [M]odern English, from affectation and false refinement, had . . . corrupted their language, by throwing out the guttural sounds, altering the pronunciation and the quantity, and disusing many words . . . of great significance . . . [T]he works of our best poets, such as Chaucer, Spenser, and even Shakespeare, were become . . . unintelligible to the natives of South-Britain, whereas the Scots . . . understand them without the help of a glossary." (199–200)

If Scots are ghostly presences in the print capital of London, in Lismahago's portrayal they haunt the present with their fullness of understanding of its past language and canonical literature, now lost to Londoners. In an era increasingly obsessed with the language and literature of the past – the more Gothic and impenetrable the better – the periphery, and the archaic language still residing there might, like that literature, become revalued.[54]

However generously or ungenerously we want to interpret Lismahago's assertions, one element of his argument stands: "peripheral" speakers of English can speak it well, perhaps even more clearly, than their English counterparts. Thomas Preston has argued that much of what Lismahago argues here "was generally accepted by the linguists of

Smollett's day."[55] Matthew's rejoinder to him doesn't so much argue against his point as assert a different cause – Scots speak a version of English more easily understood because they speak it as a second language and have not yet assimilated its music or cadence. Lismahago responds that the Scots cadence is more pure and understandable than the English, and firmly locates linguistic stability – and the continuity of literary value – at the nation's periphery. Even the reported language of Lismahago – whom we are told speaks with a Scots accent – is accent free. Yet what are we to make of the interpretation of peripheral language in relation to that of Tabitha and Win? Here are "peripheral" figures who write a version of the language which deviates wildly from standard English. Interestingly, in spite of its highly improper appearance on the page, Win's language is sanctioned by linguistic history. In her study of Win's spelling and likely pronunciation in relationship to key pronunciation guides of the day, Louise Hanes has shown that repeatedly Win's language accurately reflects historical forms of pronunciation. For example, in writing "creeter" for "Creature," Hanes tells us, Win resists what some might see as corrupting innovation in the eighteenth century. Hanes writes, "The change in sound from [t] to [~c] occurred in the eighteenth century," and quotes Robert Nares, a published orthoepist of the time, as writing, " 'I know not whether we ought in any instances to give way to this pronunciation, which has been creeping in upon us very perceptibly for some years past'" ("Pronunciation," 8). In another instance, Tabitha writes "lacksitif" for "laxative," replacing [v] with [f], and Hanes notes "the OED records the sound of [f] where [v] should appear in the fourteenth through the fifteenth centuries" (9). She goes on to remark that Gary Underwood associates the devoicing of [v] with the Welsh dialect. Here is one instance where an older form continues to exist in the periphery, and throughout her analyses of Win's peculiar usages Hanes notes how once-acceptable usages come to be considered regional dialectics. W. Arthur Boggs has even argued that "quite a number of Win's usages which today have a colloquial or proverbial flavor also turn out to be standard eighteenth century" usage ("Some Standard," 305), so we might assume that Smollett's novel played some role in the outmoding of formerly acceptable writing, shaping standard English by associating language he found distasteful with the crude female figures of Win and Tabitha.

In caricaturing this language as distasteful, however, Smollett suggests that the language of the past is not to be as valued as that into which citizens are educated, uncoupling tradition and custom from the "standard." This observation works against or exposes the limits of Johnson's ostensible model of linguistic legitimacy, where "correct" language is that validated through age-old custom. Standard English is instead standard because it is what the privileged classes of the center use or are learning to use at a particular historical moment. Perhaps it is more accurate to say that Hanes's evidence suggests that Smollett shared Johnson's dilemma: "correct" standard language was continuously in flux, and even custom changed frequently, in effect working against itself. Interestingly, however, it is not women in this case who are responsible for "giving birth" to fashionable neologisms, as Tabitha speaks the old-fashioned language which has lost its legitimacy to encroaching London barbarisms. Instead, educated men revise and distribute, through institutional systems and cultural productions, this "new" language.

Finally, however, while on the one hand the text seems to invite us to associate the strange, old language with Celtic peripheral space, on the other hand, it ultimately refuses to valorize that "corrupt" usage with *any* geographical location. Boggs has shown that the language of Win's and Tabitha's letters is a composite language, and not anyone's realistic idiolect. Win, for instance, has never been outside of Wales (before this expedition), and yet she speaks a bizarre mixture of Welsh, standard English, Cockney, and Scots. Both Win's and Tabitha's pronunciation sometimes suggests the influence of Welsh Gaelic, but at other times it does not. As Boggs puts it, "Smollett counted on the provincial linguistic ignorance of his English readers not to know when he was pulling their linguistic legs" ("Win Jenkins," 337); he was, it seems, a sort of trickster translator. In a particularly astute move, Smollett sets up a false linguistic core/periphery, English/Celtic distinction that utterly crumbles once its surface is scratched. Boggs's assessment is suggestive: "Smollett ... created a rich and persuasive speech which turns out to be no speech at all" (337). In the language of Tabitha and Win, then, we have a kind of linguistic no man's land. Yet unlike Johnson's ideal national language of "nobody," this "no speech" represents the dystopia against which Smollett aims to define the standard. If the English "nobody" is a mythic, idealized everybody, the Celtic "nobody" is the horrifying figure of incoherent dismemberment. For this dialect exists nowhere and bespeaks no alternative cultural community or identity – instead it is a form of Babel. Tab's and Win's "deviant" use of language simply locates them outside of a literate British national community, and not inside an alternative, peripheral community. This historical information on the ultimately placeless or diffuse character of incorrect language, positions it not as the language of any language community *per se*, but rather as a cipher through which to define and limit a standard. If the deceptively particular and physical language of Win and Tabitha turns out to be particular to no one, standard English must be somebody's, its general, abstract character relocated to a specific British body of language users.

Smollett moves back and forth between extolling the language of either the periphery or center, reminding us of the ambivalence we have been observing throughout this work: is Scotland's language ontologically "other," disorganized, polyvocal, in need of total linguistic conversion, or is it the linguistic remnant of an earlier, less corrupt Britain? Views of Scots Gaelic were undergoing a sea change by the end of the eighteenth century, as the remote language of the Highlanders was becoming fodder for legends of an originary British culture. Jery anticipates such views as he views "with enthusiastic pleasure" the Highland landscape with the "Poems of Ossian" in mind. Ossian's poems, he writes, "are in every mouth – A famous antiquarian of this country . . . can repeat them all in the original Gaelick [sic], which has a great affinity to the Welch [sic]" [240]. Jery makes much of the "affinity" between Scots Gaelic and Welsh, asserting, "I make no doubt but that they are both sprung from the same origin" (240). In these "peripheral" languages, origins remain legible; continuity in time and space are assured. Such beliefs were, as we shall see in Chapter 5, the basis of the "Celtomania" of the century's end, as the quality of continuity, of visible connection to the past, became increasingly important to cultural nationalist rhetoric.

Yet Smollett is ultimately distanced from that movement. For him, location has little bearing on who speaks proper English. Anyone – not just peripheral Celts – might speak a corrupt language, a fact that turns out to be central to the notion of a contrasting correct standard language which both English and Scottish might use. In fact, the case for the identity of Lowland Scot and English "stock" is evidenced in the oral language of a Highlander. Just after the passage cited above, Jery notes:

I was not a little surprised, when asking a Highlander one day, if he knew where we should find any game? He replied, '*hu niel Sassenagh*,' which signifies no English: the very same answer I should have received from a Welchman . . . The Highlanders have no other name for the people of the Low-country, but Sassenagh, or Saxons; a strong presumption that the Lowland Scots and the English are derived from the same stock. (240)

This passage reveals the tensions at the heart of Smollett's cultural work. On the one hand, it suggests the originary, authoritative status of Gaelic langauges. Welsh and Scots Gaelic languages turn out to be "the very same," providing strong evidence of the connection between these peoples. Is the work of this passage, then, to suggest the commonality between "Celtic" regions? Or, on the other hand, is it doing the work of consolidating Lowland Scot and English? After all, the authority of the ancient Gaelic word turns out to provide evidence that Lowland Scot and English are "derived from the same stock."

We have seen how, for Smollett, region and gender are factors in the construction of an exclusive national language community, but I want to close by returning to the question of class, a question frequently missing from analyses of national cultural formations. Even between the illiterate women a subtle linguistic class marker exists. Mugglestone writes, "Win's mistress shares her maid's every linguistic idiosyncrasy with one exception, that of [h]-usage . . . [I]t is the use of <h> which provides a clear marker of their social differentiation" ("Ladylike," 141). Class overlays, and at times overrides, linguistic national membership. A presumably lower-class London woman uses the corrupt language associated with the flawed Celtic dialect, for instance, in a fictional letter Smollett writes in *The Briton*. Assuming the personae of a "Winifred Bullcalf" (perhaps the female equivalent of John Bull) – said to be the basis for Win Jenkins – Smollett writes:

Mr Brittin, Althof my neighbour Firken says you can't rite English, therefore must be a Scotchman; and being a Scotchman, you have no right to call yourself a Brittin; and as how you are a vagabond people, that come over . . . with every fair wind, like locusts to devour us; yet I knows what's what. (295, No. 11, 7 August 1762)

Here Smollett reconstitutes what it means to be British. In placing this language, whose own writer "can't write English" next to the language of the author of *The Briton*, written in a scholarly King's English, with such flourishes as "I shall dedicate this paper to my correspondents, and the more earnestly wish their letters may prove agreeable to the reader, as their future interposition may afford me a comfortable respite from my own labours" – Smollett recasts the circle of Britishness. If Smollett satirizes Bullcalf's neighbor Firkin's claims that *The Briton*'s author is not a Briton because he can't write English, he reaffirms the link between Britishness and polite language – and shows that he writes it better than English natives.

It is not entirely clear that Bullcalf is outside of the national circle here – for she defends "Mr Brittin" and wisely asserts that "there are good and bad of all countries." What is clear is that those given to malapropisms should not be in positions of authority. Bullcalf certainly is not, yet even she can recognize and complain that "Sir Dogberry Verges" – a reference to the Dogberry of Shakespeare's *Much Ado about Nothing*, arguably the first malapropos purveyor of early modern English literature – was made a knight for "speechifying."[56] Bullcalf writes:

> he bespoke my husband to hollow among the mob at Temple-Bar and Guild-Hall, as having a special good counter-tenor voice; and I'll assure you he did not spare it . . . all that my husband got for tearing his pipes to pieces, was poor five shillings and half a gallon of new rum. Now, I knows as how they want voices to rail at your countryman . . . but I am resolved they shall no more dance to his pipe, unless he is better paid for his music – My husband can hollow bass as well as treble. – A word to the wise, Mr. Brittin. (295–6 No. 11, 7 August 1762)

"Dogberry," a friend of Pitt's, deserves this knighthood less than Bullcalf herself; he merely enlists the loudest voices of the mob to rail against Bute and his fellow Scots. Bullcalf, despite her flawed English, gets at the truth of the matter: Dogberry exploits empty voices to "hollow" (holler), thereby shouting down opposition with sheer noise, rather than engaging in rational, polite discourse. The Scotophobia Dogberry's mob mindlessly mouths is no more than meaningless sound. While *The Briton*'s editor appeals to a disembodied, seemingly "disinterested" language of reason, Bute's opponents assemble only the "good counter-tenor voice[s]," particularly the unambiguously embodied force of their "pipes," to mount their irrational critique. The mob, whose voices, Bullcalf hints, are available to the highest bidder, and the poor-spoken leaders who seek to manipulate them, violate the linguistically stratified structure of the nation. The politician speaks below his stratum, the mob, above. If we recall the figuration of the disembodied Celtic editors as "voices and nothing more," we might imagine that Smollett's periodical piece anticipates that figure and uses it against his English opponents. It is the English mob and corrupt politicians, and not the Scottish literati, who exploit hollow voices, especially in that they promote the use of embodied voices not in private spaces on the private day of Sunday, but in public spaces for public occasions. It is they who speak and create a confusion of tongues.

The standard English Smollett masters and promotes is posed – even constituted – as distinct from the no man's land of a subliterate usage, a dangerous hybrid of British languages. In detaching linguistic and cultural identity from spatial locations, Smollett makes it available to Scots and English alike. Core/periphery spatial distinctions give way to distinctions of linguistic competency and, finally, taste – which are in turn distinctions of class. Smollett thus limits the appreciation of fine English to those schooled in the nuances of critical reception. While Smollett has turned to linguistic practice as a means of effacing the hierarchies of region, there can be no question that this move depends on establishing a new set of hierarchies that trouble – in fact, render implausible – the inclusive posturing of nationalist rhetoric. The final irony is that in his last novel Smollett, the ambivalent figure, himself the speaker of a hybrid language, locates the nation in a virtuous, insular periphery whose identity he then effaces by denying it its own language. His last novel fails to resolve the opposition between these two models of the nation – spatial and linguistic. That failure bespeaks the oscillating, unstable character of the Scottish negotiation of British identity. His awkward and finally unsuccessful manipulations of spatial and linguistic nationalism reflect Smollett's own ambivalence regarding the challenges of defining an Anglo-British nation and its relationship to a Celtic periphery – instrumental though he was in defining both.

CHAPTER 4

The figure of the nation: polite language and its originary other

Hundreds of miles from London, Lowland Scottish merchants, lawyers, and literati worked as hard as Lowland London dwellers like Smollett to perfect their English.[1] Issues of the monthly *Scots Magazine* from 1761 reveal that middle-class Edinburghers understood mastering polite English as not simply a means of self-aggrandizement but also as an avenue of participation in the strengthening of the British nation. The July issue, for instance, features a pages-long reprint of the *Monthly Review*'s glowing appraisal of Thomas Sheridan's *British Education; or, The Source of the Disorders of Great Britain* (1756). The review echoes the Irish actor-turned-elocutionist's alarmist critique of British education and British oratory and, consequently, the languishing condition of the English language and the British nation whose political health depends upon it. In that same issue, a listing of goings-on in Scotland announces Sheridan's arrival in Edinburgh and reproduces a copy of his advertisement for his upcoming lectures on "elocution" and "the English tongue." Whoever wrote the copy for Sheridan's ad targeted his market well. In a town in which a rising elite sought full legitimization as Britons through heightened language skills, whose curiosity would not be piqued (and purse strings loosened) by the promise the ad makes? Sheridan, it explains,

will point out the true source of the difficulty (at present thought to be insuperable) which all foreigners, as well as natives of different kingdoms and counties, that speak a corrupt dialect of English, find in the attainment of the right pronunciation of that tongue.
  In the close he will point out an easy and practicable way of reducing the living tongue to a standard ... that the adult ... and the rising generation in this country may be taught to speak in its utmost purity.[2]

With an admission price of one guinea, Sheridan's lectures packed the assembly hall with those who could afford to embark on the trusted path of linguistic improvement to augmented social respectability. In a four-week-long course which met every Tuesday through Friday, Sheridan lectured to a standing-room-only crowd of "more than 300 gentlemen, the most eminent in this country" (390); the time commitment alone suggests the diligence of these earnest gentlemen. Following on the heels of this success, Sheridan offered a two-week-long course "chiefly for the use of the ladies" and published his lectures.[3] Sheridan's lectures, with their stress on correct pronunciation and affective oral delivery, were likely entertaining oratory. More important, he was a role model who provided a living example that dialect speakers such as himself – whose language was practically "foreign," as he puts it – could achieve a carefully studied verbal agility and compelling eloquence that resulted in personal and civic betterment.[4]

The Scots' interest in linguistic improvement and in the entwined national and personal character of perfected oral delivery remains evident in the following August issue of the *Scots Magazine*. This issue offers a continuation of the extended reprint of the review of *British Education*, with its admonition that only nations possessing a clear standard language can hope to preserve their culture in the distant memory of future generations, and that only the practice of oratory can lead to such a language. The issue also contains a report from the newly formed "Select Society for promoting the Reading and Speaking of the English language in Scotland," whose members included, among other luminaries of the Scottish Enlightenment, Hugh Blair, William Robertson, and Adam Ferguson. Initiated in the wake of Sheridan's lectures and seeking to redress "the disadvantages under which [Scotsmen] labour, from their imperfect knowledge of the English Tongue and the impropriety with which they speak it," the Society hired instructors to teach elite Scots "to avoid many gross improprieties . . . which render the Scotch dialect so offensive" (440). The Select Society (1754–63), from which the Society for promoting English originated, provided an ideal space in which its members could try out the proper diction and polite conversation they were learning. Composed for the most part of lawyers, landowners, merchants, and other upper- and upper-middle-class men – including Adam Smith, David Hume, Lord Monboddo, and Simon Fraser – the Select Society held weekly debates for "the improvement of the members in the art of speaking."[5]

Anyone familiar with Jurgen Habermas's writings on the development of the bourgeois public sphere will recognize in such mid-eighteenth-century Lowland societies a revealingly peculiar illustration of that social configuration. Habermas describes how with the rise of commercial exchange, "A far-reaching network of horizontal economic dependencies emerged that in principle could no longer be accommodated by the vertical relationships of dependence."[6] The polite social, particularly verbal, interaction critical to linguistic refinement also supplied the social-structural basis of those emerging horizontal relationships. Facilitating new structures of social organization and authority, the public sphere is where "private people come together as a public" (25). In the intimate homosocial domains of the Lowland clubs, polite conversation not only offered a chance to exercise one's "supraregional" English, but also provided the form for the social alliances of emerging political structures within a newly incorporated Britain. Although relentlessly "male dominated," as Paul Bator puts it, in the "close-knit, familial culture of convivial clubs and philosophical societies," the emphasis on inter-subjective relations in the establishment of non-feudal models of community – what some have called a feminization of culture – is very much in evidence.[7] Habermas observes that these discussion groups were "guided specifically by such private experiences as grew out of the audience-oriented subjectivity of the conjugal family's intimate domain" (28). Such societies approximate, on a small scale, the link between affective relationships and national sentiment that Burke later described: "We begin our public affections in our families. No cold relation is a zealous citizen. We pass on to our neighborhoods our habitual provincial connections. The love to the whole is not extinguished by this subordinate partiality. Perhaps it is a sort of elemental training to those higher and more large regards by which alone men come to be affected."[8]

This "intimate" version of the sphere is also the site of linguistic estrangement. Adam Smith writes, "We in this country are most of us very sensible that the perfection of language is very different from that we commonly speak in."[9] At once the civic-minded town fathers administering the betterment of the language – Smith and Blair lectured in rhetoric and belles lettres – they were also the recipients of such improvement.[10] Comprising a shadow public sphere, these Scottish writers narrated their relationship to proper language in ways which could conceal their secondary status. Like earlier English writers who set about to polish the English tongue, these Scots stressed the "naturalness" of polite language.[11] The means by which these affluent Lowlanders were coming to English could not be a pedagogy of blunt rules; they were training their ears to distinguish effective elocution and practicing proper English through elevated discussions of taste. As commentators on eighteenth-century linguistic practices and theories have noted, mid-century writers and educators – both English and Scottish – were committed to establishing endless, often minute rules of correct usage and polite style.[12] My emphasis, however, is on the ways in which these rules were not warranted on the authority of law and logic alone (although these, of course, remain a factor) but also on the authority of subjectively experienced aesthetic effects. The emphasis on taste relocated the determination of appropriateness from strict external rules to the individual's sense of correctness. The authority of "proper" language thus derived not from English rulers but from Scottish subjects as individuals.[13]

Striking in its bleak exemplification of cultural assimilation, the rush to imitate a standard English which could convince one's readers and listeners of the "naturalness" of the Lowlanders' English has occasioned a number of fruitful studies regarding the cultural ambivalences of such efforts and the fascinating ways in which the periphery ends up shaping "central" culture.[14] What I am especially interested in tracing, however, are the ways in which the peripheral status of these writers influenced not only English language practices and institutions of cultural transmission but also the very terms of national linguistic attachments – and their contradictions. Drawing from aesthetic theory and referring to the "beauty," "force," and "pleasing" effects of correct language, they appeal to an internalized, even physically registered, appreciation of language able to mediate between individual subjects and the national collective. Scottish borrowings and modifications of a pre-Kantian aesthetic discourse which makes room for the body and its responses to material language help shape such national formations as the new British rhetoric, the institutionalization of college literature, and the production of modern subjectivity itself. Their work has become paramount to the understanding of the place of language in the ideology of British cultural nationalism. The underlying force that brought about the claim to identification with proper English was a self-governing relationship to that tongue. Engaging the individual by equating language with taste was a subtle, understated and highly effective means to develop patriotic devotion to "proper" English. The elites learning to speak, write, and appreciate "proper" English strove to emulate and articulately admire "beautiful" language, which was also a modest, refined language that could dampen the enflamed language of civil war and Jacobite rebellions. In addition, in the face of an increasingly commercial community whose social cohesion was disintegrating into private interests, polite language could knit together a society of like-minded users of beautiful language. Delicate, pliant language could minimize political difference and ardent, potentially uncontrollable feelings in favor of a sense of propriety and the inducement of love; as Burke had written, beauty is "that quality . . . in bodies by which they cause love."[15] This emphasis on control in beautiful language might account, in part, for the decline in "eloquence" that Nicholas Hudson and Adam Potkay have documented, for eloquence might produce "the violent emotions of the nerves" (121) Burke associates with beauty's opposite, the sublime.

It is, however, in such sublime oratory that Sheridan provides his instruction in proper English. And it is to the feminizing dangers of obeying the binding regulations of written language that he points when stressing the need for powerful oratory.[16] As the theories and practices of an aestheticized polite language introduce the body, they also police it.[17] In warning of the dangers of "contracting from early childhood, and moulding into unnatural forms, the faculties of speech, which are amongst the most noble . . . possessed by man," Sheridan compares the linguistic constraints of the rules of writing and reading to a repugnant restrictive custom, the binding of women's feet in China.[18] Yet, of course, his lectures in eloquence carefully script the delivery of oral language, "reducing the living tongue to a standard," as his own advertisement describes it, and it is difficult to see in what ways his own instruction was not a "binding" of sorts. Alternatively, since it ravishes and transports, oratory might be said also to feminize its audience, which makes it difficult to support a rigid opposition between sublime and beautiful and "masculine" and "feminine" language.

The tensions between nature and culture in their aesthetic considerations of language were certainly not unique to "Celtic" writers.[19] However, as elite "outsiders" attempting to internalize "national" language, their circumstances placed particular pressures on their contributions to that aesthetic discourse. Their position was further complicated by the fact that the "nature" which sat uncomfortably alongside the "second nature" of their own relationship to British culture was, in one form, located just north of them, and, in another form, amongst them, in communities of lower social classes. The ambiguities around "native"/unlearned and "foreign"/learned language and between refined language, often gendered female, and unrefined language, often gendered male, haunt the lectures and writings of these rhetoric instructors. So too does the spectre of originary, perhaps Gaelic-speaking language communities, who, Lowlanders believed, spoke a noble, free, sublime language before the confining agents of literacy and literate education descended upon them. As educated Lowlanders recognized the opportunities presented by assimilating the "beautiful" language they believed their peers to the south spoke, they distinguished themselves from the sublime language of their northern neighbors and the rude language of "untaught" peasants. Yet in moments of awareness of the disciplining, alienated, and doubled character of the national "natural" language, a myth of precommercial community and its sublime language is retrojected. This past, pristine, and uncorrupted version of the community spoke an originary language which ties the mythic originary nation together in ways a beautiful language promises to but cannot restore or build.

BEYOND REASON: POLITE ENGLISH AND THE LANGUAGE OF FEELING

In the opening passage of the posthumously published transcript of Smith's lectures, physical response to language and the distinction between foreign and native are intertwined:

Perspicuity requires not only that the expressions we use should be free from all ambiguity proceeding from synonymous words, but that the words should be natives (if I may [say] so) of the language we speak in. Foreigners, though they may signify the same thing, never convey the idea with such strength as those we are acquainted with and whose origin we can trace.[20]

While the directive to avoid foreign words was at least as old as Quintilian's *Institutes*, unlike Quintilian, Smith invokes a nearly sense-based criterion for judging native and foreign, since native words are not simply those "whose origin we can trace" but those which convey ideas with "strength."[21] The naturalization of the native/foreign distinction is critical, for those who speak and write English well, including, of course, Smith's students, could identify themselves as natives, as opposed to foreigners. Further, even more than Johnson (unlike Johnson, he is even suspicious of Latinate terms), Smith restricts native words to Anglo-Saxon terms, thus rejecting English's mongrel mix of Roman, Celtic, Norman, and Teutonic origins.[22]

This passage moves from a discussion of "native words" to "foreigners," a virtual personification of foreign words as the unwelcome ambassadors of foreign lands, which, as in Johnson's *Dictionary*, naturalizes the distinction between native and foreign peoples. Smith follows his point with an illustration:

> we may see an instance of this in the word 'Unfold' – a good old English word derived from an English root, consequently its meaning must be easily received. This word, however, has within these ten years been . . . thrust out of common use by a French word of not half the strength or significance, to wit 'develop'. This word tho [sic] of the same signification with unfold can never convey the idea so strongly to an English reader. (1–2)

On the one hand, Smith asks his audience to consider as synonymous two words that have, in some ways, different senses. On the other hand, Smith displaces what difference he believes does exist to the distinction between their status as "foreign" and "native" words. Like Johnson, Smith laments that "new words are continually pushing out our own original ones, so that the stock of our own is now become but very small and is still diminishing" (2), and he again invokes physical sense, arguing that the English word's meaning is "received" more strongly. This is an "aesthetic" understanding of language, to the extent that sensual perception, and not reason, legitimates the continued use of "unfold"; one derives meaning from one's native tongue effortlessly, where the world with which one is familiar matches up with the words one has presumably known since childhood – and these words, in turn, have been part of the lexicon since the "childhood" of the nation.

Native words elicit different sensual responses from foreign ones and their physical impact underwrites native status. One can tell that a word is "native" if one is "pleased" or "taken" by it (2). Here Smith maps national difference onto the body, as the body is affected more strongly by its own native language. Words, in this instance, signify more than a thing or idea. "Native" words call up feelings and are able to evoke a sense of their users' and hearers' relationship to each other. Language operates, then, in the same way that the idea of being native and belonging to the nation are supposed to: through "natural" affect, not arbitrary laws. Difference between native and foreign is relegated to "gut" reactions to proper English, not only at the level of diction and syntax on the page, but also, throughout the second half of the eighteenth century and beyond, through the properly pronounced language of its native speakers.[23] After a portion of a lecture devoted to correct pronunciation, Smith adds:

> what has a greater effect on the sound of the Language than all the rest is the harmonious and sonorous pronunciation peculiar to the English nation. There

is a certain ringing in their manner of speaking which foreigners can never attain. Hence it is that this language which when spoke [sic] by the natives is allowed to be very melodious and agreable [sic], in the mouths of strangers is strangely harsh and grating. (18)

Language and the theories surrounding and constructing it aspire to their most effective and subtle naturalization of the nation when they reach, or claim to reach, a true link to national character that is beyond mere reason. While Benedict Anderson focuses on the experience of an intranational simultaneity that a standard print vernacular constructs, the discourse surrounding tasteful language use and appreciation developed in Scotland draws an even tighter point of commonality between the nation's members than a cognition of shared experience in time: the reader or listener "feels" national community through a collective aesthetic response to the well-spoken or well-written vernacular.[24]

While Smith and Blair do not discount rules and in fact are busy laying them out for their students, they do link them to an authority that exceeds the bounds of logic.[25] Although Leonard emphasizes the appeal to logic by eighteenth-century grammarians, he does show how, in objecting to placing prepositions at the end of a sentence, Blair "treats the problem wholly as a matter of securing forceful effect or pleasing structure" (*Doctrine*, 98). Smith outlines a rule: "it is a great defect in the arangement [sic] of a sentence when it has what they call a tail coming after it . . . This is always avoided by placing the terminative and circumstantiall [sic] term before the attributive . . . [I]f these rules be observed the expression . . . will have more force" (21). As he warns against the "splitting of particles," Blair too cautions, "In such instances, we feel a sort of pain, from the revulsion, or violent separation of two things, which by their nature should be closely united."[26] Referring to traditional rhetorics as "a very silly set of books" (23), Smith identifies and catalogs the feelings roused in reading and hearing different writers, from "pleasing anxiety" (88) and "lively and shocking . . . impression" to the raising of "sympatheticall [sic] affections" (90). In their belletristic discussions of language they followed Thomas Reid who had argued that one could not lay down general rules, that "taste and judgment were above rules" (Lothian, xxxviii). Rules, according to Sheridan, could even play a corrupting role in one's use of language.[27] Grammatical rules were, to Smith, imperfect and flawed since they were "only accommodated to the most plain and vulgar expressions" (22). For Blair, "No grammatical rules have sufficient authority to control established usage" (179).[28]

In elaborating a model of signification that moves beyond abstract laws, Smith and Blair participate in sweeping changes in theories of representation and linguistics. Stephen Land, for instance, has tracked a move from a more representational understanding of language – a "picture theory" of language – to the recognition that "the meaning of the sign may involve more than is contained in the referent."[29] Land highlights Burke's role in this transformation, arguing that Burke revealed "a rhetorical surplus in language" (48). In Burke's theory of language, gone is the logic of equivalence between word and thing or idea; gone too is the conviction that to grasp language is primarily to know grammar and the workings of its rational principles. Unlike painting, which offers the "pleasure of imitation," and architecture, which "affects by the . . . law of reason" (*Inquiry*, 149), "Poetry and rhetoric," Burke writes, "do not succeed in exact description . . . [T]heir business is to affect rather by sympathy than imitation" (159). It is for this reason, Burke believes, that words have "sometimes a much greater . . . share in exciting ideas of beauty and of the sublime" (149) and are, in fact, "much more capable of making deep and lively impressions than any other arts" (158).

In his most extreme theorization, Burke believes that affecting language moves its listeners and readers without their forethought and even "prevent[s their] understanding." He writes, "Whenever the wisdom of our Creator intended that we should be affected with any thing, he did not confide the execution of his design to . . . reason; but he endued it with powers and properties that prevent the understanding . . . seizing upon the sense and imagination" (97).[30] At work in the belief in an affective language that might "seize sense" is the emerging model of a "new psycho-perceptual system," as G. J. Barker-Benfield has called it, which identified a physiological, nerve-centered basis to feeling, perception, and the soul itself.[31] Most boldly put, language establishes and reflects national affinities by inducing something close to, but not quite, bodily sensations which are then reflected upon and refined in the polite conversation of criticism. Referring to this physical sense of language, Sheridan writes, "There are other things which pass in the mind of man, beside ideas; as he is not wholly made up of intellect, but on the contrary, the passions, and the fancy, compose great part of his complicated frame," and the communication of these feelings must take place "by sensible marks" (*Lectures*, 99). Blair seems to reference the "psycho-perceptual" directly when he writes in his *Lectures* how the best language would invoke "sense and perception" and "appeal . . . to feeling" by consulting "our own imagination and heart" (vol. I, 31).[32] According to Nancy Struever, as these men formulate the relationship between language, cognition, and cultural identity, they "consider sentiment as well as reason, feeling as well as circumstantial fact," even if those sensations, once aroused, were quickly controlled.[33]

When these writers apply aesthetic discourse to the use of English and its appreciation, the role of an English vernacular in consolidating a national "consensual" community becomes obvious, for this application limits the potentially transnational appeal of aesthetic discussions to a community of those who speak and can thoroughly value the same language. In the case of language, then, aesthetic discourse is not necessarily a "defensive consciousness" (*Civilised*, 2) only "devoted to aristocratic values" (26), as Daniel Cottom sees it. Instead, aesthetic discourse incorporates the claims to superior and refined judgment of an aristocratic class as it assists in the restructuring of class in broader national terms. Referring to the increasingly national direction of the alterations in linguistic theory, Murray Cohen sees a shift occurring toward the end of the eighteenth century where language becomes an object "not structurally isomorphic to the order of things . . . but a collection of native habits . . . that could be studied rhetorically as effective and affective speech."[34] Smith, for example, argues that particular styles arise "from the nature and temper of the nation" (Bryce, 162), and Blair believes that "different countries have been noted for peculiarities of Style, suited to their different temper and genius" (*Harding*, vol. I, 184). Attesting the cross-class national inclusiveness of aesthetic response, Joseph Addison had written that folk songs such as "Chevy Chase" are popular because "it is impossible that anything should be universally tasted and approved by a multitude though they are only the rabble of a nation, which hath not in it some peculiar aptness to please and gratify the mind of man."[35]

If we return to this section's opening quotation, however, we find a brief aside which might function as one point among many where the mythical linguistic nationalism Smith articulates begins to unravel in the Scottish context. The student transcriber has marked Smith's statement "(if I may [say] so)." Why might Smith ask permission to expostulate on natives and foreigners? Such hesitation calls to mind Smith's own status. In what sense can Smith, born in Scotland, in a newly consolidated "Britain," be considered a native? In what way can he deem the English he now uses – as opposed to the Scots language widely used in Edinburgh – "native" to him?[36] Smith believes that "the words of another language may ... be naturalized by time and be as familiar to us as those which are originally our own" (1). Yet his distinction between foreign and native still militates against a total erasure of difference over time, for "here likewise we may see the effect of the words being well known to us or not" (1). Smith states that a word must be "long introduced amongst us" to carry power: How long would it take for speakers of Scots and Gaelic to recognize English as their "native" tongue and to respond to English words in that way? And yet, for the new British subjects of Scotland, the sooner they could form such a relationship to the English language, or claim to, the sooner their status as British nationals could be affirmed – along with its material privileges. Smith's initial call for using native language evokes an integral, pure nation and concomitant language yet also locates the nation within a larger transnational context.

Not only Sheridan, Smith, and Blair, the developers of the linguistic aspects of this discourse, but also Burke and Francis Hutcheson, its more general theorists, were non-English British nationals.[37] Both inside and outside of the British linguistic community, these writers would find the amphibious discourse of aesthetics particularly appealing. Elizabeth Bohls describes the dual character of the aesthetic, writing that "aesthetic perception ... was abstract, without being cerebral; rooted in the senses, it nonetheless transcended the private interests traditionally associated with them, opening a space for consensus."[38] Itself doubled, somehow managing to be both universal and particular in scope and to be positioned somewhere between bodily sense and mental reason in its workings, the aesthetic discourse upon which the judgment of polite language depends holds particular allure for those "borderline" Scottish subjects hoping to situate themselves as "natives" within an at-times unwelcoming British nation. Neither pure abstraction nor total embodiment, tasteful language appeals to subtle physical responses, forever universalizing while also relativizing them.

The "disinterested" character of the aesthetic that appealed to elite Lowlanders entails a semi-permeable universality, oscillating between inclusion and exclusion regarding social class.[39] Some writers, such as Shaftesbury, writing in the early part of the century, were outspokenly single-minded in the belief that the community capable of tasteful response and discussion was limited to the upper classes with the time and means to refine their responses. Yet others, such as Hume and Burke, were more ambivalent and, at points, widened the potential community of taste.[40] For Burke, the standard of "taste is the same in all human creatures" (*Inquiry* 11). "I never remember that any thing [sic] beautiful . . . was ever shewn," he insists, "though it were to an hundred people, that they did not all immediately agree that it was beautiful" (15). In these more inclusive models of taste, where the emphasis is not primarily on class difference but rather on common human responses, those responses remind subjects of their commonality. Smith writes, "The Rules of Criticism . . . turn out to be some Principles of Common Sence [sic] which every one assents to" (55). Like aesthetic discourse, the related discourse of common sense has, as Summers describes it, a "paradoxical status as a criterion that might be either relative and consensual or absolute and universal" (*Judgment*, 327). Just as the inclusiveness of the British nation is undercut by the tacit exclusion of non-natives such as Scots, so the inclusiveness of aesthetic judgment is unavoidably undermined by class distinctions.[41] Similarly, according to Potkay, a related "politeness is an eighteenth-century ideology in formation, intended to consolidate the members of the gentry and professional classes, and to differentiate this group from a 'vulgar' underclass."[42]

What further inclusion is possible – of lower classes, of provincial regions – comes not through shared responses or language but through imitation.[43] This is why elaboration of codes of usage is necessary at all. Linked to the "custom of the country," proper national language, Smith admits, is from "some particular part of the nation . . . formed of men of rank and breeding. The easiness of those persons [sic] behaviour is so agreable [sic] and taking that whatever is connected with it pleases us. For this reason we love both their dress and their manner of language" (4). Standard English is again aestheticized – lower classes and provincials imitate their "betters" because their behavior and language are "agreeable" and "pleasing" – yet this is an aesthetic response once removed, not a "nature" but a second nature. The perspective here – not of imitated but of imitator – is as telling as the comparison of "agreeable" language to dress: both suggest that the easiness of this language is not natural to the admirer but must be learned, put on, at best, and repeated in ways one hopes will appear natural.

Thomas Miller argues that the tasteful criticism learned and practiced by Lowland Scots was a resistant response to "centrifugal" trends such as the spread of cheap print literacy. "Efforts were made to contain the educated culture," Miller writes, "by formalizing the conventions of correct expression . . . modeling the process by which individuals were to internalize 'a spectator within the breast' to judge changing mores with tasteful self-restraint" (*Formation*, 58). In Miller's analysis, Smith's impartial spectator indexes Smith's own status as a Scot as it internalizes "the outsider's dialectical awareness of cultural differences in the form of a second self who monitors, enabling one to identify with those properties and perpetuate their authority by demonstrating that they are second nature" (26). In perceiving the analogies between the provincial's position and that of the impartial spectator, Miller provides a long overdue contextualization of Smith's moral philosophy. I would, however, like to tease out the implications of the "dialectical awareness" between insider and outsider and the notion of "second nature," a little further. One way of going about that is to unpack the relationship between class, the focus of Miller's discussion, and nation, which complicates the exclusionary rhetoric of class. The appeal to taste was particularly meaningful for Lowland Scots precisely because by embracing a class-based discourse of polite refinement, elite Lowlanders could distance themselves from other Scots while approximating a "British" sensibility; once again difference in region is overwritten by difference in class. In this way, the colonial contribution to national ideology – and its linguistic practices – works in tandem with the naturalization of class difference.

This position, however, is analogous to that of the "vulgar" who must work to imitate "proper" language and to convince observers of the "naturalness" of this delivery. The mimicry connoted by the figure of "the great inmate" – Smith's other name for the internalized impartial spectator – problematizes the "second nature" status of assimilation in interesting ways. If this imitation of polite language was restrictive, it was also, as John Dwyer argues, more crucial as a binding agent for the Scots than the English, who had the notion of the "ancient constitution" to back up their national sense of identity.[44] For both Scots and English, the aesthetic is overlaid with multiple and contradictory pressures: for inclusion and exclusion, for national and class consolidation. Invoking "polite language" and its aesthetic effects in the absence of more material forms of social cohesion, these writers occupy an inescapably conflicted position. If the impartial spectator within allows one to "stand back and compose" him or herself, as Luke Gibbons theorizes, that relational sense of self-composition, its dependence on an impartial shading into "imperial spectator" must at the same time be concealed. That concealment takes place through the appeal to the aesthetic.[45] The psycho-perceptual grounds the sense of self-composition endangered by the notion of an impartial/imperial spectator. Thus I respond to Gibbons's argument that "though fellow-feeling as the language of the heart might appear to be most amenable to ties . . . of family, friends and community . . . self-command and nobility of sentiment . . . may be jeopardized by local and affective ties, by being too attached, as Edmund Burke would have it, to our 'little platoon'" (287). While such a threat to self command might be posed, that affective realm is demanded by the elite Scottish Briton. Equating taste with the language of English aristocrats, particularly its polite use during Queen Anne's reign, Scottish literati, for example, avidly read and discussed the *Tatler* and *Spectator* papers, admiring the plain style deployed in a chummy, "lighter species of essay-writing."[46] In fact, as early as 1712, Edinburgh Easy Club members read aloud the *Spectator*, adopting its principles of sociability and taste. In a 15 August 1712 letter, the secretary wrote to the authors of the *Spectator*, in a tone noticeably reflecting that of the paper itself:

none of an empty, conceited, quarreling temper can have the privilege of being a member, for we allow all the little merry freedoms among ourselves, rallying one another at our meetings without the least appearance of spleen upon account of whatever we discover to be amiss or weak in any circumstance of our conversation which produced rather love than dislike. (McElroy, 35)

The fetishization of polite interaction continued in Scotland long after the vogue of Addison had passed in Britain, largely because of the ongoing need to imitate polite "Englishness."

What is especially interesting about the Scottish situation, then, is the fact that the performed, artificial quality of the "national" language could never be wholly forgotten.[47] Consider Blair's description of the simplicity of plain language, which he contrasts to the rules-based exclusivity of Renaissance public display of command over a complex system of figures. The veneration of plain language, in contrast, was seen to divulge the private man as an equal but distinct subject in the conversations among these gentlemen. Blair contrasts tasteful "modest" language to the pomp of the court:

More studied and artificial manners of writing, however beautiful, have always this disadvantage, that they exhibit an author in form, like a man at court, where the splendour of dress, and the ceremonial of behaviour, conceal those peculiarities which distinguish one man from another. But reading an author of simplicity, is like conversing with a person of distinction at home, and with ease, where we find natural manners, and a marked character. (391)

Simple language mutes the hierarchies of the court, emphasizing instead the increasingly "horizontal" social organization claimed by the ideology of nationalism. On the other hand, plain language, because it is beyond rules, helps "distinguish one man from another" – the public sphere is, after all, constructed of individuals coming together as private subjects. The subject is best known only in the most private of circumstances, but Blair's term "natural manners" hints that even this unveiled "private" subject must be, in actuality, carefully premeditated by the speaker and mediated by a "proper" language which does not come naturally. The most intimate basis of sociability is also the most constructed, the most "horizontal" also the most differentiating. Similarly, just after his discussion of "common sense," Smith suggests a similar notion of the fabrication of self, writing, "For what . . . makes a man agreable [sic] company, is it not, when his sentiments *appear* to be naturally expressed?" (55, italics mine). Similarly, in the "unassuming" language Smith endorses, "the perfection of style consists in express[ing] in the most concise, proper, and precise manner the thought of the author . . . so that all seemed natural and easy" (51). Smith refers to "seeming" naturalness, pointing to the underlying constructedness of this natural and easy language. While the performative and learned quality of speaking and developing an ear for a polite version of one's "native" language is common to all speakers, that condition is dramatically highlighted in the case of these Scots. Scottish students, after all, were the first to learn "natural" English in a lecture hall. As they imagined the improvement of both themselves and the British nation through perfecting their English, these Scots illustrate the ways in which national membership is actually dependent upon manufacturing the linguistic self, not appealing to quasi-instinctive practices and feelings attached to national identity. They exemplify not the self-affirmation but the self-construction demanded by national membership – a constructedness, however, not unique to the Scots.

ANTINOMIES OF CIVILIZATION: ADVANCED AND ORIGINARY LANGUAGES

Their attraction to aesthetic discourse and their imitation (and development) of "beautiful" English stem, in part, from these Lowlanders' position as "peripheral" figures. It is also informed by the uncomfortably close position they hold to their more ruthlessly, and unwillingly, incorporated neighbors to the north, as well as to the presence of Scots peasants and workers stubbornly resistant to full linguistic assimilation.

A comparison of Highlander and Lowlander, particularly in their relationship to the English language, would seem absurd to most successful Lowlanders. Yet – also in the summer of 1761, the summer of Sheridan's celebrated lectures – a letter written by one of the Commissioners of the Annexed Estates (the administrative body supervising the expropriation of Jacobite estates) connects the subduing of the Highlands and the Lowland lectures in rhetoric. The commissioner assures his London correspondent that he is carrying out the king's instructions regarding the running of the estates: "The knowledge of what is acceptable to the King . . . makes us happy and easy in the Execution of our Duty."[48] Just after this, the writer goes on to affirm the success of Blair's course in "Rhetoric and Belles Lettres" in recruiting and educating students into polite English letters, writing that "his lectures meet with great approbation he [sic] has really a great genius in his profession, which I think must in time bring additional numbers of schollars [sic] to the college." Making the connection between Lowland and Highland assimilation – and London's interest in such projects – explicit, the writer also suggests that the Crown Rents, presumably from the annexed estates, could be used to pay a handsome stipend to Blair.

In striving to distinguish themselves from Highlanders, Lowlanders distanced them and their language through the narrative of conjectural history. Within this schema, the polite language of the Lowland elite signaled their society's advanced status in a four-stage chronology of human societal development. Such history is purely speculative, "utilized," as John Christie has put it, "when we are unable to ascertain how men have actually conducted themselves . . . [T]he history it recovers is always of a modernity already prescribed and inscribed within the subject of that historical process."[49] Important for the ways in which it promoted an understanding of culture within the context of a particular society's relations of production and technologies, conjectural history did, nonetheless, propound the position of Lowlanders as further along on the spectrum of a universal history, as evidenced, in part, by their linguistic culture. Elaborating on the recent high water marks of social advances of his society, Blair writes that "language is become a vehicle by which the most delicate and refined emotions of one mind can be transmitted" (vol. I, 98). In this improving age, he believes, a great deal of attention has been paid to "the beauty of language, and the grace and elegance of every kind of writing. The public ear is become refined" (7). Conjectural history establishes a mutually defining distinction between "primitive" and "advanced" languages and, importantly, transfers class and regional distinctions to a temporal schema ranging from "barbaric" to "civilized."

It is, however, precisely this projected primitive society and its "powerful" and "uncultivated" language, be it in the semi-preserved form of a long-lost Gaelic epic or in residual form in quickly vanishing vernaculars of the Scottish "folk," for which Lowlanders become nostalgic as they confront their own doubled position.[50] Too frequently, figures such as Blair and Smith and even Johnson are represented as single-minded proponents of a "polite" English print culture. Such characterizations come at the expense of exploring their ambiguities on this subject, ambiguities arising in part from the complexities of appealing to affective language and of situating language within the frame of a nation that was viewed as at once culturally pure, even exclusive, and at the same time progressive, commercially and imperially expansive. The second half of this chapter explores the ways in which this tension produces apprehensions that the language of refinement was also a hobbled language, its tasteful control diluting its power.[51] It is this vision that makes possible the reclamation of "originary" Gaelic langauges, as I shall examine in this chapter and the next. It also provides the basis for Edinburgh literati's "appreciation" of Robert Burns, which I want to spend a very brief moment pondering.[52]

In many ways, Samuel Johnson's (and Tobias Smollett's after him) authoritative refiguring of class and gender linguistic distinctions as instead cultural, ethnic, and/or national set the stage for the revaluation of "regional" languages, such as Scots or Scots Gaelic. The construction of a standard language produces at the same time, and of necessity, an understanding of what does not qualify as standard. That process of establishing a standard also narrates the basis of exclusion in fairly precise terms – unacceptable words and grammatical forms used by "lower" classes, for instance, are re-narrated as corrupt "particular" practices to a "universal" standand or as "outsider" language to the true "insider" language of the British nation. Such re-narration situates excluded class and regional practices in a relatively similar position in relation to the standard language. We have already seen how Robert Fergusson deployed that region/class conflation to wield a "criminally" particular, materially concrete language and poetics that could militate against class and regional domination at once.[53]

Oddly, it is also this redefinition of what in reality were once dominant languages amongst various classes and in diverse places as "outlaw" that dictated the very terms of their re-absorption. As a standard

English became increasingly recognizable – through the circulation of the best-selling abridged version of Johnson's *Dictionary* and of published lists of "Scotticisms," through wide attendance at popular lectures such as Sheridan's, and through readerships of novels modeling "corrupt" and standard English, such as Smollett's or even Henry Fielding's – the reincorporation of "outsider" languages *as* marginal languages became possible. It is likely on these terms that Scottish "improvers" could comfortably celebrate Burns. Robert Crawford notes, for instance, that Blair's recommendations to Burns as he commenced editing a new edition of his poems "did not involve alteration to the Scots language of the poems. Clearly, for Blair, Burns's position as an outsider licensed his use of the 'dialect'."[54]

It is in his unabashed particularity that Burns could be taken up, especially as a British cultural nationalism predicated on a "culture of diversity" and "contintuity" moved into the ideological foreground. Thus, as more than a few commentators have noted, Burns's use of "unpolished" vernacular Scots languages shores up "the concept of the 'Heaven-taught ploughman'" – connoting, as it does, both the cultural marginalization of embodied labor and the purity and innocence of divinely received (not socially bestowed) knowledge – and "fitted well into . . . the spirit of the age."[55] Burns, authenticated through his use of particular languages whose origins could be traced to local social worlds, becomes, in turn, metonymically representative of a receding authentic Scots culture, with the stress on Scottish national culture, not class, and on a language in need of redemption, no longer potentially dominant. If, as Peter Murphy argues, Burns pulls off "a difficult trick, to be both locally authentic and nationally representative," it is also in those terms alone that the trick could be sanctioned by an Anglo-British readership. Even when we take into account Burns's use of standard English alongside different Scots registers, the very "pluralism" suggested by his linguistic variety seemingly authenticates each "dialect" – or, more accurately, relegates certain languages to "authentic dialect" status. Alternative nation re-scripted as local region, working and peasant class re-classified as marginal – these are the pre-set terms upon which Burns could be incorporated as a "British" poet.[56] It is at the moment that Johnson's displacement of class difference for national difference attains purchase in Edinburgh literati circles that Burns becomes safe for their consumption.

On these specifically regional terms, and with consignment of regional culture to "the past" in the face of a modernizing, cosmopolitan present, Burns's poems received high accolades. In fact, the literati identify his "rustic" verse as possessing qualities "opposite to the sort of composition taught by the teacher of Rhetoric and Belles Lettres."[57] As we shall see below, this characterization of his verse as representative of the vibrancy and power said to be missing from refined English resembles characterizations of the language of remote, originary Highland communites. "A striking example of native genius," Burns, Mackenzie wrote in his review of his *Poems*, reflected "the darkness of distant and remote periods."[58] It has become a commonplace in analyses of the "primitivism" of the mid-eighteenth century to describe the popularity of Burns, or the related nostalgia for a Highland past, as a return to and re-appreciation of suppressed, neglected, and disappearing (or nearly dead) cultures. This commonplace, in turn, informs a reading of Burns as the consummate British poet, negotiating and synthesizing disparate components of a new British nation. Yet I find more convincing recent critical appraisals that have emphasized the inventive quality of Burns's multiple languages, withholding the designation of "native authenticity."[59] Such analyses confirm my own sense of the force of Burns's poems as deriving from both a powerful poetic agency and a refraction of intra-national linguistic contest and struggle. Although, as some have pointed out, Burns does vacillate in his characterization of poverty and peasant life – is it a virtuous domain, all the more cozy for its lack of excess riches, or is it a scourge? – he often refuses to articulate marginalization with national status. It is difficult, for instance, to read "To a Louse" or "Epistle to Davie, a Brother Poet" as Scots nationalist in tenor, emphasizing as they do class divisions; the speaker of the latter poem admits, as he views his social "betters", to "hanker, and canker,/ To see their cursed pride."[60] It is his emphasis on these divisions which hollows out the idea of an authentic, singular Scots national character and provides the dynamism and energy of Burns's poetry. Edinburgh literati misrecognize this energy as a function of the poetry's local origins and "pastness," and a similar recognition, I shall argue, informs their nostalgia for ancient Gaelic languages.

Thus it is an ancient, endangered Scots national character that provides the backdrop for the literati's angst over the weakened status of their own polite language and culture. Blair writes that "to be beautified ... is in truth [to be] weakened" (vol. I, 68) and that the prolixity of our language 'enfeebles' it ... our style is less compact; our conceptions being spread out among more words, and split, as it were, into more parts, make a fainter expression when we utter them" (173–4). Smith derides "the prolixness, constraint, and monotony of modern languages" (Bryce, 226). Like Chesterfield before him, Smith genders polite linguistic production, noting, "It is commonly said, also, that in France and England the conversation of the ladies is the best standard of language, as there is a certain delicacy and agreeableness in their behaviour and address" (2).[61] The idea of a female authority in language usage, however, does not sit well with these gentlemen, and G. J. Barker-Benfield describes one articulation of that danger:

> David Fordyce, another fellow of Smith's in the Edinburgh elite, advocated the softening of male ferocity into a new male ideal in which 'gentleman,' 'man of worth,' and Christian 'all melt insensibly and sweetly into one another.' Marking out the same, refined, gender gauge, however, he said, 'I do not mean that the mind I speak of will become feminine.' The qualification recorded a risk. (*Culture*, 140)

The longing for a past "masculine" language reflects that discomfort; the martial communities of which "masculine" language was a product counter the "effeminacy" of polite contemporary homosocial groupings. Originary language was a sublime language of presence, one which foregrounded the body without, at the same time, circumscribing it, a language far from the learned language of the lecture hall.

"We must have recourse to the deserts and the wilds; we must go back to the age of hunters and of shepherds" (vol. II, 314), Blair writes, "to explore" that "first language." In originary language, as these descriptions go, word maps world, but not because it has been artificially made to do so, as is the case with "advanced" language, but because a sign shares the same temporality as an event, capturing the event's all-at-onceness. Speakers of originary language do not need to break one event into divided parts and draw them out in a linear syntactical structure to represent it.[62] For Blair, "Words, as we now employ them ... may be considered ... as arbitrary, or instituted, not natural signs of ideas. But there can be no doubt ... that language, the nearer we remount to its rise among men, will be found to partake more of a natural expression ... in its primitive state, be more picturesque ... more expressive by sound of the thing signified" (vol. I, 106). He reiterates, "Our conceptions being spread out among more words, and split, as it were, into more parts, make a fainter expression when we utter them" (vol. I, 175) and "that luggage of particles ... which we are obliged always to carry along with us, both clogs style and enfeebles sentiment" (vol. I, 154). Smith too distinguishes the prolix language of the day from the speculative "first formations" of languages, as he calls it. He states, "Impersonal verbs, which express in one word a complete event, which preserve in the expression that perfect simplicity and unity which there always is in the object and in the idea, and which suppose no . . . metaphysical division of the event into its several constituent members . . . would, in all probability, be the species of verb first invented" (Bryce, 216). Smith's originary language, then, is pre-metaphysical, close to nature or paralleling nature in its expression of events.

Many have accounted for these appeals to (and the appeal of) an originary language as a dialectical response to the standardization of language or the inscription of the oral into the rules and categories of writing, and it is certainly true that these writers held that logocentric vision of a fundamental rift between orality and literacy.[63] My point is to calibrate this movement in terms of the historical linguistic formations of British empire and nation. Both the operation of imperial grammar and the less repressive but still normative discourse of polite (national) taste are in large part responsible for this nostalgic construction, in that they both function to eliminate the sense of contestation and antagonistic difference from language, which, in turn, removes its sense of immediacy. These writers construct and then confront a set of restrictive rules which seem to render their own language dry and prolix, or beautiful and, consequently, in their minds, effeminate and servile. Alternatively, communication within "originary" communities is believed to be non-sequential and directly connected to the event it communicates, forming a powerful, direct address impossible to a decorous social world and its recoil at enthusiastic, spontaneous, and overtly political language.

These writers associate an originary language with an oral society closer to what they see as a virtuous national community than the polite society in which they live. Smith reconstructs the scene of the first formation of languages: "the first savage inventors of language, we shall suppose, when they observed the approach of this terrible animal [a lion], were accustomed to cry out to one another, *venit*, that is, the lion comes . . . this word thus expressed a complete event, without the assistance of any other" (Bryce, 216). His construction assumes a language community small enough to be present in the same place, at the same time, to apprehend and communicate the approach of a lion. Even Johnson, in his *Journey to the Western Islands of Scotland*, repeatedly engages such fictive constructions. He continually teases his Scottish traveling companion, Boswell, about the uncivilized character of Scotland. And yet he speculates, on looking at a Highland landscape, that "it affords a generous and manly pleasure to conceive a little nation . . . where, in contempt of walls and trenches, every man sleeps securely with his sword beside him; where all, on the first approach of hostility, come together at the call to battle, as at a summons to a festal show."[64] Here is a national community so natural that it does not even need to be marked by walls or trenches. All members of the language community are present, and one call hails the nation spontaneously and heroically.[65] Although "in nations, where there is hardly the use of letters, what is once out of sight is lost for ever. Their only registers are . . . practical representations," this oral and visual language is more immediate and compelling in its signification.

These myths of origins provide a story designed to validate the present by locating in the past the qualities the contemporary nation claimed but could not in fact possess. Its members within earshot of each other, these originary communities are close enough to share the same visual field, and, importantly, the same interest as a community, all oriented toward its defense. The raising of the sword, the anxious cry – we can imagine flailing arms and an alarmed facial expression from the shouter of "venit" – invoke a language community present and attentive, linked in a moment of urgent communication. Derrida demonstrates how Rousseau believed that "only an innocent community, and a community of reduced dimensions . . . only a microcosm of . . . freedom, all the members of which can . . . remain within range of an immediate and transparent, a 'crystalline' address, fully self-present in its living speech can suffer . . . the insinuation of writing."[66] Societies predicated on this "proximity in the face-to-face of countenances and the immediate range of the voice" are more "socially authentic."

This concept of an oral and gestural language predicated on physical presence of members of a community stands in direct contrast to "imperial grammar" with its requisite "disembodiment" of language, an abstraction from differentiating particulars. Yet if these visions provide a fleeting model of the tribal origins of the nation, a Utopia where the corruptions of commerce and foreigners could no longer pose a threat, they can in no way serve as a strategy for stabilizing the modern imperial nation, where, as Burke had put it, there was a huge gap between an "order" and its "execution." At the very basis of the modern nation's ability to invent itself are the claims to stretch over time and space – modern nations are by definition larger than the size of a community where members all know each other. As well, the context of empire cannot be far from Blair's assertion, inasmuch as he foregrounds written language's ability to roam through space when he describes how writing allows the writer to speak to these distant regions, but not to be spoken back to. For him writing is "an improvement" over speech (vol. I, 125), by which we can "send our thoughts abroad and propagate them through the world. We can lift our voice . . . to speak to the most distant regions of the earth" (vol. I, 135). Such "extension," however, was also viewed as inevitably corrupting; as Derrida notes in Rousseau's writing, "Social distance, the dispersion of the neighborhood, is the condition of oppression, arbitrariness, and vice." The written language – needed for communicating over distance and between nations – not only falls short of participating in and perfectly mimicking actual experience, but also begins the corrupting spiral of language into increasing metaphysics and distance from nature. This might account for many eighteenth-century writers' odd characterizations of writing as dead and powerless, especially when this was an age marked by journalistic interventions in hotly contested political dramas. These writers thus partake in a "metaphysics of presence," which Derrida critiques in Rousseau, who mistakenly "opposes speech to writing as presence to absence and liberty to servitude" (168). In this "classical ideology" Derrida observes, "writing takes the status of a tragic fatality come to prey upon natural innocence, interrupting the golden age of the present and full speech" (168), interrupting "self-presence" with an "'exterior,' 'sensible,' 'spatial' signifier" (98). For Derrida, "self-presence" – the self-presence, say, of Smith's originary impersonal verb, "venit" – "has never been given but only dreamed of and always already split" (112).

In his deconstruction of the opposition between speech and writing Derrida maintains that "all societies capable of producing, that is to say of obliterating, their proper names, and of bringing classificatory difference into play, practice writing in general. No reality or concept would therefore correspond to the expression, 'society without writing'" (98). Derrida views the desire for the "self-presence" attributed to "oral" language as a desire to suppress the otherness that differentiates one signifier from another. This formulation is especially useful in the specific context of eighteenth-century Britain. The desire for immediacy or "self-presence" in language is also a desire to suppress the contested, multivalent character of language, shutting out the possibility of multiple, disputed meanings, an important goal for a national language, especially in the context of empire. Expansion and its threat of disruption, as well as the internal divisions within Britain itself, produced this desire for a unitary, uncontested language at the same time that it produced a desire for a compound language capable of capturing heterogeneity. The concept of an originary "self-presence" would be all the more urgent for Scots. Their polite language doubled, undeniably "fabricated," these Scots posit an alternative, originary language and link it to political agency. Indebted to writings of the ancients on the subject, Blair cites Longinus when confidently asserting, "High, manly, and forcible Eloquence is, indeed, to be looked for only, or chiefly, in the regions of freedom" (vol. II, 9). In his own age's "metaphysical refinement," Blair writes, "oratory degenerates from a masculine strain to a trifling and sophistical art" (vol. II, 16). Spoken language is

superior in point of energy and force . . . [T]he voice of the living speaker makes an impression on the mind, much stronger than can be made by the perusal of any writing. The tones of voice, the looks, the gesture . . . render discourse . . . infinitely more clear, and more expressive than the most accurate writing [and] remove ambiguities. (vol. I, 136)

Such moving interaction is also the ideal condition, we might recall, of the polite societies and clubs so popular in eighteenth-century Edinburgh. Yet polite verbal exchange is not hyperbolic oratory, and the period's discounting of the latter produces an ambivalence. Blair accuses Cicero of "too visible a parade of eloquence" and notes that his contemporaries reproached him as "swelling." The devaluation of writing does not necessarily propel "nonalphabetic signs" into a superior position. As Derrida argues, "By one and the same gesture, (alphabetic) writing, servile instrument of a speech dreaming of its plenitude and its self-presence, is scorned and the dignity of writing is refused to nonalphabetic signs" (110). So although civilized societies characterize their written language as weak, they still refuse "dignity" and sophistication to the "nonalphabetic signs" of so-called uncivilized societies. The resulting ambivalence works in two ways. First a continuing hankering for moving oratory is simply displaced to a nostalgia for a no longer available classical eloquence or originary language. Second, the appropriate space for affecting speech was no longer the public forum but the small circle of private acquaintance. Blair himself was a preacher, but this was not public, directly linked to the course of government, in the same way that Demosthenes's "pulpit" had been. Closer to this new private world of orality are the clubs in which Smith and Blair debated regularly. Their lectures, which devoted some space to emotive oratory, were also oral performances, but the lectures were initially held at private sites, only later to be officially institutionalized in the universities. Even the recordings of Johnson's witty rejoinders in the polite world of London coffee-houses might be linked to this turn to a privatized oral space. This is especially true considering the characterizations of his verbal repartee as more forceful than his own writing. In the small private domains that now functioned as stand-ins for a once publicly-executed democracy, swelling oratory would prove unnecessary and overpowering.

The notion of an originary, martial community and its sublime language, however, continued to exert a pull on these writers. While the supplementary character of this retrojection is clearly at work, it elucidates the immense and unanswerable contradictions of that notion of "aesthetic" national language to which it acts as a supplement. Consequently, not only the division between speech and writing but also between the figurative and the literal and between the beautiful and the sublime that these writers seek to establish all undo themselves in the course of their writing. Thus, Blair argues that first languages were highly figurative, and necessarily so because of both the barrenness of those languages and the sense of awe and wonder caused by the lack of experience and knowledge in early "savage" states. Blair claims, "Let nature and passion always speak their own language, and they will suggest figures in abundance" (vol. I, 360). Yet Blair sees "figures in abundance" as also a source of linguistic power. His relationship to figures is, thus, more complicated than is suggested by Potkay's assertion that "Enlightenment intellectuals regretted that the primitive [including their 'bold figuration'] was still with them; they were determined, however, to exclude its influence from mature, rational discourse" (*Eloquence*, 43).[67] According to Blair, figurative language both "gives pleasure" and "makes us advance in knowledge" (vol. I, 343) – attributes associated with the polite "native" language Smith and Blair were hoping to cultivate. Metaphors would also be especially important to a polite national language because they are often culturally specific, drawing from the everyday, from local landscape and geography and from regional customs and habits. Usually particular to a specific vernacular, metaphor assembles a community whose members share time and space coordinates necessary to comprehend its reference points. Aiming for a compromise style, Blair recommends a mixture of figurative and plain language, for "it is the union of these two kinds of composition, of the French earnestness and warmth, with the English accuracy and reason, that would form, according to my idea, the model of a perfect Sermon" (vol. II, 119).

The figural/literal division takes a more complex form with Smith. Although he warns against "allegorical, metaphorical, and such-like expressions . . . apt to make one's style dark and perplexed" and the "dungeon of metaphorical obscurity" (5), a strict duality between grammar and figure does not exist in Smith's model of language development, because, as Christie points out, "the generative act of grammar is openly characterized as figural" ("Adam Smith's," 226). That is to say that Smith sees the first words as having no generalization or abstraction – a speaker refers, for instance, not to *a* lion but *the* lion. The naming of qualities in abstraction after that first moment – the name for a specific lion becomes the name for all lions – is akin to metaphor in that a transfer takes place from particular to general via resemblance.

Then too, the conventional gendered associations of sublime and beautiful language begin to unhinge when Blair, after Burke, characterizes sublime language, in opposition to beautiful, as more forceful.[68] It inspires "terror" (vol. I, 55) and "raises the mind much above its ordinary state; and fills it with a degree of wonder and astonishment, which it cannot well express" (vol. I, 46). While the speaker or writer of sublime expression is in an empowered, masculine position, the listener or reader experiencing terror and astonishment is no longer in the masculine position of control. Sublime language might be the label for the excess of feeling that the appeal to the body always threatens. Alternatively, and paradoxically, in valuing a plain and clear style over which the reader, writer, or listener maintains control, Smith and Blair fear relinquishing those qualities capable of producing moving language.

Like the positions constituted by sublime language, characterizations of beautiful language also fluctuate. Sheridan envisions not "refined" language but "natural" language as beautiful, writing of "language which requires neither study, art, nor imitation; which spontaneously breaks out in the exactest expressions, nicely proportioned to the degrees of his inward emotions" (*Lectures*, 105). If contemporary English no longer possesses the forcefulness of an ancient eloquence, nor bespeaks manly democracy, it also lacks the truly beautiful elements – melody, softness – able to elicit refined aesthetic effects.[69] Smith believes that the terminations first created in the originary language were produced from "that love of similarity of sound" (Bryce, 208) no longer catered to in contemporary language. Smith looks to the inflected language of the ancient Greeks and Romans for such mellifluence.

As many have noted, Blair departs from Smith, deploying terms from the aesthetic of the beautiful to talk not exclusively about the language of

Greek and Roman antiquity but about a past Gaelic language which combined noble barbarity and its "strong and vivid" figures (vol. I, 273) with civilized manners and tender sentiments.[70] It is no accident that the convergence of events of 1761 includes the publication of James Macpherson's *Poems of Ossian*, poems Blair describes as conveying a "delicacy of sentiment" (96) and "wrought . . . with the most exquisite sensibility and delicacy" (107). (And in this year Macpherson took up residence in a building in which Blair himself lived.) Blair prizes a (seemingly) unartificial Gaelic language, for it conveys meaning through sympathy. In "A Critical Dissertation," he admits it is surprising to identify these elements in the language of a "rude age," but he argues that in those barbaric societies men "display themselves to one another without disguise," (89) a description strangely reminiscent of the "author of simplicity" he praised in the passage cited above. Blair's assessment of the poems of Ossian is informed by a specifically Scottish agenda, and the divergence between his analysis of the Highland culture and Johnson's is registered in Johnson's polemical refusal to acknowledge the least legitimacy of the poems of Ossian. And yet we find a surprising affinity between the two thinkers. Blair projects a martial community, ringing with immediacy, not unlike Johnson's vision.[71] He writes of the ancient Highlanders, "They had no expedient for giving the military alarms but striking a shield" ("Critical Dissertation," 104), resembling Johnson's image of an immediate, non-arbitrary language.[72]

His ambivalent Scottish affinities led Blair to claim that Gaelic was the original language of Britain, for contemporary English, with its "deficiency in harmony of sound" (vol. I, 176), has no relation to the originary language of England. Instead, he writes, "The language which is, at present, spoken throughout Great Britain, is neither the antient [sic] primitive Speech of the island, nor derived from it; but is altogether of foreign origin. The language of the first inhabitants of our island, beyond doubt, was the Celtic/Gaelic." This "Celtic" was "very expressive and copious, and one of the most ancient in the world," a notion to which we shall turn in the final chapter (vol. I, 169). Efforts to claim an originary language were not unique to Scottish intellectuals. John Horne Tooke, in *Diversions of Purley* (London, 1798), with its speculative etymologies, tries to demonstrate how English is an offshoot of a universal, iconic language. Thomas Astle, who analyzed the alphabet in *The Origin and Progress of Writing* (London, 1784), and L. D. Nelme, in *An Essay Towards the Investigation of the Origin and Elements of Language and Letters* (London, 1772), both argued that the Anglo-Saxon tongue was the closest to the first language. Precisely because it had been characterized as barbaric, and therefore linked to that originary stage, however, Gaelic was newly valorized as the originary language. A new generation of scholars believed that Gaelic, unlike English, had withstood Roman conquest and therefore maintained those sublime, barbaric, masculine qualities long defunct in English. John Grant writes, "Every one acquainted with it (the Celtic) and enticed with a taste to relish its beauties, must acknowledge its energy and descriptive powers."[73] Legion are the critics who followed in Blair's wake, praising the immediacy and physical power of oral Gaelic. John Pinkerton writes that the ancient bards affected "the passions and the ear. Their mode of expression was simple and genuine. They of consequence touched the passions truly and effectively," and asks, "Is not the war-music of the rudest inhabitants of the wilds of America or Scotland more terrible to the ear than that of the best band in the British army?"[74] The strength and simplicity at which refiners of English aimed are naturally available to the Scottish; their ballads, Pinkerton writes, have "a great advantage in point of touching the passions. Their language is rough and unpolished, and seems to flow immediately from the heart . . . They possess the pathetic power in the highest degree, because they do not affect it" (xxxv). Gaelic, these writers assert, pre-existed the troubling, corrupt gap between word and thing, and nature and artifice. As such, it has something to teach users of English.

COMMERCE AND CORRUPTION: LANGUAGE, EMPIRE, TRANSLATION

These characterizations of Gaelic reflect the particular pressures on Scots as they theorized the relationship between language, culture, and history. Robert Crawford and Penny Fielding have deftly argued that nostalgic histories of an oral Gaelic past represent "a skilled effort at cultural translation, turning Scottish matter of an unacceptable kind into a form acceptable" (Crawford, *Devolving*, 36). My aim in this final section is to explore eighteenth-century British perceptions of "international" commingling as corrupting discrete "national" languages, for this belief puts in place a nationalist rhetoric now so common as to be transparent: namely that there were social bodies akin to nations before there were imperial ventures. Thus, for Smith, Blair, Sheridan, and even Johnson, there was once a pristine, originary language understood by a single linguistic community, and it is not sheer time, the movement through developmental stages, which erodes that ideal originary language. Specifically, commerce – the production of goods for exchange and, at an advanced stage, global search for raw goods and markets – is the source of languages' corruption.[75]

Tastemakers of English, Smith, Blair, Sheridan, and Johnson record reservations about their project, viewing their society's "commercial language" – an inevitable product of the global exchange of goods increasing throughout this period – as capable of "confounding" meaning.[76] Commerce also betokens a particular stage of society, characterized in part by leisure and an attendant curiosity. This curiosity also "necessarily produce[s] . . . contempt of our native literature."[77] In addition, the leisure of commerce contributes to the use of metaphors and figures, potentially dangerous to stable language. Johnson writes, "Figures, criticisms, and refinements are the work of those whom idleness makes weary of themselves."[78] Further, because England has reached the commercial stage, "the knowledge of the common people of England is greater than that of any other vulgar" and yet this has the undesirable effect of "enabl[ing] those to talk who were born to work."[79] Johnson describes both women and "common people" seized by the "rage of writing." He writes, "The cook warbles her lyrics in the kitchen, the thrasher vociferates his heroics in the barn . . . our girls forsake their samplers to teach kingdoms wisdom."[80] Finally, increased commercialization also leads inevitably to the traffic in language itself. As language becomes a commodity through print, it is especially subject to the corrupting forces of subdivision and alienation. Johnson also argues that his ideal, a language "without alteration," is "without books, or . . . with very few" (*Journey*, 25).[81] Cynical after his Grub Street experiences, he complains that too many books printed in a language "enervate" the language, tending towards "refinement, fashion, trend, style, and corruption." Print, and the increased production of ideas and words that come with it, undermines the constancy of a language.

What seems especially dangerous about print for Johnson is its ability to circulate at distances far from its initial context, the antithesis of those mythic originary linguistic communities. Most dangerous of all is the fact that commercial activity entails the exchange of language between nations, an exchange facilitated by a "distancing" linguistic abstraction. Thus, despite his protracted advocacy of free trade in *The Wealth of Nations* (1776), Smith too betrays a fear of the impact of such commercial movement on national languages. He regards the intermingling of nations as responsible for the fall of language from an inflected, melodious condition to "prolix, constrained and monotonous" one, yet such "mingling" is exactly what takes place in international commerce. Smith argues that isolated originary language would have continued becoming increasingly perfect and inflected "had it not become more complex in its composition, in consequence of the mixture of several languages with one another, occasioned by the mixture of different nations" (Bryce, 220). He describes how native speakers of an originary language "had acquired it at so very early a period of their lives, so insensibly, and by such slow degrees, that they were scarce ever sensible of the difficulty." However,

when two nations came to be mixed with one another, either by conquest or migration, the case would be very different. Each nation, in order to make itself intelligible to those with whom it was under the necessity of conversing, would be obliged to learn the language of the other. The greater part of individuals too, learning the new language, not by art, or by remounting to its rudiments and first principles, but by rote, and by what they commonly heard in conversation, would be extremely perplexed by the intricacy of its declensions and conjugation. They would endeavour, therefore, to supply their ignorance of these, by whatever shift language could afford them. (Bryce, 220)

Like Johnson but in contrast to the imperial grammarians, Smith is suspicious of translation. Necessitated by "conquest and migration," it changes language, adding loan words and forcing a dependence on the more prolix and adulterating metaphysical adjective, which, along with the auxiliary verb, was easier to remember than complicated conjugations and declensions. The translation and "rote" learning – a phrase reminiscent of the SSPCK's instruction – signals not linguistic power but weakness. Foreign invaders, merchants, and colonial subjects need to learn the language not "by art or remounting to its rudiments and first principles but by rote." This description suggests that transparent exchange between languages cannot take place – that each language has its own distinctive "first principles," a belief which diverges from the basic tenets of imperial grammar.[82] Like Smith, Johnson sees detrimental linguistic consequences, for commerce, "however necessary . . . as it depraves the manners, corrupts the language; they that have frequent intercourse with strangers . . . must in time learn a mingled dialect" (*Journey*, 25). Moreover, the process by which foreigners – both those "temporally" foreign, i.e. belonging to different "stages," and those "spatially" foreign – learn is inauthentic. A non-native will never have the same relationship to the language as a native, and in attempting to imitate it they will corrupt it.

Given Smith's evaluation of the source of the wealth of nations – unregulated international exchange – his analysis of its linguistic repercussions is surely troubling to his narrative. What is especially unusual about his argument is that while he identifies a tendency toward commerce as endemic to human nature, writing of the human "propensity to truck, barter, and exchange" he poses this tendency as destructive of the first principles of distinct, originary languages.[83] Most important, this view naturalizes the social form of the nation – intranational exchange, of both things and words, can take place as long as it is restricted to those within the "nation's" linguistic boundaries. This retrojection of a pre-commercial community with a natural, original language, which was at the same time a stable national language, is, however, an allegory for the goals of the present. The desire for a pre-exchange Utopia and an equally Utopian language, which reflects and produces that community, inheres in the anxiety produced by the related but competing ideological demands of imperialism and nationalism. Once, such a narrative goes, uncorrupted communication was possible in an originary community that pre-existed exchange. This exchange, the basis of an originary national linguistic community, stands in contrast to a commercial inter-linguistic exchange responsible for corrupting those first languages. Consider for example, Burke's remark on the distance between the North American colonies and England, "Seas roll and months pass between the order and the execution."[84] In contrast to originary language communities, Burke describes this imperial realm as having a weak, disempowered mode of communication. Further, we might ask, what is the status of the nation when commercial empires operate under a free trade principle which purports to recognize no borders in trade or production? The border between Scotland and England is just such a fraught instantiation of this problem. While Smith calls for the lifting of trade restrictions between nations, he does not make an equivalent case for "free trade" between national languages, such as Scots and English.

Smith's distinction between healthy international commerce and its attendant unhealthy translation is not the only way of understanding this relationship. V. J. Peyton sees it quite differently, arguing that "English is superior because it is easy to learn," and that its "copiousness," from the many foreign words that have become a part of it, "makes the stock rich."[85] Linking word exchange between languages to profit, Peyton writes, "We raise a profit of new words from the same stock, which yet in their own country are not merchantable." If Peyton sees an analogy between international exchange of words and things, where international exchange of words adds to their value, just as exchange of things across space seemingly adds to theirs, Smith insists on a total detachment, an inverse relationship, between these two phenomena. This detachment has two important consequences. First, it separates linguistic/cultural value from monetary value, locating them decisively in two distinct realms. Second, the linguistic/cultural value achieved through intranational exchange – and not international linguistic exchange or imperial commerce – becomes available as the core basis of the nation. This understanding of the origin of the nation as divorced from the economic makes possible the notion of a cultural nationalism distinct from a nation-state *per se*, a possibility which, as Tom Nairn has shown, was key for eighteenth- and nineteenth-century Scots, offering a non-threatening site of national identity.[86]

In positing a cultural basis of the nation preceding an economic one, Smith inaugurates an understanding of the nation which could be applied not simply to the Scottish nation, but to all nations, including Britain itself. The modern nation, however, is not predicated on a body of individuals, sharing a national culture, who then seek a state formation. Instead, the nation-state as we know it, and as Smith knew it, appears in response to transglobal commerce and answers the need for a home base bureaucracy to protect and administer that commerce.[87] It is, then, only at the "commercial stage," which Smith and others saw as anathema to pure "national" languages, that the actual idea of a standard national language begins to emerge at all. These standard languages help facilitate the management of a home market that has arisen in the context of global trade. Thus, what Smith perceives as leading to the national language's destruction is, rather, responsible for its creation. While arguing against this seemingly unassailable link between isolation and linguistic purity might seem counterintuitive, Nancy Dorian provides extensive evidence demonstrating that it is not the isolation or smallness of a geographic region that makes for a homogeneous language. She writes, "Discernible differentiation is evident within amazingly small areas: The village of Leurbost, in Lewis . . . is about two miles long, which is apparently enough for minor dialectal differences to manifest themselves from one end to the other."[88] Whence, then, comes the now unquestioned assumption that commercial expansion weakens once pure, homogeneous languages? For Smith, the pressures of translation and interlinguistic intermingling split linguistic expression, drawing it out in time in a syntax composed of increasingly metaphysical terms. Christie suggestively sees this as a sort of "division of referential labor" developing within language signification, as expression is broken down into repeatable syntactical fragments necessary for exchange purposes ("Adam Smith's," 221). The analogy of relations of production to relations of signification is helpful in understanding how these writers came to site an "originary" language in the Highlands. In *Wealth of Nations* Smith argues that the division of labor "must always be limited by the extent of that power [of exchanging], or, in other words, by the extent of the market" (31). He (mistakenly) observes that in the Highlands of Scotland, there is minimal market activity and, consequently, very little division of labor. Similarly, isolated as he believed them to be, their linguistic exchange small, the Highlands suffered a minimal division in linguistic labor too.

Many, including Johnson, shared this assessment of the Highlands as a pre-exchange world. He "observes" that people make clothes and grow food only for their own use and do not fatten their cows for the market. Of course, by the time Johnson reached the Highlands (1775), they had been effectively colonized: the Disarming Act of 1746 had made illegal both the carrying of weapons and the wearing of plaids, and the "improvement" of the Highlands – their integration into the exchange economy of capital – was well under way.[89] Yet Johnson attempts to maintain the fiction of an isolated community untouched by the logic of exchange value, even when he is confronted with the most exaggerated evidence to the contrary. For instance, he gives a coin to a woman for milk and assumes that she is unfamiliar with this act of exchange, later learning that the woman has twelve milk cows and sells a great deal of milk. On another occasion, he wonders at the fact that Highlanders "were afforded so much luxury" (such as jams) that were not indigenous to that part of the world, and this observation begs the question of exchange in the Highlands. Nonetheless, Johnson (and Smith and Blair) continues to maintain that Highlanders' geographically imposed isolation from the outside world, including that world's commerce, is responsible for the purity of their language, writing that in the Highlands, "words could continue to express the same notions by the same sign."

These lingering conceptions of the Highlands as pre-commercial and consequently linguistically pure have long led scholars down a cul-de-sac as they have attempted to understand the Highlands in relation to the construction of British cultural identity in the eighteenth century. In his thorough-going attack of such notions of the Highlands as precommercial, Ian Carter writes, "A cultural preference in the Lowlands, for wages in kind rather than money, produced a paradoxical situation in the early stages of agricultural improvement, when rents were paid in money more frequently in the 'archaic' Highlands than the 'modern' Lowlands."[90] Just as the Highlands were being integrated within a globalizing monetary economy, narratives arose regarding the Highlands' noncommercial status, their "isolation," and their cultural and linguistic purity. If the narratives did not produce the modernization, we must at least grapple with their contemporaneous relationship.

The radical shifts that took place throughout the eighteenth century which metamorphosed a once-criminal language into an originary, powerful language will be the subject of the next chapter, but what I want to highlight in this chapter, in conclusion, is the way in which Highland communities come to represent a site of shared language capable of eliciting the aesthetic effects of immediacy and sense-based communal affiliation in ways in which the English Lowland Scots, refined to the same purpose, could not. We seem to have arrived far afield from our starting point, the polite milieu of Edinburgh. On the one hand, we have. The distance between an interest in taste and its refined language in the mid-eighteenth century and national philologies and their privileging of, or at least interest in, "rude" language is real. And yet, on the other hand, what we have been trying to trace are the connections between these discourses, the spaces opened up by the writings of Smith, Blair, Sheridan, and even Johnson that enabled this shift.[91] The world of polite letters, so central to an emerging aesthetic naturalization of a proper national "tongue," was not simply for Smith and Blair, but also for Johnson, a fraught world, producing its own disabling limits. If, as English is standardized, its restricted users begin to view it as empty of the direct forcefulness appropriate to the national community, a linguistic aesthetic develops, in part, to fill that gap, with its emphasis on quasi-somatic responses to the physical world – in particular, the space and language of the nation. The immediacy of contested language, seen in imperial grammar and polite discourse as an excessive quality of language, gets displaced to the past, to the distant, to the colonized, to the barbaric, which are then deemed natural, masculine, and sublime – redolent of the originating moment of the nation. It remained, however, for that excess to be recognized as a part of the everyday language of the embattled linguistic community inhabited by these writers, the self-dividing struggle at the heart of the nation.

CHAPTER 5

"A translator without originals": William Shaw's Scots Gaelic and the dialectic of (linguistic) empire

In 1778, at the behest of Samuel Johnson, university-educated Highlander William Shaw published the first Scots Gaelic grammar in English, *An Analysis of the Galic* [sic] *Language*, and in 1780 published the second Scots Gaelic/English vocabulary after MacDonald's, *A Galic* [sic] *and English Dictionary*. Shaw owns that "to the advice and encouragement of Dr. Johnson, the friend of letters and humanity, the public is indebted for these sheets."[1] If Johnson's encouragement is surprising given his notorious belittlement of the Highlanders' language, so too is the support of the illustrious list of English, Lowlander, and British-allied Highlander subscribers. The SSPCK ordered twenty copies, and several Writers to the Signet in Edinburgh, James Boswell, Adam Smith, James Macpherson, Hanover-supporting Campbells, English and Lowland dukes and earls, and Mr. Cumming "Watchmaker to his Majesty," all subscribed too. Overall, the subscription list reads like a virtual "who's who" of Scottish and English "improvers," and despite occasional references to his "Galic readers," Shaw's grammar is not written primarily for Gaelic speakers but for that educated class of British readers.[2] If to the "colonial" administrators moving through the space of the Highlands in the early eighteenth century Gaelic posed a problem whose solution was its eradication, its status in the later eighteenth century was very different. Consider the patronage of the Duke of Argyle, also on the subscribers' list. His family had played a key role in consolidating British rule in Scotland, cozying up to the English rulers early on and winning the enormous spoils of such an allegiance. The Duke himself was "deeply involved in schemes for civilizing the Highlands," and his support of Shaw's celebration of Gaelic is somewhat difficult to square with the fact that he "thought a resemblance or identity of language of such real national importance, that he is said to have furnished Mr. Hume with the materials of his printed collection [of Scotticisms]."[3] Yet in a post-Culloden revised symbolic economy,

Gaelic figures as a linguistic relic – the spoils or lucre of English military conquest that could now be claimed as a "national treasure" of Great Britain. In the sea change in attitudes towards a once-menacing Gaelic, the reduced threat of the distant Highlands, as opposed to the perilous proximity of Lowlanders to and in England, had made the waters of Gaelic safe for the likes of even the most Anglicized of patrons.

The revaluation of Gaelic was made possible, even necessary, by the pressures of an imperial grammar which associated Gaelic with a particular, national linguistic character while ascribing, and in some senses disabling, a universal, ahistorical character to English. To be more specific, if Argyle's patronage suggests the tension between a new interest in historical linguistic difference and the demand for a national "identity of language," Shaw resolves this tension by straddling two distinct understandings of language, one of fairly recent invention: privileging the relations between language and culture, but severing Gaelic from social history to make it a metonym of a once-grand society; one of older vintage: the belief in universal grammatical structures that could transcend time and space.[4] While subjecting Scots Gaelic to rigorous grammar tables foreign to its very structure, Shaw also praises Gaelic as "one of the greatest living monuments of antiquity" (*Analysis*, x), evocative of a "pleasing melancholy" as it calls up "thoughts on the instability of the highest temporal grandeur" (x).[5] The emphasis on Gaelic particularity and ancientness cannot be said to mark a clear departure from approaches to Gaelic that sought to translate it into a universal key. Rather, it is precisely that universalizing linguistic frame which simultaneously produces an understanding of English as universal, abstract, and trans-historical and Gaelic as particular, embodied, "historied," and feminized.[6] Crucially, Shaw's descriptions of an inherently "local" Gaelic and its relationship to "global" linguistic structures are more accurately understood as *constituting* those linguistic categories. In focusing not on imperial or national linguistic categories *per se*, but instead on the process by which one can be said to produce the other and vice versa, I invite a wider application of Lawrence Grossberg's argument that we see "context not as place, but as the becoming of place and space."[7]

Shaw's linguistic work was part of a groundswell in interest around things "Celtic" starting in the 1760s. This Celtomania was marked by the eager reception of publications praising the ancientness and sublimity of the Highlands, a phenomenon we have already begun to think about in Blair's writings. William Gilpin's *Observations, Relative Chiefly to*

Picturesque Beauty, Made in the Year 1776 on Several Parts of Great Britain, Particularly the Highlands and Thomas Pennant's *A Tour in Scotland MDCCLXIX* reflect the incorporation of the Highlands into fashionable circuits of tourism, and engravings of Highland scenes commemorate this new appreciation of those landscapes.[8] As one skeptical commentator complained in 1787, "This may be called the Celtic Century, for all Europe has been inundated with nonsense about the Celts."[9] Although interest in Gaelic languages was not entirely new – Welsh antiquarian Edward Lhuyd's *Archaeologia Britannica, Giving Some Account of the Languages, Histories and Customs of the Original Inhabitants of Great Britain* was published in 1707, for instance – these earlier texts are not as dramatically oriented to issues of Gaelic and British cultural identity.[10] By the mid-eighteenth century, however, the problem arose of negotiating the relationship between the British nation and the "Celts" – a name applied to but not adopted by Highlanders, and originally meaning "other."[11]

While some have argued that this "Celtomania" marked a shift to a "multicultural" model of the British nation, I read Shaw's linguistic work to interrogate conventional models of multiculturalism which begin with the assumption of discrete local cultures whose distinction is marked by equally discrete local languages. Howard Weinbrot, while acknowledging the compromised character of the Celtic culture ensconced in the "multicultural" society that arose in eighteenth-century England, nonetheless argues that "each [Hebrew and Celtic strains] contributes to the English assumption of a polyglot synthetic culture" (*Britannia's*, 571). Robert Crawford, from a different cultural-political location altogether, argues that "if . . . we ignore matters of local origin, then we perform an act of naive cultural imperialism" (*Devolving*, 130). Yet Crawford's position is difficult to distinguish from Weinbrot's when he writes, "*Waverley* is a Scottish and a British book . . . about the construction of a new, culturally eclectic unity – Great Britain – but it is also about the need to preserve the cultures within that unity." For both, the merging of local cultures and languages into a larger social body – be it Britain, England, or Scotland – might take the form of a destructively absorbing incorporation or a diversified amalgamation; either way, cultural identity is founded on a by-turns happy and unhappy coupling of local and global, variously defined as regional/national and national/imperial cultures.

It is impossible, however, to speak about the local cultures "synthesized" and "preserved" in a British union without speculating on the ways in which such "synthesis" and the terms of incorporation change the very meaning of what it is that is being preserved. Instead, a transnationalism which initially eradicated the local now constructs a new version of it for use in an Anglo-British historiography and for sale in the cultural marketplace – Shaw's *Analysis*, after all, went through three editions in eight years. English writers and Scottish assimilationists define the English of Britain's metropolitan center as modern, in contrast to the peripheral Gaelic of an "anachronistic space."[12] That "anachronistic space," existing somehow outside of history, also becomes representative of history itself. Thus, Edward Snyder describes the literary Celtic Revival as a "movement among English men of letters who were united by a common desire to infuse into English poetry the mythology, the history, and the literary treasures of the ancient Celts."[13] Alternatively, to a host of Highland scholars interested in forwarding what Colin Kidd has referred to as "Celtic Whiggism," the particularity of Gaelic represented a testament to the ancient history of a continuous – superior – Celtic culture with direct links to contemporary English liberty.[14]

The multiculturalism of Celtomania is flawed in ways which still haunt multiculturalism under liberal pluralism. David Lloyd critiques this multiculturalism's division of the cultural from the political and economic for the purposes of commodification:

> Liberal pluralism . . . continues to legitimate the assimilation of minorities by abstracting ethnic cultural phenomena, whether food or music or literature, from the material grounds of their existence . . . namely, as belonging in a separate, recreational sphere whose significance derives precisely from its apparent autonomy from either economic or political considerations. The work of rationalization and homogenisation continues apace in these spheres.[15]

In that commodification the dominant culture assimilates "marginal" cultures, but the reclamation of Gaelic did not simply reflect the fact that Highland culture was now safe for mere consumption. Gaelic cultural productions now offered motifs and models of literary production available for poaching in the interest of an Anglo-British cultural nationalist agenda. Thus, as Katie Trumpener has shown, the nationalist maneuvers of such texts as mid-century Gaelic ballad translations were borrowed and transformed by English writers in works such as Thomas Gray's *Bard*.[16]

While Gaelic offered an important national historical linguistic remnant in the face of modernizing English, its particularity helped consolidate the Celtic periphery in the second wave of British imperial ventures. That the multiculturalism of Celtomania might help enable Anglo-British hegemony is evident in changing attitudes towards Highland language instruction. If the repression of Gaelic accompanied the expansion of British empire inward, Shaw's accommodationist use of Gaelic was one means of enlisting the Highlanders' support in the expansion of empire outward.[17] This shift in attitudes towards the Highlands was related, as many have noted, to the effectual suppression of their armed resistance, for the importance of establishing a uniform identity is often most pronounced not in moments of relative political quietude (as in post-Culloden Britain) but when a society is least unified.[18] In opposition to the early pedagogical practices of the SSPCK, Shaw advocates teaching Highlanders to read the Scriptures in their own language. He believes that "there is no equal number of people in Britain so useful to the state. Upon every emergency they supply our navy with good seamen, and our armies with valiant soldiers" (*Analysis*, vxvii) and that the use of the Gaelic language will assure the Highlanders' allegiance to British empire; he writes, "Strip them of their dress, language, the name and honour of Gael, and they soon degenerate . . . a Galic speech ha[s] always inspired them more than the consecration of the colours" (*Analysis*, 17). Gaelic language and clothing are the polite, feminized cultural artifacts covering a regressive – and potentially fractious – "masculine" Highland political body. The Celtomaniacs making a place for Gaelic language and literature in the purely cultural realm of a "multicultural" British society frequently gender the language female and characterize it as weak, defenseless, and in need of the male philologist who will save it from total extinction.[19] While this is easy enough to recognize in the writings of English-assimilating philologists, I also want to point to the limitations of this model in "Celtic Whig" narratives of the ancient Gaelic language, as they remain stranded in the fictions of this particular multiculturalism's highly conventional conceptions of gender and necessary occlusions of class divisions.[20]

"SHAW CONTRA SHAW"

In establishing Gaelic as particular and English as universal, Shaw first had to position himself in relationship to the two, and attempted to locate himself in a "larger" British "neutral" universality against a "smaller" Gaelic particularity. Like MacDonald, Shaw was raised in the Highlands and, having spent time at university in the Lowlands, was called upon to locate himself in the shifting Scottish/English cultural and political terrain. Unlike MacDonald, Shaw headed south, taking a position as a tutor in London, and, ultimately, finding favor from Samuel Johnson, and he remains perhaps best known for his biography, *Memoirs of the Life and Writings of the Late Dr. Samuel Johnson* (1785).[21] On the heels of his *Analysis* and *Dictionary*, Shaw published in London, with the help of Johnson, *An Enquiry Into the Authenticity of the Poems Ascribed to Ossian* (1781), one of several texts attempting to expose the poems of Ossian – that lightning rod of mid-century Scottish/English culture wars – as Macpherson-penned forgeries. As a native-Gaelic-speaking "expert" prepared to delegitimate the notion of a written Scots Gaelic, Shaw was of vital importance to Johnson, who maintained that an essentially oral ancient culture could not have produced those texts.[22] His affiliation to Johnson located Shaw quite firmly in an Anglo camp, for the *Enquiry* appeared not long after Johnson's *Journey*. Many Scots felt, as Donald Macnicol did, that Johnson "hated Scotland; that was the master passion and it scorned all restraints."[23]

Both Shaw and Johnson, however, construct Englishness as the space of disinterested scholarship – Shaw accuses John Clark, who had defended Ossian's authenticity, of being "interested greatly in this controversy" because he was "nearly related to Mr. Macpherson, was his pupil when he taught a parish school" (*Enquiry* 2nd edn., 75). While the tag of partiality persistently stuck to the defenders of the authenticity of the Ossian poems, Shaw maintains that inasmuch as he disputes the poems' authenticity, his is a trustworthy, objective scholarship.[24] One's ability to occupy the position of enlightened, neutral scholar is, it seems, measured by one's distance from a Scottish/Gaelic – not British/English – cultural affiliation; he writes, "I can shew Dr. Johnson that there is *one* Scotchman who loves *truth* better than his country . . . [I] am unbiased and uninfluenced" (*Enquiry*, 21). Alternatively, unacceptable is movement between English and Scottish identification.[25] After Shaw's *Enquiry*, which dismissed the possibility of a coherent Gaelic language and culture, John Clark published a scathing rejoinder in *An Answer to Mr. Shaw's Inquiry*. Central to his denouncement of Shaw are his observations regarding Shaw's wavering between Highland and English sympathies.[26] Clearly miffed by Clark's condemnation of his fluctuating sympathies, in the second edition of his *Enquiry* (1782), Shaw complains, "I am shown, *Shaw contra Shaw* and at variance with myself" (78) and defends his movement between cultural, religious, and political sympathies writing, "The world will surely expect more veracity from a man who has changed sides by conviction than from one who resolves to stay forever where he happens to stand" (78). Attacked for his ready rejection of place and its loyalties, Shaw affirms the value of movement between, rather than a stable location within, particular culture and the proclivities such location would demand.

Shaw ascribes fixed location and its attendant affiliations to writers on the periphery; more cosmopolitan thinkers, like himself, transcend location in their ability to realign themselves in particular situations. In this "partitioned" quality and in the authorial voice he assumes regarding his *Dictionary* he angles for the type of authority earned by Johnson in his beleaguered, overworked author pose. He complains of the "drudgery" of his lexicography, writing, "Having thus collected my materials at a considerable expense and waste of time, I sat down to arrange the whole, probably sacrificing more useful pursuits." Similar to Johnson, in his preface he grumbles about the extensiveness of his searches for new words as "a progress into almost every corner of the Highland part of the continent," where he was "exposed to much fatigue and many inconveniences."[27] At the same time, like Johnson, he also insinuates a linguistic authority which gives lie to such humble posturings, boasting, "I have had access to know and understand the language as well as any man living" (*Enquiry*, 36). Most important, he adopts Johnson's alienated, collector's stance in relation to his own language: Gaelic, like Johnson's ideal English, is corpse-like, as Shaw continually refers to "preserving" its "remains." Just as in Johnson's *Dictionary* the native speakers of English can make little claim to an authoritative knowledge of the collection of English, so Highlanders are indolent and "inactive ... in the cause of their expiring language" (*Dictionary*). In fact, Sir James Foulis, "although of the Low Country of Scotland, and consequently once a stranger to the Galic, by study is now better acquainted with it than many of the natives" (*Dictionary*). Shaw's copying of Johnson's stances, however, does less to subvert colonial relations, as other moments of colonial mimicry might be said to, than to point to the "colonial" nature of Johnson's own project.

In his *Enquiry*, Shaw dismisses one of the "translators" of the Ossian poems as a fabricator: a "translator without originals." Yet the same could be said of Shaw in relation to his *Analysis* and *Dictionary*. While almost any critic who has had occasion to has remarked on the limitations, mistakes, and all-around inadequacies of Shaw's linguistic works, we need to investigate the larger cultural forces and concomitant linguistic assumptions behind some of the patterned errors of his works.

Shaw's grammatical works are, as Sher writes, a "good scam" ("Percy," 216), but for a scam to work, it must develop and play to a set of cultural expectations, and here I want to investigate those expectations around the global status of English. In his Johnsonian effacement of his own agency Shaw implies that he merely unearths the universal principles concealed by a corrupted, material Gaelic. Citing James Harris's *Hermes: or a Philosophical Inquiry Concerning Language and Universal Grammar* (1751) as one of the three books he "found of the most use" (*Analysis*, xx) in his preparation of the *Analysis*, Shaw clearly employs its theory of universal grammar: a belief, as Noam Chomsky describes it, that "the general features of grammatical structure are common to all languages."[28] If grammars in general give less of a sense of history or discrepancy between usages than dictionaries in which etymologies document change, the universal grammar vision exaggerates that ahistorical quality.[29] The "universal grammar" to which Shaw molds Gaelic is in fact Latin grammar, which, although plagued by complex laws, provided the basis of grammatical structure for European languages; it was believed to be a stable – because dead – language. Like many writers of this period, Shaw, seemingly swayed by an emerging Romantic ethos of cultural relativism, remains firmly entrenched in a neoclassical belief in universality.[30]

Key to this position is the conflation of the universal and "not Gaelic." Shaw sees an oral Scots Gaelic as so lacking in regulation that he describes this rule-giving as initially being a personal pet project.[31] He writes in the introduction, "I thought, for my own private amusement, of subjecting it to certain rules, to be observed when I had occasion to speak it" (*Analysis*, xviii).[32] Shaw believes that without books, Gaelic speakers cannot understand their own language (xvi), especially the ways in which it conforms to language's general philosophy. His task, therefore, is to "reduce to a rule a language without books, and having no standard but the judgement of every speaker" (xix).[33] Similarly, although the British had only begun to stabilize their own spelling of English, largely through the efforts of harried printers, Shaw accuses the Highlanders of uniquely disordered linguistic practices when he observes, "At present I much doubt whether there be four men in Scotland that would spell one page the same way" (*Analysis*, xvi). This portrayal of a recreant Gaelic, however, raises some important questions. If he will return Gaelic to the principles of "universal grammar" to "fix" its orthography, how did Gaelic speakers deviate from them in the first place? If the language needs to be written in order to maintain those general principles of grammar, what kind of universality is it? What is the relationship between writing and speech if speech, instead of being the source of knowledge about the general philosophy of Gaelic, is the means of corrupting it? How could a principally oral culture such as Gaelic be said to represent a continuous community and culture if it is subject, as Shaw suggests it is, to unbridled linguistic multiplicity and corruption?

Alternatively, like Johnson before him, Shaw claims to respect the customary linguistic practices of native speakers, offering his assurances that "the Gaelic reader will find no innovation in orthography; for I have considered it my business rather to record words as they've been written in the ancient Irish manuscripts, and will not alter them according to the philosophy of language" (*Dictionary*). And as in Johnson's *Dictionary*, such alterations do, nonetheless, take place. Shaw fails to record the fact that Irish and Scots spellings are often different and Shaw ignores just about every single Scots Gaelic spelling included in MacDonald's *Vocable*.[34] He also rejects both structural linguistic change through time and the significance of regional language distinctions. When Shaw's Highland sources for his *Dictionary* began charging him per word, he simply moved his research to Ireland. Ignoring major differences between Scots and Irish Gaelic, the resulting entries provide no sense of the complex regional variances of the Scots Gaelic lexicon throughout the Highlands or even the difference between Irish and Scots Gaelic. It is little wonder that many subscribers refused payment upon receipt of the *Dictionary* and that Highland subscribers testified against Shaw in a court case about that non-payment, claiming, "He discovered no inclination to tarry long in any one place, . . . was not sollicitous [sic] to hold conversation or enter into any correspondence with those who were deemed deeply conversant in the Gaelic language" (Sher, "Percy," 216–7). Disregarding a standard that values past practices reflected in etymological consistency, Shaw establishes his own principles for correct usage based in part on what looks appropriate on the page to readers of English. He writes, "Some write the termination *fhear* in place of *oir*, affecting an idle knowledge in the etymology of words, at the expence of hurting the eye of every reader with the bristly appearance of an useless assemblage of consonants" (*Analysis*, 90–1). In rejecting the propriety of an etymology, Shaw espouses a stance toward customary Gaelic linguistic practices similar to the SSPCK's, who had hoped "to cure old prejudices . . . [and] root out old opinions and practices, big with folly and absurdity."[35]

To revise Gaelic, Shaw turns to the grammatical tables of grammar handbooks. In replicating the forms of a Latin grammar, Shaw furnishes a sense of controlling knowledge over a threateningly renegade Gaelic. The *Analysis* features isolated words from Gaelic reduced to items in a table. This relocation effaces the multiple meanings of Gaelic words and fills them with meaning as signs affirming the universality of Latin/ English grammatical categories. Shaw's tables recall Roland Barthes's discussion of his experience of reading a sentence in his Latin grammar meant to function as a grammatical example. The Latin sentence "is evidently there to signify something else to me."[36] Similarly functioning as a second-order semiological system, Shaw's tables reduce signs to mere signifiers in a new chain of signification regarding the universality of English/Latin language structures. His text consists of pages and pages of tables. In them the suggestive significance of "assemble," for instance, is emptied out. The *OED*, for instance, records multiple definitions of "assemble" extant in 1778, the publication year of the *Analysis*. These include, but are not limited to, "to bring together (persons) into one place or company; to gather collect, convene," "to bring together things into one place or mass," "to couple (sexually)," and "to congregate, meet." Shaw's *Analysis* gives no sense of whether the Gaelic *cruinich* refers to all of these, or none (Fig. 5).

Filtering out such "noise," Shaw uses the language of equivalence throughout his analysis, as in "*Ei*, equivalent to the English *not*," or "*so* equal to the English termination *ble*" (98) and dismisses even the definitions of MacDonald's glossary as not equivalent enough, writing that in MacDonald's *Vocable*, "most things are expressed by circumlocution" (xv). In Shaw's *Dictionary*, no English term receives a more detailed entry than a one-word Gaelic equivalent, such as

> *Abhar, abhair*, m. I. a cause
> *Accair*, m. 2. an anchor
> *Adharc*, adhairc, f. 2 a horn (*Analysis*, 153).

Further, we might read Shaw's "universalizing" treatment of Gaelic as a reflection of an Enlightenment thought imbricated in increasingly dominant imperial capital relations. In their critique of an instrumental reason Theodor Adorno and Max Horkheimer describe the logic of the *ratio*: "what was different is equalized . . . The identity of everything with everything else is paid for in that nothing may at the same time be identical with itself; . . . it excises the incommensurable."[37] While the language of equivalence is unavoidable in any discussion of

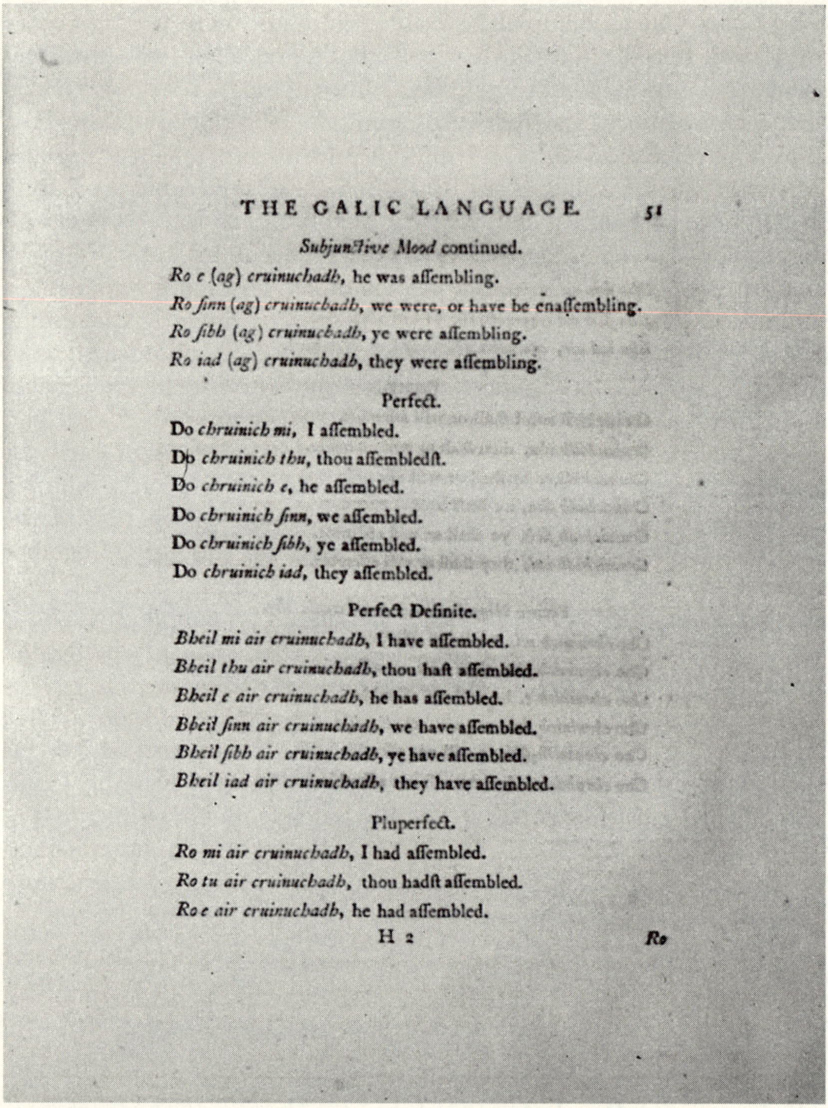

THE GALIC LANGUAGE. 51

Subjunctive Mood continued.

Ro e (ag) cruinuchadh, he was assembling.
Ro sinn (ag) cruinuchadh, we were, or have be enassembling.
Ro sibh (ag) cruinuchadh, ye were assembling.
Ro iad (ag) cruinuchadh, they were assembling.

Perfect.

Do chruinich mi, I assembled.
Do chruinich thu, thou assembledst.
Do chruinich e, he assembled.
Do chruinich sinn, we assembled.
Do chruinich sibh, ye assembled.
Do chruinich iad, they assembled.

Perfect Definite.

Bheil mi air cruinuchadh, I have assembled.
Bheil thu air cruinuchadh, thou hast assembled.
Bheil e air cruinuchadh, he has assembled.
Bheil sinn air cruinuchadh, we have assembled.
Bheil sibh air cruinuchadh, ye have assembled.
Bheil iad air cruinuchadh, they have assembled.

Pluperfect.

Ro mi air cruinuchadh, I had assembled.
Ro tu air cruinuchadh, thou hadst assembled.
Ro e air cruinuchadh, he had assembled.

H 2   Ro

Figure 5. From William Shaw, *An Analysis of the Galic Language*, 1778. Courtesy, The Lilly Library, Indiana University, Bloomington, Indiana.

translation, Shaw's logic of equivalence is important for its simultaneous association of Gaelic with particularity and Latin and English with universality.[38] He consistently lists declensions of Gaelic nouns in a system based on the familiar Latin declension. For instance,

> N. [nominative] *Ossag*, a blast.
> G. [genitive] *Ossaig*, of a blast.
> D. [dative] *Dh'ossag*, to a blast
> A. [accusative] *Ossag*, a blast.
> V. [vocative] *Ossaig*, O blast!
> A. [ablative] *Le ossag*, with a blast. (*Analysis*, 25)

Yet Shaw admits towards the end of his *Analysis*, "We cannot with strict propriety say that the Galic has an accusative, because the nominative and the accusative are always the same" (109). Similarly, Shaw refers to a Gaelic ablative – a Latin case that does not exist in an inflectional form in Gaelic.[39]

When Gaelic refuses to fit the Latin grammatical structure in these ways, Shaw locates the fault not in his project of forcing Gaelic into an equivalent Latin structure but in the Gaels themselves, whose error-ridden oral linguistic practices have destroyed their comprehension of their language. In discussing Gaelic prepositional pronouns, Shaw remarks, "Here I think it proper to interdict the false constructions common in conversation [such as] *gam*, instead of *ag mo*; as *ag mo bhuairadh*, disturbing or tempting me ... The cause of this mistake, I am certain, is writing from the ear only, without an allowance for velocity of sound" (110–11). Shaw makes the peculiar argument that in transcribing an oral language, the ear cannot be trusted. Written Gaelic replicates a defective oral pronunciation, and so words must be made up to fit conventions of Latin grammar. What sounds like one word, "*gar*" or "*gam*" is really two: "*ag ar*" and "*ag mo*," representing the separate verb and pronoun of Latin grammar that Shaw believes Gaelic speakers have mistakenly contracted into one.[40]

While linguistic relativists make much of the significance of the tense structures of a particular language in relation to the particular world view of its speakers, Shaw rejects the possibility of distinct tense structures in different languages, writing, "Some say a language has only as many tenses as are regularly formed without the auxiliary, yet I am of opinion, a verb cannot be better conjugated than by stating it in all its different times of action whatsoever" (46).[41] Similarly, instances of the most obvious differences between Gaelic and Latin or English receive no mention at all. There is no reference in Shaw's *Analysis*, for instance, to Gaelic's emphatic form of personal pronouns. Since there is no equivalent for this form in English – save italics and underlining – it would not fit into Shaw's universalizing model. Shaw also leaves unremarked the fact that the Indo-European first person pronoun does not appear in the nominal in the Celtic languages. One difference – Gaelic's "personification" of all objects, animate and inanimate, and thus its lack of an equivalent to the English neuter pronoun, "it" – is mentioned, but only as a source of ridicule. Shaw snickers, "This is what renders the Gael's first attempts to speak English so ridiculous, every substantive being either . . . he or she" (11–12). Shaw adopts a similar tone when attempting to resolve the "problem" of the multiply signifying Gaelic morpheme "A." He exasperatedly asserts, "I leave it to any one who has the least knowledge of grammar, whether it be possible for even those who naturally speak the language, to distinguish the one [meaning] from the other, where the whole may recur twice or oftener in one page. In order therefore to settle the whole, I have consulted the genius of the language, and dismissed them all except three, which I explain as follows" (106). Even his contemporaries – the SSPCK's translators McFarlane and Stewart – "have written this letter of many meanings without any fixed rule" (105). In opposition to common practice, he offers his own "right orthography" and "grammatical system" (126). In his restriction of the use of "A" and other Gaelic terms Shaw tosses aside old uses for a future clearer Gaelic more readily accessible to foreign readers. A morpheme so dependent on the context of the particular sentence in which one finds is too free-wheeling a linguistic element to fit into "fixed" categories for translating the language.

The insertion of Gaelic into neoclassical – "timeless" – linguistic values also takes place in the literary realm. Shaw closes his *Analysis* with Gaelic translations of Pope and Sterne.[42] In translating the language into conventional literary values, such translations both reflect and contribute to the aestheticization of Gaelic, through which it is schooled in the accomplishments of a later, more polished English society. Shaw, however, also drives home the distinguished antiquity of Gaelic when he offers translations of poems of Ossian and, appropriately, Tacitus's "The Speech of Galgacus," which a footnote states was "pronounced at the head of an army of Caledonians, when about to engage the Roman army on the Grampian Hills" (132). In reminding his readers of this shared historical moment of the Romans and the Caledonians, Shaw recalls the ancient glories of that Gaelic victory. Ancient eminence is still to be found in the language itself, as "the original simple principles of the Galic, make it far excell any of the modern, and rival the most ancient languages" (97). The past that eighteenth-century readers and writers constructed was no longer quickly measured against the ancient world and found wanting, particularly when it was this Gaelic past of renown.

GAELIC AND THE PLACE OF HISTORY

As discussed in Chapter 4, contemporary writers believed that the Highlands had withstood the cultural and linguistic pollution of a globalizing modernization. Shaw's association of universal grammatical structures with Latin and English are, thus, only half of the story. That half is much more useful for a colonial discourse which, as we have seen in Chapter 1, depends upon notions of universal equivalence for seamless linguistic exchange. A language capable of calling up ancestral heritage and evoking the physical sentiment of national affiliation, however, figures centrally in cultural nationalist discourse. In summarizing the various schools of thought on the origins on Britons' rising fascination with a misty, noble past, Patrick Wright has hypothesized that

[For some it] came to be articulated against Enlightenment ideas of progress and reason, while others place more emphasis on an aesthetic and neo-pastoral impulse which turns into a demand for preservation as it recoils from the rampant urbanity of a brutal industrial capitalism . . . emphasis should also be placed on the consolidation of the imperial nation-state; for whatever else it may involve, preservationism has certainly played its part in a nationalization of history which enables the state to project an idealized image . . . of its own order against a geographical and historical background of its own selection.[43]

Similarly, Ian Haywood links the "proliferation" of historical treatises in the eighteenth century to "the need to define the historical shape of national societies and in particular to describe their origins."[44] This interest in the history of the British nation is also inextricably tied to the simultaneous expansion of the British empire. Haywood writes, "The British Empire was rapidly expanding. Among historians, the most difficult task in the aggrandizement was the portrayal of a nation's genesis" (35) and Wright links "preservationism" to "the consolidation of the imperial nation-state" (49).

Yet that imperial expansion is believed to modernize the center and its language, so that they can no longer be the visible site of national pastness. Ironically, it is those very imperial relations which produce a sense of Gaelic as particular and old – making it available for national reclamations in producing English as universal and Gaelic as particular. Thus, if "the intellectual strategy of Celticism is the annulment, elision or denial of history," it is also, paradoxically, the construction of a "preservation" of history in those very terms.[45] At work in these constructions of "Celtic" culture, then, are also constructions of the understanding of history itself, where history becomes not an ongoing process of change and struggle, but a sheer pastness emptied of such contents. Shaw, through the imperial grammar he deploys, empties English of the possibility of carrying the burden of that materiality and historicity, displacing that ideological cargo to Gaelic. His aim being "to prevent [Gaelic's] dying without even a sigh" (*Analysis*, xxiv), Shaw caters to an emerging nostalgia for things old and "British."[46] If the British empire sanctions itself by *distinguishing* itself from its colonial "anachronistic" cultures spatially visible in "panoptical time," the British nation legitimates itself by *identifying* itself with a visible past at the edges of its geographically defined borders. The trajectory of Gaelic from index of colonial outsider status to vital marker of an inclusive British ancestry forms a continuous arc. In fact, as John Clark argues, an ability to retain history is built into the very structure of Gaelic: "the Celtic language was constructed on principles the best calculated for preserving as well as describing events. Every accent struck with such force upon the mind, that the memory had little trouble in retaining a composition of great length" (see note 50, 11). In what we might call a linguistic "dialectic of empire," Gaelic must be reclaimed as part of a "multicultural" Britain because it is seen as possessing those qualities of venerable age and moving specificity.[47] The "developing interest in English, Welsh, and Scottish ethnicity" (Weinbrot, *Britannia's*, 542) should be seen in this light: the new, tolerant "multicultural" view of Gaelic is produced in part out of an imperialist philological discourse that has named Gaelic as local to a global English. To borrow from Castells's terminology, while reversing his claim, the dynamics of the "space of flows," rather than suppressing, reinforces a particular, and ideologically useful, "space of place," inaugurating an understanding and appreciation of Gaelic as local.

Unlike other colonial languages, Gaelic functions as both colonial and national sign. If earlier writers had connected native Americans to the ancient Picts, this proximal instance of Celtic cultural continuity was even more compelling. Stuart Piggot writes, "The early antiquaries illuminated the prehistoric past by ethnographical analogies drawn not from remote trans-Atlantic savages, but from survivals in the British Isles themselves."[48] In fact Shaw attempts to consolidate Gaelic-speakers within a specifically British frame by establishing the "outsider" status of a third group, native Americans. Shaw's insistence that the SSPCK teach the Scriptures to Highlanders in their native language – a privilege "never denied to the most savage Indians" (xvii) – indicates his belief that these two colonial populations are distinguishable; unlike the native Americans, the Highlanders are not "savage," as evidenced in the greatness and age of their Gaelic language.

Gaelic, in fact, might be an even more inherently national language. These characterizations of the powers of Gaelic, like Macpherson's descriptions of ancient Celts, naturalize the nation in martial terms.[49] Shaw writes:

Sounds are either quick or slow, rough or smooth, strong or feeble. From the various modifications of these in a language, may be discovered, the manners, temperament, and feelings of a people . . . the genius of [Gaelic] is . . . to rouse the soul to feats of arms, or inspire pity in the restless breast. (113)

The "genius" of Gaelic's material sounds kindles the very activities and sensibilities central to nationalist rhetoric: military prowess and fellow feeling. John Clark identifies a congruent Gaelic literary sensibility; in his *Works of the Caledonian Bards* (1778) he asserts that the key tenets of their ancient poetry were "Never to forsake a friend, nor fear a foe" (18).[50] Likewise, John Smith tells of the exhortations to sociability and doughty battle to be found in the literary traditions of the Celts.[51] These particular qualities and the nationalist sentiments they elicit are presumably less perceivable in the voiceless word on the page and the hollow tables designed to showcase universal grammatical case and tense, associated, as we have seen, with English and Latin.

Shaw's writings bestride a dualism between a synchronic and an increasingly important diachronic pole of language. An "invisible" English undergirds the synchronic linguistic principles to which a visible and visibly retrograde Gaelic is contrasted, a language which, although it is too "particular" to move through space, expands back in time in that contraction of space. If English and Latin are applicable across time, Gaelic represents the past, which, it turns out, Shaw privileges when he writes, "The human mind, with great longing, looks back into the past, less interested in many particulars of the present, which it overlooks, and of the future, which it enquires not after" (*Analysis*, x–xi). Although he attacked the authenticity of the Ossian poems, Shaw was himself capable of pathos-laden sentiments regarding the ebb of the memory of "the Gael's" history, plaintively writing:

When I look back into the former times of the Gael, whose history a native might be supposed more immediately fond of, finding it so much involved in obscurity, or suppressed and obliterated by the policy of a neighbouring monarch, I could sit down and weep over its fall, execrating the policy of usurping invaders. (xi)

As Gaelic represents the cultural vestiges of an irrecoverable past, Shaw's "joy in grief" at the vision of a fading material Gaelic is a spectacular staging of diachrony.[52] These are fairly damning words indeed, seeming to comment directly on the work of groups such as the SSPCK. In his criticism of their failure to teach the Scriptures in Gaelic, Shaw reproachingly asks, "Is the Society for Propagating Christian Knowledge only a name?" (xviii).

WHOSE OLD COUNTRY?

The extent to which the imperial nation-state can claim "historical" colonial linguistic cultures as its own is limited, even in the relatively proximal case of Scots Gaelic. Highland writers made their own play to reappropriate that local history for distinctly Scottish cultural national narratives. These, however, remain trapped in the terms that the imperial nation-state has already established. In the title of this subsection I refer to Wright's title, *On Living in an Old Country: The National Past in Contemporary Britain,* to invoke not only Britain's sense of itself as increasingly defined by its past, but also to point to the instability of the collective body its memory assembles – an instability hinted at in Wright's subjectless title. Highland philologists claims of Gaelic's ancientness and power, for instance, respond to a crisis in *Scottish* nationalist historiography. As Kidd shows, transformations in eighteenth-century Scottish historiography meant that Scottish history could no longer be said to comprise a continuous movement from past liberty to future Scottish national progress. While Thomas Innes had proven that the Scots could not trace a monarchical lineage all the way back to a first Celtic king, as previously had been argued, the sociologists of the Scottish Enlightenment had demonstrated that liberty could not be linked to Scotland's historic feudal social institutions. In these narratives, the distinctive qualities of Scotland's legal and political past had no place in Scotland's – or Britain's – future. Kidd writes:

> The new history of liberty in Scotland was based on the insight that true liberty was a by-product of modernity . . . and that Scottish society had been more backward and benighted than England's. Modern liberty had come to eighteenth-century Scotland, not because of native developments, but from the incorporation of Scotland within England's realm of liberty by the Union of 1707. (*Subverting*, 269–70)

Key elements of the claims of Scottish political continuity had been disputed, and those elements of Scotland's political past that distinguished it from England in the present marked it as a cultural and political throwback. The future belonged to a Scotland that could relinquish its socio-political history as it rode the coat-tails of an English modernity to progress and liberty. In these circumstances, language remained one of the few platforms from which to make the argument regarding a continuous and dignified Scottish past that could be successfully linked to a Whig interpretation of that history.[53] "Celtic Whiggism," as Kidd labels the bid for a salvageable Scottish history of liberty, "was the culmination of a tradition of Whig responses to the destructive scholarship of Father Innes which sidestepped the weak ground of diplomatic scholarship for alternative scholarly terrain, most notably linguistics" (224). Scottish whig historians, then, insisted that the language of the Celts held particular properties that made it a more inspirational language of nationalist pride and liberty than English, earnestly promoting a "Celtomania that ennobles the Celts and their language as radically poetic and free."[54]

Thus writers such as David Malcolme, in arguing Gaelic's ancientness, attempt to rectify the "regicide" committed by Innes's much "mistaken" account of royal genealogy.[55] Not only did Malcolme meet with the approval of such bodies as the General Assembly of the Church of Scotland, members of the Faculty of Advocates, and professors of Divinity at the University of Edinburgh, but he also imagined that these seemingly arcane philologies would have a much wider readership. He emphasizes accessibility when, in his octavo-sized volume *Letters, Essays and Other Tracts* (1744), he reprints sections of Lhuyd's preface and sections from his glossary of Irish/English because in its original folio size it could not be "carried about." In this legitimating move Malcolme insists, "I have a great deal more pleasure in inquiring into the antiquities and curiosities of my own country, than of any other, even those of ancient Greece and Rome,"[56] and, similarly, in his *Gaelic Antiquities* (1780) John Smith describes his work as a corrective, "that the antiquities of our own country are too much neglected, whilst those of other nations are eagerly . . . enquired into" (1). Like the late eighteenth-century Orientalists that Said describes, who set themselves up as "hero[es] rescuing the Orient from . . . obscurity, alienation, and strangeness," Shaw and his fellow Scots "reassert the values" of ancient Gaelic (*Analysis*, 121). Unlike those Orientalists, however, they see themselves as "native" – albeit distantly – of that dying culture, suggesting one way in which we might revise Said's model to more closely account for the ways in which nation and empire work with and against each other.

It is important to point out, however, that even the most strident of these texts never goes so far as to question the 1707 Union or even, in most cases, the propriety of the spread of English to these lands. No longer jealous of each other's claims to ancient fame, John Macpherson optimistically writes that, England and Scotland "are now so much blended with one another, that whatever throws lustre upon the one, ought to be reckoned an acquisition of reputation to the other" (*Critical*, vii). Likewise, although Malcolme hopes to show that "Scotch" might help illustrate the languages of the Old Testament, he also insists that "this design will be so far from hindering the spreading of the English Language, that on the contrary, in my Way of managing it, it will considerably help diffuse it, and will . . . fall in with the . . . laudable Designs, and Intentions of the Society for propagating Christian Knowledge" (Letter 11). Unlike MacDonald's appeal to Gaelic's former glory in hopes of its future resurrection, Shaw's and his fellows' appeal to Gaelic's ancientness entombs the language and its culture in the past; in many "Celtomaniacal characterizations" of Gaelic it is, as a result, not only feminized but strangely sexualized. John Clark, in his introduction to selected *Works of the Caledonian Bards*, asks of a personified and neglected Gaelic language, "Hast thou in vain display'd thy breast, adorn'd/With the inviting charms of rhet'ric's pow'r" and "Has no sweet, bold poetic son of thine, /Held forth thy richness in luxuriant strains?" (24). Gaelic is at once sexual and maternal, the reference to a son, of course, connects the reception of the mother tongue to the biological moment of receiving mother's milk, in this case, unnaturally refused. In contrast to English, a disempowered and feminized Gaelic (her inviting charms easily shunned) is sidelined.

It is significant that in Clark's literary representations of Gaelic, it is never depicted on its own, but always in the shadow of a more powerful and all-encompassing English, a figure for the interdependence of the characterizations of both that I have been arguing. In his verse introduction to his English "translations" of Gaelic verse, John Clark seeks the approval of "ghosts of bards" not to resurrect the Gaelic tongue but simply to illustrate the power of the English tongue which has vanquished it. At the introduction's fascinating conclusion he writes:

> Come, then, Britannia's voice of modern days! . . .
> Assist, while in thy mirror I display,
> And trace the beauties of thy rival's face;
> That men may know the conquest thou hast made
> And view her strength who sank beneath thy arm
> Not small the vict'ry – heavenly were her charms!
> And tho' she fell, she justly claims a tear. (27–28)

In a powerful image of cultural absorption, Clark depicts his English translation of Gaelic verse as a mirror capable of reflecting the trace of a now-vanquished Gaelic. Interestingly, Gaelic is no longer embodied; "her" memory can only be called up by a victorious English in a spectral mirror image. It is important to note the shift from MacDonald's gendering of Gaelic which connoted the powerful reproductive capacities and strengths of that Splendid "Granddam" to Clark's feminization which connotes a beautiful but defeated state. Again associated with sentiment, able to "claim a tear," Gaelic's powerful charms, delineated in Clark's translations into English, finally serve to illuminate the strength of English. While in Shaw's writing a polite and beautiful Gaelic language successfully placated and covered a threatening Celtic masculinity, in Clark's writing such a threat has been dissolved. A universally spoken English conceals and absorbs a withdrawn female Celtic beauty. He writes, "Thus we, in vain attempt, in borrowed words,/ To draw aside the veil that keeps thee hid,/ And shew thee to admiring eyes, array'd/ In beauty, strength, and majesty sublime" (24).

Importantly, the forces and dynamics creating an "intermingled" England and dictating the uneven, gendered terms of the narratives of the Celtic/English relationship in Matthew Arnold's *On the Study of Celtic Literature* (1867), that Robert Young so accurately describes, were already at work in the eighteenth century.[57] Clark's image anticipates Arnold's later vision of a hybrid English, composed of a masculine Saxon and feminized Celtic, a vision which reaches its zenith when Arnold argues for – and wins – the establishment of a Celtic Chair at Oxford University in the interest of recuperating a version of Celtic linguistic and literary past for English use.[58] Although Arnold develops his distinctions between the English and the Celts through a much more developed racial discourse, he makes use of a model of intermingling not unlike that of these earlier writers. Importantly, he discovers the detritus of a Celtic past in contemporary English culture through linguistic evidence. We might see the work of Shaw and the other Celtomaniacs, then, as sowing the seeds for Arnold's highly influential cultural theory regarding the place of "the Celtic" in English culture.

THE TRANSLATED TRANSLATES: CELTOMANIA'S IMPAIRED RESISTANCE

I want to end by teasing out the implications of a nascent Gaelic nationalist rhetoric's attribution of originary status to Gaelic. Its special imaginative qualities sprang, in part, from its ancient and divine status. Closer to the original, godly language of Hebrew than English could claim to be, Gaelic – which some even saw as the linguistic progeny of the language of Noah's grandson Gomer – would be not simply equal but superior to an upstart composite English. Since it retained its original structures, it might be Gaelic, then, and not English, that bore a close resemblance to the classical languages that were the source of universal grammar structures. After praising the abundance of (material) "primitives" of Gaelic, Shaw claims, "Terms can easily be rendered from the Greek into the Galic, by decomposing them in the original, and then translating and joining them afresh; an advantage of which no modern language is possessed" (98). This concept, in ways unacknowledged by Shaw, reverses his claims around English and universal grammar. Gaelic's very historicity in this case ceases to signal a particularism and localism and instead refers to its past universal globalism. A floating signifier, Gaelic then becomes a highly mobile cultural marker capable of constructing the "particularity" of its contemporary speakers as well as the "universality" of its past speakers, and, finally, the premier status of the people(s) of the Highlands as the first and continuous speakers of this language. When Shaw writes, that "an acquaintance with the Galic, being the mother-tongue of all the languages in the west, seems necessary to every Antiquary who would study the affinity of languages, or trace the migrations of the ancient races" (xxiii), we see that if Gaelic is one of many "local" languages incorporated into a "global" British culture, the terms of the local/global binary do not remain secure. These Scottish writers adopt the universalizing claims which had been made, to trace the circle back, around English in response to its confrontations with Gaelic.

In his *Critical Dissertations* (1768), perhaps the most linguistically oriented of all of these works, John Macpherson maintains that the present-day Highlanders are the most ancient inhabitants of Britain and demonstrates, through a series of rather serpentine etymologies, this ancientness with such examples as the correspondence between ancient Gaelic words and present-day place names. Out of this highly charged historiography came ever broader claims about the Gaelic language. Wild speculation regarding Gaelic's status reached beyond claims that it was the ancient language of Britain, to projections of it as "the mother tongue of all languages" (Shaw, *Enquiry*, xxiii). A veritable cottage industry of amateur philologists set about writing speculative histories of the language regarding that ancient universality. In 1755 Jerome Stone, a St. Andrews-educated Highlander, took it upon himself as his "avocation" to write "An Enquiry into the Original of the Nation and Language of the Native Scots with Conjectures about the Primitive State of the Celtic, and other European Nations." (Stone died before completing this work.)[59] Extremely nationalist in tone – if we may use that term at such an early date in Scotland – Stone's manuscript argues that Celtic "was once the universal speech of Europe" and that it is the closest to the "original language." John Macpherson, too, "took pleasure in tracing other languages to that general source [Gaelic] of all antient and modern tongues of Europe" (*Critical*, v). Stone defends his point by citing *Cratylus* and arguing that, like the first language described in that text, where there is a "connection betwixt the very sounds of the first language and the ideas they served to express," in Celtic "the onomatopoeia, or resemblance betwixt the sounds, and ideas are perfectly astonishing. There is scarce an animal, domestic or wild, whose natural cry can be imitated by human organs, but has a name in the Irish exactly imitating their own sound." And here we can note the unswerving particularity of this language, tied as it is to the very fauna of the region. Similarly, in 1764 Rowland Jones, a Welshman, published a tract entitled *The Origin of Language and Nations*, which argued that "Celtic has the best claim to be the first language."[60] Jones turns to the most arbitrary of representational systems – the alphabet – in an attempt to demonstrate how even this system shares a relationship of resemblance to the things signified and how that relationship is grounded in the Celtic language. He writes, for instance, that the letter "L" "seems to express extension, as in the Celtic word for space, place, a yard, the ground." Further, "The letter S or ~ is a letter of sound, formed probably from the flowing motion of the waves of the sea, and sounded like their hissing sound; which in the Celtic is Sio, and Si-an . . . whence probably the word sea." Jones counters theories of arbitrary sign systems, so essential to the project of imperial grammar, as we have seen. He writes, "Human language has been considered by some, as nothing more than that of the Hottentots, which they suppose to be mere inarticulate sounds; others, with Mr. Locke, imagined that it is consisted only of mere arbitrary sounds, without any connection with nature." Celtic languages, Jones insists, represent truly human, motivated, immediate, and iconic language. In an extraordinary move, Jones claims that "Celtic even received no alteration at Babel."

The linguistic writings of these philologists in their simultaneous advancement and refusal of a narrative that marks Gaelic as the perennially local language in the face of an omnitemporal global English, make use of the gap informing the local/global nation/empire binary to sunder it. The rhetoric of the newly formed British state, then, did not exert total control over the inclusion of the Gaels into its heterogeneous body politic. Once again, the very transactions that might cement the Highlands to the British state through linguistic and cultural relations incite positions unforeseen by and resistant to that control. One final example might serve to illustrate the force of these oppositional readings. Importantly, this illustration demonstrates the reinjection of agency into the disempowered subjectivity suggested in the figure of "panoptical time." Amateur philologist D. Macpherson who was attempting to locate "British" history in Celtic roots, ends by inverting the imperial grammar to which the Gaels and their language had been subject. Arguing that Gaelic was the first language of England, he writes, "Ask a Highland child what London means, he will reply 'city on the marsh,' which is what it was anciently."[61] Here the Highland child, the pedagogical subject of a rote, "imperial grammar," as we have seen in Chapter 1, re-emerges as the person capable of giving the English their language. Over time, the space where London is located has itself been transformed. No longer recognizable as the "city on the marsh," its inhabitants have suffered an equally significant distancing from the root meanings of the words of their language. For them, the word "London" in English has become arbitrary and its original meaning unavailable; we might even describe its use by Londoners as "rote." "London," however, remains literal for the Highland child, who continues to understand the direct meaning of the word over time. Dramatically telling about D. Macpherson's narrative is its redirection of the image of the "backward" Gaelic-speaking child in need of advancement: Macpherson refigures the reading child as one whose living linguistic ties to the past are suppressed only at the dearest cost to British self knowledge. Wonderfully demonstrative of a symbolic reclamation of the Gaelic speaker, not taught, the child teaches, and his lessons are as natural as Adam's naming of the animals.

The Highlander D. Macpherson narrates the Highland child as the displaced, wrongly marginalized source of Britain's language and understanding of its own identity. In his choice of a child as central figure in this Gaelic myth of origins, one might argue that the power of Gaelic is now recast and reclaimed as non-threatening – in the form of a child. Yet the child who is, in this example, keeper of the past, is also a projection into the future. In his vindication of the Gaelic language through the figure of a speaking – not writing – child, Macpherson attempts to catapult the Gaelic-speaking nation out of a moribund past and to resituate the language as able to represent world and word outside of a purely local context.

Shaw, like D. Macpherson, clearly believes that some cross-cultural linguistic meaning is possible. Yet unlike Macpherson, Shaw attempts to forestall the contradictions of a simultaneously imperial/national British culture. For Shaw, it is the Anglicized "unbiased" Scot, able to reject the partiality of the Scot, who is best able to translate between these cultures. He assures his readers of the possibility of transparent translation when he accuses James Macpherson's Ossian poems of having been "too animated with Ossian's spirit" to be correct. In other words, to return to the terms with which I opened this chapter, in Shaw's view Macpherson's work is too culturally biased to represent anything close to the transparency of "true" translation. Alternatively, John Clark, who assumes the position of mere "translator" of a series of "Caledonian" poems, suggests that Gaelic's power resists translation. He writes, "The majesty, and beautiful energy of the Galic, appear no where so conspicuous, as when a translation of the compositions is attempted" (8). The Gaelic poems are "inimitable in an English version" (19). These Scottish writers inhabit opposing fields of either universal language (be it English or Scottish based) or linguistic relativism, yet as they leave the binary between them intact, one is left wondering if there is anything in between those terms.

Simply reversing the local/global binary, however, Macpherson and his fellow Highland philologists who projected an originary, universal

Gaelic stopped short of the most radical claims to be made around their language. As bilingual speakers of a universally valued English and a Gaelic disappearing from public use, their impulse to revalue Gaelic is easy to understand. The terms in which they revalued that language reflected, however, not the imperatives of a newly Gaelic and rebellious literate community, as MacDonald's had, but the consequences of a successful curtailing of the ability to imagine and enact any such resistance, as Gaelic became a means of defining Englishness by comparison and contrast in a multicultural integration. If the English, Lowland, and Highland writers who constructed the terms of the Celtic/English linguistic relationship stopped short of embracing the radical implications of transnational translation, we must move beyond their frame of understanding. By historicizing this early wave of British multiculturalism, we might be better able to imagine alternative conceptualizations of language and language communities, and their ongoing relationships and struggles.

Epilogue
Jane Austen's language and the strangeness at home in the center

We started with a look at colonial pedagogy in the far-flung regions of the Highlands, considered the role of Scottish "expatriates" in shaping standard English in their representations of English and its "dialects," analyzed English instruction in the peripheral centers of Scotland, and examined speculations regarding an ancient Gaelic language. Interspersed in these discussions have been observations regarding the mutually informing relationships between English and Scottish linguistic technologies and subjects, with Johnson's *Dictionary* functioning as a case in point. It is time to return to the "center" and reconsider the ways in which central and marginal language practices and theories worked both to define and de-center that center. The Jacobite Gaelic poet wandering the mountain nooks of the Hebrides, the broad-Scots-speaking expatriate fearfully silent in hostile London streets, and the Highland poet ventriloquizing a mythical bard musing on the mist-covered heaths of ancient Caledonia *are* incalculably distant from the users of proper English in the domiciles in the "heart" of England famously typified in the heroes and heroines of the novels of Jane Austen. Yet it is to her works that I now turn for a closer look at representations of the language which, unlike Scots, Scots Gaelic, or a recognizably dialect-inflected English, was at home in the center. Interested in the experiences of a gentry located in the lush green Home Counties and offering only fleeting impressions of spaces beyond fashionable watering holes and country residences, let alone the country of England, Jane Austen's novels have come to signal to generations of critics and readers the Englishness of England. One of the most apparent distinctions between Austen's writings and those of the Scottish writers we have considered is the abashed Scottishness of the Scottish writers and the frank Englishness of Austen. The narrator in *Emma*, for instance, describes, "a sweet view – sweet to the eye and the mind. English verdure, English culture, English comfort."[1] While the writings of Smollett, Smith, and Blair go to some lengths to minimize Scottish difference, particularly at the linguistic level, and the works of Shaw and James Macpherson praise Gaelic linguistic difference only as it once existed in an irretrievable past, Austen's novels relish the language and manners of a distinct contemporary Englishness. If one strand of Austen criticism (and adaptations) has come to understand the experience of a particular class – if itself a gradated and heterogeneous one – as metonymically representative of English experience in general, that move has been predicated, in part, on the belief in an ideal, transcendent "proper" English.[2] For the idea that there is a general "Englishness" which one class most closely approximates is homologous to the idea that there is one general, ideal language – seldom fully realized – which this particular class is seen to speak and write in its close to purest ("dialect-less") form.

It might well seem perverse that I should want to focus on Austen's English in this epilogue to a study largely devoted to the ways "outsiders," such as Scots, were uncomfortably entwined in the formation and at times resisted the adoption of standard English. Yet the ideological intersection between class, language, and nation seemingly at work in her novels is also troubled in them. This is an especially important point, in that it belies the naturalization of a unitary English linguistic identity that a focus on Scottish ambivalence alone would suggest. The accepted wisdom from critics of Scottish literature has been that in Scottish writers the private, domestic, "authentic" Scottish self is at odds with a public, "inauthentic" writing of that self in English. What I have been arguing, however, is that that dichotomy – or more accurately, conventional interpretation of it – is false, for it posits an "authentic" private, native Scots and Scots Gaelic language in contrast to an inauthentic public, foreign English language. By this logic, the speakers of polite English, understood as the language of both public and private experience in England, would speak a singular language untroubled by the cultural dualism from which the Scots suffered. My point in arguing against the authentic/inauthentic linguistic dualism attributed to the Scots has not been to expose the "invented tradition" of what had formerly been claimed as an "authentic" suppressed Scottish culture, but rather to defy a logic, which, when followed through to the English context, would naturalize the "native" language of England, confirming one of the most basic claims of English nationalism.[3] I emphasize an alienation within the "private" language of Austen's novels, for too often that language is linked to and used as proof of an "authentic" private, domestic life that reflects and betokens an "authentic" national public life with which it is continuous. If, in English nationalist constructions, the private sphere of little England and its language assert an "authentic," organic, singular cultural and political experience against the doubled cultural and political experience ascribed to the Scots, Austen's representations of that world and its language ultimately offer no such hope.

Although issues of gender have informed the analyses of each chapter, those issues are most clearly foregrounded in this epilogue. Heretofore, discussion has focused on male writers. In the Scottish context it is fair to say that those figures publicly negotiating and shaping Anglo-British linguistic identities were men. We now know that women were prominent writers of Scots Gaelic poetry in the eighteenth century.[4] In Edinburgh women did attend separate lectures in English elocution, as we noted in Chapter 4, and women would comprise a significant segment of the readers of English grammars on both sides of the border. Yet the public sphere in which newly acquired linguistic habits would be exercised was a male homosocial domain, as was the publishing sphere of the antiquaries promoting Celtomania. Women, as we have also noted, were at times invoked as the source of truly polite language, yet it is interesting to observe that while women did, of course, publish, particularly novels, throughout the eighteenth century, more often than not when a feminine linguistic propriety was demonstrated in a novel's pages, it was through a narrative transvestitism.[5] In Samuel Richardson, for instance, the moral and linguistic authority of his female protagonists are ventriloquized through a male author. Alternatively, Charlotte Lennox's best-selling *Female Quixote* authorizes an appropriate language and representational system for its female heroine through the instruction of a Dr. Johnson-like figure. By Jane Austen's era, however, domestic space had become a naturalized domain of a female authority underwriting major shifts in middle-class ascendance within a reconceived British nation.[6] To reveal Austen's reification of the "natural" English language of that space is to understand the estrangement at the heart of British linguistic nationalism central to these new configurations. If her works represent a culmination of the feminization of culture integral to a rising cultural nationalism, we shall also see that gender plays a decisive role in both building and eroding the language – class–nation nexus.

Discussions of Austen's novels frequently begin and end with their language, for in the novels "proper" English is a device for assessing character; worthy characters display their command over befitting language (and disreputable characters, such as John Thorpe, Lucy Steele, Lydia Bennet, and Augusta Elton, use improper language all the more reprehensible for their unconsciousness of its transgressions), and narrators and characters alike puzzle over and evaluate language in post-mortem appraisals of casual conversations and minute analyses of letters.[7] The content of Willoughby's rejection letter to Marianne is, for instance, no more outrageous to Elinor than that "such language could be suffered to announce it."[8] He is, in turn, slightly redeemed when he reveals that the letter was written in "my wife's style. . . . [T]he original was all her own" (315). The question of style is the key criterion of judgment, but Austen is finally ambivalent on the notion of a "true English style." On the one hand, she represents understatement and laconicism as that true style, as we shall consider directly. She also renders that "safety zone" of national feeling beyond language unavailable, inherently estranged from itself. In *Emma*, a rare moment of oral representation (signified in the contraction "d'ye") conveys a humble and unselfconscious Englishness. The greetings of the two Knightley brothers are described: " 'How d'ye do, George?' and 'John, how are you?' succeeded in the true English style, burying under a calmness that seemed all but indifference, the real attachment which would have led either of them, if requisite, to do every thing for the good of the other" (90). *Emma* contains frequent references to a quietly proud Englishness that reveals itself in modest, "common" language, and it is not surprising to find in this novel, written during the Napoleonic wars, comparisons of this Englishness to an inferior French national character expressed through showy adherence to linguistic rules. Knightley dismisses Frank Churchill in saying, "No, Emma, your amiable young man can be amiable only in French, not in English. He may be very 'aimable,' have very good manners, and be very agreeable; but he can have no English delicacy towards the feelings of other people: nothing really amiable about him" (134–5). The transposition of one letter, from "amiable" to "aimable," linguistically marks profound national difference, contrasting the outward show of a skin-deep and Frenchified geniality (Knightley translates a French "amiability" into the equivalent of an ill-mannered English "aimability") to English feeling so deep as to be beyond obvious articulation (a diametrically opposed English meaning of "amiability").[9] Consider also Elinor Dashwood's recognizably "English" suppression of expression when her sister's recovery "led to no outward demonstrations of joy, no words, no smiles. All within

Elinor's breast was satisfaction, silent and strong" (275). Polite English is subdued, decorous to the point of not sharing but screening feeling. Alternatively, the most verbose outpourings of national pride come from the mouths of odious characters, such as Augusta Elton, who speaks in endless and therefore empty superlatives about "the best fruit of England" (324) and about her region as the best of England, the "garden of England" (245). And so, while the vulgarisms and improprieties of peripheral dialects provide the humor in *Humphry Clinker*, it is Augusta's husband's "parade of speeches" that "incline [Emma] to laugh" (75). The "female" grammatical blunders of Win and Tabitha repulse, but in Austen it is "the fine flourishing letter" (134) of a Frank Churchill which "disgusts" Knightley.

We have already remarked on Adam Smith's and Hugh Blair's endorsement of a language that departs from the ostentatiousness of "courtly pomp." Like Smith and Blair, Austen's upstanding characters speak and laud a plainness they believe to be peculiar to the English. Think, for instance, of the worthiness of Robert Martin's plain letters as opposed to Elton's hyperbolic style in *Emma*. If proper English reflects linguistic principles, the most important of those is the concealment of any overt rules in favor of a seemingly humble, open, and "self-revealing" style. Contrast Lady Catherine's, or most egregious of all, Mr. Collins's overly formal language to autodidact Elizabeth Bennet's language.[10] If theirs is a language of external rules of etiquette, hers is one of well-spoken fellow-feeling, drawing on those psycho-perceptual sentiments discussed in Chapter 4. More unambiguously admirable, Knightley speaks "in plain, unaffected, gentlemanlike English" (407), which registers a deeply interiorized sense of rightness in its hearers. Its alternative, spoken by Augusta Elton, "hurts the ear." Renowned for depicting the flawless English of the estimable inhabitants of those at-times claustrophobic English private spaces, Austen's novels suggest that for those English men and women proper usage comes "naturally." Tom Nairn, who has commented on a characteristically British distaste of principles, describes the quasi-physical reverberations of the spoken English word's impact on its British hearers: "speech is the nerve of 'class'; 'class' is the nerve of the 'Unwritten constitution' where power is wielded through majestically descended 'conventions,' and the complex of these customs compose a traditional moral identity which is the framework of British nationalism."[11] Not based on external principles, proper language comes from the "heart" and subtly registers social identity and stratification on the body.

As it privileges individual style, however, the "plain" language that seems to emphasize personal delivery over external laws has a double-edged relationship to class, for "style" both confirms, while leaving room for talented individuals to negotiate, class ranks. Blair, it will be recalled, stressed a linguistic practice that would allow the revelation of the "private" person through individual style. The patrician Mr. Knightley attests the probity of this belief when he recognizes, "One man's style must not be the rule of another's" (*Emma*, 404). Although Knightley is upper gentry, his sanctification of individual style speaks not to the concerns of an aristocracy bent on protecting their authority but to the interests of a middle class hoping both to reaffirm generally while overcoming personally the fixed strata of linguistic difference.[12] Observable throughout the late seventeenth and eighteenth centuries, the transformation in defining polite language, from stately eloquence to a refinement that stresses not flourish but sincerity, is linked to the emergence of a middle class appreciation of style.[13] Fredric Jameson has historicized the concept of style, arguing that:

> What we call style is a relatively recent phenomenon and comes into being along with the middle-class world itself. It may be thought of as a consequence of the abandonment of that classical system of education which was built around Latin and Greek texts; for style is essentially that which in modern middle-class culture replaces the rhetoric of the classical period.[14]

The shift from an aristocratic classical rhetorical tradition to a middle-class "stylistics" was also a shift from ancient languages to a newly valued written and spoken national vernacular, open to individuals with the wherewithal to learn to use this language effectively. This would include women, who had been for the most part shut out of training in classical languages. The flexibility of elite status put many in the position we have analyzed in the case of the middle-class Scots; while money alone could not confirm elite standing, many attempted to prove their insider status not through non-negotiable blood lineage, which they could not claim, but through decorous manners, particularly fine linguistic practice, all the more compelling for being a reflection of the individual's inherent value. Convinced of the political repercussions of Austen's transformed language, Armstrong writes, "It is a curious twist of cultural history that such a language as hers would help to create a standard for polite English that would be shared by the newly empowered groups who read novels. Only this specialized language, it appears, could set their particular kind of literacy apart from those above and below them on the social ladders, and at the same time identify the particular interests of this class of people with those of the entire society" (*Desire*, 136). In their conversations, morally upstanding and right-judging characters demonstrate their ability to use proper language alongside their ability to exercise critical judgment in perceiving and expressing minute distinctions.

Mastery of a "plain" style that could reveal individual worth offered the means of advancement in a world of shifting class configurations, yet that language and the feminine private sphere to which it was linked also offered stability in the face of such social transformations. When a rising commercial and industrial capitalism revealed the Manichean struggles between classes that agrarian feudalism had held in check, or at least obscured, in its emphasis on patronage and paternalism, a renewed and redefined domestic space came to be seen as the last preserve of a shared culture of affect.[15] If some of Austen's critics have effectively conflated the experience of one class with those of the whole nation, they have done so in part by drawing from a set of representations of women and domestic experiences, and, significantly, the language of that private sphere.[16] As Austen continues to be inscribed within ideologies of English nationalism, that inscription has taken place specifically through the concrete texture of her representations of heart and hearth.[17]

Language is at the center of this transformation-cum-preservation. While the force of the realignments of the agrarian gentry and the mercantile class was subtly transforming the social map of Britain, language could offer national continuity across time and space, providing one of the key defining marks of gentility in a relatively open elite. Unlike the elevated writerly language of classically educated men and male-identified women raised with no regard to "feeling," the "preferred" style of Austen's characters comes from "female gossip and conversation."[18] In her use of the common language of the "private" sphere, Austen is especially effective at, as one critic has put it, reconciling particular and general. This, as we have seen, was a problem for Johnson in compiling his *Dictionary*. Myra Stokes, in her study of that language, writes, "*particularity* was . . . a word to raise a shudder . . . used 'in a sense of contempt' [Johnson's *Dictionary*, 1755, sv adj. 6] of conduct that singled out an individual and drew the wrong kind of attention to itself, which was 'peculiar so as to excite surprise and wonder' [*OED* adj. 7c]."[19] The particular language represented as general in the *Dictionary* was, in some senses, the language of nobody. Austen's fictional technique offers a more compelling construction of the particular as general, for the fictional characters who speak it are those "nobodies in particular" Gallagher describes as the locus upon which readers develop a modular sympathy transferable to multiple and shifting affiliations. Austen's revaluation of the particular makes it convincingly resonant of "general" meaning, an achievement based largely on her use of language. Of Austen's language Norman Page writes, "How is this sense of the far-reaching importance of the local and the ephemeral conveyed? Largely . . . by stylistic means: it is Jane Austen's finely controlled use of language which brings to the reader's attention the true import of episodes and conversations apparently slight in themselves" (*Language*, 9). Austen's "finely controlled use of language," then, is capable of making the emphatically local concerns of small talk at the breakfast table, for instance, of "far-reaching importance." Miss Bingley's petty and disparaging remarks regarding Elizabeth's three-mile walk to see her ailing sister, "to walk three miles, or four miles, or five miles, or whatever it is, above her ancles in dirt, and alone, quite alone . . . seems to me to shew an abominable sort of conceited independence" (82), show instead a new model of respectable womanhood. Austen endows the ephemeral with significance beyond its own particular space and time, and it is that perceived ability – to make the shreds and patches of everyday life speak to a larger national experience, to transcend spatial and temporal dimensions through a particular shared language – that is the basis of nationalist ideology. In nationalist myth, the local reflects and attests the interests and language of a general, national community across space and time. In rendering the detail "general," the language of her novels seems to cease to speak for a particular class and instead speaks for and in a narrative of common, cross-class national experience. Austen, as a novelist of the private, elite-yet-common life of the nation, represents a crucial moment in English linguistic nationalism, capable as she was at weaving the potentially counter-nationalist constructs of class and gender into a coherent national linguistic culture.

Austen's novels, however, do not escape the reification of language that the incongruity between informality and precision, between particular and general would suggest, and that reification places these emblems of English literary nationalism closer to the Scottish writings we have examined than we might initially suspect. Because of the social weight riding on "private" language and conversation – even the most commonplace exchanges yield subtle discriminations – , a sort of alienation emerges. The ostensibly casual conceals a rigorous exactitude, as language bears the weight of displaying the sensibility that makes one worthy (or not) of elite status. As I discuss how and why this is the case, I ant to reconsider the relationship between language, the feminization of culture, and the reconfiguration of social power so forcefully described by Armstrong. While Armstrong's case for the relocation of power in a feminized culture of polite (linguistic) manners is convincingly put, the room it leaves for the potential disruptions caused by that rhetoric's internal contradictions, let alone resistance to it, is slender to null. Other writers, such as Deidre Lynch, Maaja Stewart, and Susan Fraiman, problematize the claims made around the domestic scene, locating the domestic within particular histories – and within larger global frames.[20] In doing so, they reveal the discontinuities at work in Austen's representation of what might be misread as a homogeneous space of domestic life. If we apply their critique – and the ways in which it helps us to see how Austen's writing actually makes the familiar strange – to her language, we will begin to see that while a "doubledness" is evident in peripheral writers, a doubledness of a different sort is also at home in the center.

Sensitive to the "exilic marginality" of writers such as Conrad and observant of the "double view of imperialism" to which this marginality leads, Edward Said, Fraiman argues, has a blind spot when it comes to perceiving the equally doubled position of the bourgeois woman. Austen, Fraiman writes, "was arguably a kind of exile in her own country," revealing the doubled relationship the bourgeois woman might have to the national expansionist project and its appropriation of the domestic. Like the Scot, both inside and yet also outside the relationships of economic and political power, women too had "to excel still further" (Mugglestone, *Talking*, 164) in gentle manners, including language use. Some might dispute the extent to which Austen and her women characters could be said to be "exiled" from the benefits of colonialism. If her position as a "bourgeois woman" alone leaves us unconvinced of her "doubled" status, we might be additionally persuaded by a similar doubledness in her position as a bourgeois woman writer. The title of Mary Poovey's important work *The Proper Lady and the Woman Writer* gets at the mutually exclusive positions of the two, even when the woman's writing modeled proper behavior and language. As mothers instructing children and as wives displaying through their linguistic purity their sexual virtue, women were ostensibly the guardians of the proper language upon which a family's social status stock might rise.[21] And yet their public display of this proper language in writing continued to be viewed as illegitimate. If, as Armstrong suggests, Austen (neither mother nor wife) was central in establishing the new terms of polite, female-directed discourse, the legacy of the taint of scandal associated with a woman in the public position of writer – even when she wrote to promote all that was proper – could not be wholly left behind. As transmitters and sites of legitimate language use, women were at the same time alienated from it. If, as feminist historians have argued, women became virtual "unpersons" after marriage and compensated for this status through increased "attention to other aspects of social identity" (Poovey, *Proper*, 201), language was one of the most important of those "aspects." Once again, as in the case of the Scots in the center of print production, or the curious and improbable figure of the entirely disinterested language user, this formulation poses a dilemma. The most proper of languages, that of polite women, again turns out to be the language of nobody, a propertyless "unperson".

Much excellent feminist scholarship has attended to the doubled position of the bourgeois woman and the woman writer, but my argument is that the significance of this doubledness, the estrangement of the language of the woman in the center of the home, has implications beyond gender relationships. This is precisely because it is on a feminized language that the particular-as-general national identity is sited. The very act of writing the particular as general is informed by an initial and originary estrangement. Austen's fiction, in this sense, is representative of this dilemma, and we shall first explore this position through the paradox of the need to learn a "natural" language, before discussing her unique reflections on and exposure of this position. Like the Scottish Enlightenment thinkers we have discussed, Austen was highly aware of the ways in which "proper" English bears the double burden of building sympathetic community "naturally" while also being learned. As much as Austen's novels seem to favor heartfelt speech over pompous, rules-driven grammar, the sense that this language needed to be assimilated by some characters, that grammatical gaffes had to be rooted out, was never far away. While remaking language, Austen did not, could not, dismiss the authority of figures such as Johnson, even in his derogation of specifically "female" abuses of language. Myra Stokes's study of Austen's language reveals the sense of the specifically female character of language misuse that Austen inherits from Johnson. Stokes writes, "Gender distinctions can to some extent be observed to operate within the body of fashionable cant. Such intensifiers as *frightful* and *horrid* Dr Johnson specifically designated as 'women's cant'... in their looser role as mere emphatics they are distinctly more common amongst the female contingent of Jane Austen's fashionable silly or ungenteel" (italics author's, *Language*, 19). Catherine Morland's informal tutor, Henry Tilney, insists, like Johnson, on using words with precision and abandoning those words, such as "nice," for which specificity is no longer available. It is true, as several critics have noted, that there is a less than full sanction for Henry's "ever finding fault with [his sister, Elinor] for some incorrectness of language."[22] The peril of Elinor and Catherine's being "overpowered with Johnson and Blair" (96) by Henry on the long journey to Northanger Abbey lends little approval to his endeavors to improve their language. Yet a Johnsonian regard of language and "female" barbarisms such as Henry exhibits is internalized in the novels, and surely Elinor's language, the language Henry aims to correct, represents a language in need of such correction. Emma, who for all her faults remains a proper speaker and complains of "the licentiousness of that woman's [Augusta's] tongue" (255), also needs to learn proper regard for the plain style of Robert Martin. If Austen's language draws from a feminized speech, it is a disciplined form of that speech which is promoted, while other female barbarisms are warned against.

The learning displayed in the pages of her books would likely have an impact beyond those pages. There were many readers for whom the act of reading and (partially) comprehending the subtleties of Austen's language would provide the only, and incomplete, means of registering membership in the novels' particular society represented as general.[23] Clearly external to it, the lower gentry and down to servants able to read Austen's novels would be the most salient examples of readers for whom the national linguistic culture was alien, as they needed to learn it from a book. Although Austen's works were not bestsellers, generally selling only one to two thousand copies in six months (in contrast to the 10,000 copies of Scott's *Rob Roy* sold in a fortnight, for example) her novels were favorites on the circulating library circuit, where readership numbers are more difficult to determine.[24] Limited to a largely female readership with the leisure time for novel reading, Austen's readership would have been, nonetheless, wider than the relatively privileged gentry represented in the pages of her books. If, as Roger Sales has argued, Austen's novels' glimpses into fine estates and upper-gentry homes offer a kind of domestic tourism to less privileged readers, they offer a kind of linguistic tourism, showcasing high-end use of the language unfamiliar to many outside the pages of her books – and belittling "substandard" usage, a usage perhaps more familiar to some of her readers, in linking it to *outré* characters.[25] Making this language available to such readers was not the same as making it their own, however, and it is in this educative role – the necessity of making the national/natural known – that this literature exposes the alien quality of what are claimed as "national" linguistic traditions.

Moreover, the polite language of Austen's novels was not "common" to anyone. Austen's representation of "proper" language was also for her, as it was for Johnson, an attempt to reconstruct linguistic practices. Like Johnson's, hers is a rewriting of language that suggests an uncomfortable transformation of the very precedent it claims to follow. The spoken language of Austen's characters far surpassed the speech of even the most genteel subjects. Stokes observes that the language castigated in Austen's novels – the "horrids" and the "frightfuls," the solecisms, and grammatical errors of the discreditable characters, for instance, "would, in fact have been not at all abnormal in the speech of perfectly genteel and well-educated speakers, if their letters are anything to go by – even ungrammatical *don't* and *was*" (*Language*, 21). Reading these novels would be a linguistic education not only for those readers borrowing Austen's novels from the circulating library but even for those reading her novels at court.[26] Who, from any class, for instance, could hope for the composure and linguistic mastery necessary to compose the parallelisms, qualifying clauses, and antitheses that Elizabeth manages in the heat of her shocked response to Darcy's declaration of love?

> You dare not, you cannot deny that you have been the principal, if not the only means of dividing them [Jane Bennet and Mr. Bingsley] from each other, of exposing one to the censure of the world for caprice and instability, the other to its derision for disappointed hopes, and involving them both in misery of the acutest kind. (222)

It is this refined articulateness and her accusation of Darcy's lack of it, his failure to speak in a "gentleman-like manner" (224), that confirm Darcy's sense of Elizabeth's worth. While many might consequently aim for a similar linguistic control, it is clear that such language is not the common speech of anyone, and the consciousness of imitation in anyone who attempted to make it their common speech would be difficult to erase.

Like Johnson's *Dictionary*, Austen's works, in which linguistic propriety features so constantly, are also documents of the impossibility of word-world correspondence and of the common language that might collectively articulate such correspondence. Austen's language and its users were far from occupying the "golden age of cultural homogeneity" that writers such as Q. D. Leavis had imagined, an age when, as Leavis mourns, writers like Austen could "use quite simply . . . phrases like 'honour' [and] 'manly virtue' [and] . . .be sure of being understood."[27] If Austen is representative of a doubled relationship to "natural" language, she is distinctive in her canny display of the ways one could consequently *not* be sure of being understood. A close examination of any one of a number of seemingly "simple" terms suggests that Austen uses them in ways which highlight a multiplicity of meaning.[28] Is "fluency," for instance, a sign of character or a character flaw? Henry Tilney, "talked with fluency and spirit," and his witty dissection of the pro forma social exchanges at Bath certainly endears him to the skeptical reader, his sincerity a welcome breath of relief from the stuffy pomp of the ball. Yet that "fluency" is also behind his ungracious commentaries on the misusage of Catherine's or his sister's speech. Further, fluency is precisely what Knightley loses in moments of deepest-felt sentiments and what escapes Elizabeth Bennet and Elinor Dashwood as they bump into a recognition of deeper truth. Consider too the way in which the familiar term "happiness" is made strange in *Sense and Sensibility*. If we think we have some fixed idea of what the word "happiness" means, myriad contingencies thicken the term in this novel, making it virtually opaque. Is it something one earns through their "sufferings . . . and . . . constancy" (323), as Elinor seems to think Colonel Brandon does? Or is it something that forces beyond one's control predetermine, as in Elinor's explanation of the injury to Willoughby's happiness derived from "too early an independence" (319) bestowed upon him by his guardians? Or is it simply a matter of one's own wise or foolish choices, as Elinor suggests moments later when she blames Willoughby's choice of a wife for his "unhappiness" (320)? It might be some combination of external forces and one's choices, as in Marianne's "unhappy prepossession" for Willoughby, a prepossession, which, had he acted differently, might have been a happy one. Can one experience true happiness if one remains ignorant of certain facts? Elinor dreads telling Marianne of the enduring love Willoughby has confessed for her, for fear that Marianne, upon hearing this news, could never "be happy with another" (323), yet without that knowledge, any happiness Marianne experienced would be, presumably, illusory. While happiness is undoubtedly what everyone wants for their loved ones, Marianne's "unhappiness" (322) renders her "dearer" to her mother. And yet Mrs. Dashwood's "greatest happiness would lie in promoting

[Marianne and Brandon's] marriage" (326). This then leads to reflections on the notion of a parent's happiness; is it to see one's child enter into an economically sound, if relatively passionless marriage? Can Mrs. Dashwood feel the unmitigated happiness she claims in settling her daughter in this way, still knowing that Marianne's heart has been so severely broken? At the very least, as in Johnson's list of sixty-six definitions for the word "to stand," "happiness" is alienated from a stock familiarity. To be sure, Austen heaps shade upon shade of meaning here, but at what point does this linguistic density not only offer nuances of meaning but begin to occlude it?

If we pursue the aforementioned figure of Austen as "exile" for just a moment, we find a possible point of unexpected resonance between Austen's defamiliarizing use of language and Theodor Adorno's own calls for an alienation of "native" language as he warns that "the returning exile must combine his love for the language with an untiring vigilance regarding all the swindle it promotes."[29] As one writer has put it, "Adorno advocates a distance toward so-called 'natural' ways of speaking and feeling," and in doing so he critiques the naturalization of 'home,' and 'heart-felt nationalism'."[30] While Adorno makes the case for introducing strange words into discourse to achieve *Verfremdung*, my point is that we might read Austen as achieving a similar alienation effect. She does this on a number of levels; perhaps the most compelling and immediate instances that come to mind are literal materializations of language in *Emma*, such as the minute analysis of Frank Churchill's handwriting or more dramatically the children's' "box of letters" with their alphabet contents "scattered over a table" (313). *Emma* also illuminates the doubledness of language in word games that demand the addition of meaning to otherwise arbitrary letters, as in "M A" for Emma (336), in charades that insist on recognizing the doubled meaning of a pun, as in Elton's combination of "court" and "ship," and in statements that reduce linguistic signs to sheer arbitrariness, as in Emma's reference to herself and Knightley as N and M after the *Book of Common Prayer*, where the letters stand for the names of those to be married (420).[31]

It should go without saying, but I do want to make clear here, that I am not arguing that Austen consciously deployed strategies of alienation effect to the same ends more than a century before German Marxists promoted those strategies. What I am saying, however, is that her use of language does make the familiar strange and that this defamiliarization is all the more significant given that, to a much greater extent than her predecessors, she foregrounds interiority, private feeling, and domestic depths of sentiment in her novels. Whether through the endowment of language with a talismanic status, as in Darcy's memorization of the exact language of Elizabeth's criticism, or in the abstraction of language in Knightley's translation of every phrase of Frank Churchill's letter, language is much more than the sum of its parts, more than mere means to the end of straightforward communication. Austen's novels reveal what is, in fact, a truism of all linguistic interaction: none, and least of all those languages that claim to be homely, domestic, familiar, can escape the foreignness at their heart. As George Steiner writes, "Any model of communication is at the same time a model of translation, of a vertical or horizontal transfer of significance. No two historical epochs, no two social classes, no two localities use words and syntax to signify exactly the same things, to send identical signals of valuation and inference" (*After*, 47). If translation between two national languages openly advertises the estrangement involved in its meaning making, Austen's novels expose the strangeness of the most familiar and private linguistic exchanges as they unpack the layers of meaning embedded within them.[32]

What makes Austen's use of language particularly uncanny, *unheimlich*, and unhomely, is the way it crosses back and forth between unfamiliar and familiar. While the syntax of some of her characters is notable precisely for its innovation, Austen still, for the most part, "uses ordinary correct English."[33] The narrative voice frequently assumes a "what we all know" familiarity, but frequently presents such "common knowledge" in an alienating syntactical frame. This linguistic alienation is all the more strange given that it is often the familiar language of a heroine's intimate thoughts. Consider Emma, thinking to herself about what she (wrongly) perceives to be Mr. Elton's "passion" for Harriet: "Mr. Knightley saw no such passion, and of course thought nothing of its effects; but she saw too much of it, to feel a doubt of its overcoming any hesitations that a reasonable prudence might originally suggest; and more than a reasonable, becoming degree of prudence, she was very sure did not belong to Mr. Elton" (61). This is a rather tortuous construction to convey what one might more likely think of as "passion knows no bounds, especially in the imprudent"; ironically, it is an overly analytical phrasing of the idea that passion can overcome reasonably prudent expression.

While Armstrong is right to point out that, "the preferred style for writing has its source in common English," the conclusion she draws is tendentious. Does Austen's language truly "derive its value from its capacity to communicate the author's feelings without inflating or concealing them" (*Desire*, 149)? I would argue, to the contrary, that although the language gives the appearance of openness through the use of common terms, it is invariably clouded over by contingency and difference. Thus, two oppositional statements can both seem true. Elinor's common sensible reasoning and plain language in ascribing blame for Willoughby's behavior to – "too early an independence and its consequent habits of idleness, dissipation, and luxury" (319) – is countered by her own equally uninflated and rational assessment – "the whole of his behaviour . . . from the beginning to the end of the affair, has been grounded on selfishness" (338) – yet both seem possible.

I have already pointed to the peculiar nature of a proper language of power as it is entrusted to and modified by the exilic figure of the bourgeois woman for whom that language is one of the key sources of power. I have also argued that the novels' work as instruction – making the unfamiliar familiar to a body of readers – denaturalizes proper language. In addition, I have been demonstrating that the use of language in the novels, the linguistic density, the common diction in uncommon syntax, makes alienation inescapable on a formal level. This defamiliarization of language is probably most notable in her use of irony. Even if the users of language know better, there is a tacit understanding that particular words name particular shared ideas; it is this understanding – however much it demands a suspension of disbelief – which allows some belief in communication to exist. We have seen how an exaggerated version of such linguistic transparency underlies the possibility of translation within imperial contexts. Yet irony is the opposite of the transparency of imperial grammar; irony depends upon disrupting one-to-one correspondence between word and thing in order to make an alternative meaning, for it is, at its most basic moment, saying one thing and meaning another. If a reader thinks she knows what a "faultless" "style of letter writing" means, her understanding of Henry's use of those words must shift by the end of his sentence explaining that writing might be considered "faultless" even when three damning qualities are in evidence: "a general deficiency of subject, a total inattention to stops, and a very frequent ignorance of grammar" (15). In the specific context of Henry's represented speech act, full comprehension depends upon an ironic inversion of meaning. Similarly, if a reader can think of a word or words to name the situation of Robert and Lucy Ferrars and Fanny and John Dashwood, in which "jealousies and ill-will continually subsist between Fanny and Lucy, in which their husbands of course took a part, as well as the frequent domestic disagreements between Robert and Lucy themselves," (364) the narrator's word for it, "harmony," ironically alters the usual expectations of that term.

Through techniques many critics have analyzed, Austen's narrators and the methods of narration convey much of the duplicity of meaning, her innovative narrative modes emphasizing the yawning breach between word and world, and the meaning to be found in that gap. In the opening pages of *Sense and Sensibility*, for instance, the narrator refers to Robert Ferrars as "promising" (15). It is only much later in the book that Robert is introduced, his full boorishness depicted, and the high irony of that choice of language revealed. The "decent philosophy" (321) with which the neighborhood takes up the news of Lydia's poor marriage is more immediately ironic, as is the accusation of "insensibility" and "hardheartedness" (256) at Elizabeth's and Jane's failure to mourn the departure of the regiment from their neighborhood. In simple language Austen inhabits and overturns the quotidian verbal form of the maxim in her heavily ironic and well-known opening sentence to *Pride and Prejudice*: "It is a truth universally acknowledged, that a single man in possession of a good fortune, must be in want of a wife . . . this truth is so well fixed . . . that he is considered as the rightful property of some one or other of their daughters" (51). Such an anomalous construction – a "universal truth" which is obviously not universal – forces the reader to recognize the inversion of meaning in the narrator's use of "truth" and "universally" and perhaps even to reflect on the truth claims of all maxims. Simple language and an understated irony contribute to the strangeness that gets stranger on the second reading the sentence demands. A particular readership – those able to appreciate the humor of this irony – is assembled in such constructions. That particular group, in turn, recognizes an alternative "universal" truth about marriage markets and the powers of self interest to delude interlocutors.

This is a meaning making through alienation of word and world, as are the ironic depictions of reprehensible characters. Saying one thing and revealing another is the means through which the less-than-worthy characters of Austen's novels often unwittingly reveal themselves. Augusta Elton's virtual stream of consciousness monologues disclose the emptiness – and unintended fullness – of her language:

Maple Grove – cultivation – beds when to be renewed – gardeners thinking exactly different – no general rule – gardeners never to be put out of their way – delicious fruit – only too rich to be eaten much of – inferior to cherries –

currants more refreshing – only objection to gathering strawberries the stooping – glaring sun – tired to death. (324)

Augusta's language conveys meaning not through a transparency between word and thing but through contradictions and the gaps between words. Her expressed joy at harvesting England's bountiful garden dwindles into exhaustion, and the end of the monologue undoes its beginning as the narrator represents it. Alternatively, saying one thing and concealing another is one condition of polite conversation itself, as evidenced especially in Elinor Dashwood's diplomatic verbal responses to awkward social situations. As Lucy Steele boasts of Edward's desire for her picture, Elinor exercises an excruciating scrupulousness in answering simply, "You are quite right," (126) suppressing much of the sentiment we know her to feel. When her sister abruptly leaves the room on Lucy Steele's arrival, Elinor politely offers, "My sister will be equally sorry to miss the pleasure of seeing you" (210) – far from the truth of things, as the reader knows. Both cases instantiate the failure of language if not to signify, then to signify in any remotely straightforward way. As many critics have pointed out, it is upon the inevitable misfirings of communication which so many of Austen's plots turn, but it is especially important for our purposes to note that polite conversation, far from being an open exchange of one's innermost sentiments, is more often a concealing of them.

Mannered dialogue requires one to hold one's tongue, but Austen imparts characters' secret (impolite) thoughts through representing internal monologues. Sharp and witty, such remarks continuously force a consciousness of the doubled character of much social linguistic interaction. For instance, responding to a vulgar comment by Harriet, "Emma felt the bad taste of her friend, but let it pass with a 'very true . . . '" (48). When told of Mrs. Martin's opportunistic promotion of her son's merits to Harriet, Emma thinks to herself, " 'Well done, Mrs. Martin! . . .You know what you are about'" (24). Characters themselves also double meaning in wry diction in open dialogue as well, as when Knightley ironically refers to Emma's "genius for foretelling and guessing" (33). When Emma tells an imploring Harriet that regarding Robert Martin's marriage proposal, "I shall not give you any advice . . . I will have nothing to do with it. This is a point which you must settle with your own feelings" (46), we well know that the opposite is true, given what the narrator has already told us – and the advice Emma herself offers a few lines later.

We might, if we re-invoke Fraiman's notion of exile, link Austen's use of irony and other linguistic strategies to the awkwardly doubled position to which Austen and other contemporary women writers attempted to respond.[34] Sharing with Johnson and the Augustans a sense of the imperative to correct and teach the "proper" language, Austen, however, in her position as a woman and as a writer depicting a private interiority of female characters, resists rather than repeats the language of her "forefathers." Like other critics I harbor a skepticism of the claims made of Austen's unambiguous homage to Augustan authorities such as Johnson and am especially interested in the terms upon which she has been enlisted in that lineage of national literary tradition. As Page describes it, her linguistic project is difficult to distinguish from Johnson's, for "Austen's greatness lay in exploiting the distinctive strengths of the English language as she found it, and in resisting some of the influences which were at work to change it even as she wrote."[35] If Austen was creating a new language of power, one might argue that she legitimated this language by announcing her familiarity with the linguistic traditions and conventions of previous generations. Yet such an announcement also indicates the performative quality of Austen's use of language; she was, no doubt, like all women who dared to write in this period, aware of how her language would be read with and against the language of her canonized male predecessors. And here again, this sense that she and other women writers must prove themselves through a display of mastery over the language approximates the position of writers such as Blair, gratified, one suspects, by the praise of such authoritative writers as Johnson.[36]

When we consider the images through which her relationship to the "bard" and the "Great cham" have been figured, we see an analogy between Austen's position and that of the "marginal" writers we have considered, inasmuch as she is described as a talented imitator of a dominant world view and its language. Descriptions of Austen such as C. S. Lewis's: that she was the "daughter of Samuel Johnson" and she "inherits his common sense, his morality, even his style" and that Johnson provided her mind's "hard core" embarrassingly and predictably position Austen as the soft woman to the hard man, the child to the adult.[37] Other figurations are less jejune and still more revealing. Mary Lascelles introduces the figure and relations of pedagogy, accounting for Austen's linguistic achievements as a result of her having "trained herself in Johnson's school." Consider also A. C. Bradley's description of Jane Austen's writing as a kind of ventriloquy of Samuel Johnson. He writes, "When she speaks her mind fully and gravely she speaks for Johnson too." Similarly, figuring their relationship as one of convincing mimicry, Lewis writes "the language of the two writers, the terminology they use, is sometimes so close that one can hardly distinguish one from another."

As we have already seen, Johnson's own authority in matters of linguistic stability was vexed, and he acknowledged his own, and anyone's, inability to fix the language. Critics invested in his cultural authority, however, established him as the founding father of grave sentiments expressed through proper English. Equally interesting are Austen's negotiations of this Augustan legacy as well as the terms upon which later critics attempted to insert her into it. As we have emphasized, the relations of pedagogy, the performative acts it requires, and the self-division and maneuver available in its seeming repetitions are not always controllable. Austen's female "dummy" to Johnson's male ventriloquist does not suggest an openly confrontational role. And yet, the voice, the persona, and the message all change in the act of ventriloquy. Austen's writing is especially jarring in its movement between an eighteenth-century poetics which borrowed heavily from its masters such as Johnson and "common" language, particularly a plain diction. In his study of Austen's language, for example, Page argues that Austen's writings resemble the upper limits of an Augustan rhetorical tradition, as she makes use of dazzling zeugma, parallelisms, and antitheses, but that she also uses what R. W. Chapman had described as Johnson's "language everyone now writes." In the use of zeugma such as, "she meditated, by turns, on broken promises and broken arches," however, or in the strangely apt yoking together of unlike terms, as in "Tilney's and trap-doors" (*Northanger Abbey*, 74), Austen deploys traditional rhetorical forms in unconventional yet strikingly efficient ways. In his reflections on Samuel Johnson's influence on Austen, Knud Sorensen has assembled a number of examples of Austen's use of Johnson's favored syntactical constructions only to turn them on their head. For instance, Austen borrows his "peculiar way of varying his adverbs, as in: 'calamities sometimes to be sought, and always endured' (*Rambler*, IV, 178)" (396). Yet consider the humorous result of her borrowing; she describes Catherine Morland: "for she was often inattentive, and occasionally stupid" (396). Sorensen also points out that while Johnson's formal parallelisms offer "rough semantic conformity between the members," Austen's similar parallelisms have a purposeful lack of such conformity, as in her description of "parties of ladies . . . in quest of pastry, millinery, even . . . of young men" (*Northanger Abbey*). Sorensen calls Austen's appropriative use of

Johnson's syntax "Johnsonese with a difference" and it is that difference that I want to stress.[38]

Consider Austen's use of "flirtation" as the narrator describes Emma's thoughts on her public repartee with Frank Churchill:

Emma, glad to be enlivened . . . gave him all the friendly encouragement, the admission to be gallant, which she had ever given in the first . . . period of their acquaintance; but which now, in her own estimation, meant nothing, though in the judgment of most people looking on it must have had such an appearance as no English word but flirtation could very well describe. (332)

We might recall here Johnson's scornful reference to this word as "a cant word" used by women and his refusal to include a direct, contemporary definition of this word and Chesterfield's description of its "birth" out of a woman's mouth. In Emma's reflection of the animated display of teasing exchange between herself and Frank Churchill, she insists that there is only one word for their appearance. Though the word was not wholly incorrect – it was, after all, in the *Dictionary* – Austen claims a legitimacy for it certainly not granted by Johnson. A kind of mimicry, however, the use of "flirtation" oscillates here between rebellion and imitation. If we imagine Austen to be using it confrontationally to Johnson's disapproval, we must note too that it describes an appearance and not the actual thing. Those observing them would name it one thing, but, Emma thinks to herself, they are deceived by appearance. What they name is not the actual thing itself, and there is likely no exact word to describe the appearance of flirtation which is not flirtation at all. In this sense "flirtation" remains an unfixed and suspect term. And yet it is, Emma assures, an act for which no other word will do. In contra-distinction to the *Dictionary*, Emma proclaims its aptness, even as it names an appearance and not the "real" thing.

While the argument has been made that Austen disrupts "patriarchal" ideology in the very act of performing various literary codes, I am interested in examining this estrangement in the realm of language in particular. Claudia Johnson, for instance, has argued that Catherine Morland's seemingly unreasonable fears of Captain Tilney's tyranny are actually borne out in his subsequent behavior towards her. Henry's means of proving the absurdity of Catherine's fears is an appeal to national character: "We are English . . . consult your own understanding . . . your own observation of what is passing around you. Does our education prepare us for such atrocities? Do our laws connive at them? Could they be perpetrated without being known in a country like this, where social and literary intercourse is on such a footing?" (182). When Henry turns out to be wrong, when his father *is* guilty of cruel behavior, is the groundwork of his argument – the critical superiority of the English – also up for dispute?[39] Further, just preceding this lesson is another, on language. Henry corrects Catherine's solecism, "Promised so faithfully! A faithful promise! that puzzles me. I have heard of a faithful performance; but a faithful promise – the fidelity of promising!" (180). Henry's own faith in an English language free of contradiction might be as misguided as his belief in an England in which a high level of "social and literary intercourse" guarantees the absence of tyranny. His emphatic and unseemly exclamations suggest as much – not to mention the fact that the phrase "promised faithfully" can be found in the writing of Henry Fielding himself.[40]

If we have seen how Austen repeats but transforms the language of the Augustans, her narrative techniques stress a similar doubling. Austen's "repetitions," which are not quite the same, trouble notions of imitation and cultural transmission, and they occur in their most interesting form in her use of free indirect discourse, a much discussed narrative mode which I here want to link back to the figure of mimicry.[41] As a representation, in a sense a repetition of a character's inner thoughts, we might imagine free indirect discourse as a kind of mimicry of that character's inner language. The omniscient narrator pretends to a kind of transparent repetition in revealing hidden thoughts of the heroines. Yet the narrator also manipulates the message heavily by alternately deleting and overstating aspects of the character's thoughts – pure repetition is impossible here, just as it is in the act of mimicry. As the narrator "describes" one of Emma's "inner" monologues, for instance, the reader becomes aware of her less than benevolent motives for taking Harriet under her wings:

But in every respect as she saw more of her, she approved her, and was confirmed in all her kind designs.

Harriet certainly was not clever, but she had a sweet, docile, grateful disposition; was totally free from conceit; and only desiring to be guided by any one she looked up to. Her early attachment to herself was very amiable; and her inclination for good company, and power of appreciating what was elegant and clever, shewed that there was no want of taste . . . Altogether she was quite convinced of Harriet Smith's being exactly the young friend she wanted – exactly the something which her home required. (22)

This narrator, witness to the thoughts within the recesses of Emma's mind, resembles nothing so much as Adam Smith's "spectator within the breast." Yet, as is obvious from the revelation of selfish considerations running alongside Emma's belief in her altruism regarding Harriet, this instance of narrative "mimicry," like Smith's impartial spectator, betrays the doubledness and ambivalence endemic to that figure. In repeating the means by which Emma justifies her relationship to Harriet to herself, the narrator reveals to the reader all that is wrong with those justifications; Harriet is the friend Emma "wants," not because she is her equal in "cleverness," but because she is "docile," ready and willing to attach herself to Emma's opinions and advice.

We might note too that this passage, which reveals through a technique of telling narrative "mimicry" sentiments which Emma would not admit and of which she might not even be aware, has as its own subject Harriet's mimicry of Emma, a mimicry which initially delights the eponymous heroine. Emma hopes she will talk through Harriet, that Harriet will adopt her language, manners, values, and powers of discrimination. In free indirect discourse the narrator depicts her declaring, "She would improve her; . . . she would form her opinions and her manners" (20). Emma's efforts to create in Harriet a mimic of herself, and Harriet's earnest yet flawed attempts to imitate the mannerly decorum of Emma, represent a mimicry "which," as Emma puts it, "her home required." It is all the more portentous that when Emma partially succeeds, when Harriet begins to take on what she misperceives Emma's perspective on appropriate matches for Harriet, Harriet transmogrifies into a monster. Like Dr. Frankenstein, Emma, upon hearing Harriet's declared mimicry, "I never should have presumed to think of it at first . . . but for you," bemoans, "Oh God! that I had never seen her!" (373). Harriet's is not the haunting mimicry of the peripheral subject, but a doubledness at the center, in the home in the Home Counties. If Austen's novels can be said to instruct, they also problematize the moment of instruction; the impossibility of instruction, the performance and repetition it requires and the doubledness they entail, are located in the very center of home and of nation.

Emma's ultimate inability to shape the "outsider" Harriet into the insider that she is not certainly bears the conservative, static vision of class many readers have noted.[42] While not declaring it outright, Austen leans towards the impossibility of improvement; ability to make tasteful discriminations and to use English in a way reflective of those abilities, she hints, might be a factor of "nature" and beyond education. Emma herself is properly "instructed" by the novel's end, but Knightley dismisses his role in that process. Like "thousands" of others, Knightley remarks, she will "correct herself" (419) not through anyone's assistance, but because "nature gave [her] understanding: – Miss Taylor gave [her] principles" (419). The likes of Harriet would have neither access to such a worthy governess, nor possess the "nature" of an elite woman like Emma. I have been arguing that much of Austen's work makes the familiar – particularly domestic language – strange, but if her novels ultimately keep class bounds intact, they would merely maintain the familiar, in this case class hierarchy, as familiar. In order to re-affirm my argument, I will not point to other instances in which Austen's novels seem to sanction what was, after all, the characteristic class fluidity between various strata of the gentry and mercantile classes.[43] Instead, I want to insist on the significance of the subtle formal techniques through which Austen's texts question not only the "nativeness" of native language and the naturalness of the heart and home that language would bespeak but also the very possibility of reproducing that language and its consciousness. If even the narrative voice "reflecting" the thoughts of characters refracts those thoughts, betraying a doubled meaning alien even to the awareness of the character's innermost thoughts, what moment of imitation is not a moment of distorting mimicry? While such warping mimicry is recognizable in the context of peripheral subjects, my point here is that it is inescapable – even required, as Emma says – within that most English of country homes, the homophonically suggestive "Hartfield."

The subjective estrangement embedded in Austen's linguistic and narrative structures points towards the difficulty, even impossibility, of reproducing identity through time and space.[44] The abstraction of language necessary to facilitate its spread across generations and classes leaves it open, as it did for Scottish peripheral writers, to transcoding. If language is the medium of English national continuity, Austen throws the limits of that language into high relief. Strong feelings leave Emma's "tongue motionless" (390) and Knightley unable to "make speeches," and, it turns out, "Seldom, very seldom, does complete truth belong to any human disclosure" (391). One might be tempted to say that Austen merely posits a deeply felt national affinity which is beyond language, but her texts are far too verbally rich to leave it at that. If, as we have seen, at points the novels pose a "typically English" realm of deeply felt sentiments beyond language, the narrative technique of free indirect discourse estranges that very interiority. Characters' feelings are revealed to be opaque to themselves – and linguistic alienation invades and overturns even a wordless sentimentality.

The double meaning of irony, overstatement, and contradiction depends upon a community willing and able to read that secondary meaning against the word's basic meaning. In this sense, it depends upon and forms a community of language users through inversion.[45] The novels, then, might be said to form specific, if short-lived and sporadic, reading communities precisely in the gaps that mark the inability to sustain meaning, forming community negatively. These are not "national" communities – they are much more well defined, ephemeral, and limited than that. But they do suggest group identities formed in relation to language and print, a group identity claimed for but impossible to realize in the form of a nation-state.[46] It is then, finally, not only those in power who have the ability to use language as "an instrument of ironic exclusion," as George Steiner has argued (*After*, 33). The model of reading communities formed in the very negation of the possibility of plain sentiment and a plain language resembles those "dystopic" language communities Pratt has described, formed not so much from shared meaning, as from a negative distancing from the "common," "native," and "conventional" language. If this is the case, then Austen functions as a double agent; inside the language of power, affirming and undermining its canons of "proper" literacy. Ultimately, her impact depends on the position of her various readerships. To those whom she is most clearly "instructing," it is not at all clear that their instruction through invitation to imitation works at any level. In fact, as I have been arguing, the texts demonstrate the impossibility of that imitation, emphasizing the alienation incumbent in such efforts.

If Austen criticism has shifted from readings of her as demure conservative ideologue to wily feminist combatant and now ambivalent transcoder, that shift has depended on our own revised understandings of the structure of cultural, national, and linguistic identities. To claim that all identities are inter-dependent and relational is not new. To expose language as perhaps the most unstable of identity sites, the point at which any notion of continuous national identity collapses, however, remains a heretical claim. This understanding of linguistic and cultural identity was one that an unlikely collection of writers, from Alexander MacDonald to Samuel Johnson, from Adam Smith and Hugh Blair to Jane Austen, helped shape, yet their writings have long been put to quite the opposite use. The point is to question such claims, far and near.

Despite the semi-chronological structure of this study, I have tried to trouble the notion of a straightforward and linear movement from one way of understanding language and the significance of its practice to another. Between the universality of imperial grammar and the particularity of national language we find not so much a gulf of time as simultaneous and mutually determining movements. Both influenced each other, both shared assumptions about the intersections of language and identity, and both exhibited an unavoidable ambivalence in regards to those connections. As those two understandings of language and their relationship to culture work in tandem, we stand to gain through reading "central" English writers in relation to their "peripheral" contemporaries. Not the least of those gains is a more complex understanding of the genealogy of claims to national language and the possibility of reading back into the "standard" the dense histories it has rendered opaque.

To recognize that the relationships between two understandings of language and the worlds in which they intervened are intricate and endlessly complex also suggests that the purview of my own project has had to remain partial and fragmentary. One of the main purposes of this work has been to re-situate particular visions of language in particular historical contexts in the hopes of understanding the ways in which material relationships, political formations, and cultural and linguistic theories and practices might be interrelated. In turn, it is my hope that historicizing such relationships will invite further investigations of those matrices in relation to other historical moments, including our own. Thus, in a continuation of this work, one might consider the ways in which the Celtic revival gave way to an understanding of Englishness itself as a special ethnicity, with its own attendant studies of the English language's historical philology. Conversely, early inscriptions of Gaelic within the history of the English language might be traced to the parallel reclamation of colonial languages within the "story of English" so proudly told today. That story has been most fully articulated in the *OED*. James Murray, a Scot who referred to himself as "a nobody," cited numerous Scottish writers copiously. Yet this seems less a case of Samuel Johnson's worst fears coming home to roost than of Smith's and Blair's highest aspirations of assimilation coming true. Alternatively, in the rising Scottish nationalist sentiments reflected and produced in the wake of the vote for a separate parliament, it is important to recall the complexities of cultural identities to which linguistic practices, theories, and representations have pointed historically. Such knowledge should make us particularly wary of claims of a past unified language and people – this ever receding possibility is a construction, in both England

and Scotland, of a national collectivity that never was or could be. If anything, language is the moment at which the inequalities upon which the idea of national identity is based become apparent. While such claims need to be assessed within their own historical moment and global context, part of that contextual moment is what has come before.

Similarly, the social context of eighteenth-century theories of universal grammar is a part of the seemingly remote context of twentieth-century understandings of language, including the idea of transformational grammar. If Chomsky himself invokes the Cartesian linguists, we cannot consider their influence strictly in terms of an abstract history of ideas. An awareness of the historical location of Cartesian linguistics might, in turn, have some bearing on our assessment of the efforts to construct artificial intelligence, or more modestly, on our evaluation of the promotion of translating software now available that promises "transparent translation." While these conceptualizations of language have their own contextual histories, part of those histories remains the legacy of eighteenth-century conversations.

I have set myself the impossible task of trying to talk about both imperial and national pressures on ideas and practices of language in the eighteenth century, which makes a map of further trajectories of this project potentially infinite. If the attempt to discuss these two linguistic theories in relation to both political formations has meant a sacrifice in the depth of research, the gesture is an important one, despite the sacrifice, because it underwrites my most important claim, and the one that, at my most ambitious, I hope will bear some trace in future treatments of the linguistic and cultural formulations of this period. We simply cannot talk about national notions of linguistic identity outside of political and linguistic relationships of empire. Their mutual interdependence is one of the most significant factors in the ambivalencies I have tracked, and their reciprocal development is the means of their ideological undoing. In a world in which languages slip away in the face of a dominant English and in which people continue to die in defense of a separate national – linguistic – identity, that fact remains as pressing as ever.

Notes

INTRODUCTION

1 The phrase is G. Gregory Smith's from *Scottish Literature: Character and Influence* (London: Macmillan, 1919), p. 4. Helpful analyses of this dualism include Ian Duncan, "The Upright Corpse: Hogg, National Literature and the Uncanny," *Studies in Hogg and His World* 5 (1994): 29–54; Susan Manning, *The Puritan Provincial Vision: Scottish and American Literature in the Nineteenth Century* (Cambridge University Press, 1990); Caroline McCracken-Flesher, "English Hegemony and Scots Subjectivity: Calvinism and Cultural Resistance in Nineteenth-Century 'North British' Novels" (Ph.D. Dissertation, 1987); and Karl Miller, *Doubles: Studies in Literary History* (Oxford: Clarendon, 1985).
2 Robert Louis Stevenson, *The Strange Case of Dr. Jekyll and Mr. Hyde* (New York: Bantam, 1978, org. 1886), pp. 88 and 39, respectively.
3 Murray Ritchi and Denis Campbell, "Scotland Decides Yes Yes" *The Herald*, 9 December 1997.
4 See Michael Hechter, *Internal Colonialism: The Celtic Fringe in British National Development* (Berkeley: California University Press, 1975).
5 Leith Davis, *Acts of Union: Scotland and the Literary Negotiation of the British Nation 1707–1830* (Stanford University Press, 1999).
6 This might account for why the initial emphasis on linguistic homogenization was much more pronounced in the Highlands (and Wales and Ireland) than in India – see Gauri Viswanathan, *Masks of Conquest* (New York: Columbia University Press, 1987), or Africa – see Sue Zemka, "The Holy Books of Empire: Translations of the British and Foreign Bible Society," in *Macropolitics of Nineteenth-Century Literature*, eds. Jonathan Arac, Harriet Ritvo (Philadelphia: Pennsylvania University Press, 1991). In yoking together critical texts focusing on the diverse spaces of India, Africa, and Scotland, I do not mean to suggest that the ideologies of literacy, the technologies of translation, and the representations of "other" languages in each of these situations is not particular to their historical context. Yet where I do see isomorphic qualities between them, I shall identify them.
7 In the literature produced in this juncture of linguistic cultures G. Gregory Smith points to the "stress of foreign influence and native division" reflected in a "Caledonian antisyzygy" (4). David Daiches names the split resulting

from imposed bilingualism a "dissociation of sensibility" in *The Paradox of Scottish Culture* (London: Oxford University Press, 1964), while Kenneth Simpson conceptualizes a "projection of self-images" available to multilingual writers but recuperates an essential notion of identity with such phrases as "multiplicity of voice, fragmentation of personality" in *The Protean Scot: The Crisis of Identity in Scottish Literature* (Aberdeen University Press, 1988), p. 2. Essayists in the journal *Scotlands* 1 (1994) and in *Celticism*, ed. Terence Brown (Amsterdam: Rodopi, 1996) make salutary arguments for a new image of Scottish literary culture not simply as a native tradition fractured by foreign influence but as "pluralistic, synthetic ... international" ("Introduction") and acknowledge, "A growing wariness of notions of an essentialist Scotland" (Robert Crawford, "Bakhtin and Scotlands," in *Scotlands*, pp. 66–80), and I write in their spirit.

8 Homi Bhabha's "The Ambivalence of Colonial Discourse," in *OCTOBER: The First Decade, 1976–1986*, ed. Annette Michelson et al. (Cambridge, MA: MIT Press, 1987) is my starting point for this discussion, although this "ambivalence" takes very different shapes in different situations, and part of my project will be finessing those differences by taking into account the historical specificity of each case.

9 See Jurgen Habermas, who sees the power to exercise and publicize such judgments as fundamental to participation in the public sphere in *Structural Transformation of the Public Sphere*, trans. Thomas Burger (Cambridge, MA: MIT Press, 1989).

10 See *The Scottish Invention of English Literature*, ed. Robert Crawford (Cambridge University Press, 1998) and Thomas Miller, *The Formation of College English: Rhetoric and Belles Lettres in the British Cultural Provinces* (Pittsburgh University Press, 1997).

11 See Benedict Anderson, *Imagined Communities* (London: Verso, 1987); Gerald Newman, *The Rise of English Nationalism: A Cultural History, 1740–1830* (New York: St. Martin's, 1987); Linda Colley, *Britons: Forging the Nation 1707–1837* (New Haven: Yale University Press, 1992). These works, however, stop short of fully illustrating the inequities upon which the nation is formed.

12 See Robert Crawford, *Devolving English Literature* (Oxford: Clarendon, 1992); Simon Gikandi, *Maps of Englishness: Writing Identity in the Culture of Colonialism* (New York: Columbia University Press, 1996); Anne McClintock, *Imperial Leather: Race, Gender and Sexuality in the Colonial Contest* (New York: Routledge, 1995); Felicity Nussbaum, *Torrid Zones* (Baltimore: Johns Hopkins University Press, 1995); Katie Trumpener, *Bardic Nationalism: The Romantic Novel and British Empire* (Princeton University Press, 1997); and Kathleen Wilson, *The Sense of the People* (Cambridge University Press, 1996).

13 See Habermas, *Structural*, and Michael Warner, *The Letters of the Republic* (Cambridge, MA: Harvard University Press, 1990). The mutually dependent linguistic relationship corresponds to the relationship between nation and empire. These sociopolitical formations initially worked with each other; the British empire arose because commercial interests were looking to

expand ever increasing markets; the English and then British nation developed as a centralized core for controlling and consolidating those interests. This view is central to my project.

14 Patrick Brantlinger and Richard Boyle have demonstrated the connection between Hyde and nineteenth-century caricatures of the Irish in "The Education of Edward Hyde: Stevenson's 'Gothic Gnome' and the Mass Readership of Late-Victorian England," in *Dr Jekyll and Mr Hyde – After 100 Years*, eds. William Veeder and Gorden Hirsch (Chicago University Press, 1988), pp. 265–82. This would be a good place to note that consideration of the Irish and Welsh, while vital to a full understanding of the internal "grammar of empire" is beyond the scope of this project.

15 See Miller and Luke Gibbons, "The Sympathetic Bond: Ossian, Celticism, and Colonialism" in *Celticism*.

16 Although she is less interested in language *per se*, Leith Davis makes a similar point regarding the representative status of Scotland in *Acts of Union*.

17 Murray Pittock describes Colley's history as an "incremental" or Whig history "in which the metropolis, the center, the imperial state makes sense of its achievements," and argues that Colley is guilty of a "developmental, progress-oriented minimizing of difference," and while his own history might be guilty of overstating the importance of Jacobitism, his emphasis on the gaps in Colley's history – Ireland, Scottish Episcopalianism – are well taken. *Poetry and Jacobite Politics in Eighteenth-Century Britain and Ireland* (Cambridge University Press, 1994), pp. 1–2.

18 Ferdinand de Saussure, *Course in General Linguistics*, trans. Wade Baskin (New York: McGraw-Hill, 1966), p. 9, and V. N. Volosinov, *Marxism and the Philosophy of Language*, trans. Ladislav Matejka and I. R. Titunik (Cambridge, MA: Harvard University Press, 1973), p. 58, respectively.

19 Charles Jones, "Scottish Standard English in the Late Eighteenth Century," *Transactions of the Philological Society* 9 (1993), pp. 95–131. See also his *A Language Suppressed* (Edinburgh: State Mutual Book and Periodical Service, 1996); K. J. Kohler, "A late eighteenth century comparison of the 'Provincial dialect of Scotland' and the 'Pure Dialect,'" *Linguistics* 23 (1966), pp. 30–69; A. J. Aitken, "The Scottish Vowel Length Rule," in eds. M. Benskin and M.L. Samuels, *So Meny People, Longages and Tonges* (Edinburgh University Press, 1981), pp. 131–57.

20 See John Guillory, *Cultural Capital: The Problem of Literary Canon Formation* (Chicago University Press, 1993).

21 Murray Cohen's *Sensible Words: Linguistic Practice in England 1640–1785* (Baltimore: Johns Hopkins University Press, 1977) and Stephen K. Land's *From Signs to Propositions: The Concept of Form in Eighteenth-Century Semantic Theory* (London: Longman Publishers, 1974) provide thorough formal analyses of these theories, and I cite their work frequently but use it as a springboard for considering the social repurcussions of these theories. Other works do consider their social role; see Hans Aarsleff, *From Locke to Saussure* (Minneapolis: Minnesota University Press, 1982); John Barrell, *English Literature in*

History, 1730–1780, An Equal Wide Survey (London: Hutchinson, 1983); Tony Crowley, *Language in History* (London and New York: Routledge, 1996); Roy Harris, *The Language-Makers* (Ithaca: Cornell University Press, 1980); and Michel Foucault, *The Order of Things* (New York: Vintage Books, 1973). I add to these by examining the relations of empire and nation to these theories.

22 Noam Chomsky, *Cartesian Linguistics* (New York: Harper & Row, 1966), p. 59. There is a wide range of material that falls under the category of theories of universal grammar, not to be confused with the also prolific discussions around universal languages, which posit not a mind/language symmetry but a natural world/language symmetry. For a recent study of this material see Robert E. Stillman, *The New Philosophy and Universal Languages in Seventeenth-Century England* (Lewisburg: Bucknell University Press, 1995).

23 Such claims are not easily characterized as inherently progressive or reactionary. In some ways they confirm the "Enlightenment humanitarian ideals of universality, sameness and equality" Robert Young has identified in *Colonial Desire: Hybridity in Theory, Culture and Race* (New York and London: Routledge, 1995), p.8. Similarly, regarding philology, Edward Said asks, "For what was philology on the one hand if not a science of all humanity, a science premised on the unity of the human species and the worth of every human detail, and yet what was the philologist on the other hand if not... a harsh divider of men into superior and inferior races?" *Orientalism* (New York: Vintage, 1979), p. 133.

The debate on universal grammar encompasses characterizations of the discourse of reason itself. Partha Chatterjee insists that reason's complicity with empire cannot be dissolved, writing, "Enlightenment itself, to assert its sovereignty as the universal ideal, needs its Other; if it could ever actualize itself in the real world as the truly universal, it would in fact destroy itself." *Nationalist Thought and the Colonial World* (Minneapolis: Minnesota University Press, 1993), p. 17. My position is close to that of Max Horkheimer and Theodor Adorno in *Dialectic of Enlightenment*, trans. John Cumming (New York: The Seabury Press, 1972); I remain open to the alternative possibilities of reason in different historical moments.

24 James Knowlson notes that proposals for a universal language scheme "arose partly out of an awareness of the problem of communicating with people who spoke non-European languages – an awareness that grew as the reports and journals published by travellers and missionaries introduced readers to the seemingly strange languages of the Far East or West." *Universal Language Schemes in England and France 1600–1800* (Toronto University Press, 1975), p. 8. In "Language and Difference: The Problem of Abstraction in Eighteenth-Century Language Study," *Journal of the History of Ideas* 54 (1993), James Paxman observes, "As... explorers, missionaries, and travelers expanded knowledge of the world's languages faster than ever before, language philosophers faced the need to integrate within speculative theory the astounding diversity they saw in the ways people named ideas and even, apparently, in the ideas they named" (19).

Universal grammar also bears a close relationship to commercial interests and capital accumulation of the period. We might point to the earlier linguistic projects of the Royal Society, which "looked forward to providing English merchants with the advantage of a universal grammar" (Cohen, *Sensible Words*, p. 2). Similarly, Marc Shell has related this understanding of language to the discourse of Enlightenment and the practice of commerce, seeing it as originating from a "concern for commercial and political concord, as well as an 'enlightenment' search for affinity among languages or for a universal language." "Babel in America: or, The Politics of Language Diversity in the United States," *Critical Inquiry* 20 (1993), p. 106.

As Ellen Meiksin Wood writes, "The tradition of linguistic austerity is traceable at least to the seventeenth century, and its association with developments in the political economy of England is direct and explicit enough to accommodate even the crudest application of the base-superstructure metaphor." *The Pristine Culture of Capitalism: A Historical Essay on Old Regimes and Modern States* (London: Verso, 1991), p. 82.

25 *Encyclopaedia Britannica, or a Dictionary of Arts and Sciences . . . by a Society of Gentlemen in Scotland* (London, 1775). Cited in Sterling Andrus Leonard, *The Doctrine of Correctness in English Usage 1700–1800* (New York: Russell & Russell, 1962), p. 48.
26 Roy Harris, *The Language-Makers* (Ithaca: Cornell University Press, 1980).
27 Similarly, Land writes that the "propositional 'deep' structures" at which the Port Royal arrive "are not a product of linguistic development but rather the primeval formal base upon which language is by 'transformational' rules constructed" (*From Signs*, p. 83). Aarsleff also writes "the *Grammaire générale et raisonnée* includes no concept of development" and "seeks no reduction to the original parts out of which all the rest might . . . have evolved" (*From Locke*).
28 See, for instance, John Locke's provisions against the meretricious charms of metaphor and rhetoric in his *Essay Concerning Human Understanding*, in "Book III, Of Words," ed. Roger Woolhouse (London: Penguin, 1997) p. 452.
29 My focus on male authors in most of the book speaks to the ways in which a male-dominated public sphere – in conversation and print – formed the basis of discussions about language. However, recent work, including Douglas Gifford and Dorothy Macmillan, eds., *A History of Scottish Women's Writing* (Edinburgh University Press, 1997) and Clifford Siskin's paper on "The Fair Intellectual Club" (presented at the Women Writers' Conference (1999), Albuquerque, NM) promise to complicate these formulations in interesting ways.
30 Benedict Anderson, in his book *Imagined Communities*, has traced the coalescence of events in Europe which led to the dramatic shift from hierarchic dynasties organized around a sacred language incomprehensible to most dynastic subjects to "horizontal, boundary-oriented communities" organized around a standard vernacular. My indebtedness to and revisions of Anderson's important work will be in evidence throughout this book.

31 The connection of a standardized language to state power was by no means new to the eighteenth century; its key practitioners in the eighteenth century were intimately familiar with a classical body of literature which discussed the administrative and power-legitimizing uses of a standard. Harris has argued that the construction of a standard in ancient societies assumed what is now called the "classical fallacy," the idea that there is only one proper, correct usage of a language. (See also Guillory, *Cultural Capital*.)

32 Peter Womack, in his comprehensive and deft analysis of representations of the Highlands, writes, "Ironically, the government's determination that Highland difference should end led to its representation, with unprecedented concreteness and detail" (5), yet the structuring of Highland difference was "incompatible with 'improvement'" (21). Alternatively, if the logic of improvement "had been as universal as it claims, there would have been no Highland myth" (26). *Improvement and Romance: Constructing the Myth of the Highlands* (London: Macmillan, 1989).

33 Murray Cohen regards "the major difference between seventeenth- and eighteenth-century ideas of language: in the earlier period the basic linguistic unit was the letter, sound . . . or word: later, it is the syntactical function" (*Sensible Words*, p. 51). Word and syntax took on different valences in these two oppositional visions of language. Eighteenth-century "linguists repeatedly cite the distinction between the arbitrariness of words and the universality of syntax" (56). The word, because (in theory) its very arbitrariness demands agreement on usage based on the custom of a particular society, would be unavoidably culturally specific. John Henley, like many of his peers, perceives the individual word as repository of history and site of cultural difference, writing, "What diversifies a Language, is, the different Sets, and Molds of Words: . . . the latter [is] very seldom [accountable], if ever, from any other Cause but the Genius, commerce, and Manner of the People,"*Compleat Linguist* (London: J. Roberts, 1719), Number III, p. vii. Etymologies were deemed inappropriate for inclusion in early eighteenth-century grammars. Through this gesture, we might infer that in this view of language, words, like women in the eighteenth century, "should have no history." Alternatively, etymologies become an increasingly important component in the dictionaries produced later in the century and into the nineteenth century, culminating in the achievement of the *OED*

34 These might be roughly linked to Sterling Andrus Leonard's identification of "two contrasting theories of usage . . . one assumes the power of reason to remold language completely, and appeals to various principles of metaphysics or logic. . . . The other, recognizes language . . . as a vastly complicated and often haphazard growth of habits stubbornly rooted, the product of great variation in social soil and climate," in *The Doctrine of Correctness in English Usage, 1700-1800* (New York: Russell and Russell, 1962), p. 13.

35 Different claims might be made about them in different contexts – radicals of the 1790s advocated the usage of a rational style in their pamphlets, while the use of highly figurative vernaculars might mean something different

outside of a ruling nationalist context. See Olivia Smith, *The Politics of Language* (Oxford University Press, 1984).

36 Hechter distinguishes this colonialism from colonization, the physical settlement of land, but in a few instances such colonization did take place in the Highlands (*Internal Colonialism*, p. 32). James I established colonies on the Islands of Scotland, giving over the island of Lewis to Lowland adventurers, for example. Later, an eighteenth-century pamphleteer proposed Highland colonies which would follow the Roman model, arguing, "As the wisdom, virtue, and bravery of the Romans deservedly gained them the empire of the world, what better pattern can be proposed for imitation?" (Anonymous, *Some Remarks on the Highland Clans and Methods Proposed for Civilizing Them* [Edinburgh, 1750]). At various points, English-allied Lowlanders planted non-Highland tradesmen in Highland locales to create "manufacturing colonies" and in the wake of the Jacobite rising of 1745 colonists from the English-allied clan Campbell settled the annexed lands of defeated Jacobite chiefs. See Eric Cregeen, "The Changing Role of the House of Argyll in the Scottish Highlands," in *Scotland in the Age of Improvement*, eds. N. T. Phillipson and Rosalind Mitchison (Edinburgh University Press, 1970).

37 Even in terms of economics, the evidence is incomplete. Hechter's language is not likely to inspire confidence in a skeptical reader: "It is *likely* that the profits which derived from the vastly increased trade between England and the Celtic periphery accrued mostly to England. *It is reasonable to suppose* that . . . the English took a disproportionately great share of this commerce" (italics mine, 89).

38 What distinguishes an internal colonial model from a "diffusion" model, according to Hechter, is precisely the avoidance of assimilation. More attentive to the cultural elements of their colonial status, Womack also makes use of this spatialized model, describing England's relation to the Highlands as a core/periphery relationship: "to the extent that a given part of the world is assimilated into the system, and its social and economic life subordinated to the requirements of the whole, it enters into a client relationship with the core – that is, it is peripheralized" (*Improvement*, p. 166).

39 Tom Nairn voices a similar point in *The Break-up of Britain* (London: NLP, 1970).

40 Sympathetic to criticisms of Hugh Trevor-Roper's essay in *The Invention of Tradition*, eds. E. J. Hobsbawm and T. O. Ranger (Cambridge University Press, 1983), I argue for the necessity of a critique of England's own invented traditions.

41 In his descriptions of the dovetailing interests of the gentry and merchant class interest in this period, Terry Eagleton suggests a hermetic, unchallenged domination in *The Ideology of the Aesthetic* (London: Blackwell, 1990). This formulation was developed in the 1970s by Tom Nairn, and Perry Anderson "Components of the National Culture," *New Left Review* 50 (1968). Similarly, Anderson's description of the cultural formation of the nation rarely delves into instances where pockets of a nation's members might

protest. For a recent critique of this vision of the nation, especially in terms of its failure to consider gender in any significant way, see Wilson's *The Sense*, and James Chandler, "Devolutionary Criticism: Scotland, America, and Literary Modernity," *Modern Philology* 92 (1994), pp. 211–19.

42 I am referring not only to lexical heterogeneity but also to differences of pronunciation. Drawing from Nairn, Meiksin Wood notes, "Britain ... is ... distinctive in the extent to which sound patterns, the conventions of pronunciation, predominate over other linguistic criteria of social difference. What is remarkable is the relative weakness of its linguistic hierarchy in syntactic form" (*Pristine Culture*, p. 82).

43 Manuel Castells, *The Informational City* (Oxford: Basil Blackwell, 1989), p. 342. Tom Foster has pointed out the pertinence of this work for my argument.

44 Thus, Ian Carter argues that the economic status of the eighteenth-century Highlands was far from an "antediluvian province of England" (279). Instead, their deep integration into a global profit system, particularly in their cattle trade and kelp industry, was responsible for a later economic decline when these industries receded. I do, however, differ from Carter's conclusions that a "metropolitan/satellite" relationship is the most accurate understanding of the Highlands relationship to Britain. "The Highlands of Scotland as an Underdeveloped Region," in *Sociology and Development*, eds. Emanuel de Kadt and Gavin Williams (London: Tavistock, 1974), pp. 279–311. See also A. J. Youngson, *After the Forty-Five: The Economic Impact on the Scottish Highlands* (Edinburgh University Press, 1973) and Malcolm Gray, *The Highland Economy 1750–1850* (Edinburgh: Oliver and Boyd, 1957).

45 Robert J. Foster, "Making National Cultures in the Global Ecumene," *Annual Review of Anthropology* 20 (1991), pp. 236–60, esp. p. 245.

46 Mary Louise Pratt, "Linguistic Utopias," in *The Linguistics of Writing*, ed. Nigel Fabb (New York: Methuen, 1987).

47 Lynda Mugglestone, *'Talking Proper': The Rise of Accent as Social Symbol* (Oxford: Clarendon, 1995).

48 I take this term "Anglo-British" from Colin Kidd's *Subverting Scotland's Past: Scottish Whig Historians and the Creation of an Anglo-British Identity, 1689–1830* (Cambridge University Press, 1993). For Kidd, even when it has been assisted by Scots, the construction of "Britishness" has not been Anglo-Scottish but instead has been dependent upon "English ideals" and "on a historical allegiance to England's evolving constitution of crown and parliament" (1). "Anglo-British" suggests both English and Scottish involvement in its building but holds that the resulting political entity was not an amalgam of English and Scottish cultures and histories.

49 On his "partitioned" quality, see Fredric Bogel, "Johnson and the Role of Authority" in *The New 18th Century*, eds. Felicity Nussbaum and Laura Brown (London: Methuen, 1987), pp. 189–209 and Deidre Lynch, " 'Beating the Track of the Alphabet': Samuel Johnson, Tourism, and the ABCs of Modern Authority," *ELH* 57 (1990), pp. 357–405.

50 Simpson, *The Protean Scot*, p. 16. Smollett's feat, according to Simpson, is his ability to render in Standard English these "organic" Scottish literary traditions, and Simpson's extensive enumeration of those earlier traditions – "vivid representation of the physical" (18), "incongruity in the interests of social satire" (19), "propensity... to the unusual or grotesque," (23), and use of animal imagery – is useful but has a way of shoring up notions of a fixed national identity expressed through the nation's canonical texts. Damien Grant essentializes a Scottish literary aesthetic when he writes, "The Scots have always been renowned for their hospitality to words, their love of dense and complicated verbal surfaces." *Tobias Smollett: A Study in Style* (Manchester University Press, 1977), p. 83.

51 Hugh Blair, *Lectures on Rhetoric and Belles Lettres*, ed. Harold F. Harding, 2 vols. (Carbondale: Southern Illinois University Press, 1965) and Adam Smith, *Lectures on Rhetoric and Belles Lettres*, ed. J. Bryce (Oxford Univeristy Press, 1983). See Crawford, *Scottish Invention*; Miller, *Formation*; Adam Potkay, *The Fate of Eloquence in the Age of Hume* (Ithaca: Cornell University Press, 1994); and Franklin Court, *Institutionalizing English Literature: The Cultural Politics of Literary Study, 1750–1900* (Stanford University Press, 1992).

52 David Lloyd writes, "Both imperialism and nationalism seek to occlude troublesome and inassimilable manifestations of difference by positing a transcendent realm of essential identity." *Nationalism and Minor Literature* (Berkeley: California University Press, 1987), p. x, and Chatterjee, *Nationalist*.

53 V. I. Lenin, *The Right of Nations to Self Determination* (London: International Publishers, 1951).

54 Alok Yadav, "Nationalism and Contemporaneity: Political Economy of a Discourse," *Cultural Critique* 26 (1993–4): 191–229. See also Benita Parry, "Resistance theory/theorising resistance or two cheers for nativism," in *Colonial Discourse, Post-Colonial Theory*, eds. Francis Barker, Peter Hulme, and Margaret Iverson (Manchester University Press, 1994), pp. 173–96.

55 Thus I disagree with Tom Nairn, who dismisses "internationalism" as mere orthodoxy. It is a strange orthodoxy that "would keep its options permanently open." Nairn's chief argument, that the "non-logical, untidy, refractory, disintegrative, particularistic truth of nation-states" is a "reality," which those who critique it naively refuse to acknowledge is difficult to distinguish from a position that would accuse feminists or anti-racists of a similar naiveté. *Faces of Nationalism* (London and New York: Verso, 1997) pp. 25–46.

56 William Strunk, Jr. and E. B. White, *Elements of Style* (New York: Macmillan, 1979).

57 If the origins of English literature are to be found in the more robust cultural nationalisms of its Celtic periphery, Trumpener *is* quick to point out that the origins of that cultural nationalism are in turn to be found in "reactions to Enlightenment programs for economic improvement, read as a form of political and cultural imperialism" (*Bardic Nationalism*, p. xi). More than any other's, Trumpener's deep analysis of Celtic cultural nationalisms reveals

the ways in which they are "enmeshed both in the project of empire ... and in the process of class stratification" (30). Yet that understanding of class stratification is not in evidence when she describes Scots Gaelic as "the most important shared property of the national community" (86). It is this notion of "shared property," with its echoes of national linguistic community and cross-class cultural value, which gives me pause.

1 SCRIPTING IDENTITY

1 Society in Scotland for Propagating Christian Knowledge (hereafter SSPCK) (Edinburgh, 1716). British administrators mistakenly used "Irish" as a synonym for Scots Gaelic.
2 (Edinburgh, 1751). Translations taken from *The Poems of Alexander MacDonald*, trans. Rev. A. MacDonald (Inverness: Northern Counties Newspaper and Print Co., 1924).
   "Malcolm Canmore" was King of Scotland, 1057–93. "Gall" refers to someone not a member of the Gaelic ethnolinguistic community. See Donald MacAulay, "Canons, Myths and Cannon Fodder," *Scotlands* 1 (1994), pp. 35–54.
3 For an introduction to MacDonald's work see Derick Thomson, "Gaelic Poetry in the Eighteenth Century: The Breaking of the Mould" in *The History of Scottish Literature*, vol. 2, ed. Andrew Hook, pp. 175–89 and *An Introduction to Gaelic Poetry* (Edinburgh University Press, 1987).
4 One recent example of this re-thinking of British literature is Robert Crawford's "Native Language," *Comparative Criticism* 18 (1996), pp. 71–90.
5 Michael Hechter makes a convincing if overly general argument about the colonial economic status of Wales, Ireland, and Scotland in *Internal Colonialism: The Celtic Fringe in British National Development* (Berkeley: California University Press, 1975), p. 32.
6 Murray Pittock, *Poetry and Jacobite Politics in Eighteenth-Century Britain and Ireland* (Cambridge University Press, 1994) and Thomson, "Gaelic Poetry in the Eighteenth Century."
7 Alexander MacDonald, *A Gaelic/English Vocable* (Edinburgh: Robert Fleming, 1741).
8 Tony Crowley discusses English instruction in Ireland, but he moves directly from the extirpation of Gaelic to the Celtic revival, missing out on a crucial moment of resistance in MacDonald's writings. *Language in History* (London and New York: Routledge, 1996).
9 Manuel Castells, *The Informational City* (Oxford: Basil Blackwell, 1989), p. 342.
10 Mary Louise Pratt, *Imperial Eyes: Travel Writing and Transculturation* (London: Routledge, 1992), p. 7.
11 Malcolm Chapman, *The Gaelic Vision in Scottish Culture* (London: Croom Helm, 1978).
12 John MacInnes, *The Evangelical Movement in the Highlands of Scotland* (Aberdeen University Press, 1951), pp. 3, 247.

13 Sara Suleri, *The Rhetoric of English India* (Chicago University Press, 1992), p. 5.
14 Tom Nairn, *The Break-up of Britain* (London: NLP, 1970), p. 134.
15 Cited in SSPCK, *An Account of the [SSPCK] from its Commencement in 1709 . . . with Regard to Religion* (Edinburgh: A. Murray and J. Cochrane, 1774), p. 3. English assertions of political – through cultural – authority over the "Celtic fringe" extend back to the Henrician Reformation in 1534. As Victor Durkacz puts it, an unassimilated Celtic periphery was the "Achilles heel of the Protestant succession." *The Decline of the Celtic Languages* (Edinburgh: John Donald Publishers, Ltd., 1983).
16 T. C. Smout cites Alexander Webster's 1755 estimate: "just over half the people had lived north of a line from the Firth of Tay to the Firth of Clyde" in *A History of the Scottish People 1560–1830* (London: Fontana Press, 1985), p. 241.
17 *A Summary Account of the Rise and Progress of the SSPCK* (Edinburgh, 1783).
18 Scottish Records Office (SRO) GD 95 10.
19 On the SSPCK's founding, see M. G. Jones, *The Charity School Movement: A Study of Eighteenth-Century Puritanism in Action* (London: Frank Cass, 1964).
20 Durkacz, *The Decline*, p. 47. The 300,000 figure comes from MacInnes, *Evangelical Movement*, p. 248. John Withers believes that census records show a traceable link between the schools and the spread of English. *Gaelic in Scotland 1698–1981* (Edinburgh: John Donald Publishers, 1984), p. 5. But John Crawford writes, "the SSPCK . . . failed in the larger objective of making English the primary language" in "Policy Formulation for Public Library Provision in the Highlands of Scotland," *Journal of Librarianship* 16 (1984), p. 96.
21 See Rosalind Mitchison, "The Government and the Highlands, 1707–1745," in *Scotland in the Age of Improvement*, eds. N. T. Phillipson and R. Mitchison (Edinburgh University Press, 1970). But see also Smout, less convinced of its weakness, *A History*, p. 207. The Society's 1783 *Summary Account* determinedly proclaims, "though we regret the failure of public aid . . . it is rather an . . . incentive to private beneficence," (Edinburgh, 1783), p. 20.
22 Bruce Lenman writes, "They were all obsessed with their own version of progress by stadial progression. A nation only deserved respect if its history showed a progressive development of politeness and propriety" in "Empire and Opportunity," paper presented at American Society for Eighteenth-Century Studies, April 1996. See also Crawford, *Devolving English Literature* (Oxford: Clarendon, 1992), pp. 18–40 and my Chapter 4.
23 Further, as Frederick Mills has argued, the work of the SSPCK reflected the "revised ecclesiastical policy of the British government" so important to the success of the House of Hanover in consolidating Anglicans and Presbyterians. "The SSPCK in British North America, 1730–1775," *Church History* 63 (1994), pp. 15–30, eps. p. 18.
24 Alok Yadav argues, "denigration of Scots Gaelic as illiterate and meager was . . . the assertion of a cultural hierarchy structured to reinforce English

superiority," in "Nationalism and Literature in Eighteenth-Century Britain," Ph.D. Dissertation, 1993, p. 87.
25 *Selections from the Prison Notebooks of Antonio Gramsci*, eds. Quentin Hoare and Geoffrey Nowell Smith (London: Lawrence and Wishart, 1971), p. 57. Gauri Viswanathan cites this passage to describe English instruction in India in *Masks of Conquest* (New York: Columbia University Press, 1987), p. 1. See also *The Lie of the Land: English Literary Studies in India*, ed. Rajeswari Sunder Rajan (Oxford University Press, 1992).
26 Louis Althusser, "Ideology and Ideological State Apparatuses," in *Lenin and Philosophy* (London: Monthly Review, 1971). The Commissioners of the Forfeited Annexed Estates ran these schools from 1752 to 1784.
27 Nancy Dorian, *Language Death: The Life Cycle of a Scottish Gaelic Dialect* (Philadelphia: Pennsylvania University Press, 1981), p. 28.
28 SSPCK, *Abridgement of the Statutes of the Society* (Edinburgh, n.d. 1732?), p. 30, reads "June 6, 1723 *Item* That all the Scholars be exhorted to learn to speak *English*, and that none who can speak it be allowed to speak *Irish*, except when turning it into *English*, and that Censors be named to delate Transgressors therein."
29 National Library of Scotland (NLS). MS 17504 ff 58. Less a blanket almsgiving than a means of social discipline, charity organizations legitimated as they put to social use their members' newly acquired wealth in what Jones sees as an alliance of puritan ethics and capitalism (*Charity School*, p. 7). MacInnes describes the SSPCK as a "philanthropic society, organized on the lines of a joint-stock company" (*Evangelical Movement*, p. 236).
30 D. J. Withrington, "The SPCK and Highland Schools in Mid-Eighteenth Century," *Scottish Historical Review* XLI (1962), pp. 89–99.
31 *Abridgement of the Statutes of the SSPCK*, p. 33.
32 Pierre Bourdieu, *Language and Symbolic Power*, trans. Gino Raymond and Matthew Adamson (Cambridge, MA: Harvard University Press, 1991), p. 46.
33 While Chapman helpfully calibrates the complex matrix of forces behind language change in the Highlands, his dismissal of its reflection of any form of cultural oppression overstates the case. *The Celts: The Construction of a Myth* (London: Macmillan Press, 1992), pp. 99–106.
34 Here I use the Gaelic-derived Scots term to connote both "English speaking" and, variably, Lowlander and Englishman or woman. *The Concise Scots Dictionary*, ed. Mairi Robinson (Aberdeen University Press, 1991).
35 SRO GD 95 2/2, 22 March 1718.
36 A. Cowper and I. Ross, *Eighteenth-Century Schoolmasters in Strathbora* (Edinburgh, 1980).
37 SRO GD 95 2/7, 14 June 1756.
38 SRO GD 95 2/2, 4 November 1717.
39 Cowper and Ross, *Schoolmasters*. The Society also records that after the 1715 rebellion "few students remained," SRO GD 95 2/2, 1 May 1718. Perhaps related to the high level of suspicion in this era, rumors also circulated about the motives of the Society. Meeting minutes mention "a foolish report

spread that the Society's schools were intended as a seminary for the plantations" SRO GD 95 2/1, 13 January 1715.

40 MacInnes, *Evangelical Movement*, p. 247.

41 Robert Wallace, *Ignorance and Superstition a Source of Violence and Cruelty, and ... Cause of the Present Rebellion* (Edinburgh, 1746), p. 20.

42 MacInnes, for instance, notes that in the eighteenth century "the standard of culture among the tacksmen and smaller gentry of Skye and the Hebrides was very high. To be able to converse in Latin was a common accomplishment among them" *Evangelical Movement*, p. 228.

43 Cited in Ronald Black, "Mac Mhaighstir Alasdair: the Ardnamurchan Years," *Society of West Highland and Island Historical Research* (1985) pp. 3–43, esp. p. 11.

44 Maurice Lindsay, for instance, writes, "throughout the seventeenth century, the Makars had been largely, though not totally, forgotten," *History of Scottish Literature* (London: Robert Hall, 1977), p. 169.

45 Black, "Mac Mhaighstir," p. 4. See also J. L. Campbell, "Alexander MacDonald: Portrait of a Traditionalist," *Scots Magazine* 24 (1934–1935), pp. 61–76; Derick Thomson, "Alasdair Mac Mhaigstir Alasdair," *An Gaidheal* 47 (1952); *Dictionary of National Biography*, vol. XXII, pp. 471–3; *Companion to Gaelic Scotland*, ed. Derick Thomson (Oxford: Blackwell, 1983).

46 The parallels the Anglo-British imagined between Highlanders and other colonial populations are evident in the missionary activities and colonial rhetoric regarding those activities applied to both. The SSPCK sent missionaries to Georgia to minister both to the Gaelic-speaking population who had been settled there and the "native Indians." See *An Account*, p. 14. See also Roger Emerson, "American Indians, Frenchmen, and Scots Philosophers," *Studies in Eighteenth-Century Culture*, v. 9 (Madison: Wisconsin University Press, 1979), pp. 211–36 for descriptions of the Highlanders and their American "cousins"; and Donald Meek, "Scottish Highlanders, North American Indians, and the SSPCK," *Records of the Scottish Church History Society* 23 (1989), pp. 378–96, esp. p. 383.

In Scottish Enlightenment theories, both populations shared an anachronistic position on a universal chronology of human development. Sir James Stuart, for instance, compared the Highlands to the England of 400 years ago. In *Time and the Other* (New York: Columbia University Press, 1983) Johannes Fabian discusses the ways in which anthropological discourses employ notions of temporal distance as a means of "othering" communities under study.

47 Peter Womack, *Improvement and Romance: Constructing the Myth of the Highlands* (London: Macmillan, 1989).

48 William Robertson, "The Situation of the World at the Time of Christ's Appearance: A Sermon Preached before the SSPCK" in *State of the SSPCK ... in 1754* (Edinburgh, 1755), cited in Womack, *Improvement*, p. 22.

49 Jonathan Arac situates negative identity formation within a socio-political context, writing, "imperialism names a historically crucial process by which

an 'other' conceived as exotic is represented and subordinated for the purpose of strengthening the worldly place of a metropolitan state," in *Macropolitics of Nineteenth-Century Literature*, eds. Jonathan Arac and Harriet Ritvo (Philadelphia: Pennsylvania University Press, 1991); while Edward Said assigns to it a more universal status, writing, "modern and primitive societies seem thus to derive a sense of their identities negatively.... space acquires emotional and even rational sense by a kind of poetic process, whereby the vacant or anomalous reaches of distance are converted into meaning for us here," in *Orientalism* (New York: Vintage, 1978), pp. 54–5. Most important for our purposes is the figuring of difference through language. David Spurr, after Hayden White, notes that one of the qualities of the "other" is "linguistic confusion," in *The Rhetoric of Empire* (Durham and London: Duke University Press, 1994), pp. 76–7, and Olivia Smith points out, "civilization was largely a linguistic concept, establishing a terrain in which vocabulary and syntax distinguished the refined and civilized from the vulgar and savage," in *The Politics of Language 1791–1819* (Oxford: Clarendon Press, 1984), p. vii.

50 David Lloyd writes of this general phenomenon, "Reduction to a single common form for human identity is the end that hegemonic colonialism is forced to pursue in the face of the multiplicity of resistant cultural and social forms contained within any empire" in *Nationalism and Minor Literature* (Berkeley: California University Press, 1987), p. x.

51 Womack maintains that Britain's rational economistic approach to the Highlands and its exotic characterizations of the Highlands were reciprocal, the image of an exotically "different" Highlands suppressing the disruptions of economic improvement (*Improvement*, p. 3). Of the rise of capital relations in the Highlands, Eric Cregeen writes, "inevitably the disintegration of the traditional social structure was accompanied by the growth of a new pattern of relationships based on commercial values. The chief became a landlord ... treating the land no longer as a means of supporting a warlike following but as a source of revenue and as a commodity to be bought and sold," in *Scotland*, eds. Phillipson and Mitchison, p. 9.

52 SSPCK Annual Sermon, 1790, cited in MacInnes, *Evangelical Movements*, p. 244.

53 SRO GD 95 10.

54 The interest in Indian "improvement," Viswanathan notes, was intended to redress "abuse of power by the Nabobs" and "the damage done to India following early British conquests" (*Masks*, p. 25). Meek tracks the SSPCK's movement from efforts to "debarbarize" the Highlanders to an increased "awareness of the need to evangelize a culture different from their own" ("Scottish Highlanders," p. 378).

55 Thomas Randell, *Christian Benevolence, A Sermon Preached before the [SSPCK] at their Anniversary Meeting* (Edinburgh, 1763), pp. 93–5.

56 Anonymous, *The Highland Complaint* (Edinburgh, 1737), p. 41, following quote, p. 14.

57 Homi Bhabha, "The Other Question...," *Screen* 24 (1983), p. 23.
58 Bhabha, "The Ambivalence of Colonial Discourse," in *OCTOBER: The First Decade, 1976–1986*, ed. Annette Michelson, *et al.* (Cambridge, MA: MIT Press, 1987), p. 318.
59 Eric Cheyfitz, in *The Poetics of Imperialism* (Oxford University Press, 1991), p. 35, shows how the English colonialist in North America both "recognizes cultural difference as linguistic difference... and obliterates this difference in a belief in the power of eloquence to act immediately on the Indians." See also David Cairn and Shaun Richards, *Writing Ireland: Colonialism, Nationalism and Culture* (Manchester University Press, 1988).
60 *Present State of the Society in Scotland for Propagating Christian Knowledge, Giving a Brief Account of the Conditon of the Islands* (Edinburgh, ?), p. 40.
61 This practice parallels the English SPCK's methods with working-class English children, an alienation of the native population's language we shall take up in Chapter 2. (Jones, *Charity School*, pp. 77–83.)
62 Scholars have attributed *Journall and Memoirs of P – C – Expedition into Scotland by a Highland Officer in his Army* (*Lockhart Papers*, vol. II [London: William Anderson, 1817]) in which the author refers to "the Duke of Athole to whom some of us had been known in the year 1715" (480) to MacDonald.
63 The Society emphasized reading, although some students did learn to write. See Smout, "Born Again at Cambuslang: New Evidence on Popular Religion and Literacy in Eighteenth-Century Scotland," *Past & Present* 97 (1987), pp. 114–27.
64 Sue Zemka, "The Holy Books of Empire: Translations of the British and Foreign Bible Society," in *Macropolitics of Nineteenth-Century Literature*, p. 109.
65 Both this quote and the following are from *An Account*, p. 2.
66 Assessments of literacy's impact range from Claude Levi-Strauss, *Tristes Tropiques* (Paris, 1955) trans. John and Doreen Weightman (London: Cape, 1973); Marshall McLuhan, *Gutenburg Galaxy* (Toronto University Press, 1988); and Walter Ong, *Orality and Literacy: The Technologizing of the Word* (London: Methuen, 1982), who all insist on both cognitive and social structural changes in the move to literacy, to Jacques Derrida, *Of Grammatology*, trans. Gayatri Spivak (New Haven: Johns Hopkins University Press, 1976) and Roy Harris, *Language-Makers* (Ithaca: Cornell University Press, 1980), who insist on the essential textuality of oral communication. Most useful is Eric Havelock's recognition of "different systems with different effects" and his insistence on "not a history of writing but a history of reading," *The Literate Revolution in Greece and Its Cultural Consequences* (Princeton University Press, 1982), pp. 55–6.
67 Harris, *Language-Makers*, p. 6.
68 E. P. Thompson, cited in R. A. Houston, *Scottish Literacy and the Scottish Identity* (Cambridge University Press, 1985), p. 194. Houston writes, "oral tradition is a complex and demanding artistic form, not just a poorly developed sort of literary tradition."
69 *A Summary Account*, p. 4.
70 John Crawford, "Books, Libraries and the Decline of Gaelic on the Island of

Arran," *Library Review* (1987), p. 87. Ian Duncan, however, has pointed out to me the atypical character of Arran.
71 Zemka writes, "Time and time again, the fantasy of the Bible's reception abroad is the same: missionaries find non-Christians in a state of apprehensive desire for religious enlightenment, and once they read or hear the New Testament, they spontaneously endorse an understanding of it sympathetic to Protestant faith," "Holy Books," p. 111, following point, p. 116.
72 Jo Willison, "A Narrative of the extraordinary Work at Cambuslang in a letter to a Friend, May 8th, 1742." Reproduced in *Historical Collections Relating to Remarkable Periods of the Success of the Gospel*, ed. Rev. John Gillies, (Kelso: John Rutherfurd, 1845), pp. 434–6.
73 While Gaelic had been "a vital and literate culture" in the sixteenth and seventeenth centuries, it had "lapsed out of texts," with only the odd and neglected religious tract, Psalter, and Old Testament (in classical Irish Gaelic) making their way into print – but never widespread distribution – by the mid-eighteenth century. Houston, *Scottish*, p. 76, and Derick Thomson, *Why Gaelic Matters* (Edinburgh: Saltire Society, 1984).
74 Black, *Mac Mhaighstir*, p. 17.
75 Withers, p. 123.
76 SRO GD 95 1/2, 10 August 1721.
77 SRO GD 95 1/2, 4 November 1725.
78 Letter to William Drummond in James Boswell, *The Life of Samuel Johnson*, ed. Bergen Evans (New York: Random House, 1965), p. 144. While notorious for his hostility towards Gaelic culture, Johnson also had a copy of MacDonald's glossary.
79 John Balfour, *Robe's Monthly History* VI (June 20, 1744), p. 39.
80 Brian Street, *Literacy: Theory and Practice* (Cambridge University Press, 1984), p. 97. My thanks to Srinivas Aravamudan for this citation. Similarly, Viswanathan admonishes that the reading experience is not "a direct and open source of attitudes, beliefs, and ideas whose transmission is entirely unmediated by the political and historical realities that in fact affect and influence the processes of education" (*Masks*, p. 17).
81 David Murray discusses the significance of the often concealed role of the colonial translator in *Forked Tongues: Speech, Writing, and Representation in North American Indian Texts* (Bloomington: Indiana University Press, 1991).
82 Tejaswini Niranjana describes translation theory as assuming, from the past few centuries to the present, an "empiricist-idealist framework" and "a naively representational theory of language." *Siting Translation: History, Post-Structuralism, and the Colonial Context* (Berkeley: California University Press, 1992), pp. 50–1. Similarly, Harris has commented on the "odd idea" that language is translatable, "where native words are regarded as items which have their equivalents, more or less, in other languages" (*Language-Makers*, p. 4).
83 My understanding of the theory of language operating in the context of Highland pedagogical practices is distinct from Richard Kroll's analysis of early eighteenth-century linguistic theories in *The Material Word: Literate*

Culture in the Restoration and Early Eighteenth Century (Baltimore: Johns Hopkins University Press, 1991). While it might be true, as Kroll argues, that philosophers did not view language as transparent, but rather as a "fully mediated vehicle of knowledge," this view of language could hardly be afforded by colonial administrators who were not likely to have shared the playful, contingent view of language. In other words, like literacy, linguistic theories shift between contexts.

84 Cited in Thomas Sprat, *The History of the Royal Society*, 2, section xx, (London, 1667). See also R. F. Jones, "Science and English Prose Style," in *The Seventeenth Century: Studies in the History of English Thought and Literature from Bacon to Pope* (Stanford University Press, 1965). Stephen K. Land describes this linguistics: "seventeenth-century philosophers thought of language as an aggregate of signs rather than a system. . . . their attention was given chiefly to the relation between the individual sign and the thing it represented." *From Signs to Propositions: The Concept of Form in Eighteenth-Century Semantic Theory* (London: Longman, 1974), p. 2. Not everyone agrees that this was the dominant view of language in the period. See Robert Markley, *Fallen Languages: Crises of Representation in Newtonian England, 1660–1740* (Ithaca: Cornell University Press, 1993) and Brian Vickers, "The Royal Society and English Prose Style: A Reassessment," in *Rhetoric and the Pursuit of Truth: Language Change in the Seventeenth and Eighteenth Centuries* (Los Angeles: William Andrews Clark Memorial Library, 1985).

85 Such an image of language extended into the nineteenth century, as later Bible Societies stressed the use of "easy and simple diction" in translation, believing, as Zemka has written, that "every language has its idiom of unadorned, plain style prose, free from rhetorical embellishment (the universal idiom of rational, empirical communication)."

86 Theodor Adorno and Max Horkheimer directly link this way of thinking to the instrumental reason of Enlightenment thought, critiquing the theory of language to which it gives rise: "the most recent school of logic denounces – for the impressions they bear – the words of language, holding them to be false coins better replaced by neutral counters." *Dialectic of Enlightenment*, trans. John Cumming (New York: The Seabury Press, 1972), p. 5. On equivalence they write, "bourgeois society is ruled by equivalence. It makes the dissimilar comparable by reducing it to abstract quantities" (7).

87 Several writers have even theorized the co-development of alphabets and coins, suggesting that literacy itself is coterminous with the rise of commerce. See, for instance, Marc Shell, *The Economy of Literature* (Baltimore: Johns Hopkins University Press, 1978), p. 11; Ong, *Orality*, p. 99; and Harris, *The Origins of Writing* (LaSalle, Illinois: Open Court, 1986), pp. 71, 134. Although in need of more historical specificity, Jean-Joseph Goux's observation that "the history of societies shows a complex objective correspondence between forms of economic exchange and forms of signifying exchange" remains important. *Symbolic Economies After Marx and Freud*, trans. Jennifer Curtiss Gage (Ithaca: Cornell University Press, 1990), p.

110. Nor should we forget that the use of bank notes and notes of credit demands literacy skills. Houston writes, "Paradoxically, it was tenant farmers in areas of Scotland where transport was most difficult who would have more involvement with marketing . . . since landlords preferred money rents to the problems of moving bulk products over difficult terrain. Thus, even 'backward,' relatively remote parts of Scotland were generating substantial amounts of paperwork at this time" (*Scottish Literacy*, p. 143).

88 The glossary form participates in – and perhaps helps shape – seventeenth-century linguistics. Murray Cohen describes how in seventeenth- and early-eighteenth-century linguistic work "the most important parts of any system are its basic elements" and "language makes visible sense" (5) and can be "touched, tabulated and visualized" in *Sensible Words*, p. 8.

89 Campbell, "Alexander MacDonald," p. 63.

90 Peter Murphy writes, "The problem with Gaelic, what made it so 'foreign,' was not that it was especially difficult to learn, but rather how it had to be learned . . . Gaelic had to be learned from the mouth of an actual speaker (an actual Highlander)." "Fool's Gold: The Highland Treasures of Macpherson's Ossian," *ELH* 52 (1985) pp. 567–91.

91 John Stuart, son of James, supervised the translation of the first two parts of *Leabhraiche an t-scann tiomnaidh*, the Old Testament (Edinburgh: William Smellie, 1783–7) and translated the third part. John Smith of Campbeltown translated the fourth part.

92 Donald Meek, "The Gaelic Bible," in *The Bible in Scottish Life and Literature*, ed. David Wright (Edinburgh: Saint Andrew Press, 1988), pp. 9–23, p. 18. The seventeenth-century translations of Bedell conformed to the classical Gaelic of Scottish and Irish manuscript culture.

93 The fact that this missionary group printed the first books in Gaelic anticipated this role of colonizing missionaries in many other contexts of British empire, notably Bengal. See Partha Chatterjee, *The Nation and its Fragments* (Princeton University Press, 1993), p. 7.

94 John Crawford writes that "the evangelical movement encouraged the translation of English Puritan Divines into Gaelic" ("Policy Formulations," p. 98) and that such publications sparked a revivalism which in turn increased the demand for Gaelic publications. Between 1811 and 1830 a movement for Gaelic schools emerged.

95 Benedict Anderson, *Imagined Communities: Reflections on the Origin and Spread of Nationalism* (London: Verso, 1983), p. 47.

96 Space does not allow a discussion of the reception of MacDonald's glossary outside of the Highlands. Paul DeGategno takes that up in "'The Source of Daily and Exalted Pleasure': Jefferson Reads the Poems of Ossian" in *Ossian Revisited*, ed. Howard Gaskill (Edinburgh University Press, 1991), pp. 94–108. DeGategno writes of the irony of Jefferson's eager use of the glossary to learn Ossian's language: "Jefferson overturned the design of one people to deny the intellectual freedoms of another" (100).

97 Niranrjara, *Siting Translation*, p. 10. George Steiner also critiques the "context-free system" and "formal codification" of translation. *After Babel: Aspects of Language and Translation* (Oxford University Press, 1975).
98 SRO GD 95 2/2, 2 February 1719.
99 SRO GD 95 6, 2 June 1745, p. 271.
100 Black, *Mac Mhaighstir*, pp. 12–13.
101 Nancy Dorian makes the point about Gaelic linguistic diversity in *Language Death*.
102 In this overly simplistic characterizations of "older form(s) of globalisation," Lawrence Grossberg falters in an otherwise helpful essay. "The Space of Culture, the Power of Space," in *The Post-Colonial Question: Common Skies, Divided Horizons*, eds. Iain Chambers and Lidia Curti (London and New York: Routledge, 1996), p. 182.
103 Donald MacAulay, "Canons, myths and cannon fodder," *Scotlands* 1 (1994), pp. 35–54.
104 In his avowal of Gaelic's ancientness MacDonald had many colleagues, including fellow Highlander David Malcolme who "had traced the antiquity of the Celtic languages" (Black, *Mac Mhaighstir* p. 26). Even the seemingly maverick poem in praise of Gaelic had a predecessor in Maighstir Iain's "erudite but powerful congratulatory ode in – and about – Gaelic" (published in Edward Lhuyd's *Archaeologia Britannica* [Oxford, 1707], Black, *Mac Mhaighstir*, p. 11). I focus on MacDonald because his case reveals the ways in which these constructions of Gaelic are explicitly tied to Anglo-British institutions of literacy instruction.
105 Katie Trumpener, *Bardic Nationalism* (Princeton University Press, 1997).
106 *Poems of Ossian*, trans. James Macpherson (London: Cadell and Davies, 1807), p. 240.
107 Black, *Mac Mhaighstir*, p. 27.
108 Crawford, "Native Language," p. 79.
109 Black, *Mac Mhaighstir*, p. 14.
110 Of course, Macpherson's publication of *Poems of Ossian* – in English – exploits those technologies as well, but in locating the bardic figure in the past and downplaying his own role as author interceding in events of his own day, he situates those technologies at a far remove from the direct action of the bard.
111 See Thompson, *Gaelic*, p. 32. David Daiches, in *The Paradox of Scottish Culture* (London, 1964), p. 94, asserts that MacDonald initiated "an indigenous Scottish movement, in which for the first time Scots Gaelic developed a tradition independent of the formal rhetorical training of the Irish schools."
112 Derick Thomson, "Mac Mhaighstir Alasdair's Nature Poetry and its Sources," in *Gaelic and Scots in Harmony*, ed. Derick Thomson (Glasgow University Press, 1988), p.157.
113 Many critics have noted his familiarity with conventions of classical, English Augustan, and even contemporary Scots vernacular revival poetry;

113 Chapman and Thomson identify the influence of James Thomson's "The Seasons" in his nature poetry.
114 Daiches, *Paradox*, p. 66.
115 I will depart from Robert Young's reading of Stevenson's novella as an English "fantasy of crossing." Instead, I want to insist on the specifically Scottish context of crossing at work in this story. *Colonial Desire: Hybridity in Theory, Culture and Race* (London and New York: Routledge, 1995), p. 22.
116 Robert Louis Stevenson, *The Strange Case of Dr. Jekyll and Mr. Hyde* (New York: Bantam, 1978), p. 57.
117 Lori Chamberlain, "Gender and the Metaphorics of Translation," *Signs* 13 (1988), pp. 464–72.
118 Teaching literacy in English, however, "colonizes" that potentially private moment of reading, complicating these strict dichotomies.
119 Chatterjee, *The Nation*, p. 6.
120 Murray Pittock, *Inventing and Resisting Britain* (New York: St. Martin's Press, 1997), p. 116.
121 See Laura Murray, " 'Pray Sir, consider a Little': Rituals of Subordination and Strategies of Resistance in the Letters of Hezekiah Calving and David Fowler to Eleazar Wheelock, 1764–1768," *Studies in American Indian Literatures* 4 (1992), pp. 48–74, esp. p. 68.
122 His poems have appeared in a number of editions throughout the nineteenth and twentieth centuries. Chapman and Campbell, in "The Expurgating of MacMhaighstir Alasdair," *Scottish Gaelic Studies* 12 (1971), pp. 59–76, discuss a nationalist hagiography's expurgation of his lewd and militant material in these collections.
123 Interestingly, MacDiarmid also produced an edition of MacDonald's final poem, "*Birlinn Chlann Raghnaill*," his most consciously traditional (and least "transcultural") poem. See Thomson, *Introduction*, pp. 172–8.
124 Here I differ from Yadav. He helpfully notes that "'anti-essentialist' perspectives on English 'national character' were articulated in close relation to the support of dominant political realities" – think of Defoe's triumphant *True-Born Englishman*. Yet he also argues that, consequently, "the positing of natural facts can be an ambiguous strategy of delimitation and resistance to subsumption, and we have therefore to be cautious about simply launching into a critique of . . . essentialist nodes in counter-hegemonic discourses." This "the enemy ideology of my enemy's ideology must be my friend" formulation has too long led to an uncritical support of nationalism – a disastrous *cul de sac* for progressive movements. *Nationalism*, p. 57.
125 Alfred Arteaga, *An Other Tongue* (Durham, NC: Duke University Press, 1994), p. 18.
126 By mid century, particularly around the time of the Scottish Earl of Bute's reign as prime minister, migrant Lowland Scots and Highlanders were conflated in the imagination of the English, both figured in that persistent trope of foreignness: contamination and, relatedly, invasion.

2 "A GRAMMARIANS REGARD TO THE GENIUS OF OUR TONGUE"

1 Richard Helgerson examines Elizabethan efforts "to have a kingdom of our own language" in *Forms of Nationhood: The Elizabethan Writing of England* (Chicago University Press, 1992). The contradictions he observes in Spenser's formulation, in which a "dynastic conception of communal identity" sits uncomfortably next to a "postdynastic nationalism" (2) were no longer pressing in the eighteenth century, yet the distinction Helgerson perceives between national representation that "based its claim to cultural legitimacy on removing itself from popular culture . . . being less like the people and more like the aristocratic cultures of Greco-Roman antiquity" and modern nationalism which "since the late eighteenth century, has characteristically based itself on the recovery (or the invention) of a 'national' folk and on a reduction in the depth of class divisions" (10–11) informs Johnson's own movement between nationalist rhetorics of exclusion and inclusion.

2 Luke Gibbons, "The Sympathetic Bond: Ossian, Celticism, and Colonialism," in *Celticism*, ed. Terence Brown (Amsterdam: Rodopi, 1996), p. 275.

3 I take the figure of "nobody" from Catherine Gallagher's discussion in *Nobody's Story: The Vanishing Acts of Women Writers in the Marketplace, 1670–1820* (Berkeley: California University Press, 1994). In this period in England "Nobody" also signified a common person, a suggestive double meaning I discuss later in the chapter.

4 Allen Reddick's comparison in *The Making of Johnson's Dictionary* (Cambridge University Press, 1990), p. 177.

5 Samuel Johnson, *Plan of a Dictionary* (1747) (Menston, UK: Scolar Press, 1970). *Dictionary* references are to the first edition (London: William Shahan, 1755).

6 Benedict Anderson, *Imagined Communities* (London: Verso, 1987). Marshall McLuhan writes, "Nationalism depends upon or derives from the 'fixed point of view' that arrives with print," in *The Gutenberg Galaxy* (Toronto University Press, 1988) p. 220. See also Alvin Kernan, *Printing Technology, Letters and Samuel Johnson* (Princeton University Press, 1987).

7 Scott Elledge, "The Naked Science of Language, 1747–1786," in *Studies in Criticism and Aesthetics, 1660–1800*, eds. Howard Anderson and John Shea (Minneapolis: Minnesota University Press, 1967), Reddick (*The Making*), and Howard Weinbrot, "Samuel Johnson's *Plan* and Preface to the *Dictionary*: The Growth of a Lexicographer's Mind," in *New Aspects of Lexicography*, ed. Howard Weinbrot (Carbondale: Southern Illinois University Press, 1955) have argued that neither Johnson nor his *Dictionary* were prescriptive, and hints of prescription in the *Plan* reflect Johnson's attempt to appease the *Dictionary*'s early quasi-patron, Lord Chesterfield. Donald T. Siebert, "Bubbled, Bamboozled, and Bit: 'Low Bad' Words in Johnson's *Dictionary*," *SEL* 26 (1986), pp. 484–95, shares this viewpoint, arguing that Johnson's inclusion of "low words" indicates he was not a "rigidly prescriptivist lexicographer." But see also James H. Sledd and Gwin J. Kolb, *Dr. Johnson's*

Dictionary: Essays in the Biography of a Book (Chicago University Press, 1955), DeWitt T. Starnes and Gertrude E. Noyes, *The English Dictionary from Cawdrey to Johnson 1604–1755* (North Carolina University Press, 1946), and Elizabeth Hedrick, "Fixing the Language: Johnson, Chesterfield, and *The Plan of a Dictionary*," *ELH* 55 (1988), pp. 421–42 for views of Johnson's prescriptivism. Despite Johnson's own anti-prescriptive attitude, it is important to note that before communicating anything else, the *Dictionary* communicates a conception of language as ordered and unitary. We would do well to consider the *Dictionary* not in terms of Johnson's intentions, but in the symbolic market in which it participates. For a discussion of the "symbolic market" of languages see Pierre Bourdieu, *Language and Symbolic Power* (Cambridge, MA: Harvard University, Press, 1991).

A parallel difficulty emerges around the vacillating rhetorical position of Johnson's authority. See Martin Wechselblatt, who describes Johnson's "displacement and recovery of authority as an ahistorical condition of all questioning of authority" in "Finding Mr. Boswell: Rhetorical Authority and National Identity in Johnson's *A Journey to the Western Islands of Scotland*," *ELH* 60 (1993), pp. 117–48, and Steven Lynn, "Locke's Eye, Adam's Tongue, Johnson's Word: Language, Marriage, and the 'Choice of Life'," *The Age of Johnson* 3 (1990). Deidre Lynch reads "Johnson's own peculiar duality" as produced by a crisis in authority wrought by the rise of the (literary) market in " 'Beating the Track of the Alphabet': Samuel Johnson, Tourism, and the ABCs of Modern Authority," *ELH* 57 (1990), pp. 357–405.

8 John Barrell, *English Literature in History, 1730–1780* (London: Hutchinson, 1983), p. 113.
9 The notion of "grammar in general" resembles the beliefs of natural law theorists Grotius and Pufendorf, who, Peter Stein writes, "sought to establish the existence of certain universal legal principles which are binding on all men, irrespective of the time and the place . . . They had the same certainty and generality as a proposition of mathematics." Pertinent to my linking of these attitudes to empire, Stein writes of such axioms, "They could then be regarded as the basis of an international law." *Legal Evolution: The Story of an Idea* (Cambridge University Press, 1980), pp. 3–4.
10 Robert Lowth, *Short Introduction to English Grammar* (Leeds: J. Binns, 1794), p. iv, following quote, p. vii.
11 As late as 1799, for instance, Hugh Mitchell cites Lowth directly in arguing that students should be taught their native tongue in relation to universal grammar. See *Scotticisms, Vulgar Anglicisms, and Grammatical Improprieties Corrected* (Glasgow: Falconer and Willison, 1799), p. vi.
12 A. D. Horgan, for instance, points to Johnson's description of Shakespeare's style as "ungrammatical" as evidence of Johnson's belief in general grammar. *Johnson on Language* (London: Macmillan, 1994), p. 87.
13 Hedrick, "Locke's Theory of Language and Johnson's *Dictionary*," *Eighteenth-Century Studies* 20 (1987), pp. 423–44 and Murray Cohen, *Sensible Words*

(Baltimore: Johns Hopkins University Press, 1977) locate Johnson's work in the juncture between an older, Lockean theory of language and an emerging linguistic historicism. I link those linguistic models to imperial and national views of language, respectively.
14 But see Wechselblatt, "The Pathos of Example: Professionalism and Colonialization in Johnson's Preface to the *Dictionary,*" *Yale Journal of Criticism* 9 (1996), pp. 381–403.
15 Linda Colley, *Britons: Forging the Nation* (New Haven: Yale University Press, 1992), p. 85.
16 Johnson reportedly responded to Dr. Adams's doubt that he could complete the *Dictionary* in three years, when the French Academy of forty members had taken forty years, "Let me see; forty times forty is sixteen hundred. As three is to sixteen hundred, so is the proportion of an Englishman to a Frenchman." James Boswell, *The Life of Samuel Johnson,* ed. Bergen Evans (New York: The Modern Library, 1965), p. 52. Geoffrey Hughes lists some of the French terms Johnson excluded with their earliest *OED* citation: champagne (1664), coursage (1481), bourgeois (1564), and facade (1656) in "Johnson's Dictionary and Attempts to 'Fix the Language,'" *English Studies in Africa* 28 (1985), pp. 99–107.
17 George Caffentzis links attempts to stabilize linguistic value to imperial commerce in *Clipped Coins, Abused Words and Civil Government* (Brooklyn: Autonomedia, 1989).
18 A. Archibald Land, *A Key to the Art of Letters* (London: 1700). Cited in Tony Crowley, *Language in History* (London: Routledge, 1996), pp. 71–2.
19 J. C. D. Clark, *Samuel Johnson: Literature, Religion, and English Cultural Politics from the Restoration to Romanticism* (Cambridge University Press, 1994), p. 75.
20 For a consideration of the shift in the "official language" from classical to vernacular see Joseph Levine, *The Battle of the Books* (Ithaca: Cornell University Press, 1991). In *Johnson's* Dictionary *and the Language of Learning* (North Carolina University Press, 1986), Robert DeMaria offers quotations revealing Johnson's conflicted relationship to Latinate language (pp. 169–70, 172).
21 Anderson calls the nationalist imperative to claim ancient status "subjective antiquity" (*Imagined Communities,* p. 14). On the appeal to the past specific to the politics of eighteenth-century Britain see Isaac Kramnick, *Bolingbroke and His Circle: The Politics of Nostalgia in the Age of Walpole* (Cambridge, MA: Harvard University Press, 1968).
22 Jonathan Swift, *Proposal for Correcting, Improving and Ascertaining the English Tongue* (London, 1712).
23 "Preface to Shakespeare," in *The Yale Edition of the Works of Samuel Johnson,* ed. Arthur Sherbo (New Haven: Yale University Press, 1968), vol. vii, p. 110. Attempting to preserve literary meaning over time, Johnson's *Dictionary* resembles early Western dictionaries, which offer translating quotations to help readers understand a fading classical Greek.
24 Letter to Thomas Warton 16 July 1754. *Letters of Samuel Johnson,* ed. Bruce Redford (Princeton University Press, 1982), vol. I, p. 80.

25 DeMaria notes the *Dictionary*'s indebtedness to "encyclopedic historical works that flourished in the seventy years after the Restoration" (*Johnson's Dictionary*, p. 11), but I want to highlight its specifically Anglo-British emphasis. Johnson hopes to "add celebrity to *Bacon*, to *Hooker*, to *Milton*, and to *Boyle*" and writes against "favour of foreign authors and of contempt for our native literature" in *Idler* 91, 6 January 1760.
26 Cited in Carey McIntosh, *Common and Courtly Language, The Stylistics of Social Class in 18th-Century Literature* (Philadelphia: Pennsylvania University Press, 1986), pp. 19, 76.
27 Raymond Williams writes, "in the stabilization of a 'national' language, and then within that centralizing process of a 'standard' wholly native, authentic and long-standing variations become designated as culturally subordinate" (i.e. "dialects"). *Keywords* (Oxford University Press, 1983), p. 105.
28 John Donald comments, "the nation is not so much identity as 'hierarchically organized values, dispositions, and differences'" Cited in *Cultural Institutions of the Novel*, eds. Deidre Lynch and William Warner (Durham, NC: Duke University Press, 1996), p. 171. See also Crowley, *Language*, pp. 71, 76, 88 and Barrell, *English*, pp. 110–75.
29 Olivia Smith notes the use of imperial terms, "civilized" and "barbarian", to mark intra-national linguistic divides. *The Politics of Language 1791–1819* (Oxford University Press, 1984).
30 Barrell describes the mid-century rhetoric of grammar as fulfilling "egalitarian aspirations even as it suppresses difference" (*English Literature*, p. 112).The rhetoric around literacy worked in a similar way in this period. Kathleen Wilson argues that if literacy is the point of entry for some, that point is more aptly understood as a continuum which shades into exclusion for many. "Citizenship, Empire, and Modernity," *Eighteenth-Century Studies* 29 (1995), p. 75.
31 The authoritative introduction to English dictionary history is Starnes and Noyes, *English Dictionary*.
32 Michel Foucault, *The Order of Things* (New York: Vintage, 1973), p. x.
33 See, for instance, James Lightbody, *Mariner's Jewell* (London, 1695). Interestingly, that other print production of nationalist consciousness, the newspaper, also appeared alongside and facilitated imperial commerce. See Jurgen Habermas, *The Structural Transformation of the Public Sphere*, trans. Thomas Burger (Cambridge, MA: MIT Press, 1991), pp. 16–22.
34 Judith Anderson, *Words that Matter* (Stanford University Press, 1996).
35 See also John Bullokar, *An English Expositor or Compleat Dictionary* (1616); Thomas Blount, *Glossographia* (1656); and Edward Phillips, *The New World of English Words* (1658).
36 V. N. Volosinov, *Marxism and the Philosophy of Language*, trans. Ladislav Matejka and I. R. Titunik (Cambridge, MA: Harvard University Press, 1986), pp. 71–7.
37 Raymond Williams, *Marxism and Literature* (Oxford University Press, 1977), p. 25.

38 Edward Said, *Orientalism* (New York, Vintage, 1979), p. 20.
39 See Sterling Andrus Leonard, *The Doctrine of Correctness in English Usage 1700–1800* (New York: Russell & Russell, 1962) and Joel Reed, "Restoration and Repression: The Language Projects of the Royal Society," *Studies in Eighteenth-Century Culture* 19 (1989), pp. 399–412. See also Walter Mignola's documentation of the mutual development of Spanish vernacular grammars and Spanish empire in *The Darker Side of the Renaissance* (Ann Arbor: Michigan University Press, 1996).
40 Letter to William Samuel Johnson 9 March 1773. *Letters*, Redford, ed., vol. I, p. 81. See also Wechselblatt "The Pathos" and Steven Scherwatzky, "Johnson, *Rasselas*, and the Politics of Empire," *Eighteenth-Century Life* 16 (1992), pp. 103–13.
41 Johnson's *Journey* is notorious for its sweeping generalizations regarding Scots Gaelic. See Katie Trumpener, *Bardic Nationalism, The Romantic Novel and the British Empire* (Princeton University Press, 1997), pp. 67–127. Johnson writes, "Cromwell, when he subdued Scotland, stationed a garrison ... the soldiers seem to have incorporated afterwards with the inhabitants ... for the language of this town has been long considered as peculiarly elegant." (Note the one-way direction of this linguistic influence.) *A Journey to the Western Islands of Scotland*, ed. Peter Levi (Harmondsworth, UK: Penguin, 1984), p. 51. On literacy and colonial improvement see Johnson's letter of 25 September 1770 to his former Jamaican servant, Francis Barber. *Letters*, Redford, ed., vol. I, p. 350.
42 W. K. Wimsatt, *Philosophic Words* (Hamden, CT: Archon Books, 1968).
43 Lord Monboddo, for instance, writes that a dead language exists in greater purity, and with less hazard of corruption, than while it continued to be spoken. *Of the Origin and Progress of Language* (Edinburgh: 1773–92), vol. I, pp. 405–6. Although Johnson differed from him on many points, he shared this view.
44 This structure reflects a Lockean movement from simple to complex ideas, as Hedrick notes. She adds, however, that Johnson's definitions of complex ideas are rarely Locke's "combinations of simple ideas." I am indebted to Hedrick and to DeMaria (*Johnson's Dictionary*, p. 165).
45 Johnson writes of metaphors such as "body politic," "In these imaginary similitudes, the same word is used at once in its primitive and metaphorical sense ... These parallels therefore have more of genius and less of truth; they often please but never convince." *Idler* 34, 9 December 1758.
46 See Homi Bhabha, "DissemiNation: time, narrative, and the margins of the modern nation" in *Nation and Narration*, ed. Homi Bhabha (London: Routledge, 1990).
47 Ruth Salvaggio, *Enlightened Absence: Neoclassical Configurations of the Feminine* (Urbana and Chicago: Illinois University Press, 1988), p. 11. Alternatively, Luce Irigaray's vision of language as a phallocentric ordering system is diametrically opposed to Johnson's vision. See *This Sex Which Is Not One*, trans. Catherine Porter (Ithaca: Cornell University Press, 1985). See also

Carol Fabricant, "Binding and Dressing Nature's Loose Tresses: The Ideology of Augustan Landscape Design," *Studies in Eighteenth Century Culture* 8 (Madison: Wisconsin University Press, 1979). Fabricant links the language of landscape design, where an all-powerful gardener "shapes and cultivates" a limitless feminized nature, to concepts of ownership (specifically enclosure) and "sexual forms of possession" (117).

48 Similarly, Salvaggio points to Bacon's self-described project of the "penetration of nature" (*Enlightened Absence*, p. 17).

49 Hedrick writes, "For Johnson, circulation of illegitimate words is domestic and political rebellion . . . In language . . . fatherhood is the basis for moral order." ("Fixing," p. 426).

50 David Hume, "Of the Rise and Progress of the Arts and Sciences," in *Essays Moral, Political and Literary*, ed. Eugene Miller (Indianapolis: Liberty Classics, 1987), pp. 111–37.

51 Philip Dormer Stanhope, fourth Earl of Chesterfield, *The World*, No. 100, 28 November 1754.

52 Chesterfield, *The World* 101, 5 December 1754.

53 Patricia Parker, *Literary Fat Ladies: Rhetoric, Gender, Property* (London: Methuen, 1987), p. 8.

54 For a discussion of Johnson's gendered conceptions of linguistic production and his estimation of orality, see my "Dr. Johnson Eats his Words," *Language Science* 22 (2000), pp. 295–314.

55 *Idler* 77, 6 October 1759.

56 Allon White, *Carnival, Hysteria, and Writing: Collected Essays and Autobiography* (Oxford: Clarendon Press, 1993), p. 125.

57 See Ernest Gellner, *Nations and Nationalism* (Oxford: Basil Blackwell, 1983) for the importance of these "day-to-day" cultural phenomena to nationalist rhetoric.

58 Jerome Christensen, *Practicing Enlightenment* (Madison: Wisconsin University Press, 1987), p. 15.

59 Crowley's use of Bourdieu's concept of a habitus is helpful here. He defines it as "a system of disposition which acts as the principle of generation and structuration of practices and representations which can be objectively 'regulated' and 'regular' without being reducible to rules" (*Language in History*, p. 82. See my Chapter 4.

60 See David Paxman, "The Genius of English: Eighteenth-Century Language Study and English Poetry," *Philological Quarterly* 70 (1991), pp. 27–46.

61 Cited in J. G. A. Pocock, *The Ancient Constitution and the Feudal Law* (New York: W. W. Norton & Company, 1967), pp. 33–4.

62 Wechselblatt compares the epistemological structure of common law "with its 'immemorial' origins supplemented retroactively by *subsequent* 'precedent'" to the rhetorical strategy of national identity, which "always contains 'a minus in the origin,' in need of regular resupplying by subsequent instances" – "Finding." p. 131). Bhabha also writes of the "tension in signifying the people as an *a priori* historical presence, a pedagogical object;

and the people constructed in the performance of narrative, its enunciatory 'present' marked in the repetition and pulsation of the national sign" ("Dissemination," p. 299).
63 Cited in E. L. McAdam, *Dr. Johnson and the English Law* (Syracuse University Press, 1951), p. 96.
64 Adam Smith, *Edinburgh Review* 1 (1755).
65 Like Lynch, I find Stewart's discussion of the collection useful, in *On Longing: Narratives of the Miniature, the Gigantic, the Souvenir, the Collection* (Baltimore: Johns Hopkins University Press, 1984), p. 152. Invested with both a use and exchange value, the position of the word in the *Dictionary* also suggests a commodity logic. Differences between words are effaced in the abstraction of their appearance on a list and by the equivalence implied in the construction or a definition. See Karl Marx, *Capital*, trans. Samuel Moore and Edward Aveling (New York: International Publishers, 1967), p. 37.
66 I adapt this term "linguistic patrimony" from Nestor Garcia Canclini's concept of cultural patrimony as "constitut[ing] the least suspicious resource for guaranteeing social complicity. That group of goods and traditional practices that identify us as a nation," and "the perennial character of these goods makes us imagine that their value is beyond question and turns them into a source of collective consensus, beyond the divisions among classes, ethnic groups, and other groups that fracture society." *Hybrid Cultures: Strategies for Entering and Leaving Modernity* (Minneapolis: Minnesota University Press, 1995) p. 108.
67 Ernest Renan, "What is a Nation?," trans. Martin Thom, in *Nation and Narration*, ed. Homi Bhabha (New York and London: Routledge, 1990) pp. 18–22.
68 The twentieth-century "Creole Hypothesis" recognizes English as a product of linguistic contact. Nicole Z. Domingue writes, "The 'unbroken continuity' of English has been observed by many . . . it is however possible to interpret the same linguistic facts . . . to show that the language of Chaucer is not a modernized form of OE but a linguistic innovation, the result of the contact of several languages – in fact, very much alike [sic] a creole," in "Middle English: Another Creole?" *Journal of Creole Studies* 1 (1977), pp. 89–100. See also Patricia Poussa, "The Evolution of Early Standard English: The Creolization Hypothesis," *Studia Anglica Posnaniensia* 14 (1982), pp. 69–85. Alok Yadav shared these references with me.
69 Some critics have identified Johnson's attention to English grammar as the *Dictionary*'s most important contribution. See Jeffrey T. Gross, "Dr. Johnson's Treatment of English Particles in the *Dictionary*," *University of Mississippi Studies in English* 2 (1981), pp. 71–92. Johnson's attention to the peculiarities of English syntax suggests a more complicated vision of grammar than the unconscious reliance on Harris's notion of universal grammar argued by Horgan.
70 The same holds true for his references to the Irish, as in " 'There flocked unto him all the scum of the Irish out of all places' Spenser." Yadav notes

that Johnson does not even include definitions for "Gaelic," "British," or "Scots," in "Nationalism and Literature in Eighteenth-Century Britain," (Ph.D Dissertation, 1993).
71 James G. Basker, "Scotticisms and the Problem of Cultural Identity in Eighteenth-Century Britain," *Eighteenth-Century Life* 15 (1991), pp. 81–95.
72 This achieves on a linguistic level the temporal "othering" Johannes Fabian describes in *Time and the Other* (New York: Columbia University Press, 1983).
73 Basker notes that the warning labels did not appear in the abridged version. Alternatively, some Scots terms included in the *Dictionary* no longer circulate in English, as in "Juking, in Scotland . . . any complaisance by bending the head" or "klick, in Scotland it denotes to pilfer or steal away suddenly with a snatch" or "liard, in Scotland denotes gray-haired."
74 To those who would argue that the language of the Scots was merely a dialect, one writer has succinctly responded, in Scots, "A language is a dialect wi' an army an navy!" Billy Kay, *Scots: The Mither Tongue* (Edinburgh: Mainstream Publishing, 1986), p. 11.
75 John Ray, *Collection of English Words not Generally Used* (London: 1674).
76 See Lynda Mugglestone, *'Talking Proper': The Rise of Accent as Social Symbol* (Oxford: Clarendon, 1995), p. 26.
77 Wimsatt notes, "The *Dictionary* contained many words that "had attained archaic status at the date when Johnson used them" (*Philosophic Words*, p. 92).
78 I say "at least" because this was the number produced by a search of the *Dictionary* on CD-ROM (Cambridge University Press, 1996), which is, however, not entirely reliable – many instances failed to appear in this search.
79 Bourdieu, *Language*, p. 60. Johnson's *Dictionary* does not quite fit Bourdieu's model: "The dictionary . . . assembles, by scholarly recording, the totality of the linguistic resources accumulated in the course of time and, in particular, all the possible uses of the same word," but it does claim that totality. Bourdieu's assertion that the "normalized language" represented in dictionaries is "capable of functioning outside the constraints and without the assistance of the situation" squares with Johnson's early lexical hopes.
80 John Willinsky's observation of the *OED*'s assembling of writers that makes them appear "as if these word workers had for a thousand years been engaged in the common project of giving meaning and form to this one language" applies too to Johnson's presentation. *Empire of Words: The Reign of the* OED (Princeton University Press, 1994), p. 6.
81 There are parallels here to Thomas Reinert's discussion of the dilemma of fame in *Regulating Confusion* (Durham, NC: Duke University Press, 1996), pp. 18–45.
82 Barrell writes, "it must be open, then, only to those who perform no regular, determinate task to comprehend and describe the relations between such tasks" (*English Literature*, p. 34). It is the language of the impossible figure of the spectating gentleman, capable of a general overview of an ever more complex society.

83 In this way, language might be said to resemble other eighteenth-century "bodily" markers, such as beauty marks, meant to distinguish one from the anonymity of the crowd. See Reinert's discussion of the work of Richard Sennett (*Regulating*, pp. 5–7, 31).

84 Similarly, Garcia Canclini writes of all national monuments: they "present the collection of heroes, scenes, and founding objects. They are placed in a square, a public territory that does not belong to anyone in particular but to 'everyone'" (*Hybrid Cultures*, p. 133).

85 Johnson himself might be said to occupy an "outsider" position. As Olivia Smith (and Raymond Williams before her) points out, "scholars such as Johnson who had received a classical education without having the social status which usually accompanied it, played a major role in fixing usages of language as means of class distinction" (*Politics of Language*, p. 17).

86 This sense of language depends not simply upon the idea that one class and its language might be conventionally understood as superior, but rather on the possibility that a permanent, "general" version of the language could be said to exist at all. See Christina Ross, "The Natural law of Standard English and the Practical Criticism of Emily Dickinson" (Ph.D. Dissertation, 1995).

87 In his analysis of Cawdrey's *Table Alphabeticall*, White writes, "The double movement of instruction, which preserves the hierarchy of discourse in the very act of apparently trying to abolish it, is clearly revealed ... Holding out the tantalizing promise to the reader that she will gain skill and power through the purchase of the book, it nevertheless places her precisely as an outsider to her own national language, by and in the very act of producing the 'table alphabeticall'" (127).

88 See Crowley on the empowerment of the bourgeoisie through their developing confidence in their language in terms of Habermas' theory of the bourgeois public sphere (73). See also Susan Fitzmaurice-Wright, "The Commerce of Language in the Pursuit of Politeness in Eighteenth-Century England," *English Studies* 4 (1998), pp. 309–27.

89 Harvey Graff states, "perhaps thirty percent of the lower class youngsters learned their letters through charity schools," in *Legacies of Literacy* (Indiana University Press, 1991) p. 239. Johnson took a great interest in such charity schools, both Scottish and English.

90 Stephen J. Greenblatt, "Learning to Curse," in *First Images of America: The Impact of the New World on the Old*, ed. Fredi Chiapelli (Berkeley: California University Press, 1976), pp. 561–80.

91 For a discussion of its reception see Arthur Sherbo. "*Nil Nisi Bonum*: Samuel Johnson in *The Gentleman's Magazine*", *College Literature* 16 (1989), pp. 168–83. In a letter to Charles Burney (24 December 1757) Johnson complains that "among all my acquaintances there were only two who ... did not depress me with threats of censure from the public." Suggestively, in the same letter Johnson describes one positive review in the *London Chronicle* which compares him to Caesar. *Letters* vol. II pp. 157, 160.

92 *The Poems of Robert Fergusson*, vol. II, ed. Matthew P. McDiarmid (Edinburgh and London: Blackwood & Sons, 1956), pp. 204–6. See also Trumpener's discussion, *Bardic Nationalism*, pp. 86–7.

93 See "To the Principal and Professors of the University of St. Andrews on their Superb Treat to Dr. Samuel Johnson," in *Poems*, ed. McDiarmid. Instead of serving Johnson "snails and puddocks" "frae France and Spain" the professors should have served "Imprimis . . . a haggis fat" and "Secundo . . . a gude sheep's head . . . And four black trotters clad wi' girsle."

94 Archibald Campbell, *Lexiphanes, a Dialogue* (London: 1767). Campbell's Scottish affiliations are noticeable in his extended footnotes quarreling with Johnson's definition of oats.

95 This is also a reversal of characterizations of Irish and Scots Gaelic-inflected English. Trumpener writes of "Lilli burlero," (1687), the "ubiquitous anti-Jacobite song of the Williamite wars . . . sung throughout the eighteenth century, to mark the defeat of their cause, the verse mocked both the nonsensical sounds of Gaelic and Irish English" (*Bardic Nationalism*, p. 46).

96 Marie-Helen Huet, *Monstrous Imagination* (Cambridge, MA: Harvard University Press, 1993), p. 136.

97 T. Collinson's letter to Dr. John Sims, Edinburgh University Library MS.La.II.647/91. A language scholar familiar with recent appointees at Oxford, he speaks highly of Horne Tooke.

98 George Mason, *A Supplement to Dr. Johnson's English Dictionary* (London, 1801).

99 That Johnson faced this accusation from all sides – both from those who felt the *Dictionary* did not represent simple, polite "modern" English and from those who felt it did not contain enough of English's noble, older, "Gothic" terms suggests more than a generalized carping. Jonathan Brody Kramnick has made a convincing argument regarding Johnson's rejection of both of these positions in relation to literary criticism, and a parallel argument pertains to his lexicographical choices. See *Making the English Canon: Print, Capitalism and The Cultural Past, 1700–1770* (Cambridge University Press, 1998). Yet if the Gothic and modern are more easily dismissed as mistaken literary critical positions, Johnson could not confine words used now or in the distant past to the dustbins of history quite so easily.

100 Cited in Sledd and Kolb, *Dr. Johnson's*, p. 35. Johnson responds to attacks of his use of hard words in *Idler* 70, 18 August 1759: "words are only hard to those who do not understand them; and the critic ought always to inquire, whether he is incommoded by the fault of the writer, or by his own. Every author does not write for every reader; many questions are such as the illiterate part of mankind can have neither interest nor pleasure in discussing, and which therefore it would be a useless endeavour to level with common minds."

101 The *OED* lists as a contemporary definition of "Hottentot": "a person of inferior intellect or culture; one degraded in the scale of civilization, or ignorant of the usages of civil society."
102 See Smith, *Politics of Language*. Stephen Prickett, however, refutes Smith's (and Marilyn Butler's) claims that Tooke "favoured the legitimacy of 'vulgar' speech" and argues that the wacky etymologies and Socratic dialogue of *The Diversions* worked instead towards establishing that the politics of right had been "laid down from the very beginning of language in the human psyche itself" (16). See "Radicalism and Linguistic Theory: Horne Tooke on Samuel Pegge," *Yearbook of English Studies* 19 (1989), pp. 1–17.
103 Tooke had many supporters, including Charles Richardson, who credited him with straightening out Johnson's muddle of metaphorical and literal usage. *Illustrations of English Philology* (London: Gale and Fenner, 1815).
104 Susan Stewart has argued that "the model which linguistics has assumed, whereby stable languages eventually become creolized, has been moving backward; instead, we might assume creolization at the point of origin and view stabilization of the linguistic system not as the normal but as the restricted case." "Shouts in the Street," *Critical Inquiry* 10 (1983), p. 273.

3 WOMEN, CELTS AND HOLLOW VOICES

1 So central is Dickens to Anglo-British identity that his likeness appears on British currency (which remains the last and most virulently fought-over vestige of national iconography in the wake of European Union).
2 *The Concise Scots Dictionary*, ed. Mairi Robinson (Aberdeen University Press, 1985). Johnson's *Dictionary* lists the sound/sense echo of the origins of "clink": "perhaps softened from clank, or corrupted from click," it means "to strike so as to make a small sharp noise." Aileen Douglas also notes that "clinker" signifies, appositely, "mistake" and "coal that won't burn . . . matter with which nothing can be done," in *Uneasy Sensations: Smollett and the Body* (Chicago University Press, 1995), p. 183.
3 See Paul-Gabriel Bouce, *Les Romans de Smollett: étude critique* (Paris: Didier, 1971), p. 394; Damien Grant, *Tobias Smollett: A Study in Style* (Manchester University Press, 1977); W. Arthur Boggs, "A Win Jenkins' Lexicon," *Bulletin of the New York Public Library* 68 (1964), pp. 323–30; "Dialectical Ingenuity in *Humphry Clinker*," *Papers on English Language and Literature* 1 (1965), pp. 327–37; "Win Jenkins' Archaisms and Proverbial Phrases," *The USF Language Quarterly* 4 (1965), pp. 33–6 and "Some Standard Eighteenth-Century English Usages," *The Quarterly Journal of Speech* 51 (1965), pp. 304–6; Louise Hanes, "The Pronunciation of Tabitha Bramble," *Journal of English Linguistics* 14 (1980), pp. 6–19; and Arthur Sherbo, "Win Jenkins' Language," *Papers on Language and Literature* 5 (1969), pp. 199–204.
4 See Terence Bowers, "Reconstituting the National Body in Smollett's *Travels through France and Italy*," *Eighteenth-Century Life* 21 (1997), pp. 1–25;

Michael Rosenblum, "Smollett's *Humphry Clinker*," in *The Cambridge Companion to the Eighteenth-Century Novel*, ed. John Richetti (Cambridge University Press, 1996), pp. 175–97; Kenneth Simpson, *The Protean Scot* (Aberdeen University Press, 1988); Charlotte Sussman, "Lismahago's Captivity: Transculturation in *Humphry Clinker*" *ELH* 61 (1994), pp. 597–618; and Douglas, *Uneasy Sensations*. Two exceptions are James G. Basker, "Scotticisms and the Problem of Cultural Identity in Eighteenth-Century Britain," *Eighteenth-Century Life* 15 (1991), pp. 81–95; and Robert Crawford, *Devolving English Literature* (Oxford: Clarendon, 1992).

5 In using Colin Kidd's term "Anglo-British" (with the stress on "Anglo," as discussed in my introduction), I vary from Crawford's sense of Smollett's final novel as achieving "a comparative ... framework" (*Devolving*, p. 75).

6 Of those untrustworthy translations Anne Grant, herself transplanted from England to the Highlands, observed, "In what relates to the lower class of Highlanders even he appears allowably ignorant, not knowing their language." *Letters from the Mountains Being the Real Correspondence of a Lady* (London, 1809), cited in *Tobias Smollett: The Critical Heritage*, ed. Lionel Kelly (London and New York: Routledge and Kegan Paul, 1987), p. 241.

7 Tobias Smollett, *The Expedition of Humphry Clinker*, ed. Lewis Knapp, revised Paul-Gabriel Boucé (Oxford University Press, 1992), p. 338.

8 *The Briton* No. 10, 31 July 1762, in *Poems, Plays, and* The Briton, ed. Byron Gassman (Athens, GA: Georgia University Press, 1993), p. 284.

9 Allan Ramsay, in his use of Scots vernacular, might seem a logical addition to this list. Yet I find myself persuaded by Peter Zenzinger's argument that Ramsay, as a middle-class poet aspiring to social recognition by the upper classes, was in a position that "required more deliberate distancing from his subject matter." In other words, his use of Scots was something different from a "mutinous brandishing." See "Low Life, Primitivism and Honest Poverty in Ramsay and Burns," *Studies in Scottish Literature* 30 (1998) pp. 43–58.

10 Tobias Smollett, *Present State of all Nations*, Volume 2 (London, 1768), p. 115.

11 "Percy, Shaw and the Ferguson 'Cheat'" in *Ossian Revisited*, ed. Howard Gaskill (Edinburgh University Press, 1991), p. 212.

12 If Walter Scott is to be believed, Smollett's family had ties to rebel Highlanders. In *Rob Roy* he claims that an ancestor of Smollett's (himself named Tobias Smollett), led a Highland raid. Smollett's grandfather had promoted the English/Scottish Union, but Smollett's relationship to him was antagonistic. See Robin Fabel, "The Patriotic Briton: Tobias Smollett and English Politics, 1756–1771," *Eighteenth-Century Studies* 8 (1974), pp. 100–14.

13 James Basker, *Tobias Smollett: Critic and Journalist* (Newark: Delaware University Press, 1988), p. 76 and Robert Spector, *Tobias George Smollett* (Boston: Twayne, 1989).

14 June 1756, p. 438, cited in Basker (*Tobias Smollett*, p. 76).

15 Basker notes, "to Johnson it must have seemed particularly inappropriate, perhaps even presumptuous, that Smollett should propose founding an

academy of letters in 1755, just months after Johnson had published his *Dictionary* – a work that many, including Johnson himself . . . thought had obviated the need for such a body" (29). Basker also remarks, "It didn't help that Smollett was a Scot" (*Tobias Smollett*, p. 29).
16 Rosenblum, "Smollett's *Humphry*" p. 176–7.
17 Louis Martz, *The Later Career of Tobias Smollett* (New Haven: Yale University Press, 1967), pp. 56 and 63, respectively.
18 *Monthly Review* (April 1758), cited in Paul-Gabriel Bouce, "Archibald Campbell on Smollett's Style," *Studies in Scottish Literature* 9 (1972), pp. 211–17. This is the same Campbell who authored *Lexiphanes*.
19 In *The Lounger* (1792) Jeremiah Whitaker Newman writes, "A good style has been defined, 'proper words in proper places;' and I have not met with a more just selection of appropriate terms, and descriptive expression, than in . . . Smollett," and Charles Lamb asserts that Smollett "wrote good pure English" in *Critical Heritage*, pp. 25, 260, respectively.
20 Johnson refers to Smollett as "a scholarly man, sir, though a Scot." Cited in Crawford, *Devolving*, pp. 56–8. J. C. D. Clark cites William Murphy's 1793 recording of Johnson as saying, "the impudence of a Scotsman is the impudence of a leech, that fixes and sucks your blood." *Samuel Johnson* (Cambridge University Press, 1994), p. 66. See Eric Rothstein, "Scotophilia and *Humphry Clinker*: The Politics of Beggary, Bugs, and Buttocks," *University of Toronto Quarterly* 52 (1982), pp. 65–78 and Andrew Varney "From Tennis-Ball to Fruit Tree: Smollett's Story of the Scottish Self," *The Swansea Review* 9 (1994), pp. 549–60.
21 Sterling Leonard, *The Doctrine of Correctness in English Usage 1700–1800* (New York: Russell & Russell, 1962), p. 178.
22 *The Briton* No. 11, 7 August 1762.
23 Bowers helpfully points to Bourdieu's observation that "societies that seek to produce a new man . . . set such store on the seemingly most insignificant details of *dress, bearing*, physical and verbal *manners*." Bowers adds, "It is in such details that larger ordering systems – including social and political systems – are made 'natural' to those who must conform to them" ("Reconstituting," p. 2). What remains interesting about Smollett and those responding to him are the ways in which particular verbal manners are seen as natural or not natural to the Scots. Much rides on this question, which is why a seemingly inordinate amount of detail is paid to linguistic minutiae. *The Briton*, No. 1 announces, "Though I am a NORTH BRITON, I will endeavour to write 'plain English,' and to avoid the numerous 'Scotticisms' the BRITON abounds with; and then, as the world is apt to mistake, he may be taken for a 'Scotsman,' and I shall pass for an 'Englishman.'" The periodical thus draws the lines of Britishness in stark linguistic terms.
24 *Critical Heritage*, pp. 164–5.
25 See Helen Deutsch's essay, "The Author as Monster: The Case of Doctor Johnson," in *"Defect": Engendering the Modern Body*, eds. Helen Deutsch and

Felicity Nussbaum (University of Michigan Press, 2000), and Deidre Lynch, "'Beating the Track of the Alphabet': Samuel Johnson, Tourism, and the ABCs of Modern Authority," *ELH* 57 (1990), pp. 357–405.
26 This is a reference to Thomas Sheridan, whom I discuss in Chapter 4. Cited in Tony Crowley, *Language in History* (London and New York: Routledge, 1996).
27 Reprinted in *Poems, Plays, and* The Briton, ed. Byron Gassman, O. M. Brack (Athens, GA: University of Georgia Press, 1993) pp. 49–52.
28 Smollett's politics are not easily characterized, and several critics have exposed mistaken assumptions about his Toryism and Jacobite sympathies, such as Donald Greene, "Smollett the Historian: A Reappraisal," *Tobias Smollett: Bicentennial Essays Presented to Lewis Knapp*, eds. G. S. Rousseau and P.-G. Boucé (Oxford University Press, 1971), pp. 25–56 and Fabel, *Patriotic Briton*. These essays, however, seem to overshoot the mark in denying any Jacobite sympathies in Smollett's *Tears* or later *History of England*. Crawford, in contrast, points to Grant's observation that as late as 1769, in *The History and Adventures of an Atom*, Smollett continues to attack Cumberland, the "butcher" of Culloden (*Devolving*, p. 62).
29 Douglas, *Uneasy Sensations*, p. xxviii. She writes, "His emphasis on sensation disrupts convenient accounts of how society works and gives his fiction a contentious, subversive cast. Smollett was an alien in English society, and this may explain his inability to take it entirely on its own terms."
30 Betty Schellenberg, "Imagining the Nation in Defoe's *A Tour thro' the Whole Island of Great Britain*," *ELH* 62 (1995), pp. 295–312 especially p. 302. See also Pat Rogers "Introduction," *A Tour Thro' the Whole Island of Great Britain* (New York: Penguin, 1971).
31 These include Martin Martin's *A Late Voyage to St. Kilda* (1698) and *A Description of the Western Islands of Scotland* (1703) – with a revision of Martin's style, which Johnson had attacked – and Defoe's *Tour*. That Smollett's relationship to the Highlands was fully mediated by other texts is not surprising, given that, as Anne Grant had pointed out, he "left the country so young, that he was in a great measure a stranger to the Highlands, though born a borderer on it." See Martz, *Later Career*.
32 I would not want to overstate the political tenor of this characterization, reading it as strictly Tory in character, for Schellenberg reminds us how Defoe himself was ambivalent about a monstrously growing London.
33 John Sekora, *Luxury: The Concept in Western Thought from Eden to Smollett* (Baltimore: Johns Hopkins University Press, 1977).
34 On the discrepancy between material forms and linguistic signs see Douglas, *Uneasy Sensations*, especially pp. 162–83 and R. D. S. Jack, "Appearance and Reality in *Humphry Clinker*," in *Tobias Smollett*, ed. Alan Bold (Totowa, NJ: Vision, 1982), pp. 209–27.
35 Edward Schwarzschild argues that Win's and Tabitha's malaprops "realize forces and tensions concealed by supposedly complete representations. Such words, at once multivalent and pointed, indicate the instability and

the cost of the expedition's pat resolutions," in "'I Will Take the Whole Upon My Own Shoulders:' Collections and Corporeality in *Humphry Clinker*," *Criticism* 36 (1994), pp. 541–68.

36 Several critics have commented upon Smollett's changed characterization of Scotland. Robert Mayer argues that in this recharacterization "The Union . . . is a potential solution to the woes besetting England and the challenges confronting Scotland," in "History, *Humphry Clinker*, and the Novel," *Eighteenth-Century Fiction* 4 (1992), pp. 239–55, especially, p. 250.

37 Philip Withers, *Aristarchus* (London: 1788), pp. 160–1, cited in Leonard (*Doctrine*, p. 167).

38 Mary Favret describes the role of nineteenth-century centralizing reform of the postal system, yet even earlier distribution systems facilitate a spatial cognition integral to the individual's understanding of his or her place in a national system. In *Romantic Correspondence: Women, Politics and the Fiction of Letters* (Cambridge University Press, 1993), p. 210.

39 The efficacy of the epistolary novel in this regard is related to the popularity of the letter-writing manual of this period, a sort of linguistic "conduct book." See Carey McIntosh, *Polite and Courtly Language* (Champaign: Illinois University Press, 1986) and Favret, *Romantic*, pp. 24–5, 37.

40 The link between moral and literate acuity is even more transparent in the earlier letter manuals. See Robert Adams Day, *Told in Letters* (Ann Arbor: Michigan University Press, 1966).

41 Favret writes, "Throughout the eighteenth century the letter's ability to define and confine personal experience had already been subject to a centripetal force which carried the private into the public realm, offering the individual's most intimate self for mass consumption. Epistolary fiction invaded, then shattered, the closed areas of home, family and personal identity. This literary form, which developed alongside the eighteenth century's growing faith in the value of personal – and especially feminine – experience, grew in time to betray the very individualism it promoted" (*Romantic*, p. 12).

42 For a fascinating account of the social role of embarrassment and national identity formation see Cannon Schmitt, *Alien Nation: Nineteenth-Century Gothic Fictions and English Nationality* (Philadelphia: Pennsylvania University Press, 1997).

43 Robert Adams Day observes that the British letter in particular took "an increasing negligence of form, extremely loose . . . colloquially expressed" *Told in Letters* (Ann Arbor, MI: University of Michigan Press) p. 63), cited in Favret *Romantic*, p. 24.

44 Francis Grose's *Classical Dictionary of the Vulgar Tongue* (1789) refers to "bum" as "the breech, or backside," and Johnson's *Dictionary of the English Language* defines "commode" as a "privy."

45 Nick Williams, "The Dialect of Authenticity" in *English and the Other Languages*, eds. Marius Buning and Ton Hoenselaars (Amsterdam: Rodopi, 1999).

46 Lynda Mugglestone, "Ladylike Accents," in *'Talking Proper': The Rise of Accent as Social Symbol* (Oxford: Clarendon, 1995), pp. 160–207.
47 *Rabelais and His World*, trans. Helene Iswolsky (Bloomington: Indiana University Press, 1984), pp. 145–53. As Douglas points out, Smollett's "other" languages fall short of "heteroglossia" which demands that those languages be "equally capable of being 'languages of truth'" (*Uneasy Sensations*, p. 166). And Rosenblum argues, "Although *Humphry Clinker* is sometimes treated as a venture in the gaps and indeterminacies of Richardsonian epistolarity, I think it is really more old-fashioned . . . The letters are as grounded in the authority of the gentleman as the tour itself is." ('Smollett's *Humphrey*," p. 186). As in Humphry's representation, the other "outsider" characters and their languages have, as John Richetti argues, "always already [been] transformed by comic universalizing," in "Representing an Under Class," in *The New 18th Century*, eds. Felicity Nussbaum and Laura Brown (New York and London: Methuen, 1987) pp. 84–98, 94.
48 John Gibson Lockhart, *The Life of Robert Burns* (Edinburgh and London, 1828) cited in *Critical Heritage*, p. 365.
49 Mary Louise Pratt, "Linguistic Utopias," in *The Linguistics of Writing*, ed. Nigel Fabb (New York: Methuen, 1987), pp. 48–64.
50 Ernest Gellner, *Nations and Nationalism* (Ithaca: Cornell University Press, 1983).
51 Harvey J. Graff cites this ratio in *Legacy of Literacy* (Bloomington, IN: Indiana University Press, 1987), p. 231. These numbers are notoriously difficult to pin down.
52 Kathleen Wilson, "Citizenship, Empire, and Modernity," *Eighteenth-Century Studies* 29 (1995), p. 80.
53 For a discussion of images of female consumption see Elizabeth Kowaleski-Wallace, *Consuming Subjects: Women, Shopping, and Business in the Eighteenth Century* (New York: Columbia, 1997).
54 Jonathan Kramnick writes specifically of the *English* past, "The past crystallized by the Augustans was dialectically preserved by their successors as the radiant sheen of pre-enlightened, vernacular high culture," and "the linguistic distance . . . of Shakespeare and Spenser . . . made these writers canonical" (1090) "The Making of the English Canon," *PMLA* 112 (1997), pp. 1087–101.
55 Thomas Preston, Introduction to *The Expedition of Humphry Clinker*, ed. O. M. Brack, Jr. (Athens and London: Georgia University Press, 1990), p. xxxii.
56 William Mudford writes, "Of language thus debased by ignorance and affectation, the first instance in our country is, I believe, to be found in Shakespeare's comedy of *Much Ado about Nothing*, where the sagacious and eloquent Dogberry discourses with a most profound knowledge of that mode of speech which rhetoricians denominate catachresis." Cited in *Critical Heritage*, p. 322.

4 THE FIGURE OF THE NATION

1 See Bruce Lenman, *Integration, Enlightenment, and Industrialization: Scotland 1746–1832* (London: Edward Arnold, 1981); Nicholas Phillipson, "Politics, Politeness and the Anglicisation of early Eighteenth-Century Scottish Culture," in *Scotland and England*, ed. Roger Mason (Edinburgh: John Donald, 1987), pp. 226–46; and Tom Nairn, *The Break-up of Britain* (London: New Left Books, 1977).
2 *Scots Magazine* xxiii (1761), pp. 389–90.
3 Throughout this chapter I stress the predominantly male composition of the clubs and classes organized with an eye toward English language improvement – and the tensions between this male composition and an at-times feminizing discourse of linguistic politeness. In "Robert Fergusson's Robert Burns," in *Robert Burns and Cultural Authority* (University of Edinburgh, 1996), pp. 1–22, Robert Crawford argues that these "all-male" clubs functioned as "institutions which were crucial for the circulation and maintaining of the cultural codes which characterised eighteenth-century Scotland" (8). Nonetheless, it should be noted that as early as 1717, a group of women who called themselves "The Fair Intellectual Club" emerged. "An Account of the Fair Intellectual Club," whose final page marks Edinburgh, 28 July 1719 as the place and time of its writing, describes how in "May 1717, three young ladies happened to divert ourselves by walking in Heriot's Gardens, where one of us took occasion to propose that we should enter into a society, for Improvement of one another in the Study and Practice of such Things, as might contribute most effectually to our Accomplishment." My thanks to Clifford Siskin, who is pursuing the interesting implications of such social formations, for bringing this material to my attention.
4 Sheridan's detractors feared his instruction might blur class boundaries; others dismissed his oratory as showmanship for the masses. See Thomas Miller, *The Formation of College English: Rhetoric and Belles Lettres in the British Cultural Provinces* (Pittsburgh University Press, 1997), pp. 136–40; Nicholas Hudson, *Writing and European Thought* (Cambridge University Press, 1994), pp. 76–91; and Adam Potkay, *The Fate of Eloquence in the Age of Hume* (Ithaca: Cornell University Press, 1994).
5 Ramsay of Ochtertyre, *Scotland and Scotsmen in the Eighteenth Century*, vol. I (Edinburgh: 1888), p. 321.
6 Jurgen Habermas, *Structural Transformation of the Public Sphere*, trans. Thomas Burger (Cambridge, MA: MIT Press, 1989), p. 5. The paradoxical nature of this "horizontal" character will be explored below. For an illuminating discussion of such societies and a parallel "project of civility" in "British America" see David Shields, *Civil Tongues and Polite Letters* (Chapel Hill: North Carolina University Press, 1997).
7 Paul Bator, "The Formation of the Regius Chair of Rhetoric and Belles Lettres at the University of Edinburgh," *Quarterly Journal of Speech* 75 (1989) p. 40.

8 Edmund Burke, *Reflections on the Revolution in France*, ed. J. G. A. Pocock (Indianapolis and Cambridge: Hackett Publishing, 1987), p. 173.
9 Adam Smith, *Lectures on Rhetoric and Belles Lettres*, ed. J. Bryce (Oxford University Press, 1983), p. 42.
10 Smith lectured at Edinburgh University from 1748 to 1751. Lectures transcribed by a student, based on his University of Glasgow lectures from 1762 to 1763, were not published until the twentieth century. In 1762 Hugh Blair was made "Regius Professor of Rhetoric and Belles Lettres" at Edinburgh University, the first professorship of its kind. He published his lectures in 1783. Smith's and Blair's lectures were extremely well attended. Among the "hundreds of young Scots" attending were Boswell, William Robertson, Lord Kames, future Lord Chancellor Wedderburn.
11 By "nature" these writers mean "*la belle nature*" as opposed to vulgar nature, but this distinction was not always easy to maintain.
12 In *The Doctrine of Correctness in English Usage 1700–1800* (New York: Russell & Russell, 1962), Sterling Leonard notes, "Eighteenth-century critics found a thousand positions in logic and grammar to use as points of sortie against the usage of their time" (35). Carey McIntosh shows that even the "very best writers of 1710–1740 . . . are censured for faulty pronoun reference, lack of parallel structure, incorrect parts of speech . . . and many other 'errors'" and that "nit-picking like this must have tightened the screws of linguistic self-consciousness for all new authors," in *The Ordering of English: Style, Rhetoric, Politeness, Print Culture, and the Evolution of Prose from 1700 to 1800* (Cambridge University Press, 1998).
13 Miller writes, "As provincials refashioned their own language and sensibility, they became aware of differences in cultural conventions, but teachers generally maintained that the dominant culture had a natural authority because they wanted to believe that it was based in their common nature, rather than simply being imposed upon outsiders" (*Formation*, p. 5).
14 See Miller, McIntosh, Potkay and Ian Duncan, "Adam Smith, Samuel Johnson, and the Institutions of English," in *The Scottish Invention of English Literature*, ed. Robert Crawford (Cambridge University Press, 1998); Charles Jones, "Scottish Standard English in the Late Eighteenth Century," *Transactions of the Philological Society* 91 (1993), pp. 95–131; Franklin Court, *Institutionalizing English Literature: The Culture and Politics of Literary Study, 1750–1900* (Stanford University Press, 1992); and Robert Crawford, *Devolving English Literature* (Oxford: Clarendon, 1992).
15 Burke, *A Philosophical Inquiry into the Origin of Our Ideas of the Sublime and the Beautiful*, ed. Adam Philips (Oxford University Press, 1990), p. 83.
16 Michele Cohen, however, pursues the shifting valuations of "effeminacy" in language throughout the century, showing how, by its end, the identification of polite language with a devalued effeminate, French culture led to the understanding of a specifically English language as taciturn, "sincere and manly." *Fashioning Masculinity: National Identity and Language in the Eighteenth Century* (London: Routledge, 1996) p. 3.

17 Terry Eagleton describes this ambivalent attitude toward the body in all aesthetic discourse as "a creative turn to the sensuous body, as well as an inscribing of that body with a subtly oppressive law," in *The Ideology of the Aesthetic* (London: Basil Blackwell, 1990) p. 9. See also Roy Porter, "Bodies of Thought: Thoughts about the Body in Eighteenth-Century England," in *Interpretation and Cultural History*, eds. Joan Pittock and Andrew Wear (New York: St. Martin's Press, 1991).
18 Thomas Sheridan, *Lectures on Elocution* (1762) (Menston, UK: Scolar Press, 1968), p. 3, 2.
19 Daniel Cottom describes the contradictions between the appeal to nature and culture as "tool[s] of eighteenth-century social order." My argument is that those contradictions are less containable than he imagines, particularly in the Scottish context. *The Civilized Imagination* (Cambridge University Press, 1983), p. 14.
20 Adam Smith, *Lectures on Rhetoric and Belles Lettres*, ed. John M. Lothian (London: Thomas Nelson and Sons, Ltd., 1963), vol. I, p. 1. Citations are from this edition, unless marked "Bryce," for Bryce's edition.
21 Thus, while Quintilian writes, "we understand barbarisms as being of several kinds. One, with reference to country, such as is committed when a person inserts an African or Spanish term in Latin composition," he does not invoke the aesthetic terminology of "beauty" or "strength" in justifying the use of Latin over foreign words. In fact, this fault is "sometimes excused, either from custom, or authority, or perhaps from their nearness to beauties." *Quintilian on the Teaching of Speaking and Writing*, ed. James J. Murphy (Carbondale: Southern Illinois University Press, 1987), p. 36.
22 I include Johnson, despite his altercations with Smith, because both believed in the importance of establishing a standard English. In Smith's review of Johnson's *Dictionary* (*Edinburgh Review* [1755]), despite rewriting some of Johnson's entries, he writes, "In this country, the usefulness of it will be soon felt, as there is no standard of correct language in conversation ... we would earnestly recommend it."
23 Similarly, Lynda Mugglestone notes that five times as many works on elocution appeared between 1760 and 1800 than before and that "paradigms of 'beauty' and 'ugliness' make their due appearance, further amplifying ... resonances of the standard ideology for the spoken word." She cites J. Johnston's reference to the "grating sounds" of provincial discourse", for instance. *"Talking Proper": The Rise of Accent as Social Symbol* (Oxford: Clarendon, 1995) pp. 60–61.
24 Anderson himself seems to slip into this affective apprehension of the nation. He describes the experience of national simultaneity in the group singing of the national anthem: "How selfless this unisonance feels!" *Imagined Communities* (London: Verso, 1983), p. 133.
25 Kathryn Sutherland writes, "Smith minimizes the role played by reason in man's dealing with the world." "Fictional Economies: Adam Smith, Walter Scott and the Nineteenth-Century Novel," *ELH* 54 (1987) pp. 97–127.

26 *Lectures*, (London, 1793 edition), vol. I, p. 211. Cited in Leonard (*Doctrine*, p. 95). Douglas Ehninger and James Golden note how Blair's *Lectures* demonstrate a "denial that taste is 'resolvable into operations of reason,' with the consequent elevation of emotion and sensibility." "The Intrinsic Sources of Blair's Popularity," *Southern Speech Journal* 21 (1955), p. 13. These authors cite Scot Elledge, who goes so far as to say that "Blair supplied much of [the] necessary background to . . . the new poetic theory of the romantics." "The Background and Development in English Criticism of the Theories of Generality and Particularity," *PMLA* LXII (1947), p. 177. The question of exact periodization of this shift is unfortunately beyond the scope of this chapter.

27 In *Lectures*, Sheridan notes how laws of reading corrupt oral delivery (17).

28 Hugh Blair, *Lectures on Rhetoric and Belles Lettres*, ed. Harold F. Harding, 2 vols. (Carbondale: Southern Illinois University Press, 1965), vol. I, p. 179. All citations are from this edition unless otherwise marked. Characterizing this shift as a move from general to particular, Joel Weinsheimer describes how these writers valued "acting judiciously . . . not merely in knowing what is right ideally, generally, or in the abstract, but in judging what is right here and now." *Eighteenth-Century Hermeneutics: Philosophy of Interpretation from Locke to Burke* (New Haven: Yale University Press, 1993), p. 198.

29 Stephen Land, *From Signs to Propositions: The Concept of Form in Eighteenth-Century Semantic Theory* (London: Longman, 1974), p. 35.

30 John Mullan sees the increasing interest in "'sentiment' . . . a word made variously synonymous with 'passion,' 'feeling,' 'opinion,' and 'judgment' as consistent with a skepticism about the powers of reason." Although space does not allow full engagement with contemporary theories of sentiment, the connections to my discussion of language and the aesthetic are clearly important, as sentiment is "felt in the fibers of the body" and is therefore conducive to a particularly effective consolidation of social cohesion. "The Language of Sentiment: Hume, Smith, and Henry Mackenzie" in *The History of Scottish Literature*, vol. II, ed. Andrew Hook, p. 279.

31 G. J. Barker-Benfield, *The Culture of Sensibility: Sex and Society in Eighteenth-Century Britain* (Chicago University Press, 1992), p. 8.

32 Rather than quoting instances of both Smith and Blair in all cases, let me point out here that Blair's lectures are highly derivative from Smith's. Smith, in turn, was often drawing from a body of work on rhetoric from other Edinburgh University lecturers. I will point to differences between Smith and Blair as they occur – but hope to demonstrate that they are less dramatic than many writers have proposed.

33 Nancy Struever, "The Conversable World: Eighteenth-Century Transformations of the Relation of Rhetoric and Truth," in *Rhetoric and the Pursuit of Truth: Language Change in the Seventeenth and Eighteenth Centuries* (Los Angeles: William Andrews Clark Memorial Library, 1985).

34 Murray Cohen, *Sensible Words* (Baltimore: Johns Hopkins University Press, 1977), p. xxv.

35 See *The Tatler* numbers 70 and 74. Quoted in David Summers, *The Judgment of Sense: Renaissance Naturalism and the Rise of Aesthetics* (Cambridge University Press, 1987), p. 330. Imaginative works are particularly important because, like the aesthetic, the pleasures of the imagination "are not so gross as those of sense, nor so refined as those of understanding." Summers points out the Aristotelian origins of this concept; for Aristotle "imagination is the literal crucial point at which sense and reason meet" (24).

36 Blair writes of the alienation of his "native" Scots tongue, for instance, as a premonition that the "old rustic dialect of Scotland . . . will probably be entirely obsolete, and not intelligible," yet for members of his class, this distance was already apparent (vol. II, 352). English had been in use in Lowland Scotland among sections of the middle classes since the seventeenth century. Yet this did not translate to general usage until the early eighteenth. Even then, Scots – and many dialectic versions of it at that – remained the dominant language of everyday Lowland life.

37 Like Smith and Blair, who helped found the Select Society for Promoting Reading and Speaking of English in Scotland, in 1747, Burke founded the first debating society in Dublin at Trinity College: Academy of Belles Lettres. These societies preceded such societies in England, where they did not arise until 1815 and 1823 at Cambridge and Oxford respectively.

38 Elizabeth Bohls, "Disinterestedness and the Denial of the Particular: Locke, Adam Smith, and the Subject of Aesthetics," in *Eighteenth-Century Aesthetics and the Reconstruction of Art*, ed. Paul Mattick, Jr. (Cambridge University Press, 1993) pp. 16–51, esp. p. 27.

39 Too often "disinterest" is uniformly attributed to these discussions. Ian Ross insists on the distinct character of the Scottish school, which argued that although aesthetics might have been disinterested at the level of individuals, it was not disinterested on a discursive level. He writes, "Kant refutes, or seeks to refute, the Hutcheson-Hume school, and asserts that aesthetic contemplation is disinterested, involving the free play of the imagination and understanding" in "Aesthetic Philosophy: Hutcheson and Hume to Alison," in *History*, ed. Hook, pp. 239–57, esp. p. 252.

40 Here I am more convinced by Struever's position that "Hume places more stress on the accessibility of the canons of taste" ("Conversable," p. 88) than by Cottom's uniform vision of an unvaryingly exclusive discourse. Cottom is quite right to say aesthetic standards have a stake in the ordering of society, but pressures around the "inclusiveness" of nationalist rhetoric complicate the picture.

41 The paradox of this aesthetic discourse mirrors that of the "horizontal," yet exclusive, status of the gentlemen's clubs in which these conversations took place. Although the clubs prided themselves on the equality of their members, one had to qualify to enter them, primarily by property ownership. Habermas writes, "*The fully developed bourgeois public sphere was based on the fictitious identity of the two roles assumed by the privatized individuals who came together to form a public: the role of property owners and the role of human beings pure and simple*"

(*Structural*, p. 56, italics his). Terry Eagleton writes of this public sphere, "Only those with an interest can be disinterested," in *The Function of Criticism* (London: Verso, 1990), p. 16

42 Potkay, "Eloquence and Style in the Age of Hume," *Eighteenth-Century Studies* 25 (1991), p. 50. Potkay is referring to Pocock's *Virtue, Commerce, and History: Essays on Political Thought and History, Chiefly in the Eighteenth Century* (Cambridge University Press, 1985), pp. 48–9.

43 In *Theory of Moral Sentiments* Smith holds that imitation is inferior to sympathy as a mode of interaction.

44 John Dwyer, "Clio and Ethics: Practical Morality in Enlightened Scotland," *The Eighteenth Century: Theory and Interpretation* 30 (1989), pp. 45–72.

45 The phrase is from Luke Gibbons, "Ossian, Celticism and Colonialism," in ed. Terence Brown, *Celticism* (Amsterdam: Rodopi, 1996), p. 289.

46 Cited in Jarvis McElroy, *Scotland's Age of Improvement: A Survey of Eighteenth-Century Literary Clubs and Societies* (Pullman, WA: Washington State University Press, 1969) p. 35. Interestingly, a key member of this club was Allan Ramsay, who composed poetry which included Scots terms, read it aloud to Easy Club members, and began publishing it in 1721. Although this appreciation for Scots might seem to argue against the assimilation of these Lowland men, Ramsay's poetry had little of the confrontational character of Robert Fergusson's poetry. Ramsay's verse collections included glossaries of Scots terms, suggesting a distancing of that language from Ramsay and his polite readers.

47 Duncan argues that Smith's metropolitan identity is "not natural but artificial," (41) highlighting the "expansive thrust of an argument that insists on the cultural and performative status of national identity" (41). I see Smith's understanding of identity as vacillating between this consciously performative sense and a corporeally naturalized sense.

48 8 August 1761. Author unknown. National Library of Scotland (NLS), MS. 16720/f9IRTV. To give a further sense of how important the powers in London saw this project, we should note King George III, through the help of his Prime Minister – the Scottish – Bute, arranged for Blair's appointment as Regius Chair.

49 John Christie, "Adam Smith's Metaphysics of Language," in *The Figural and the Literal*, ed. Andrew Benjamin *et al.* (Manchester University Press, 1987), p. 203. Blair outlines the four stages: "first is the life of hunters; pasturage succeeds to this, as the ideas of property begin to take root; next agriculture; and lastly, commerce." (He adds that Ossian's Poems are of the first stage.) "A Critical Dissertation on the Poems of Ossian," in *The Poems of Ossian, to which are Prefixed a Discourse and Dissertation on the Aera of Ossian*, trans. James Macpherson (Boston: Phillip Sampson, 1959), p. 102.

50 The turn to the rural as opposed to the city, to linguistic continuity as opposed to abstract and reasoned linguistic principles also confirms Martin Thom's identification of a shift from Enlightenment to Romantic understandings of the nation, a move away from "the ancient city" to "the

barbarian tribe" (1). As Johnson, Smith, and Blair describe the bands of originary langauge communities, we might also recall Thom's naming of the new nationalism "tribe-nation." See *Republics, Nations, and Tribes* (London: Verso, 1995).

51 These characterizations of ancient language were not unique to the British. Rousseau similarly characterizes ancient language as "softly crushing. . . more effective" (6), "vigorous. . . more arousing" (7), "vital" (11), "de-emphasiz[ing] grammatical analogy for euphony, harmony, beauty of sound" (15), *On the Origin of Languages*, trans. John H. Moran and Alexander Gode (Chicago University Press, 1966). Etienne Condillac describes ancient languages as "elevated, noble, act[ing] with greater force" (176), "more emotional" (202), and "metaphoric, figurative, picturesque" (227), *An Essay on the Origin of Human Knowledge* (Gainesville, FL: Scolars' Facsimiles and Reprints, 1971).

52 While the work of Burns is clearly important to discussions of Britain, Scotland, and language, I spend only a moment on him here because the Burns bicentennial anniversary has occasioned a copious amount of exhaustive critical material, and I fear a certain amount of redundancy in my discussion of him. See Crawford, ed., *Robert Burns and Studies in Scottish Literature: Special Robert Burns Issue* 30 (1998). I cite other important critical works below.

53 Kenneth Simpson draws interesting parallels between Fergusson and Burns (and, less likely, Ramsay) in relation to poetic form, marking their transformation of an English mock-heroic into "democratized heroic." See "Genre and National Identity," *Studies in Scottish Literature* 30 (1998), pp. 31–42. I am, however, uncomfortable with the notion of a "Scottish character" and a unique Scots ability to capture "ordinary human experience" which he credits in that transformation. Also interested in Burns's manipulation of poetic form and constructions of cultural identity is Douglas Dunn in " 'A Very Scottish Kind of Dash': Burns' Native Metric," in *Robert Burns and Cultural Authority*, ed. Crawford, pp. 58–85.

54 Crawford, *Devolving English Literature* (Oxford: Clarendon Press, 1992), p. 101. To use Raymond Williams's terminology, this emergent attitude was not yet dominant. In the December, 1786 issue of *The Monthly Review*, James Anderson wrote of the language in the Kilmarnock edition of Burns's poems "We much regret that these poems are written in some measure in an unknown tongue," reserving "the freedom to modernise the orthography a little . . . to render it less disgusting to our Readers south of the Tweed." Donald Low, ed. *Robert Burns: The Critical Heritage* (London: Routledge, 1974), p. 72, cited in Strauss, below.

55 Dietrich Strauss, "Some Reflections on Burns's Command of English," in *Studies in Scottish Literature* 30 (1998), pp. 76–89.

56 They are also the terms which continue to stymie Burns criticism. As Peter Zenzinger writes, "David Craig employs the terms 'the people's poetry,' and 'national poetry' as quasi-synonyms; like John Speirs, David Daiches

and, more recently, Robert Thompson and David Sampson, he stresses the communal nature of Scottish verse as opposed to the genteel, predominantly English tradition of eighteenth-century poetry." See "Low Life Primitivism and Honest Poverty in Ramsay and Burns," p. 44.
57 Crawford, *Devolving*, p. 99.
58 This review appeared in the *Lounger* (9 December 1786) and is cited by Leith Davis in *Acts of Union* (Stanford University Press, 1998), p. 123.
59 See Crawford, and Davis, Carol McGuirk, *Robert Burns and the Sentimental Era* (Athens, GA: University of Georgia Press, 1985), Raymond Bentman, *Robert Burns* (Boston: Twayne, 1987). But see also Thomas Crawford, *Burns: A Study of the Poems and Songs* (Edinburgh: Mercat, 1978).
60 Robert Burns, *Selected Poems*, ed. Carol McGuirk (Harmondsworth, UK: Penguin, 1993), p. 15.
61 See Hume's "Of Eloquence," in *Essays Moral, Political, and Literary*, ed. Eugene Miller (Indianapolis: Liberty, 1985). Struever adds, "Hume is frankly horrified at the thought of the ladies as sovereigns of both worlds, the 'public' republic of letters as well as the intimate realm of conversation, as was certainly the case in the French salons" ("Conversable," p. 94).
62 This division sounds similar to the one Michel Foucault posits in *The Order of Things* (New York, Vintage Books, 1970) between a semiotics of resemblance and of difference. Foucault argues that in the seventeenth and eighteenth centuries a "Classical" semiotic, whereby signs derived meaning through their relationship of difference from other signs, emerged. This "Classical" episteme superseded an earlier model of understanding, where signs signified through their relationship of resemblance. Although Foucault's analysis is overly general, it does provide a basic schema which can be useful, and usefully refined in this case.
63 Hudson writes, "A key theme in linguistic scholarship of the mid and late eighteenth century was that the dominance of writing and literacy in modern culture had enervated the vigours, natural 'tones' of living speech" (*Writing*, p. 92). I would, however, disagree with his characterization of these re-evaluations of orality as a uniformly "conservative tendency." Miller too asserts, "Elocutionists present some of the most obvious examples of the romantic nostalgia and stifling proprieties that shaped the formation of college English" (*Formation*, p. 139). Penny Fielding writes that "once free from its socially stigmatizing qualities, an idealized orality was a powerful mark of subjectivity" (21), but she also insists that there are too many pressures at work to see these opposing characterizations as forming a mere binary. Instead, they form "an unstable duality, each part of which is continually dividing into authentic and debased versions of itself" (16). *Writing and Orality: Nationality, Culture, and Nineteenth-Century Scottish Fiction* (Oxford: Clarendon, 1996).
64 Johnson, *Journey to the Western Islands of Scotland*, ed. Peter Levi (Harmondsworth, UK: Penguin Books, 1984), p. 98.
65 While I point to this brief, suggestive passage, I do not intend to argue that

this was a sustained position for Johnson. Boswell writes that when he commented on the happiness of the savage life, Johnson replied, "There can be nothing more false . . . Rousseau *knows* he is talking nonsense." Boswell, *The Life of Samuel Johnson*, ed. Bergen Evans (New York: The Modern Library, 1965) p. 158. (158).

66 Derrida, *Of Grammatology*, trans. Gayatri Spivak (Baltimore: Johns Hopkins University Press, 1976), pp. 119, 138.

67 We examined evidence of Johnson's hostility to metaphor. Yet on this question, as on many others, Johnson registers ambivalence. When Boswell informs him that Monboddo disapproved of his frequent use of metaphorical expressions, Johnson responds, "Metaphorical expression . . . is a great excellence in style . . . for it gives you two ideas for one; – conveys the meaning more luminously, and generally with a perception of delight." Boswell, *Life*, p. 354.

68 Following them, John Pinkerton writes of the freedom and nobility of "the original language . . . the effusion of fancy actuated by the passions: . . . uncontrouled [sic] by custom, and the manners which in an advanced community are termed polite," *Scottish Tragic Ballads* (London: J. Nichols, 1781), p. x.

69 Blair saw this shortcoming as a function of the "naturally phlegmatic" English character. Alternatively, he and his peers saw the absolutist, "arbitrary" government of France as responsible for the "effeminate" fawning language of that country (vol. II, 119).

70 See Leith Davis, "Origins of the Specious: James Macpherson's Ossian and the Forging of the British Empire," *Eighteenth-Century: Theory and Interpretation* 34 (1993) and Potkay, *Eloquence*.

71 Embedded in Blair's image of a martial community are also concerns around the modern crisis in authority. In a 10 April 1788 letter to Thomas Cadell, Blair laments the decay of Britain from its "fullest glory," a function, as he sees it, of its lack of strong leaders. He writes, "I am persuaded there is still vigour and spirit . . . in the nation, if there were any man of bold and determined spirit to take the lead, and call it forth. But Alas! where is any such public leader to be found." National Library of Scotland MS 16720 ff 88–91. Related, Blair was a member of the Poker Club, which aimed to "poke" the government into establishing a militia in Scotland. See John Robertson, *The Scottish Enlightenment and the Militia Issue* (Edinburgh: John Donald Publishers, Ltd, 1985).

72 One would think that the isolated mountain regions where "people still speak the first tongue of the first inhabitants of Britain" would come in for Johnson's highest acclaim as a space where linguistic purity and stasis has been maintained. He praises, however, not the Gaelic of the present-day Highlanders but the eloquent language now spoken by the Scottish who live in areas that British armies have occupied.

73 John Grant, *Statistical Account of Scotland*, Parish of Kirkmichael, County of Banff, vol. XII, no. 32.

74 Pinkerton, *Scottish Tragic Ballads* (London, 1781), pp. xvii and xix, respectively. Crucially important, however, is the fact that he identified the Goths, and not the Celts, as Scotland's first inhabitants.
75 Rousseau, by whom Blair was influenced, writes of the alphabet, "[It] must have been invented by commercial peoples who, in traveling to various countries, had to speak various languages, which would have impelled them to invent characters that could be common to all of them" (17). As the process of exchange produces the concept of common exchange value, Rousseau posits an analogous process in language exchange.
76 Johnson, *Journey*, p. 147. Of course, there are extensive examples of Johnson's distaste for the oral "Earse" of the Highlanders in this text, and I do not mean to read his ambivalence about print as supplanting these negative remarks about Gaelic, but only to point to a suggestive undercurrent.
77 *Idler* 91, 12 January 1760.
78 *Idler* 37, 30 December 1758. Johnson also maps this trajectory writing, "In time, happiness and plenty give rise to curiosity . . . then begin the arts of rhetoric and poetry." *Idler* 63, 30 June 1759.
79 *Idler* 7, 27 May 1758.
80 *Idler* 2, 22 April 1758.
81 Ironically, Johnson's prophecy of corruption impacts on his own work. The best-selling abridgment of his *Dictionary* – eight editions of five thousand copies each – lopped off all "warning labels" on "impure" words such as Scotticisms. And so despite himself, or at least despite his efforts to "purify" the language, Scotticisms which had been outlawed remained firmly in the lexicon. See Basker, "Scotticisms and the Problem of Cultural Identity in Eighteenth-Century Britain," *Eighteenth-Century Life* 15 (1991), pp. 82–3.
82 Christie argues that for Smith "history renders grammar plural and various" ("Adam Smith's," p. 207).
83 Adam Smith, *An Inquiry into the Nature and Causes of the Wealth of Nations*, eds. R. Campbell and A. Skinner (Oxford University Press, 1979), vol. I, p. 25.
84 Edmund Burke, *Speech on Conciliation* (London: Ginn & Co., 1900).
85 V. J. Peyton, *The History of the English Language* (London, 1771), pp. 20, 25, and 26 respectively.
86 Nairn, *Break-Up*.
87 For the interdependence of the rise of the nation-state and commercial empire see Karl Marx, *The German Ideology*, ed. C. J. Arthur (New York: International Publishers, 1985), pp. 74–9 and Chris Harman, "The Return of the National Question," *International Socialism* 56 (1992), pp. 1–62. Marlon Ross describes how, by the eighteenth century, it had become clear that the British nation depended on expansion, invoking a contemporary analogy: "cultivating a great estate is, like the cultivation of a great national culture itself, a duplicitous activity . . . it requires him to expand his domain – whether it be a bourgeois estate or a capitalist nation-state – in order to assure the continued health of that domain." "Romancing the Nation-State: The Poetics of Romantic Nationalism," in *Macropolitics of Nineteenth-*

Century Literature: Nationalism, Exoticism, Imperialism, eds. Jonathan Arac and Harriet Ritvo (Philadelphia: Pennsylvania University Press, 1991).

88 Nancy Dorian, *Language Death: The Life Cycle of a Scottish Dialect* (Philadelphia: Pennsylvania University Press, 1981). See also Magne Oftedal, *The Gaelic of Leurbost, Isle of Lewis* (Oslo: Aschenhoug, 1956), p. 14.

89 Peter T. Murphy describes how by mid century, "The old communal economy, where rent was paid in kind, and in blood in . . . military service, was not designed to satisfy the needs of [the] new way of life. The chiefs needed a transportable medium of exchange, something to translate their local wealth into a true British wealth. . . . [T]his translation, of course, is effected by money, and the eighteenth-century Highland chief began to feel the need for it. There were a number of ways to get more money out of a given estate, all of which involved 'improvement,' methods of increasing cash return through increasing productivity or changing the product itself. Improvement usually implied enclosure." "Fool's Gold: The Highland Treasures of Macpherson's Ossian," *ELH* 52 (1985), pp. 569–70. Especially interesting is Murphy's use of the term "translation," as it corroborates the language/currency comparison.

90 Ian Carter, "The Highlands of Scotland as an Underdeveloped Region," in *Sociology and Development*, eds. Emanuel de Kadt and Gavin Williams (London: Tavistock, 1974), pp. 279–311, esp. p. 289.

91 Several writers, for instance, have linked the writings of Hugh Blair to William Wordsworth. See Ehninger and Golden, "Intrinsic," p. 20 and Hans Aarsleff, "Wordsworth, Romanticism, and Language," in *From Locke To Saussure* (Minneapolis: Minnesota University Press, 1982).

5 "A TRANSLATOR WITHOUT ORIGINALS"

1 William Shaw, *An Analysis of the Galic Language* (London: W. and A. Strahan, 1778; Menston, UK: The Scolar Press, 1972), p. xxiii, and *A Galic and English Dictionary, Containing all the Words in the Scottish and Irish Dialects of the Celtic* (London: W. and A. Strahan, 1780), the pages of this book are not numbered.

2 While Macpherson's seems an odd name on this list of English-promoting literati, Colin Kidd writes, "Although Macpherson has been pigeon-holed as an early Scottish 'nationalist', his whiggism was British in scope," in *Subverting Scotland's Past: Scottish Whig Historians and the Creation of an Anglo-British Identity, 1689–1830* (Cambridge University Press, 1993), p. 233.

3 Recorded by Sir John Sinclair and cited in Robert Crawford, *Devolving English Literature* (Oxford: Clarendon, 1992), p. 23.

4 Joseph Levine observes that modern historicism "developed in two stages . . . the first stage view[s] the variety of the past and its dissimilarity from the present and yet continue[s] to maintain the universality and constancy of human nature and values." He argues a second stage, cultural relativism, was not reached in the eighteenth century, although I see hints of it in this

material. *Humanism and History: Origins of Modern Historiography* (Ithaca: Cornell University Press, 1987), p. 192.

5 Thus, Shaw yokes "two contrasting strains in eighteenth-century Scottish letters," Roderick Watson, *The Literature of Scotland*, p. 165. Leith Davis also writes of the Scots' attempts "to revive a Scottish past and to assimilate quickly into English culture." James Beattie, for instance, celebrates ancient Scotland in *The Minstrel* (1768) and derogates Scots in *Scoticisms, Arranged in Alphabetical order* (1787). *Acts of Union: Scotland and the Literary Negotiation of the British Nation, 1708–1832* (Stanford University Press, 1999).

6 While eighteenth-century linguists confronting new languages divide them into universal and different elements, David Paxman argues, "Sameness by its nature is that which can be assimilated into systematic representation. Difference is often that which cannot be systematized, tamed, domesticated, or assimilated ... descriptions of difference often reduce it to known paradigms" (21). "Language and Difference: The Problem of Abstraction in Eighteenth-Century Language Study," *Journal of the History of Ideas* 54 (1993), pp. 19–36, esp. p. 21. I would only wish to amplify the imperial character of these linguistic conceptualizations.

7 Lawrence Grossberg, "The Space of Culture, the Power of Space," in *The Post-Colonial Question*, eds. Iain Chambers and Lidia Curti (New York: Routledge, 1996), p. 177. Other critiques of a (cultural) politics which "heroizes" the local include Veit Erlmann's, who charges, "Homogenization and differentiation [are] not mutually exclusive features of musical globalization ... but [are] integral constituents of musical aesthetics under late capitalism ... the position must be questioned, then, that ... local cultures [and] diversity subvert homogeneity." "The Aesthetics of the Global Imagination: Reflections on World Music in the 1990s," in *Public Culture* 20 (1996), p. 469. My only argument is the "late capitalism" attribution.

8 See Peter Womack's analysis of Celtic fashionability in *Improvement and Romance: Constructing the Myth of the Highlands* (London: Macmillan, 1989).

9 Cited in Howard Weinbrot, *Britannia's Issue: The Rise of British Literature from Dryden to Ossian* (Cambridge University Press, 1993), p. 477.

10 Edward Lhuyd finished only the first volume, *Glossography* (London, 1707).

11 In Britain "Celt" was also applied to the Welsh and Irish. See Malcolm Chapman, *The Celts: The Construction of a Myth* (London: Macmillan, 1992), p. 33; David McCrone, A. Morris, and Richard Kiely, *Scotland the Brand: The Making of Scottish Heritage* (Edinburgh University Press, 1995); and *Celticism*, ed. Terence Brown (Amsterdam: Rodopi, 1996). Although space does not permit a consideration of it here, this last title features useful discussions of trans-European Celticism.

12 Anne McClintock's (after Johannes Fabian) name for a tropic space in which "colonized people ... do not inhabit history proper but exist in a permanently anterior time within the geographic space of the modern empire as anachronistic humans ... bereft of human agency." *Imperial*

Leather: Race, Gender and Sexuality in the Colonial Contest (New York and London: Routledge, 1995), p. 30. Chapman writes of "the Celts": "A central defining power establishes and controls fashion, and is a centre of innovation. As it elaborates new fashions, it consciously differentiates itself from the periphery, which it finds old-fashioned . . . This process has gone on for as long as we have records, and it is of the first consequence for understanding 'the Celts' and the fringe dwellers come to be seen as occupants of history, guardians of tradition" (*The Celts*, pp. 95–6). I question, however, Chapman's characterization of this process as ages old. Womack is less sweeping in range but more precise.

13 Edward Snyder, *The Celtic Revival in Literature: 1760–1800* (Cambridge, MA: Harvard University Press, 1923), p. 4.

14 Celtic Whiggism aims "to restore to Scots an ancient history replete with national pretensions and political import" – and ties to contemporary enlightened English culture. Representative scholarship includes John Macpherson, *Critical Dissertations on the Origin, Antiquities, Language, Government, Manners, and Religion of the Ancient Caledonians* (Dublin, 1768).

15 David Lloyd, "Ethnic Cultures, minority discourses and the state" in *Colonial Discourse, Post-Colonial Theory*, eds. Francis Barker, Peter Hulme and Margaret Iverson (Manchester University Press, 1994), p. 222.

16 Katie Trumpener, *Bardic Nationalism: The Romantic Novel and the British Empire* (Princeton University Press, 1997).

17 A. J. Youngson writes that from 1757 "until 1815 the recruitment of highlanders in the British army was continuous, and large numbers of these men were sent to North America to fight first in the Seven Years' War and then in the War of American Independence" in *After the Forty-Five* (Edinburgh University Press, 1973), p. 42. See also Womack, "Warriors," in *Improvement*, pp. 27–60.

18 Robert Young argues, "The notion of a fixed identity was a product of rapid change of metropolitan and colonial societies, which meant, as with nationalism, such identities needed to be constructed to counter schisms, friction, and dissent." *Colonial Desire: Hybridity in Theory, Culture and Race* (London and New York: Routledge, 1995), p. 3. Regarding language in particular, Bjorn Jernudd contends, "It is in periods of transition . . . that puristic responses [to language] are especially likely to arise" (cited in Mugglestone, *Talking Proper*, p. 73).

19 Said, in *Orientalism* (New York: Vintage, 1979), has described philology as one of various "techniques of representation that make the Orient visible, clear, 'there' in discourse about it" (22); "Philology enables a general view of human life . . . : 'Me, being there at the center, inhaling the perfume of everything, judging, comparing . . . inducing – . . . I shall arrive at the very system of things . . . There is an unmistakable aura of power about the philologist" (132).

20 Trumpener notes, in *Bardic*, both progressive and regressive tendencies in Celtic revivals. Yet while she insists on the deleterious aspect of an anti-

British Celtic nationalist campaign mounted through the cultural alone, at other points she argues for the revolutionary political intersections of eighteenth-century Celtic cultural nationalism (in contrast to its later nineteenth-century incarnations). While the case might well be made for Ireland in the 1790s, the writings of the Celtomaniacs of Scotland in this period do not lend themselves to parallel claims.

21 Shaw, *Memoirs of the Life and Writings of the Late Dr. Samuel Johnson* (1785) ed. Arthur Sherbo (Oxford University Press, 1974). Although published anonymously, twenty-two paragraphs describe Shaw's relationship to Johnson, while only ten are devoted to his *Dictionary*, making its authorship rather easy to detect.

22 Richard Sher, "Percy, Shaw and the Ferguson 'Cheat,'" in *Ossian Revisited*, ed. Howard Gaskill (Edinburgh University Press, 1991).

23 Donald Macnicol, *Remarks on Dr. Samuel Johnson's Journey to the Hebrides* (London: T. Cadell, 1779), p. 5.

24 Curiously, Thomas Curley continues to profess Shaw's unbiased position, writing that upon meeting Shaw in 1774 "conversation with a neutral Gaelic scholar [was] most welcome to Johnson," cited in "Johnson's Last Word on Ossian: Ghostwriting for William Shaw" in *Aberdeen and the Enlightenment*, eds. Jennifer J. Carter and Joan H. Pittock (Aberdeen University Press, 1987), p. 380.

25 Shaw writes, "I am not ignorant of doing what may, though innocently, incur not only the displeasure, but the resentment, of some of my compatriots, as derogating much from their supposed national honour" *Enquiry*, p. 36.

26 Shaw also "changed sides" in religious faith, leaving "the Scotch for the English communion" (*Enquiry*, p. 78) and taking an appointment as curate in Kent, arranged by Johnson. These ranging spiritual and cultural fidelities might well have been related to more temporal interests. Rejected in his application for funding for research for his dictionary by the Highland Society, Shaw turned to Johnson for succor. It was around this time that Shaw changed his tune on the Ossian question.

27 Sher also points to the echoes of Johnson's *Journey* in Shaw's texts; in the Highlands, Shaw claims, "by a certain 'intellectual retrogradation, I knew less, the more I heard of it" *Enquiry*, p. 58.

28 Although Chomsky maintains a bewildering support for these theories, his description of them in *Cartesian Linguistics* (New York and London: Harper and Row, 1966), p. 59, is helpful. Murray Cohen's objection to Chomsky's argument that nineteenth-century philologists shared beliefs of the universal grammarians is supported in the tensions I identify within Shaw's works.

29 Murray Cohen summarizes early eighteenth-century grammars that subscribe to the universality of linguistic structures. Among these are James Greenwood's *An Essay Towards a Practical English Grammar* (1711) and John Henley's *The Compleat Linguist; or, An Universal Grammar to all the Considerable Tongues in Being* (London: J. Roberts and J. Pemberton, 1719–26), of particu-

lar note because it is a collection of serially published grammars of a wide range of languages: French, Chaldee, Greek, Hebrew, Syriac, Saxon. Its purpose "was to demonstrate the Alliance there is in all that Variety," (Number x, p. i). Attached to one number in this series is an advertisement promising, "a key to the universal grammar which will explain the terms of grammar to the meanest capacity" (Number III), tantalizingly referring the reader to the "skeletal key" which will explain the basic structure behind all languages. In *Sensible Words* (Baltimore: John Hopkins University Press, 1977) Cohen writes "[Henley's] attempt at a polyglot grammar is perfectly congruent with the shared idea of linguistic universality in the early eighteenth century, for it assumes that what is universal is the 'general System of Grammar' . . . Universality is taken for granted" (p. 71). Like Henley, William Loughton, in *A Practical Grammar of the English Tongue; or, A Rational and Easy Introduction* (1734), insists that the same structures pertain to all languages. He avers, "The End and Design of Grammar in general, is the same in all Languages" (cited in Cohen, p. 72.) Cohen points out that "the basis of the universality is the correspondence between language and thought" (73). While Hans Aarsleff, in *From Locke to Saussure* (Minneapolis: Minnesota University Press, 1982) p. 169, has asserted that "there is in fact strong evidence in favor of the argument that universal grammar as a philosophical and theoretical discipline . . . had fallen into desuetude during the first half of the eighteenth century" to be later resurrected in 1754, we might explain the different chronologies Aarsleff and Cohen arrive at by noting the difference between the primary sources they examine. Whereas Cohen casts his net wide enough to include grammarians and pedagogues, Aarsleff focuses on canonical philosopher-linguists.

30 Levine describes how Edward Gibbon, for instance, despite his ruminations on the past, "accepted without hesitation values of his own time, both moral and aesthetic, and saw them as universally applicable to past and present" (*Humanism*, p. 191) . . . "even arch romantics like Warton reveal neoclassicism at their core" (195). Kidd details the belief in conjectural history amongst the most outspoken promoters of Scottish particularism.

31 For a magisterial treatment of eighteenth-century conceptions of orality, literacy, and cultural authority, see Kathryn Temple, "Johnson and Macpherson: Cultural Authority and the Construction of Literary Property," *Yale Journal of Law* 5 (1993), pp. 355–87. Here I do not mean to recapitulate the association of immediacy, presence, and "nonexploitation" with oral language, a gesture Derrida calls to our attention in *Of Grammatology*, especially pp. 101–40. Yet Derrida also writes, "One must above all avoid reversing them [arguments that see the technology of writing as a means of domination] and taking the opposite view. In a certain given historical structure . . . it is undoubtedly true that the progress of formal legality, the struggle against illiteracy, and the like, could have functioned as a mystifying force and an instrument consolidating the power of a class or a state whose formal-universal significance was confiscated by a particular empirical force" (132).

32 In a moment of startling resemblance we find that "Edward Fitzgerald, translator of the *Rubaiyat* of Omar Khayyam wrote to his friend E. B. Cowell in 1857: 'It is an amusement for me to take what Liberties I like with these Persians, who (as I think) are not poets enough to frighten one from such excursions." Cited in *Translation/History/Culture*, ed. Andre Lefevere (London: Routledge, 1992), p. 4.
33 As Chapman writes, "We have millennia of records of other people, where the accusation of *disorder* is ... the result of failure to perceive a different *kind* of order," *The Celts*, p. 162.
34 Alexander MacDonald, *A Gaelic/English Vocable* (Edinburgh: Robert Fleming, 1741).
35 *The Present State of the S.S.P.C.K.* (Edinburgh, 1756), p. 37.
36 Roland Barthes, *Mythologies*, trans. Annette Lavers (New York: Hill and Wang, 1972), p. 116.
37 *Dialectic of Enlightenment*, trans. John Cumming (New York: Seabury, 1969), p. 12.
38 It is, of course, a question of degrees. Johnson illustrates a belief in near complete linguistic equivalence when he states, "[He] will deserve the highest praise ... who can convey the same thoughts with the same graces, and who, when he translates, changes nothing but the language," in "Preface" to *Dictionary of the English Language* (London: 1755).
39 David Elton Gay has pointed out this discrepancy to me.
40 Despite Shaw's efforts, the combined form of prepositional pronouns remains "correct" usage. A recently published guide to Gaelic advises, "When using pronouns such as *mi, thu, e*, etc. (I, you, he, etc.), the pronoun becomes amalgamated within the preposition *aig* to form a new word. You say *Tha car agam*, not *Tha ca aig mi*." Boyd Robertson and Iain Taylor, *Teach Yourself Gaelic* (London: Hodder Headline, 1993), p. 37.
41 Best known is Benjamin Lee Whorf, "The Philosophy of Time," in *Language, Thought, and Reality*, ed. Richard Gale (New York: Doubleday, 1967) pp. 377–85. Whorf writes, "The Hopi language gets along perfectly without tenses for its verbs," and "I find it gratuitous to assume that a Hopi who knows only the Hopi language and the cultural ideas of his own society has the same notions, often assumed to be intuitions, of time and space that we have." Linguistic relativism has come in for strong criticism in recent linguistic scholarship, a fact which might be related to the discipline's claims to a status as a science outside of socio-historical concerns.
42 The choice of Pope is especially notable, as it reconfirms Shaw's neoclassicism. Adumbrating a dialectical movement, Levine speculates, "Perhaps it was the very triumph just then of the neoclassical style in Pope's poetry that finally ... inadvertently and paradoxically raised nostalgia for the culture of the later middle ages," *Humanism*, p. 193.
43 Patrick Wright, *On Living in an Old Country: The National Past in Contemporary Britain* (London: Verso, 1985), p. 49. See also *The Invention of Tradition*, eds. E. J. Hobsbawm and T. O. Ranger (Cambridge University Press, 1983).

44 Ian Haywood, *The Making of History* (London: Associated University Press, 1986), p. 16.
45 George Watson, "Celticism and the Annulment of History," in *Celticism*, p. 208.
46 Narratives of the space of the British Isles in history were thus themselves multi-faceted and highly "interested." Chapman outlines the competing narratives of the origins of the 'p'/ 'q' Celtic alteration, for instance, showing how invasion explanations "involve . . . arguments about superiority and inferiority, priority and modernity, origins and destinies, and relative chronology . . . insular development [explanations] substitutes instead a quiet linguistic change," *The Celts*, p. 9.
47 Womack explains the reciprocal relationship between rationalization and romanticization in the eighteenth-century Highlands, writing, "These oppositions can occasionally make the romance look like a counter ideological formation, but as their symmetry suggests, the conflict is illusory," *Improvements*, p. 3.
48 Stuart Piggot, *Ancient Britons and the Antiquarian Imagination* (London: Thames and Hudson, 1989), p. 63.
49 See Christopher Harvie, "The Scottish Intellectuals 1760–1930," in *Celticism*, p. 234.
50 Clark, *Works of the Caledonian Bards* (Edinburgh, 1778), p. 18.
51 John Smith, *Galic Antiquities* (Edinburgh, 1780).
52 Thus, David Daiches's important ancillary observation that "there is something very ironical about the spectacle of the intellectual leaders of Edinburgh theorizing about the nature of Gaelic poetry while ignoring the original Gaelic poetry being written in the Scotland of their own day" (such as the poetry of MacDonald) in *The Paradox of Scottish Culture: The Eighteenth-Century Experience* (London: Oxford University Press, 1964), p. 94.
53 Central to Kidd's study is Herbert Butterfield's concept of the Whig interpretation of history, which Butterfield defines as a history which "studies the past with reference to the present . . . [H]istorical personages can easily and irresistibly be classed into the men who furthered progress and the men who tried to hinder it." *The Whig Interpretation of History* (London: G. Bell and Sons, 1951), p. 11.
54 Cited in Weinbrot, *Britannia's*, p. 397. The characterization of Gaelic as free is analogous to Womack's observation that in the Highlands "the political problem of lawlessness inverts easily into a folk-tale image of freedom," *Improvement*, p. 12.
55 David Malcolme, *Letters, Essays, and Other Tracts illustrating the Antiquities of Great Britain and Ireland together with Many Curious Discoveries of the Affinity betwixt the language of the American Indians and the Ancient Britons . . .* (London: J. Millar, 1744). Malcolme's study of the "Scotch or Irish" language served several purposes. He writes, "These same Languages . . . will be found useful to rescue the Antiquities . . . of these Islands . . . and to confirm the Accounts which the Holy Scriptures give of Things to repel the *Deists*" (from a letter to

the Very Reverend Mr. Anderson, Moderator of the General Assembly, 1735).
56 The pages of the articles assembled in Malcolme's *Letters, Essays and Other Tracts* are not numbered consecutively. This quotation is found in the dedication.
57 Young writes of Arnold: "the force of 'modern civilization' destroys the last vestiges of a vanquished culture to turn it into an object of academic study" (*Colonial*, p. 71). Like Weinbrot, Young argues that not simply Britishness but "Englishness has often been constructed as a heterogeneous . . . composite of contrary elements" (3) and that cultural theorists such as Arnold believed, "Celtic culture must be submerged in English culture rather than set against it" (71), yet Young emphasizes the conflicting nature of that heterogeneity.
58 Matthew Arnold, See *On the Study of Celtic Literature and on Translating Homer* (New York: Macmillan, 1904), which makes constant references to the "feminine" nature of the Celts.
59 Edinburgh University Library MS. La. III. 251.
60 Rowland Jones, *The Origin of Language and Nations* (1764). Reprinted: (Menston, UK: The Scolar Press, 1972).
61 D. Macpherson, "Cursory Remarks on Verstegan's Restitution (n.d. eighteenth century), Edinburgh University Library, ms Dc.8.128.

EPILOGUE

1 Jane Austen, *Emma*, ed. James Kinsley (Oxford University Press, 1995), p. 325.
2 Many critics have asserted that a mistaken critical tradition is not wholly to blame for such ideological connections. The most well-known works of this persuasion include Marilyn Butler, *Jane Austen and the War of Ideas* (Oxford: Clarendon Press, 1975); David Aers, "Community and Morality: Towards Reading Jane Austen," in *Romanticism and Ideology: Studies in English Writing 1765–1830*, eds. David Aers, Jonathan Cook, and David Punter (London: Routledge and Kegan Paul, 1981), pp. 118–36; Gary Kelly, "Jane Austen's Real Business: The Novel, Literature and Cultural Capital" in *Jane Austen's Business*, eds. Juliet McMaster and Bruce Stovel (New York: St. Martin's Press, 1996), pp. 154–67; Alistair Duckworth, *The Improvement of Estate* (Baltimore: Johns Hopkins University Press, 1971); and Raymond Williams, *The Country and the City* (Oxford University Press, 1973). Alternatively, Roger Sales provides an excellent summary of the Victorian-era hagiography through which Austen had been claimed as part of a representation of de-politicized Regency England, representative of the splendor, gentility, and decorum ascribed to the English. *Jane Austen and Representations of Regency England* (New York and London: Routledge, 1994).
3 Those Scottish claims, if acknowledged as such, have at least the merit of a strategic essentialism absent in parallel English claims.

4 See *A History of Scottish Women's Writing*, eds. Douglas Gifford and Dorothy Macmillan, (Edinburgh University Press, 1997).
5 The term is Madeleine Kahn's in *Narrative Transvestitism: Rhetoric and Gender in the Eighteenth-Century English Novel* (Ithaca: Cornell University Press, 1991).
6 Here I draw from Nancy Armstrong, *Desire and Domestic Fiction* (Oxford University Press, 1987).
7 Norman Page concludes that "the 'triumph' of the novels is to a large extent a triumph of style," in *Language in Jane Austen* (Cambridge University Press, 1977), p. 9. Laura Mooneyham avers that Austen's "realms are language and its power," in *Romance, Language and Education in Jane Austen's Novels* (New York: St. Martin's Press, 1988), p. ix, while George Steiner insists that "the world of a Jane Austen novel is radically linguistic," in *After Babel*, (Oxford University Press, 1992 [second edition]), p. 9.
8 Jane Austen, *Sense and Sensibility*, ed. Peter Conrad (New York: Alfred A. Knopf, 1992), p. 176.
9 This confirms Michele Cohen's thesis that by the end of the century "masculine" laconicism stood for true English linguistic identity. *Fashioning Masculinity: National Identity and Language in the Eighteenth Century* (London: Routledge, 1996).
10 Jane Austen, *Pride and Prejudice*, ed. Tony Tanner (Harmondsworth: Penguin, 1985), pp. 377–8.
11 Tom Nairn, *The Enchanted Glass: Britain and its Monarchy* (London: Verso, 1988), p. 70. Cited in Meiksins Wood, p. 81. See also David Simpson's, *Romanticism, Nationalism, and the Revolt against Theory* (Chicago University Press, 1993).
12 Although I use it as a shorthand, I am uncomfortable with the imprecision of the term "middle class." By this term I mean the elite below the peerage and above yeomanry, which could on occasion include wealthy merchants, lawyers, and traders. See G. E. Mingay, *The Gentry* (London: Longman, 1976) and Lawrence Stone and Jean Fawtier Stone, *An Open Elite?* (Oxford: Clarendon, 1984).
13 This was not, however, an outright rejection of rhetoric so much as what Nancy Struever describes as "the peculiar alliance of rhetorical skills and aesthetic interests forged in the eighteenth century." Austen's texts, Struever argues, put those conversations in the mouths of fictional characters. "The Conversable World: Eighteenth-Century Transformations of the Relation of Rhetoric and Truth," in *Rhetoric and the Pursuit of Truth: Language Change in the Seventeenth and Eighteenth Centuries* (Los Angeles: William Andrews Clark Memorial Library, 1985), p. 81.
14 Fredric Jameson, *Marxism and Form* (Princeton University Press, 1971), pp. 333–4.
15 The necessity of protecting a cultural realm of lasting meaning would be especially pertinent in England, where the relative openness of the elite meant that the dictates of blood, rigidly adhered to in other European nations, did not exert a stabilizing force or provide an exclusionary criterion. See Stone and Stone, *Open Elite*, p. 3.

16 Nancy Armstrong writes, "Coming from a female source, however, the same authority appears to speak for heart and home in general and not on behalf of a particular class or dominant gender." Armstrong sees Austen as central to a novelistic tradition which restructures the domain of power in the late-eighteenth and early-nineteenth century in "The Nineteenth-Century Jane Austen: A Turning Point in the History of Fear", *Genre* 23 (1990), pp. 227–246, esp. p. 237. See also Mary Poovey, *The Proper Lady and the Woman Writer: Ideology as Style in the Works of Mary Wollstonecraft, Mary Shelley, and Jane Austen* (Chicago University Press, 1984) and Maaja Stewart, *Domestic Realities and Imperial Fictions: Jane Austen's Novels in Eighteenth-Century Contexts* (Athens and London: Georgia University Press, 1993).

17 Stewart makes an argument similar to Armstrong's, although she highlights the simultaneous conservation that accompanied the radical transformation Armstrong posits. Stewart shows how, in the wake of cultural and political instability, the home, and the women in it, become the site of cultural preservation. In the younger son's imitation of the older brother, Stewart writes, is "an assurance that some of the central values of the residual estate ideology, which is thus transformed even as it is being reproduced, will be preserved within the emergent mercantilism through the ideal female subject," p. 3. Poovey describes the ways in which women were forced to preserve the alliance of patronage in the face of the competition wrought through capitalist individualism, p. xv.

18 Armstrong, "Nineteenth-Century," p. 149. Walter Ong, however, provides an interesting twist to this formulation, noting that a classical training produced writing which was "formulaic and agonistic like oral" communication in men, and that most women writers, on the other hand, "worked outside of the oral tradition because they were outside of orally based rhetorical training of the schools." *Orality and Literacy*, (London: Methuen, 1982), pp. 109, 159.

19 Myra Stokes, *The Language of Jane Austen: A Study of Some Aspects of her Vocabulary* (New York: St. Martin's Press, 1991), p. 114.

20 Lynch, "At Home with Jane Austen," in *Cultural Institutions of the Novel*, eds. Deidre Lynch and William Warner (Durham, NC: Duke University Press, 1996), pp. 159–92 and Fraiman, "Jane Austen and Edward Said: Gender, Culture, and Imperialism," *Critical Inquiry* 21 (1995), pp. 805–21.

21 Lynda Mugglestone writes, "Guardians of the moral right and wrong, ladies were thus also to assume the role of guardians of the language" in '*Talking Proper': The Rise of Accent as Social Symbol* (Oxford: Clarendon, 1995), p. 172.

22 Austen, *Northanger Abbey* (New York: Pantheon, 1948), p. 96. See Claudia Johnson, who emphasizes the suspect nature of Henry's efforts, in *Jane Austen: Women, Politics, and the Novel*, (Chicago University Press, 1988).

23 Armstrong points out, "Fiction was the means by which this particular class ruled. For it made the once-privileged knowledge of the practices of an older land-owning society available on a mass basis – available, that is, to anyone possessing literacy and time for reading fiction," "Nineteenth-Century," p. 235.

24 See *Jane Austen: The Critical Heritage*, ed. B.C. Southam (London: Routledge and Kegan Paul, 1968).
25 Gary Kelly also notes, "Novels portrayed the manners, tastes, and power relations of the classes to which many novel readers aspired. Most novels also portrayed models for gentrified middle-class social conduct, subjective experience, class relations and negotiation with upper-class ideology and conduct" ("Jane Austen's," p. 158), and that literature "was a way to acquire linguistic capital, or knowledge of kinds of language useful in influential society" (155).
26 Southam tells us that Austen's novels were popular at court. On the fact that language ridiculed in Austen was used by even the best of speakers, K. C. Phillips writes, " 'Errors' perpetrated by the [Steele] sisters had had a very respectable ancestry, being used by earlier letter-writers of impeccable social status, and even by established authors, down to at least the middle of the eighteenth century" (lvi). "Lucy Steele's English," *College English* 59 (1969), pp. lv-lxi and *Jane Austen's English* (London: Andre Deutsch, 1970).
27 Here I quote Lynch who cites Q. D. Leavis ("At Home," 172).
28 Daniel Cottom argues, "Words that otherwise might seem to have a definite significance are disturbed by other words that would seem just as definite." *The Civilized Imagination* (Cambridge University Press, 1985), p. 116. I draw from his work by arguing, as he does, that much more is to be made of this linguistic indeterminacy.
29 Theodor Adorno, "Foreign Words," in *Notes to Literature*, trans. Shierry Weber Nicholsen (New York: Columbia University Press, 1991–2).
30 Karla Schultz goes on to note, "He calls ['strange' words] tiny cells of resistance against national sentiment, against the regressive tendency to claim as our 'own' what has been made familiar by ideological convention . . . It triggers reflection about one's position in society and about this society's social relations," in "The Strangeness of Home: Brecht's and Adorno's Dialectics." Paper presented at the Institute for Culture and Society, Corvallis, OR, 19 June 1997. See also Jameson (*Marxism*), who believes that in Adorno's theorization of form he "shows . . . how every possible idea we form about society is necessarily partial and imperfect, inadequate and contradictory."
31 See Grant Holly, "Emma-Grammatology," *Studies in Eighteenth-Century Culture* 19 (1989), pp. 39–51.
32 Inger Sigrun Thomsen writes, "Austen not only profoundly distrusted words, but . . . she actually sought to instill a similar distrust in her readers," in "Words 'Half-Dethroned': Jane Austen's Art of the Unspoken" in *Jane Austen's Business* (96).
33 R. W. Chapman cited in Page, *Language*, (10). It is significant that for this novelist for whom language is the "realm of action" (Mooneyham, ix) "her language does not habitually draw attention to itself: her attitude to style is too critical to permit 'fine writing', and her satirical sense too strong to permit elaborate effects. What is in question often involves no more than

the use of an unexpected word or phrase, or a temporary departure from normal syntax" (Page, 10). On the other hand, the claim that Austen has no distinct style reinforces the argument that Austen's novels simply use "correct" English, attributing a transparency to her writing of which we should be suspicious.

34 See Poovey, *Proper*, pp. 3–47 and Johnson, *Jane Austen*. I do not mean to suggest that these writers merely reduce Austen's ambivalence to her position as a woman. Stressing her active reworking of language in the interest of resolving potentially ideologically contradictory beliefs, Poovey has argued that "Austen developed aesthetic strategies to balance her attraction to feeling with investment in traditional social institutions" (182).

35 Page, *Language*, p. 9. He argues that Austen "inherits and preserves the great language of the eighteenth-century." Writing against this view are Thomsen, "Words," and Knud Sorensen, "Johnsonese in *Northanger Abbey*: A Note on Jane Austen's Style," *College English* 50 (1969), pp. 390–7. Austen *was*, nonetheless, an admirer of Johnson. See Claudia Johnson (78–85).

36 Several writers have discussed Austen's own consciousness of the performativity of social roles and identity. See Tanner's Introduction to *Pride and Prejudice*.

37 C. S. Lewis, Mary Lascelles, and A. C. Bradley cited in Peter DeRose, *Jane Austen and Samuel Johnson* (Washington, DC: University Press of America, 1980), p. 4.

38 For Armstrong, it is precisely through "distinguishing her polite English from the linguistic materials that she inherited from earlier novelists" that Austen is able to locate a continuously fluctuating gentry class within the power elite (*Desire*, p. 135).

39 Johnson argues that Austen uses the conventions of the Gothic novel – a genre often associated with conservative ideology – to challenge patriarchy ("Women," p. 21), and that her techniques of reduction, reversal, literalization, and hyperbole are nothing so much as performances capable of overturning conservative prerogatives.

40 Henry Fielding, *Tom Jones*, ed. John Bender and Simon Stern (Oxford University Press), p. 146, as one instance.

41 See Page's helpful discussion of this mode in *Language*.

42 See Meenakshi Mukherjee, *Jane Austen* (New York: St. Martin's, 1991), pp. 66–8.

43 The Stones, for instance, among many other historians, argue in *Open Elite* that by the sixteenth century the English elite was open enough for merchants to enter.

44 This is not an affirmation of the "inimitability" of Austen's characters but rather an insistence that those characters are not "identical" to themselves.

45 Here I want to offer an alternative take to Kelly's reading of Austen's irony. He argues that in requiring re-reading, Austen's novels are deemed "classics" which, in their then-canonical status, confirm nationalist and imperialist agendas. While such cultural work is likely going on, it is also likely that

the repetition of reading necessitated by irony is never the same, and that the classic's claim to somehow preserve continuity through time is thus short circuited.

46 Thus the effects of Austen's use of free indirect discourse parallel the effects of her parodies of generic conventions associated with female readerships. The extent of the humor relies on the reader's familiarity with the genre in the first place, as Kelly has pointed out. A general audience will likely see the joke in Elinor's teasing censure of her sister, "It is not every one ... who has your passion for dead leaves" (84), yet those most familiar with specific literary texts with "dead leaves" as their subject matter will appreciate it all the more. While some have read Austen's ironic strategies and parodies of novelistic convention as implicit critiques of the excesses of these "female" genres, and a chastening of their readerships, trapping unwary readers in their own conditioned responses, Kelly, alternatively, views this as reconstituting precisely those reading communities that critics of these genres hoped to dispel.

Bibliography

PRIMARY SOURCES

Anonymous, *Some Remarks on the Highland Clans and Methods Proposed for Civilizing Them*, Edinburgh, 1750
Anonymous, *The Highland Complaint*, Edinburgh, 1737
Arnold, Matthew, *On the Study of Celtic Literature and on Translating Homer* (1867), New York: Macmillan, 1904
Austen, Jane, *Emma* (1816), ed. James Kinsley, Oxford University Press, 1995
  Northanger Abbey (1818), New York: Pantheon, 1948
  Pride and Prejudice (1913), ed. Tony Tanner, Harmondsworth: Penguin, 1985
  Sense and Sensibility (1811), ed. Peter Conrad, New York: Alfred A. Knopf, 1992
Blair, Hugh, "A Critical Dissertation," in *The Poems of Ossian, to which are Prefixed a Discourse and Dissertation on the Aera of Ossian* (1763), Boston: Phillip Sampson, 1959
  Lectures on Rhetoric and Belles Lettres, 2 vols., London, 1793 edition and ed. Harold F. Harding, 2 vols., Carbondale: Southern Illinois University Press, 1965
Blount, Thomas, *Glossographia*, London, 1656
Boswell, James, *The Life of Samuel Johnson* (1791), ed. Bergen Evans, New York: Random House, 1965
Bullokar, John, *An English Expositor or Compleat Dictionary*, London, 1616
Burke, Edmund, *A Philosophical Enquiry into the Origin of Our Ideas of the Sublime and the Beautiful* (1757), ed. Adam Philips, Oxford University Press, 1990
  Reflections on the Revolution in France (1790), ed. J. G. A. Pocock, Indianapolis and Cambridge: Hackett Publishing, 1987
  Speech on Conciliation, New York: Ginn, 1900
Burns, Robert, *Selected Poems*, ed. Carol McGuirk, Harmondsworth: Penguin, 1993
Campbell, Archibald, *Lexiphanes, a Dialogue*, London, 1767
Cawdrey, Robert, *A Table Alphabeticall*, London, 1604
Chesterfield, Philip Dormer Stanhope, fourth Earl, *The World*, No. 100, 28 November 1754, and 101, 5 December 1754
Clark, John, *Works of the Caledonian Bards*, Edinburgh, 1778
Condillac, Etienne, *An Essay on the Origin of Human Knowledge* (1746), tr. Thomas

Nugent, London, 1756; repr. Gainesville, Fla.: Scholars Facsimiles and Reprints, 1971

Defoe, Daniel, *A Tour Thro' the Whole Island of Great Britain* (1724–6), ed. and intro. Pat Rogers, New York: Penguin, 1971

Encyclopaedia Britannica, or a Dictionary of Arts and Sciences ... by a Society of Gentlemen in Scotland, 3 vols., Edinburgh, 1768–71

Fergusson, Robert, *The Poems of Robert Fergusson*, 2 vols., ed. Matthew P. McDiarmid, Edinburgh and London: Blackwood & Sons, 1956

Fielding, Henry, *Tom Jones* (1749), ed. John Bender and Simon Stern, Oxford University Press, 1996

Gillies, Rev. John (ed.), *Historical Collections Relating to Remarkable Periods of the Success of the Gospel*, Kelso: John Rutherford, 1845

Grant, Anne, *Letters from the Mountains Being the Real Correspondence of a Lady*, London, 1809

Grose, Francis, *A Classical Dictionary of the Vulgar Tongue*, London, 1789

Henley, John, *Compleat Linguist*, London, 1719–26

Hume, David, "Of the Rise and Progress of the Arts and Sciences" and "Of Eloquence," in *Essays Moral, Political and Literary*, ed. Eugene Miller, Indianapolis: Liberty Classics, 1987

Johnson, Samuel, *A Dictionary of the English Language*, London, 1755
  Idler 2, 22 April 1758
  Idler 7, 2 May 1758
  Idler 34, 9 December 1758
  Idler 37, 30 December 1758
  Idler 63, 30 June 1759
  Idler 70, 18 August 1759
  Idler 77, 6 October 1759
  Idler 91, 6 January 1760

A Journey to the Western Islands of Scotland (1775), ed. Peter Levi, Harmondsworth: Penguin, 1984

Letter to Francis Barber, 25 September 1770. *Letters*, vol. I, ed. Bruce Redford, Princeton University Press, 1982

Letter to Charles Burney, 24 December 1757. *Letters*, vol. II, ed. Bruce Redford, Princeton University Press, 1982

Letter to William Samuel Johnson, 9 March 1773. *Letters*, vol. I

Letter to Thomas Warton, 20 March 1755 in *Letters*, vol. II

Plan of a Dictionary, London, 1747; facs repr. Menston: Scolar Press, 1970

"Preface to Shakespeare," in *The Yale Edition of the Works of Samuel Johnson*, ed. Arthur Sherbo, v. vii, New Haven: Yale University Press, 1968

Jones, Rowland, *The Origin of Language and Nations* (1764); fac. repr. Menston: Scolar Press, 1972

Lane, A. Archibald, *A Key to the Art of Letters*, London, 1700

Lightbody, James, *Mariner's Jewell*, London, 1695

Lhuyd, Edward, *Archaeologia Britannica, Glossography*, Oxford, 1707

Locke, John, *An Essay Concerning Human Understanding* (1690), ed. Roger Woolhouse, Harmondsworth: Penguin, 1997

Loughton, William, *A Practical Grammar of the English Tongue; or, A Rational and Easy Introduction*, London, 1734

Lowth, Robert, *A Short Introduction to English Grammar*, London (1762), Leeds: J. Binns, 1794

Mac Mhaighstir Alasdair, Alasdair (Alexander MacDonald), *Aiseirigh Na Seann Chanain Albannaich (The Resurrection of the Ancient Scottish Language)*, Edinburgh, 1751

MacDonald, Alexander, *Journall and Memoirs of P— C— Expedition into Scotland by a Highland Officer in his Army* (*Lockhart Papers*, vol. II [London, 1817])

A Gaelic / English Vocable, Edinburgh, 1741

The Resurrection of the Ancient Scottish Language, tr. Rev. A. MacDonald and Rev. A. MacDonald, Inverness, 1924

Macnicol, Donald, *Remarks on Dr. Samuel Johnson's Journey to the Hebrides*, London, 1779

MacPherson, James, *Poems of Ossian* (1760), London: Cadell and Davies, 1807

MacPherson, John, *Critical Dissertations on the Origin, Antiquities Language, Government, Manners, and Religion of the Ancient Caledonians*, Edinburgh, 1768

Malcolme, David, *Letters, Essays, and Other Tracts illustrating the Antiquities of Great Britain and Ireland*, London, 1744

Martin, Martin, *A Late Voyage to St. Kilda* (1698) and *A Description of the Western Islands of Scotland* (1703), ed. Donald J. MacLeod, Edinburgh: Birlinn, 1994

Mason, George, *A Supplement to Dr. Johnson's English Dictionary*, London, 1801

Mitchell, Hugh, *Scotticisms, Vulgar Anglicisms, and Grammatical Improprieties Corrected*, Glasgow, 1799

Monboddo, James Burnet, Lord, *Of the Origin and Progress of Language*, 5 vols., Edinburgh, 1774–93

Peyton, V. J., *The History of the English Language*, London, 1771

Phillips, Edward, *The New World of English Words*, London, 1658

Pinkerton, John, *Scottish Tragic Ballads*, London: J. Nichols, 1781

Quintilian, *Quintilian on the Teaching of Speaking and Writing*, ed. James J. Murphy, Carbondale: Southern Illinois University Press, 1987

Randell, Thomas, *Christian Benevolence, A Sermon Preached before the Society in Scotland for Propagating Christian Knowledge at their Anniversary Meeting*, Edinburgh, 1763

Ray, John, *Collection of English Words not Generally Used*, London, 1674

Richardson, Charles, *Illustrations of English Philology*, London: Gale and Fenner, 1815

Robertson, William "The Situation of the World at the Time of Christ's Appearance: A Sermon Preached before the S.S.P.C.K.," in *State of the Society in Scotland for Propagating Christian Knowledge ... in 1754*, Edinburgh, 1755

Rousseau, Jean-Jacques, *On the Origin of Languages* (1781), ed. and trans. John H.

Moran and Alexander Gode, Chicago University Press, 1966
Scots Magazine xxiii, Edinburgh, 1761
Shaw, William, *An Analysis of the Galic [sic] Language*, London, 1778
   An Enquiry Into the Authenticity of the Poems Ascribed to Ossian, 1781
   A Galic [sic] and English Dictionary, London, 1780
   Memoirs of the Life and Writings of the Late Dr. Samuel Johnson (1785), ed. Arthur Sherbo, Oxford University Press, 1974
Sheridan, Thomas, *A Course of Lectures on Elocution*, London, 1762; facs. repr. Menston: Scolar Press, 1968
Smith, John, *Galic* [sic] *Antiquities*, Edinburgh, 1780
Smollet, Tobias, *The Briton* No. 10, 31 July 1762, No. 11, 7 August 1762, in *Poems, Plays, and* The Briton, ed. Byron Gassman, Athens, GA: Georgia University Press, 1993
   The Expedition of Humphry Clinker (1771), ed. Lewis Knapp, revised Paul-Gabriel Boucé, Oxford University Press, 1992, and ed. O. M. Brack, Jr., Athens, GA, and London: Georgia University Press, 1990
   The History and Adventures of an Atom, London, 1769
   The Present State of All Nations, 8 vols., London, 1768
   "Tears of Scotland" (1746) in *Poems, Plays, and* The Briton, ed. Byron Gassman, Athens, GA: Georgia University Press, 1993
Smith, Adam, *Lectures on Rhetoric and Belles Lettres*, ed. J. Bryce, Oxford University Press, 1983, and ed. John M. Lothian, 2 vols., London: Thomas Nelson and Sons, Ltd., 1963
   Review of Johnson's *Dictionary, Edinburgh Review* 1 (1755)
   An Inquiry into the Nature and Causes of the Wealth of Nations, 2 vols., ed. A. Skinner, Oxford University Press, 1976
Society in Scotland for Propagating Christian Knowledge, *Abridgement of the Statutes of the Society*, Edinburgh: n.d. 1732?
   An Account of the Society in Scotland for Propagating Christian Knowledge, Edinburgh, 1716
   An Account of the Society in Scotland for Propagating Christian Knowledge from its Commencement in 1709 ... with Regard to Religion, Edinburgh, 1774
   Present State of the Society in Scotland for Propagating Christian Knowledge, Edinburgh, 1756
   A Summary Account, Edinburgh, 1783
Statistical Account of Scotland, Parish of Kirkmichael, County of Banff, vol. XII, no. 32.
Stevenson, Robert Louis, *The Strange Case of Dr. Jekyll and Mr. Hyde* (1886), New York: Bantam, 1978
Swift, Jonathan, *Proposal for Correcting, Improving and Ascertaining the English Tongue*, London, 1712
Tooke, John Horne, *The Diversions of Purley*, London, 1786; 2nd ed., 2 vols., London, 1798
Wallace, Robert, *Ignorance and Superstition a Source of Violence and Cruelty, and ... Cause of the Present Rebellion*, Edinburgh, 1746

MANUSCRIPTS

Edinburgh University Library (EUL) MS.La.II.647/91. T. Collinson Letter to Dr. John Sims
EUL MS La. III. 251
EUL MS Dc.8.128 D. Macpherson, "Cursory Remarks on Verstegan's Restitution"
National Library of Scotland (NLS) MS 17504 ff 58
NLS MS 16720/f9IRTV
NLS MS 16720 ff 88–91
Scottish Records Office (SRO) GD 95 10
SRO GD 95 1/2, 10 August 1721
SRO GD 95 1/2, 4 November 1725
SRO GD 95 2/1, 13 January 1715
SRO GD 95 2/2, 2 February 1719
SRO GD 95 2/2, 4 November 1717
SRO GD 95 2/2, 22 March 1718
SRO GD 95 2/2, 1 May 1718
SRO GD 95 2/7, 14 June 1756
SRO GD 95 6, 2 June 1745, p. 271

SECONDARY SOURCES

Aarsleff, Hans, *From Locke to Saussure: Essays on the Study of Language and Intellectual History*, Minneapolis: Minnesota University Press, 1982
The Study of Language in England, 1780–1860, Princeton University Press, 1967
Adorno, Theodor, "Foreign Words," in *Notes to Literature*, trans. Shierry Weber Nicholsen, New York: Columbia University Press, 1991–2
Aers, David, "Community and Morality: Towards Reading Jane Austen," in *Romanticism and Ideology: Studies in English Writing 1765–1830*, ed. David Aers, Jonathan Cook, and David Punter, London: Routledge and Kegan Paul, 1981
Aitken, A. J., "The Scottish Vowel Length Rule," in *So Many People, Longages and Tonges*, ed. M. Benskin and M. L. Samuels, Edinburgh University Press, 1981
Althusser, Louis, *Lenin and Philosophy*, London: Monthly Review, 1971
Anderson, Benedict, *Imagined Communities: Reflections on the Origin and Spread of Nationalism*, London: Verso, 1987
Anderson, Judith, *Words that Matter: Linguistic Perception in Renaissance English*, Stanford University Press, 1996
Anderson, Perry, "Components of the National Culture," *New Left Review* 50 (1968)
Arac, Jonathan and Harriet Ritvo (eds.), *Macropolitics of Nineteenth-Century Literature*, Philadelphia: Pennsylvania University Press, 1991
Armstrong, Nancy, *Desire and Domestic Fiction: A Political History of the Novel*,

Oxford University Press, 1987

"The Nineteenth-Century Jane Austen: A Turning Point in the History of Fear," *Genre* 23 (1990), 227–46

Arteaga, Alfred, *Other Tongue: Nation and Ethinicity in the Linguistic Borderlands*, Durham, NC: Duke University Press, 1994

Bakhtin, Mikhail, *Rabelais and His World*, trans. Helene Iswolsky, Bloomington: Indiana University Press, 1984

Barker-Benfield, G. J., *The Culture of Sensibility: Sex and Society in Eighteenth-Century Britain*, Chicago University Press, 1992

Barrell, John, *English Literature in History, 1730–1780, An Equal Wide Survey*, London: Hutchinson, 1983

Barthes, Roland, *Mythologies*, trans. Annette Lavers, New York: Hill and Wang, 1972

Basker, James G., "Scotticisms and the Problem of Cultural Identity in Eighteenth-Century Britain," *Eighteenth-Century Life* 15 (1991), 81–95

Tobias Smollett: Critic and Journalist, Newark: Delaware University Press, 1988

Bator, Paul, "The Formation of the Regius Chair of Rhetoric and Belles Lettres at the University of Edinburgh," *Quarterly Journal of Speech* 75 (1989), 40–64

Bentman, Raymond, *Robert Burns*, Boston: Twayne, 1987

Bhabha, Homi, "The Ambivalence of Colonial Discourse," in *OCTOBER: The First Decade, 1976–1986*, ed. Annette Michelson *et al.*, Cambridge, MA: MIT Press, 1987

DissemiNation: Time, Narrative, and the Margins of the Modern Nation," in *Nation and Narration*, ed. Homi Bhabha, London: Routledge, 1990

"The Other Question...," *Screen* 24 (1983), 18–36

Black, Ronald, "Mac Mhaighstir Alasdair: the Ardnamurchan Years," *Society of West Highland and Island Historical Research* (1985), 3–43

Bogel, Fredric, "Johnson and the Role of Authority," in *The New 18th Century*, ed. Felicity Nussbaum and Laura Brown, London: Methuen, 1987

Boggs, W. Arthur, "Dialectical Ingenuity in *Humphry Clinker*," *Papers on English Language and Literature* 1 (1965), 327–37

"Some Standard Eighteenth-Century English Usages," *The Quarterly Journal of Speech* 51 (1965), 304–06

"Win Jenkins' Archaisms and Proverbial Phrases," *The USF Language Quarterly* 4 (1965), 33–6

"A Win Jenkins' Lexicon," *Bulletin of the New York Public Library* 68 (1964), 323–30

Bohls, Elizabeth, "Disinterestedness and the Denial of the Particular: Locke, Adam Smith, and the Subject of Aesthetics," in *Eighteenth-Century Aesthetics and the Reconstruction of Art*, ed. Paul Mattick, Jr., Cambridge University Press, 1993

Boucé, Paul-Gabriel, "Archibald Campbell on Smollett's Style," *Studies in Scottish Literature* 9 (1972), 211–17

Les Romans de Smollett: étude critique, Paris: Didier, 1971

Bourdieu, Pierre, *Language and Symbolic Power*, trans. Gino Raymond and

Matthew Adamson, Cambridge, MA: Harvard University Press, 1991
Bowers, Terence, "Reconstituting the National Body in Smollett's *Travels through France and Italy,*" *Eighteenth-Century Life* 21 (1997), 1–25
Brantlinger, Patrick and Richard Boyle, "The Education of Edward Hyde: Stevenson's 'Gothic Gnome' and the Mass Readership of Late-Victorian England," in *Dr Jekyll and Mr Hyde After 100 Years*, ed. William Veeder and Gordon Hirsch, University of Chicago Press, 1988
Brown, Terence (ed.), *Celticism*, Amsterdam: Rodopi, 1996
Butler, Marilyn, *Jane Austen and the War of Ideas*, Oxford: Clarendon Press, 1975
Butterfield, Herbert, *The Whig Interpretation of History*, London: G. Bell and Sons, 1951
Caffentzis, George, *Clipped Coins, Abused Words and Civil Government: John Locke's Philosophy of Money*, Brooklyn: Autonomedia, 1989
Cairn, David and Shaun Richards, *Writing Ireland: Colonialism, Nationalism and Culture*, Manchester University Press, 1988
Campbell, J. L., "Alexander Macdonald: Portrait of a Traditionalist," *Scots Magazine* 24 (1934–5), 61–76
  "The Expurgating of MacMhaighstir Alasdair," *Scottish Gaelic Studies* 12 (1971), 59–76
Canclini, Nestor Garcia, *Hybrid Cultures: Strategies for Entering and Leaving Modernity*, Minneapolis: Minnesota University Press, 1995
Carter, Ian, "The Highlands of Scotland as an Underdeveloped Region," in *Sociology and Development*, ed. Emanuel de Kadt and Gavin Williams, London: Tavistock, 1974
Castells, Manuel, *The Informational City: Information Technology, Economic Restructuring, and the Urban-Regional Process*, Oxford: Basil Blackwell, 1989
Chamberlain, Lori, "Gender and the Metaphorics of Translation," *Signs* 13 (1988), 464–72
Chandler, James, "Devolutionary Criticism: Scotland, America, and Literary Modernity," *Modern Philology* 92 (1994), 211–19
Chapman, Malcolm, *The Gaelic Vision in Scottish Culture*, London: Croom Helm, 1978
  The Celts: The Construction of a Myth, London: Macmillan Press, 1992
Chatterjee, Partha, *The Nation and its Fragments*, Princeton University Press, 1993
  Nationalist Thought and the Colonial World, Minneapolis: Minnesota University Press, 1993
Cheyfitz, Eric, *The Poetics of Imperialism: Translation and Colonization from the Tempest to Tarzan*, Oxford University Press, 1991
Chomsky, Noam, *Cartesian Linguistics*, New York: Harper & Row, 1966
Christensen, Jerome, *Practicing Enlightenment: Hume and the Formation of a Literary Career*, Madison: Wisconsin University Press, 1987
Christie, John, "Adam Smith's Metaphysics of Language," in *The Figural and the Literal*, ed. Andrew Benjamin *et al.*, Manchester University Press, 1987
Clark, J. C. D., *Samuel Johnson: Literature, Religion, and English Cultural Politics from the Restoration to Romanticism*, Cambridge University Press, 1994

Cohen, Michele, *Fashioning Masculinity: National Identity and Language in the Eighteenth Century*, London: Routledge, 1996
Cohen, Murray, *Sensible Words: Linguistic Practice in England 1640–1785*, Baltimore: Johns Hopkins University Press, 1977
Colley, Linda, *Britons: Forging the Nation 1707–1837*, New Haven: Yale University Press, 1992
Cottom, Daniel, *The Civilized Imagination: A Study of Ann Radcliffe, Jane Austen, and Sir Walter Scott*, Cambridge University Press, 1983
Court, Franklin, *Institutionalizing English Literature: The Cultural Politics of Literary Study, 1750–1900*, Stanford University Press, 1992
Cowper, A. and I. Ross, *Eighteenth-Century Schoolmasters in Strathbora*, Edinburgh, 1980
Crawford, John, "Books, Libraries and the Decline of Gaelic on the Island of Arran," *Library Review* (1987), 83–94
  "Policy Formulation for Public Library Provision in the Highlands of Scotland," *Journal of Librarianship* 16 (1984), 94–117
Crawford, Robert, "Bakhtin and Scotlands," *Scotlands* 1 (1994), 66–80
  Devolving English Literature, Oxford: Clarendon Press, 1992
  "Native Language," *Comparative Criticism* 18 (1996), 71–90
Crawford, Robert (ed.), *Robert Burns and Cultural Authority*, Edinburgh University Press, 1996
  The Scottish Invention of English Literature, Cambridge University Press, 1998
Crawford, Thomas, *Burns: A Study of the Poems and Songs*, Edinburgh: Mercat, 1978
Cregeen, Eric, "The Changing Role of the House of Argyll in the Scottish Highlands," in *Scotland in the Age of Improvement*, ed. N. T. Phillipson and Rosalind Mitchison, Edinburgh University Press, 1970
Crowley, Tony, *Language in History: Theories and Texts*, London and New York: Routledge, 1996
Curley, Thomas, "Johnson's Last Word on Ossian: Ghostwriting for William Shaw," in *Aberdeen and the Enlightenment*, ed. Jennifer J. Carter and Joan H. Pittock, Aberdeen University Press, 1987
Daiches, David, *The Paradox of Scottish Culture: The Eighteenth-Century Experience*, London: Oxford University Press, 1964
Davis, Leith, *Acts of Union: Scotland and the Literary Negotiation of the British Nation 1707–1830*, Stanford University Press, 1999
Day, Robert Adams, *Told in Letters*, Ann Arbor: Michigan University Press, 1966
DeGategno, Paul, "'The Source of Daily and Exalted Pleasure': Jefferson Reads the Poems of Ossian," in *Ossian Revisited*, ed. Howard Gaskill, Edinburgh University Press, 1991
Demaria, Robert, *Johnson's Dictionary and the Language of Learning*, Chapel Hill: North Carolina University Press, 1986
DeRose, Peter, *Jane Austen and Samuel Johnson*, Washington, DC: University Press of America, 1980

Derrida, Jacques, *Of Grammatology*, trans. Gayatri Spivak, Baltimore: Johns Hopkins University Press, 1976

Deutsch, Helen, "The Author as Monster: The Case of Doctor Johnson," in *"Defect": Engendering the Modern Body*, ed. Helen Deutsch and Felicity Nussbaum, Ann Arbor: University of Michigan, 2000

Dominque, Nicole, "Middle English: Another Creole?" *Journal of Creole Studies* 1 (1977), 89–100

Dorian, Nancy, *Language Death: The Life Cycle of a Scottish Gaelic Dialect*, Philadelphia: Pennsylvania University Press, 1981

Douglas, Aileen, *Uneasy Sensations: Smollett and the Body*, Chicago University Press, 1995

Duckworth, Alistair, *The Improvement of the Estate: A Study of Jane Austen's Novels*, Baltimore: Johns Hopkins University Press, 1971

Duncan, Ian, "Adam Smith, Samuel Johnson, and the Institutions of English," in *The Scottish Invention of English Literature*, ed. Robert Crawford, Cambridge University Press, 1998

"The Upright Corpse: Hogg, National Literature and the Uncanny," *Studies in Hogg and His World* 5 (1994), 29–54

Durkacz, Victor, *The Decline of the Celtic Languages*, Edinburgh: John Donald Publishers, 1983

Dwyer, John, "Clio and Ethics: Practical Morality in Enlightened Scotland," *The Eighteenth Century: Theory and Interpretation* 30 (1989), 45–72

Eagleton, Terry, *The Function of Criticism*, London: Verso, 1984

The Ideology of the Aesthetic, London: Blackwell, 1990

Ehninger, Douglas and James Golden, "The Intrinsic Sources of Blair's Popularity," *Southern Speech Journal* 21 (1955), 12–30

Elledge, Scott, "The Background and Development in English Criticism of the Theories of Generality and Particularity," *PMLA* 62 (1947)

"The Naked Science of Language, 1747–1786," in *Studies in Criticism and Aesthetics, 1660–1800*, ed. Howard Anderson and John Shea, Minneapolis: Minnesota University Press, 1967

Emerson, Roger, "American Indians, Frenchmen, and Scots Philosophers," *Studies in Eighteenth-Century Culture* 9 (1979), 211–36

Erlmann, Veit, "The Aesthetics of the Global Imagination: Reflections on World Music in the 1990s," *Public Culture* 20 (1996)

Fabel, Robin, "The Patriotic Briton: Tobias Smollet and English Politics, 1756–1771," *Eighteenth-Century Studies* 8 (1974), 100–14

Fabian, Johannes, *Time and the Other: How Anthropology Makes its Object*, New York: Columbia University Press, 1983

Fabricant, Carol, "Binding and Dressing Nature's Loose Tresses: The Ideology of Augustan Landscape Design," *Studies in Eighteenth-Century Culture* 8 (1979)

"History, Narrativity, and Swift's Project to 'Mend the World'," in *Case Studies in Contemporary Criticism: Jonathan Swift's* Gulliver's Travels, ed. Christopher Fox, New York: St Martin's Press, 1995

Favret, Mary, *Romantic Correspondence: Women, Politics and the Fiction of Letters*,

Cambridge University Press, 1993
Fielding, Penny, *Writing and Orality: Nationality, Culture, and Nineteenth-Century Scottish Fiction*, Oxford: Clarendon Press, 1996
Fitzmaurice-Wright, Susan, "The Commerce of Language in the Pursuit of Politeness in Eighteenth-Century England," *English Studies* 4 (1998), 309–27
Foster, Robert J., "Making National Cultures in the Global Ecumene," *Annual Review of Anthropology* 20 (1991), 236–60
Foucault, Michel, *The Order of Things*, New York: Vintage Books, 1973
Fraiman, Susan, "Jane Austen and Edward Said: Gender, Culture, and Imperialism," *Critical Inquiry* 21 (1995), 805–21
Gallagher, Catherine, *Nobody's Story: The Vanishing Acts of Women Writers in the Marketplace, 1670–1820*, Berkeley: California University Press, 1994
Gellner, Ernest, *Nations and Nationalism*, Oxford: Basil Blackwell, 1983
Gibbons, Luke, "The Sympathetic Bond: Ossian, Celticism, and Colonialism," in *Celticism*, ed. Terence Brown, Amsterdam: Rodopi, 1996
Gifford, Douglas and Dorothy Macmillan (eds.), *A History of Scottish Women's Writing*, Edinburgh University Press, 1997
Gikandi, Simon, *Maps of Englishness: Writing Identity in the Culture of Colonialism*, New York: Columbia University Press, 1996
Goux, Jean-Joseph, *Symbolic Economies After Marx and Freud*, trans. Jennifer Curtiss Gage, Ithaca: Cornell University Press, 1990
Graff, Harvey J., *Legacy of Literacy*, Bloomington, IN: Indiana University Press, 1987
Gramsci, Antonio, *Selections from the Prison Notebooks of Antonio Gramsci*, ed. Quentin Hoare and Geoffrey Nowell Smith, London: Lawrence and Wishart, 1971
Grant, Damien, *Tobias Smollett: A Study in Style*, Manchester University Press, 1977
Gray, Malcolm, *The Highland Economy 1750–1850*, Edinburgh: Oliver and Boyd, 1957
Greene, Donald, *Politics of Samuel Johnson*, New Haven: Yale University Press, 1960
  "Smollett the Historian: A Reappraisal," in *Tobias Smollett: Bicentennial Essays Presented to Lewis Knapp*, ed. G. S. Rousseau and P.-G. Boucé, Oxford University Press, 1971
Greenblatt, Stephen J., "Learning to Curse," in *First Images of America: The Impact of the New World on the Old*, ed. Fredi Chiapelli, Berkeley: California University Press, 1976
Gross, Jeffrey T., "Dr. Johnson's Treatment of English Particles in the *Dictionary*," *University of Mississippi Studies in English* 2 (1981), 71–92
Grossberg, Lawrence, "The Space of Culture, the Power of Space," in *The Post-Colonial Question: Common Skies, Divided Horizons*, ed. Iain Chambers and Lidia Curti, London and New York: Routledge, 1996
Guillory, John, *Cultural Capital: The Problem of Literary Canon Formation*, Chicago

University Press, 1993
Habermas, Jurgen, *Structural Transformation of the Public Sphere*, trans. Thomas Burger, Cambridge, MA: MIT Press, 1989
Hanes, Louise, "The Pronunciation of Tabitha Bramble," *Journal of English Linguistics* 14 (1980), 6–19
Harman, Chris, "The Return of the National Question," *International Socialism* 56 (1992), 1–62
Harris, Roy, *The Language-Makers*, Ithaca: Cornell University Press, 1980
Harvie, Christopher, "The Scottish Intellectuals 1760–1930," in *Celticism*, ed. Terence Brown, Amsterdam: Rodopi, 1996
Havelock, Eric, *The Literate Revolution in Greece and Its Cultural Consequences*, Princeton University Press, 1982
Haywood, Ian, *The Making of History: A Study of Literary Forgeries of James Macpherson and Thomas Chatterton*, London: Associated University Press, 1986
Hechter, Michael, *Internal Colonialism: The Celtic Fringe in British National Development*, Berkeley: California University Press, 1975
Hedrick, Elizabeth, "Fixing the Language: Johnson, Chesterfield, and *The Plan of a Dictionary*," *ELH* 55 (1988), 421–42
  "Locke's Theory of Language and Johnson's *Dictionary*," *Eighteenth-Century Studies* 20 (1987), 423–44
Helgerson, Richard, *Forms of Nationhood: The Elizabethan Writing of England*, Chicago University Press, 1992
Hobsbawm, E. J. and T. O. Ranger (eds.), *The Invention of Tradition*, Cambridge University Press, 1983
Holly, Grant, "Emma-Grammatology," *Studies in Eighteenth-Century Culture* 19 (1989), 39–51
Horgan, A. D., *Johnson on Language*, London: Macmillan, 1994
Horkheimer, Max and Theodor Adorno, *Dialectic of Enlightenment*, trans. John Cumming, New York: The Seabury Press, 1972
Houston, R. A., *Scottish Literacy and the Scottish Identity*, Cambridge University Press, 1985
Howell, Wilbur S., *Eighteenth-Century British Logic and Rhetoric*, Princeton University Press, 1971
Hudson, Nicholas, *Writing and European Thought: 1600–1830*, Cambridge University Press, 1994
Huet, Marie-Helene, *Monstrous Imagination*, Cambridge, MA: Harvard University Press, 1993
Hughes, Geoffrey, "Johnson's Dictionary and Attempts to 'Fix the Language'," *English Studies in Africa* 28 (1985), 99–107
Irigaray, Luce, *This Sex Which Is Not One*, trans. Catherine Porter, Ithaca: Cornell University Press, 1985
Jack, R. D. S., "Appearance and Reality in *Humphry Clinker*," in *Tobias Smollett*, ed. Alan Bold, Totowa, NJ: Vision, 1982
Jameson, Fredric, *Marxism and Form*, Princeton University Press, 1971
Johnson, Claudia, *Jane Austen: Women, Politics, and the Novel*, Chicago University

Press, 1988

Jones, Charles, "Scottish Standard English in the Late Eighteenth Century," *Transactions of the Philological Society* 9 (1993), 95–131

  A Language Suppressed, Edinburgh: State Mutual Book and Periodical Service, 1996

Jones, R. F., "Science and English Prose Style," in *The Seventeenth Century: Studies in the History of English Thought and Literature from Bacon to Pope*, Stanford University Press, 1965

Jones, M. G., *The Charity School Movement: A Study of Eighteenth-Century Puritanism in Action*, London: Frank Cass, 1964

Kahn, Madeleine, *Narrative Transvestitism: Rhetoric and Gender in the Eighteenth-Century English Novel*, Ithaca: Cornell University Press, 1991

Kay, Billy, *Scots: The Mither Tongue*, Edinburgh: Mainstream Publishing, 1986

Kelly, Gary, "Jane Austen's Real Business: The Novel, Literature and Cultural Capital," in *Jane Austen's Business*, ed. Juliet McMaster and Bruce Stovel, New York: St. Martin's Press, 1996

Kelly, Lionel (ed.), *Tobias Smollett: The Critical Heritage*, London and New York: Routledge and Kegan Paul, 1987

Kernan, Alvin, *Printing Technology, Letters and Samuel Johnson*, Princeton University Press, 1987

Kidd, Colin, *Subverting Scotland's Past: Scottish Whig Historians and the Creation of an Anglo-British Identity, 1689–1830*, Cambridge University Press, 1993

Kohler, K. J. "A Late Eighteenth-Century Comparison of the 'Provincial Dialect of Scotland' and the 'Pure Dialect'," *Linguistics* 23 (1966), 30–69

Knowlson, John, *Universal Language Schemes in England and France 1600–1800*, Toronto University Press, 1975

Kowaleski-Wallace, Elizabeth, *Consuming Subjects: Women, Shopping, and Business in the Eighteenth-Century*, New York: Columbia, 1997

Kramnick, Isaac, *Bolingbroke and His Circle: The Politics of Nostalgia in the Age of Walpole*, Cambridge, MA: Harvard University Press, 1968

Kramnick, Jonathan, *Making the English Canon: Print Capitalism and the Cultural Past, 1700–1770*, Cambridge University Press, 1998

  "The Making of the English Canon," *PMLA* 112 (1997), 1087–101

Kroll, Richard, *The Material Word: Literate Culture in the Restoration and Early Eighteenth Century*, Baltimore: Johns Hopkins University Press, 1991

Land, Stephen K., *From Signs to Propositions: The Concept of Form in Eighteenth-Century Semantic Theory*, London: Longman Publishers, 1974

Lefevere, Andre (ed.), *Translation/History/Culture*, London: Routledge, 1992

Lenin, V. I., *The Right of Nations to Self Determination*, London: International Publishers, 1951

Lenman, Bruce, *Integration, Enlightenment, and Industrialization: Scotland 1746–1832*, London: Edward Arnold, 1981

Leonard, Sterling Andrus, *The Doctrine of Correctness in English Usage 1700–1800*, New York: Russell & Russell, 1962

Levi-Strauss, Claude, *Tristes Tropiques*, Paris, 1955

Levine, Joseph, *The Battle of the Books*, Ithaca: Cornell University Press, 1991
   Huamanism and History: Origins of Modern Historiography, Ithaca: Cornell University Press, 1987
Lindsay, Maurice, *History of Scottish Literature*, London: Robert Hall, 1977
Lloyd, David, "Ethnic Cultures, Minority Discourses and the State," in *Colonial Discourse, Post-Colonial Theory*, ed. Francis Barker, Peter Hulme, Margaret Iverson, Manchester Univesity Press, 1994
   Nationalism and Minor Literature, Berkeley: California University Press, 1987
Low, Donald (ed.), *Robert Burns: The Critical Heritage*, London: Routledge, 1974
Lynch, Deidre, "At Home with Jane Austen," in *Cultural Institutions of the Novel*, ed. Deidre Lynch and William Warner, Durham, NC: Duke University Press, 1996
   "'Beating the Track of the Alphabet': Samuel Johnson, Tourism, and the ABCs of Modern Authority," *ELH* 57 (1990), 357–405
Lynn, Steven, "Locke's Eye, Adam's Tongue, Johnson's Word: Language, Marriage, and the 'Choice of Life'," *The Age of Johnson* 3 (1990), 35–61
Manning, Susan, *The Puritan Provincial Vision: Scottish and American Literature in the Nineteenth Century*, Cambridge University Press, 1990
Markley, Robert, *Fallen Languages: Crises of Representation in Newtonian England, 1660–1740*, Ithaca: Cornell University Press, 1993
Martz, Louis, *The Later Career of Tobias Smollett*, New Haven: Yale University Press, 1967
Marx, Karl, *Capital*, trans. Samuel Moore and Edward Aveling, New York: International Publishers, 1967
   The German Ideology, ed. C. J. Arthur, New York: International Publishers, 1985
McAdam, E. L., *Dr Johnson and the English Law*, Syracuse University Press, 1951
MacAulay, Donald, "Canons, Myths and Cannon Fodder," *Scotlands* 1 (1994), 35–54
McClintock, Anne, *Imperial Leather: Race, Gender and Sexuality in the Colonial Contest*, New York: Routledge, 1995
McCracken-Flesher, Caroline, "English Hegemony and Scots Subjectivity: Calvinism and Cultural Resistance in Nineteenth Century 'North British' Novels" (Ph.D. Dissertation, 1987)
McGuirk, Carol, *Robert Burns and the Sentimental Era*, Athens, GA: University of Georgia Press, 1985
MacInnes, John, *The Evangelical Movement in the Highlands of Scotland*, Aberdeen University Press, 1951
McIntosh, Carey, *Common and Courtly Language, The Stylistics of Social Class in Eighteenth-Century Literature*, Philadelphia: Pennsylvania University Press, 1986
   The Ordering of English: Style, Rhetoric, Politeness, Print Culture, and the Evolution of Prose from 1700 to 1800, Cambridge University Press, 1998
McLuhan, Marshall, *Gutenburg Galaxy*, Toronto University Press, 1962
McCrone, David, A. Morris and Richard Kiely, *Scotland the Brand: The Making of*

Scottish Heritage, Edinburgh University Press, 1995
Mayer, Robert, "History, *Humphry Clinker*, and the Novel," *Eighteenth-Century Fiction* 4 (1992), 239–55
Meek, Donald, "The Gaelic Bible," in *The Bible in Scottish Life and Literature*, ed. David Wright, Edinburgh: Saint Andrew Press, 1988
  "Scottish Highlanders, North American Indians, and the SSPCK," *Records of the Scottish Church History Society* 23 (1989), 378–96
Mignola, Walter, *The Darker Side of the Renaissance: Literacy, Territoriality, and Colonization*, Ann Arbor: Michigan University Press, 1996
Miller, Karl, *Doubles: Studies in Literary History*, Oxford: Clarendon Press, 1985
Miller, Thomas, *The Formation of College English: Rhetoric and Belles Lettres in the British Cultural Provinces*, Pittsburgh University Press, 1997
Mills, Frederick, "The S.S.P.C.K. in British North America, 1730–1775," *Church History* 63 (1994), 15–30
Mingay, G. E., *The Gentry*, London: Longman, 1976
Mitchison, Rosalind, "The Government and the Highlands, 1707–1745," in *Scotland in the Age of Improvement*, ed. N. T. Phillipson and R. Mitchison, Edinburgh University Press, 1970
Mooneyham, Laura, *Romance, Language and Education in Jane Austen's Novels*, New York: St. Martin's Press, 1988
Mugglestone, Lynda, *'Talking Proper': The Rise of Accent as Social Symbol*, Oxford: Clarendon Press, 1995
Mukherjee, Meenakshi, *Jane Austen*, New York: St. Martin's Press, 1991
Mullen, John, "The Language of Sentiment: Hume, Smith, and Henry Mackenzie," in *History of Scottish Literature*, vol. 2, ed. Andrew Hook, Aberdeen University Press, 1987
Murphy, Peter, "Fool's Gold: The Highland Treasures of Macpherson's Ossian," *ELH* 52 (1985), 567–91
Murray, David, *Forked Tongues: Speech, Writing, and Representation in North American Indian Texts*, Bloomington: Indiana University Press, 1991
Murray, Laura, "'Pray Sir, consider a Little': Rituals of Subordination and Strategies of Resistance in the Letters of Hezekiah Calving and David Fowler to Eleazar Wheelock, 1764–1768," *Studies in American Indian Literatures* 4 (1992), 48–74
Nairn, Tom, *The Break-up of Britain*, London: NLP, 1970
  The Enchanted Glass: Britain and its Monarchy, London: Verso, 1988
  Faces of Nationalism, London and New York: Verso, 1997
Newman, Gerald, *The Rise of English Nationalism: A Cultural History, 1740–1830*, New York: St. Martin's Press, 1987
Niranjana, Tejaswini, *Siting Translation: History, Post-Structuralism, and the Colonial Context*, Berkeley: California University Press, 1992
Nussbaum, Felicity, *Torrid Zones*, Baltimore: Johns Hopkins University Press, 1995
Oftedal, Magne, *The Gaelic of Leurbost, Isle of Lewis*, Oslo: Aschenhoug, 1956
Ong, Walter, *Orality and Literacy: The Technologizing of the Word*, London:

Methuen, 1982
Page, Norman, *Language in Jane Austen*, Cambridge University Press, 1977
Parker, Patricia, *Literary Fat Ladies: Rhetoric, Gender, Property*, London: Methuen, 1987
Parry, Benita, "Resistance Theory/Theorising Resistance or Two Cheers for Nativism," in *Colonial Discourse, Post-Colonial Theory*, ed. Francis Barker, Peter Hulme and Margaret Iverson, Manchester University Press, 1994
Paulin, Tom, *Day-Star of Liberty: William Hazlitt's Radical Style*, London: Faber and Faber, 1998
Paxman, David, "Language and Difference: The Problem of Abstraction in Eighteenth-Century Language Study," *Journal of the History of Ideas* 54 (1993), 19–36
  "The Genius of English: Eighteenth-Century Language Study and English Poetry," *Philological Quarterly* 70 (1991), 27–46
Phillips, K. C., *Jane Austen's English*, London: Andre Deutsch, 1970
  "Lucy Steele's English," *College English* 59 (1969), lv–lxi
Phillipson, Nicholas, "Politics, Politeness and the Anglicisation of Early Eighteenth-Century Scottish Culture," in *Scotland and England: 1286–1816*, ed. Roger Mason, Edinburgh: John Donald, 1987
Piggot, Stuart, *Ancient Britons and the Antiquarian Imagination*, London: Thames and Hudson, 1989
Pittock, Murray, *Inventing and Resisting Britain*, New York: St. Martin's Press, 1997
  Poetry and Jacobite Politics in Eighteenth-Century Britain and Ireland, Cambridge University Press, 1994
Pocock, J. G. A., *The Ancient Constitution and the Feudal Law*, New York: W. W. Norton & Company, 1967
  Virtue, Commerce, and History: Essays on Political Thought and History, Chiefly in the Eighteenth Century, Cambridge University Press, 1985
Poovey, Mary, *The Proper Lady and the Woman Writer: Ideology as Style in the Works of Mary Wollstonecraft, Mary Shelley, and Jane Austen*, Chicago University Press, 1984
Porter, Roy, "Bodies of Thought: Thoughts about the Body in Eighteenth-Century England," in *Interpretation and Cultural History*, ed. Joan Pittock and Andrew Wear, New York: St. Martin's Press, 1991
Potkay, Adam, "Eloquence and Style in the Age of Hume," *Eighteenth-Century Studies* 25 (1991)
  The Fate of Eloquence in the Age of Hume, Ithaca: Cornell University Press, 1994
Poussa, Patricia, "The Evolution of Early Standard English: The Creolization Hypothesis," *Studia Anglica Posnaniensia* 14 (1982), 69–85
Pratt, Mary Louise, *Imperial Eyes: Travel Writing and Transculturation*, London: Routledge, 1992
  "Linguistic Utopias," in *The Linguistics of Writing*, ed. Nigel Fabb, New York: Methuen, 1987
Prickett, Stephen, "Radicalism and Linguistic Theory: Horne Tooke on

Samuel Pegge," *Yearbook of English Studies* 19 (1989), 1–17
Rajan, Rajeswari Sunder (ed.), *Lie of the Land*, Oxford University Press, 1992
Reddick, Allen, *The Making of Johnson's Dictionary*, Cambridge University Press, 1990
Reed, Joel, "Restoration and Repression: The Language Projects of the Royal Society," *Studies in Eighteenth-Century Culture* 19 (1989), 399–412
Reinhart, Thomas, *Regulating Confusion*, Durham, NC: Duke University Press, 1996
Richetti, John, "Representing an Under Class," in *The New 18th Century*, ed. Felicity Nussbaum and Laura Brown, New York and London: Methuen, 1987
Robertson, Boyd and Iain Taylor, *Teach Yourself Gaelic*, London: Hodder Headline, 1993
Robertson, John, *The Scottish Enlightenment and the Militia Issue*, Edinburgh: John Donald Publishers, Ltd., 1985
Robinson, Mairi (ed.), *The Concise Scots Dictionary*, Aberdeen University Press, 1991
Rosenblum, Michael, "Smollett's *Humphry Clinker*," in *The Cambridge Companion to the Eighteenth-Century Novel*, ed. John Richetti, Cambridge University Press, 1996
Ross, Christina, "The Natural law of Standard English and the Practical Criticism of Emily Dickinson" (Ph.D. Dissertation, 1995)
Ross, Ian, "Aesthetic Philosophy: Hutcheson and Hume to Alison," in *The History of Scottish Literature*, vol. 2, ed. Andrew Hook, Aberdeen University Press, 1987
Ross, Marlon, "Romancing the Nation-State: The Poetics of Romantic Nationalism," in *Macropolitics of Nineteenth-Century Literature: Nationalism, Exoticism, Imperialism*, ed. Jonathan Arac and Harriet Ritvo, Philadelphia: Pennsylvania University Press, 1991
Rothstein, Eric, "Scotophilia and *Humphry Clinker*: The Politics of Beggary, Bugs, and Buttocks," *University of Toronto Quarterly* 52 (1982), 65–78
Said, Edward, *Orientalism*, New York: Vintage, 1979
Sales, Roger, *Jane Austen and Representations of Regency England*, New York and London: Routledge, 1994
Salvaggio, Ruth, *Enlightened Absence: Neoclassical Configurations of the Feminine*, Urbana and Chicago: Illinois University Press, 1988
de Saussure, Ferdinand, *Course in General Linguistics*, trans. Wade Baskin, New York: McGraw-Hill, 1966
Schellenberg, Betty, "Imagining the Nation in Defoe's *A Tour thro' the Whole Island of Great Britain*," *ELH* 62 (1995), 295–312
Schwerwatzky, Steven, "Johnson, *Rasselas*, and the Politics of Empire," *Eighteenth-Century Life* 16 (1992), 103–13
Schmitt, Cannon, *Alien Nation: Nineteenth-Century Gothic Fictions and English Nationality*, Philadelphia: Pennsylvania University Press, 1997
Sekora, John, *Luxury: The Concept in Western Thought from Eden to Smollett*, Balti-

more: Johns Hopkins University Press, 1977
Shell, Marc, "Babel in America: or, The Politics of Language Diversity in the United States," *Critical Inquiry* 20 (1993), 103–27
The Economy of Literature, Baltimore: Johns Hopkins University Press, 1978
Sher, Richard, "Percy, Shaw and the Ferguson 'Cheat'," in *Ossian Revisited*, ed. Howard Gaskill, Edinburgh University Press, 1991
Sherbo, Arthur, "*Nil Nisi Bonum*: Samuel Johnson in *The Gentleman's Magazine*," *College Literature* 16 (1989), 168–83
"Win Jenkins' Language," *Papers on Language and Literature* 5 (1969), 199–204
Shields, David, *Civil Tongues and Polite Letters in British America*, Chapel Hill: North Carolina University Press, 1997
Siebert, Donald T., "Bubbled, Bamboozled, and Bit: 'Low Bad' Words in Johnson's *Dictionary*," *SEL* 26 (1986), 484–95
Simpson, David, *Romanticism, Nationalism, and the Revolt against Theory*, Chicago University Press, 1993
Simpson, Kenneth, "Genre and National Identity," *Studies in Scottish Literature* 30 (1998), 31–42
The Protean Scot: The Crisis of Identity in Scottish Literature, Aberdeen University Press, 1988
Sledd, James H. and Gwin J. Kolb, *Dr. Johnson's Dictionary: Essays in the Biography of a Book*, Chicago University Press, 1955
Smith, G. Gregory, *Scottish Literature Character and Influence*, London: Macmillan, 1919
Smith, Olivia, *The Politics of Language: 1790–1819*, Oxford University Press, 1984
Smout, T. C., *A History of the Scottish People 1560–1830*, London: Fontana Press, 1985
"Born Again at Cambuslang: New Evidence on Popular Religion and Literacy in Eighteenth-Century Scotland," *Past & Present* (1987), 114–27
Snyder, Edward, *The Celtic Revival in Literature: 1760–1800*, Cambridge, MA: Harvard University Press, 1923
Sorensen, Janet, "Dr. Johnson Eats his Words," *Language Science* 22 (2000), 295–314
Sorensen, Knud, "Johnsonese in *Northanger Abbey*: A Note on Jane Austen's Style," *College English* 50 (1969), 390–7
Southam, B. C. (ed.), *Jane Austen: The Critical Heritage*, London: Routledge and Kegan Paul, 1968
Spector, Robert, *Tobias George Smollett*, Boston: Twayne, 1989
Spurr, David, *The Rhetoric of Empire: Colonial Discourse in Journalism, Travel Writing, and Imperial Administration*, Durham, NC, and London: Duke University Press, 1994
Starnes, DeWitt T. and Gertrude E. Noyes, *The English Dictionary from Cawdrey to Johnson 1604–1755*, Chapel Hill: North Carolina University Press, 1946
Stein, Peter, *Legal Evolution: The Story of an Idea*, Cambridge University Press, 1980
Steiner, George, *After Babel: Aspects of Language and Translation*, Oxford University

Press, 1975
Stewart, Maaja, *Domestic Realities and Imperial Fictions: Jane Austen's Novels in Eighteenth-Century Contexts*, Athens, GA, and London: Georgia University Press, 1993
Stewart, Susan, *On Longing: Narratives of the Miniature, the Gigantic, the Souvenir, the Collection*, Baltimore: Johns Hopkins University Press, 1984
   "Shouts in the Street," *Critical Inquiry* 10 (1983), 265–81
Stillman, Robert E., *The New Philosophy and Universal Languages in Seventeenth-Century England*, Lewisburg: Bucknell University Press, 1995
Stokes, Myra, *The Language of Jane Austen: A Study of Some Aspects of her Vocabulary*, New York: St. Martin's Press, 1991
Stone, Lawrence and Jean Fawtier Stone, *An Open Elite?* Oxford: Clarendon Press, 1984
Strauss, Dietrich, "Some Reflections on Burns's Command of English," *Studies in Scottish Literature* 30 (1998), 76–89
Street, Brian, *Literacy: Theory and Practice*, Cambridge University Press, 1984
Struever, Nancy, "The Conversable World: Eighteenth-Century Transformations of the Relation of Rhetoric and Truth," in *Rhetoric and the Pursuit of Truth: Language Change in the Seventeenth and Eighteenth Centuries*, Los Angeles: William Andrews Clark Memorial Library, 1985
Strunk, William Jr. and E. B. White, *The Elements of Style*, New York: Macmillan, 1979
Suleri, Sara, *The Rhetoric of English India*, Chicago University Press, 1992
Summers, David, *The Judgment of Sense: Renaissance Naturalism and the Rise of Aesthetics*, Cambridge University Press, 1987
Sussman, Charlotte, "Lismahago's Captivity: Transculturation in *Humphry Clinker*," *ELH* 61 (1994), 597–618
Sutherland, Kathryn, "Fictional Economies: Adam Smith, Walter Scott and the Nineteenth-Century Novel," *ELH* 54 (1987), 97–127
Temple, Kathryn, "Johnson and Macpherson: Cultural Authority and the Construction of Literary Property," *Yale Journal of Law* 5 (1993) 355–87
Thom, Martin, *Republics, Nations, and Tribes*, London: Verso, 1995
Thomsen, Inger Sigrun, "Words 'Half-Dethroned': Jane Austen's Art of the Unspoken," in *Jane Austen's Business*, ed. Juliet McMaster and Bruce Stovel, New York: St. Martin's Press, 1996
Thomson, Derick, "Alasdair Mac Mhaigstir Alasdair," *An Gaidheal* 47 (1952)
   "Alexander MacDonald," in *Dictionary of National Biography*, vol. XXII, 471–3
   "Mac Mhaighstir Alasdair's Nature Poetry and its Sources," in *Gaelic and Scots in Harmony*, ed. Derick Thomson, Glasgow University Press, 1988
   "Gaelic Poetry in the Eighteenth Century: The Breaking of the Mould," in *The History of Scottish Literature*, vol. 2, ed. Andrew Hook, Aberdeen University Press, 1987
   An Introduction to Gaelic Poetry, Edinburgh University Press, 1987
   Why Gaelic Matters, Edinburgh: Saltire Society, 1984
Thomson, Derick (ed.) *Companion to Gaelic Scotland*, Oxford: Blackwell, 1983

    Gaelic and Scots in Harmony, Glasgow University Press, 1988
Trumpener, Katie, *Bardic Nationalism: The Romantic Novel and British Empire*, Princeton University Press, 1997
Varney, Andrew, "From Tennis-Ball to Fruit Tree: Smollett's Story of the Scottish Self," *The Swansea Review* 9 (1994), 549–60
Vickers, Brian, "The Royal Society and English Prose Style: A Reassessment," in *Rhetoric and the Pursuit of Truth: Language Change in the Seventeenth and Eighteenth Centuries*, Los Angeles: William Andrews Clark Memorial Library, 1985
Viswanathan, Gauri, *Masks of Conquest: Literary Studies and British Rule in India*, New York: Columbia University Press, 1987
Volosinov, V. N., *Marxism and the Philosophy of Language*, trans. Ladislav Matejka and I. R. Titunik, Cambridge, MA: Harvard University Press, 1973
Warner, Michael, *Letters of the Republic: Publication and the Public Sphere in Eighteenth-Century America*, Cambridge, MA: Harvard University Press, 1990
Watson, George, "Celticism and the Annulment of History," in *Celticism*, ed. Terence Brown, Amsterdam: Rodopi Press, 1996
Wechselblatt, Martin, "Finding Mr. Boswell: Rhetorical Authority and National Identity in Johnson's *A Journey to the Western Islands of Scotland*," *ELH* 60 (1993), 117–48
    "The Pathos of Example: Professionalism and Colonization in Johnson's Preface to the *Dictionary*," *Yale Journal of Criticism* 9 (1996), 381–403
Weinbrot, Howard, *Britannia's Issue: The Rise of British Literature from Dryden to Ossian*, Cambridge University Press, 1993
    "Samuel Johnson's *Plan* and Preface to the *Dictionary*: The Growth of a Lexicographer's Mind," in *New Aspects of Lexicography*, ed. Howard Weinbrot, Carbondale: Southern Illinois University Press, 1955
Weinsheimer, Joel, *Eighteenth-Century Hermeneutics: Philosophy of Interpretation from Locke to Burke*, New Haven: Yale University Press, 1993
White, Allon, *Carnival, Hysteria, and Writing: Collected Essays and Autobiography*, Oxford: Clarendon Press, 1993
Whorf, Benjamin Lee, "The Philosophy of Time," in *Language, Thought, and Reality*, ed. Richard Gale, New York: Doubleday, 1967
Williams, Nicholas, "The Dialect of Authenticity," in *English and the Other Languages*, ed. Marius Buning and Ton Hoenselaars, Amsterdam: Rodopi, 1999
Williams, Raymond, *The Country and the City*, Oxford University Press, 1973
    Keywords, Oxford University Press, 1983
    Marxism and Literature, Oxford University Press, 1977
Willinsky, John, *Empire of Words: The Reign of the OED*, Princeton University Press, 1994
Wilson, Kathleen, *The Sense of the People: Politics, Culture, and Imperialism in England, 1715–1785*, Cambridge University Press, 1996
Wimsatt, W. K., *Philosophic Words*, New Haven: Yale University Press, 1948

Withers, John, *Gaelic in Scotland 1698–1981*, Edinburgh: John Donald Publishers, 1984
Withrington, D. J., "The S.P.C.K. and Highland Schools in Mid-Eighteenth Century," *Scottish Historical Review* 41 (1962), 89–99
Womack, Peter, *Improvement and Romance: Constructing the Myth of the Highlands*, London: Macmillan, 1989
Wood, Ellen Meiksin, *The Pristine Culture of Capitalism: A Historical Essay on Old Regimes and Modern States*, London: Verso, 1991
Wright, Patrick, *On Living in an Old Country: The National Past in Contemporary Britain*, London: Verso, 1985
Yadav, Alok, "Nationalism and Contemporaneity: Political Economy of a Discourse," *Cultural Critique* 26 (1993–4), 191–229
  "Nationalism and Literature in Eighteenth-Century Britain" (Ph.D. Dissertation, 1993)
Young, Robert, *Colonial Desire: Hybridity in Theory, Culture and Race*, London and New York: Routledge, 1995
Youngson, A. J., *After the Forty-Five: The Economic Impact on the Scottish Highlands*, Edinburgh University Press, 1973
Zemka, Sue, "The Holy Books of Empire: Translations of the British and Foreign Bible Society," in *Macropolitics of Nineteenth-Century Literature*, ed. Jonathan Arac, Harriet Ritvo, Philadelphia: Pennsylvania University Press, 1991
  Victorian Testaments: The Bible, Christology, and Literary Authority in Early Nineteenth-Century Culture, Stanford University Press, 1997
Zenzinger, Peter, "Low Life, Primitivism and Honest Poverty in Ramsay and Burns," *Studies in Scottish Literature* 30 (1998), 43–58

Index

Note: page numbers in italics refer to figures

Aarsleff, Hans, 226n. 21, 228n. 27, 273n. 29
abstraction, in language, 10, 46, 159, 163, 166, 173, 211, 220, 271n. 6
accent, *see* Scottish accent
Act of Union, 2, 33–4, 35, 90, 118, 190
Addison, Joseph, 71, 147, 151
Adorno, Theodor, 181, 210, 226n. 23, 240n. 86, 280n. 29
Aers, David, 227n. 2
aesthetic discourse, 6, 14, 23, 141, 142, 148–9, 150, 152, 262n. 17, 264n. 41
aesthetic effects, 141, 145, 163, 185
aesthetic understanding of language, 144, 162, 171, 263n. 30
alien word concept, 69, 71
alienation effect, in Austen's novels, 204, 206, 210–13
see also estrangement
alphabet, 68–9, 161, 193, 240n. 87, 269n. 75
Althusser, Louis, 34, 235n. 26
ambivalence, 4, 6, 7, 18, 20–4, 37, 39–40, 48, 49, 51, 134, 137, 141, 161, 164, 219, 223
"anachronistic space," 175, 271n. 12
Anderson, Benedict, 18, 48, 64, 128, 145, 225n. 11, 228n. 30, 241n. 95, 244n. 6, 246n. 21, 262n. 24
Anderson, Judith, 69, 247n. 34
Anderson, Perry, 230n. 41
Anglo-British identity, 29, 31, 104–6, 114, 117, 135, 175, 231n. 48, *see also* identity
Anne (queen of England), 33, 151
Annexed Estates, 153
antiquaries, 53, 54, 187, 192, 199
Arac, Jonathan, 224n. 6, 236n. 49, 269n. 87
Aravamudan, Srinivas, 239n. 80
arbitrary sign systems, 6, 8, 194, 229n. 33
Argyle, duke of, 172–3
Armstrong, Nancy, 202–3, 205, 211, 278n. 6, 279nn. 16, 18

Arnold, Matthew, 191, 192, 277nn. 57, 58
Arteaga, Alfred, 61, 243n. 125
assimilation, 17, 18, 31, 33, 34, 40, 50, 105, 113, 114, 115, 130, 141, 150, 152, 153, 234n. 22, 265n. 46
Astle, Thomas, 164
Augustan tradition, 215, 216, 218, 242n. 113, 259n. 54
Austen, Jane,
  and alienation effect, 210–13
  Augustan tradition, 216, 218
  and Hugh Blair, 201
  and class fluidity, 220
  class/language intersection, 198
  controlled use of language, 204
  doubling techniques, 218
  Emma, 200, 201, 202, 207, 210, 211, 213, 214, 217, 218, 219–20
  Englishness represented in work, 23, 197–8, 200
  as feminist, 221
  and France, 200
  instruction in, 219
  and Samuel Johnson connections, 24, 215–17, 281n. 35
  language, in her novels, 198–200, 204
  linguistic propriety, 208
  and literary tradition, 215
  mimicry, 217–19
  Northanger Abbey, 207, 209, 212, 216, 217–18
  novels, as instruction, 207, 212
  patriarchal ideology, 217
  popularity of, 207
  Pride and Prejudice, 201, 204, 208, 213
  Sense and Sensibility, 200, 209, 210, 213, 214
  and Adam Smith, 201
autoethnographic writing, 31, 57

Bakhtin, Mikhail, 127

304 Index

Balfour, John, 44, 239n. 79
ballad form, 114, 175
Barber, Francis, 87–8, 248n. 41
bard, 165, 175
   and Austen, 215
   figure of, 53, 242n. 110
   in Scottish nationalism, 54, 55
   tradition, 58
Barker-Benfield, G. J., 146, 157, 263n. 31
Barrell, John, 64, 95, 226n. 21, 244n. 8, 247n. 30, 251n. 82
Barthes, Roland, 181, 275n. 36
Basker, James, 108, 109, 251nn. 71, 73, 254n. 4, 255n. 13
bastard words, 79
Bator, Paul, 140, 260n. 7
Battle of Culloden, 17, 21, 54, 113
Battle of the Reviews, The, 111, 113
Beattie, James, 271n. 5
Bhabha, Homi, 40, 49, 56, 225n. 8, 238nn. 57, 58, 248n. 46, 249n. 62, 250n. 67
Bible, 43, 45, 47, 48
   Bedell translation, 241n. 92
   New Testament
      bilingual printing of, 43
      translation, 48
   Old Testament, translation, 47–8, 241n. 91
   reading, and social control, 42, 239n. 71
   translations, 43, 47–8, 241nn. 91, 92
Bible Societies, 42, 240n. 85
bilingualism, 10, 30, 224n. 7
Black, Ronald, 37, 46, 56–7, 236nn. 43, 45, 239n. 74, 242nn. 100, 107, 109
Blair, Hugh, 139, 232n. 51, 263n. 28
   alienation of native tongue, 264n. 36
   ambivalence towards Scots Gaelic, 18, 143, 157–64
   appointed Regius Chair, 261n. 10, 265n. 48
   and Robert Burns, 155–6
   "Critical Dissertation, A," 164
   on eloquence, 161
   first languages, figurative nature of, 162
   on language rules, 145
   Lectures on Rhetoric and Belles Lettres, 22, 146, 153
   member of Select Society for promoting..., 139
   modest *vs.* courtly language, 151–2, 201
   national language styles, 147
   and originary language, 157–64
   on proper English, 5, 156
   sermon collection, 96–7
   on social advances, 153
   on writing, 160
body, 1, 15, 105, 112, 141, 142, 144, 146, 148, 155, 157, 163, 171, 262n. 17
   see also embodiment
Boggs, W. Arthur, 132, 133, 254n. 3
Bohls, Elizabeth, 148, 264n. 38
Boswell, James, *Life of Samuel Johnson*, 93, 239n. 78, 268n. 65
Boucé, Paul-Gabriel, 254n. 3, 255n. 7, 256n. 18, 257n. 28
Bourdieu, Pierre, 35, 93, 97, 235n. 32, 244n. 7, 251n. 79
bourgeoisie, empowerment of, 86, 105–6, 121, 135, 138–41, 202–5, 252n. 88
Bowers, Terence, 105, 254n. 4, 256n. 23
Bradley, A. C., 215, 281n. 37
British and Foreign Bible Society, 41
British identity, 24, 32, 34, 138, 139
Briton, The (Smollett, ed.), 106, 110, 135, 136
broadsheets, 98
Brown, Laura, 231n. 49, 259n. 47
Bullokar, John, 247n. 35
Burke, Edmund, 140, 142, 146, 148–9, 151, 261nn. 8, 15, 264n. 37, 269n. 84
Burns, Robert, 127, 154, 155–6
Bute, 3rd Earl of, 109, 110, 113, 136, 241n. 91, 243n. 126, 265n. 48
Butler, Marilyn, 254n. 102, 277n. 2
Butterfield, Herbert, 276n. 53

Cadell, Thomas, 268n. 71
Caffentzis, George, 245n. 17
Cairn, David, 238n. 59
Caliban (Shakespeare), 98
Calvinism, 1, 224n. 1
Campbell, Archibald, 100–1, 253n. 94
Campbell, J. L., 236n. 45, 241n. 89, 243n. 122
Canclini, Garcia, 96, 97, 250n. 66, 252n. 84
cant, 79, 82, 85, 92, 93, 94, 100, 206–7, 217
capitalism, 18, 19, 38, 47, 235n. 29, 237n. 51
   and class struggles, 203
   and language standardization, 18–19, 25, 46–7
   and literacy, 49
   and Puritan ethics, 235n. 29
Carlyle, Alexander, 115
Carter, Ian, 231n. 44, 270n. 90
Cartesian linguistics, 8–11, 223, 227n. 22
case, *see* grammar
Castells, Manuel, 18, 30, 186, 231n. 43, 233n. 9
catechisms, 57
Cawdrey, Robert, *A Table Alphabeticall*, 69, 70
Celtic
   culture, 17, 186, 232n. 57
   masculinity, 191
   original language of Britain, 164
   original speech of Europe, 193–4, 242n. 104

periphery, 3, 4, 17, 106, 120, 126, *see also* periphery
revival, 18, 23, 173–5, 222
type, 6
writers, 111–12
Celtic Whigs, 175, 176, 189, 194, 272n. 14
Celtomania, 23, 134, 173–6, 189, 192–6, 199
Celts, 6, 17, 174, 175, 271n. 11, 271n. 13
center, 7, 10, 17, 19, 20, 22, 24, 106, 107, 116, 117, 118, 119, 125, 126, 134, 137, 197, 205, 219, 222
ceolmor, 55
Chamberlain, Lori, 58, 243n. 117
Chambers, Robert, 86
Chandler, James, 230n. 41
chap-books, 98
Chapman, Malcolm, 31, 233n. 11, 235n. 33, 242n. 113, 243n. 122, 271n. 11, 275n. 33
Chapman, R. W., 216, 280n. 33
charity schools, 34–7, 41–4, 98, 235n. 29, 252n. 89
Chatterjee, Partha, 24, 48, 60, 226n. 23, 241n. 93, 243n. 119
Chesterfield, Stanhope, Philip Dormer (4th Earl of Chesterfield), 80–2, 101, 130, 244n. 7, 249nn. 51, 52
Cheyfitz, Eric, 40, 238n. 59
Chomsky, Noam, 10–11, 179, 223, 226n. 22, 273n. 28
Christensen, Jerome, 86, 249n. 58
Christie, John, 153, 163, 170, 265n. 49, 269n. 82
Church of Scotland, 58–9
Cicero, 161
civilization
  as linguistic concept, 33, 40, 66, 154, 237n. 49, 247n. 29
clans, *see* Highlands
Clark, J. C. D., 65, 245n. 19, 276n. 50
Clark, John, 177, 186, 187, 190–1, 195
class distinctions, 20, 22, 23, 25, 60, 63, 66, 88, 95, 105, 106, 108, 109, 116, 119–21, 131, 135, 137, 148, 149, 150, 156, 178, 200–2, 203, 211, 219, 220, 280n. 25
  destabilization, 119–20, 201–5
  and linguistic standards, 121, 201, 203, 256n. 23
  realignments, in eighteenth-century Britain, 86, 98, 147
  see also cross-class alliances
clubs
  all-male, 140, 260n. 3
  debate, 161
  Edinburgh Easy, 151
  Fair Intellectual, 260n. 3

Lowlands, 140, 260n. 3
Cohen, Michele, 261n. 16, 273n. 29, 278n. 9
Cohen, Murray, 147, 226n. 21, 227n. 24, 229n. 33, 241n. 88, 244n. 13, 263n. 34, 273nn. 28, 29
Colley, Linda, 7, 17, 225n. 11, 226n. 17, 245n. 15
Collinson, T., 101, 253n. 97
colonial ambivalence, *see* ambivalence
colonial culture, 5, 188
colonial discourse, 9, 29, 40, 56
colonial imagery of standardizing English, 89
colonial literacy instruction, 29, 34, 40–9, 60
colonial pedagogy, 10, 13–14, 29, 34, 40–9, 60
  and English in England, 67
colonial subjects, 44, 49, 88, 94, 98
colonialism, 2–5, 63
  internal model, 3, 16–20
  and language 4–5, 64, 71, 88, 248n. 41
  and nationalism, 4–5
  see also imperialism, internal colonialism
commerce, 46, 68, 103, 247n. 33
  and civilization, 38
  in the Highlands, 35, 46–7, 170–1
  and language corruption, 165–71
  and linguistic value, 246n. 17
  and national development, 118, 269n. 87
  and newspapers, 247n. 33
  and polyglot dictionaries, 68
  precursor to nation-state, 3, 169
  and universal grammar, 12, 227n. 24
  see also capitalism; economics; market; trade
commodity, 47, 175, 250n. 65
common law, 86–7, 249n. 62
common sense, 149, 152, 215
community, nation as, 19, 128, 221
Condillac, Etienne, 266n. 51
conjectural history, 153, 265n. 49, 274n. 30
  see also stadial history
constitution, 64, 87, 150
conversion, linguistic, 63, 97
  religious, 40–2
core, *see* center
Cottom, Daniel, 147, 262n. 19, 264n. 40, 280n. 28
Court, Franklin, 232n. 51
Cratylus, 193
Crawford, John, 42, 105, 107, 115, 234nn. 20, 22, 238n. 70, 241n. 94, 242n. 108
Crawford, Robert, 18, 26, 155, 165, 174, 224n. 7, 225nn. 10, 12, 233n. 4, 254n. 4, 256n. 20, 260n. 3, 266nn. 52, 54, 267nn. 57, 58, 270n. 3
Crawford, Thomas, 267n. 58
Cregeen, Eric, 230n. 36, 237n. 51

Creole hypothesis, 250n. 68, 254n. 104
creolization, 89, 103, 250n. 68
cross-class alliance, 55, 60, 147, 149, 204
Crowley, Tony, 226n. 21, 233n. 8, 245n. 18,
    247n. 28, 252n. 88, 257n. 26
Culloden, Battle of, 17, 21, 54, 113
    post-, 54, 65, 172, 176, 230n. 36
cultural authority, 117, 216, 274n. 31
cultural identity, 2, 32, 50, 60
cultural nationalism, 19, 24–7, 51, 52, 76, 81,
    141, 155, 232n. 57
cultural patrimony, 250n. 66
cultural relativism, *see* relativism
cultural schizophrenia, 4, 5, 6
culture
    feminization of, 80–1, 140, 199, 205–7, 279n.
        16
    literary, 29, 62, 225n. 7
    national, 3, 46, 85, 129, 185, 204
    and nature, 142, 262n. 19
    and standardized English, 63, 141
Curley, Thomas, 273n. 24
cursing, 98–9
custom, 15, 21, 25, 64, 65, 80–1, 84–7, 103, 123,
    125, 133, 149, 180, 201, 229n. 33

Daiches, David, 55–6, 224n. 7, 242n. 111, 243n.
    114, 276n. 52
Davies, John, 87
Davis, Leith, 3, 224n. 5, 226n. 16, 267nn. 57,
    58, 268n. 70, 271n. 5
Day, Robert Adams, 258nn. 39, 43
De Saussure, Ferdinand, 8, 226n. 18
debate clubs, *see* clubs
Defoe, Daniel, 71, 116, 117, 118, 243n. 124
DeMaria, Robert, 67, 68, 76, 98, 246n. 20,
    247n. 25, 248n. 44
Derrida, Jacques, 159, 160, 161, 238n. 66,
    268n. 66, 274n. 31
Deutsch, Helen, 256n. 25
dialectic of empire, 16, 20–4, 186–7, 276n. 47
dialects, 6, 48, 63, 67, 95, 116, 126, 127, 201,
    247n. 27
dictionaries
    Latin/English, 46, 69
    limitations on language transmission, 122
    polyglot, 68
    word, and multiple meanings, 73
    see also glossaries; grammar
Dictionary of the English Language (Johnson), 83
    abridged edition, 155, 269n. 81
    advertisement for, 80
    Anglo/British emphasis, 247n. 25
    arrangement, 73–4
    assistants, 96–7
    and bad taste, 100–1
    cant terms in, 92
    common words in, 86
    and correct diction, 122
    figurative language in, 75
    imperial grammar in, 21, 250n. 69
    imperial lexicographies and, 68–77
    Latinisms in, 65, 93, 99, 100, 246n. 20
    and Locke's theory of language, 245n. 13
    national literacy invitation, 99
    obsolete words in, 93
    particular *vs.* general, 203
    as pedagogical address, 97
    pregnancy motif, 101
    prescriptive nature of, 244n. 7
    price of, 75
    and primitive signification, 72–6
    quotations in, 76
    as reduction, 101
    resistance to, 99–103, 252n. 92, 253nn. 99,
        100
    Scots' words in, 90–3, 251n. 73
Disarming Act of 1746, 170
disinterestedness, 63, 148, 177, 206, 264n. 47
domestic space, *see* private sphere
Donald, John, 257n. 28
Dorian, Nancy, 34, 169, 235n. 27, 242n. 101,
    270n. 88
doubled character, in colonial subjects, 1, 32,
    49
doubled language, 84–8, 95, 96, 130, 210, 214,
    220
doubled position, of bourgeois woman, 205,
    206
doubled talk, 32–49
doubleness, 1, 6, 18, 24, 112, 205, 209, 224n. 1
    in Austen, 218
    in Johnson's *Dictionary*, 86
Douglas, Aileen, 105, 114, 254n. 4, 257nn. 29,
    34, 259n. 47
dualism, linguistic, 1, 18, 198
Duckworth, Alistair, 277n. 2
Duncan, Ian, 224n. 1, 238n. 70, 261n. 14
Dunn, Douglas, 266n. 53
Durkacz, Victor, 234nn. 15, 20
Dwyer, John, 150, 265n. 44

Eagleton, Terry, 18, 230n. 41, 262n. 17, 264n.
    41
echo figure, 112
economics
    and the Highlands, 231n. 44, 237n. 51, 270n.
        89
    international, 18
    and linguistic conversion, 39

national integration, 117
and standardization of languages, 18–19
see also capitalism; trade
Ehninger, Doublas, 263n. 26, 270n. 91
Elizabethan language, 103, 244n. 1
Elledge, Scott, 244n. 7, 263n. 26
eloquence, 79–81, 81, 121, 142, 161
embodiment, 1, 12, 15–16, 22, 23, 79–80, 96, 99–101, 106, 114–15, 128, 141, 142, 144, 146, 148, 155, 157, 163, 171, 187, 191, 201, 252n. 83, 262n. 17
Emerson, Roger, 236n. 46
emigration, 62
Emma, see Austen
encyclopedias, in Enlightenment, 78
England, middle-class in, 105, 199, 202, 278n. 12
English character, 268n. 69
English culture, *see* culture
English education, 34–5
English enforcement, 33–5
English language
  Anglo-British imposition of print, 42
  ignorance of origins, 194
  and national identity, *see* language, linguistics
  proper, 198–9, 216
  reformative powers of, 38, 43
  revaluation of, 63, 65, 244n. 1
  as universal, 173, 176, 183, 186
  see also language; standard English
Englishness, 2, 5, 7, 23, 26, 29, 34, 67, 102, 104, 113, 115, 135, 173, 177, 196–201, 217–18, 222, 277n. 57
Englightenment, 26, 32, 36, 39, 41, 62, 68, 76, 77–8, 81, 240n. 86
  and Dr. Johnson's *Dictionary*, 76
  idea of progress, 185
  ideals, 227n. 23
  language model, 8, 81, 240n. 86
  nature image, 77
  scientists, 78
  Scottish thinkers, 38, 188, 236n. 46
  vision of SSPCK, 36, 39
epistolary novels, 121–31, 258nn. 39–41
equivalence
  language of, 181, 183
  logic of, 46–7, 49, 69, 72, 76, 185, 239n. 82
estrangement, 1, 6, 24, 44, 47, 63, 66, 84, 86, 88, 199, 210, 217, 220
ethnicity, 17, 63, 102, 107, 119, 222
etymology, 13, 72–6, 79, 180, 193, 229n. 33

Fabel, Robin, 225n. 12, 257n. 28
Fabian, Johannes, 251n. 72
Fabricant, Carol, 248n. 47
Fair Intellectual Club, The, 260n. 3
Favret, Mary, 258nn. 38, 40
feeling, language of, 143–52
  see also embodiment
female, *see* women
Female Quixote (Lennox), 199
female sexuality, 127
feminization of culture, 80–1, 140, 199, 205–7, 279n. 16
feminization of Gaelic, 190
feminine nature of language, 79–84, 142, 157, 176, 190, 191, 206, 249n. 54
Ferguson, Adam, 38, 106–7, 139
Fergusson, Robert, 16, 99–101, 127, 154, 265n. 46
feudal societies, 86, 203
fiction, 96, 279n. 23
  see also novels
Fielding, Henry, 95, 155, 281n. 40
Fielding, Penny, 165, 267n. 63
figurative language
  Blair and Smith on, 162, 163
  in Johnson's *Dictionary*, 75
  see also metaphor
Fitzmaurice-Wright, Susan, 252n. 88
Fordyce, David, 157
foreign impact on language, 89–90
foreign trade, and polyglot dictionaries, 68
foreign words, avoidance of, 25, 143
Foster, Robert J., 19, 231n. 45
Foucault, Michel, 68, 226n. 21, 267n. 62
Foulis, Sir James, 178
Fraiman, Susan, 205, 214, 279n. 20
Franco-phobia, in Johnson's *Dictionary*, 65
free indirect discourse, 24, 218–20, 282n. 46
free trade, 18, 168
French Academy, 81

Gaelic
  aestheticization of, 184
  antedating Latin, Greek and French, 52–3, 173, 189, 192, 242n. 104
  associated with barbarism, 29, 234n. 24
  authoritative status of, 135
  ballad translations, 175
  Bible translations, 43, 47–8, 92, 241n. 91
  Classical, 48, 55, 241n. 92
  and classical culture, 53–4
  as colonial and national sign, 50–62, 186–7
  considered female and private, 59, 173
  cultural identity, 50–62, 174, 176
  devaluing, 29
  difficulty in translating, 195
  extirpation of, 33, 172

Gaelic (cont.)
  feminization of, 176, 190, 191, 277n. 58
  glossaries, 4, 21, 29, 44–6, 49
  history, as site of, 50–62, 173, 175, 184–6, 271n. 13
  and Latin grammar, 179, 183
  learning, 37, 241n. 90
  linguacide, 42
  linguistic identity, 50
  as linguistic relic, 51–2, 173
  literacy, 43–9
  literacy, Johnson on, 43
  literary traditions, 28–9, 32, 37, 51–5
  and masculinity, 157, 165, 171, 176, 191
  as mother tongue, 193
  national identity, 31, 48–62
  nationalistic rhetoric, 48–62, 175, 192
  oral, 16
  originary language, 23, 52–3, 164–5, 188, 189, 192–6
  as particular, 173, 175, 176, 183, 186, 194, 274n. 30
  personal pronouns in, 184
  personification of objects, 184
  poetry, 28–9, 50–7, 191, 276n. 52
  prose, 48
  reification of, 47
  revaluation of, 16, 23, 29, 52, 173, 175, 186, 193
  severed from social history, 173
  standardization efforts, 31–2, 47–9
  see also Celtic; Scots Gaelic
Gaelic/English Vocable (MacDonald), 4, 21, 29, 31, 40–1, 44–9, 50, 241n. 96
Gallagher, Catherine, 95, 96, 204, 244n. 3
Gaskill, Howard, 241n. 96, 255n. 11
Gay, David Elton, 275n. 39
Gellner, Ernest, 129, 249n. 57, 259n. 50
gender
  and Anglo-British linguistic identity, 199
  distinctions, 63
  division of labor, 58
  factors, for Smollett, 135
  and language/class/nation nexus, 199, 204
  and public sphere, 199
  roles, 58–9
  status, 108
  see also language: gender aspects
general, 6, 10, 63, 67, 92–3, 94, 103, 112, 114, 116, 134, 148, 163, 203, 204
  see also universal
general grammar, see universal grammar
General Assembly of the Church of Scotland, 189
gentry, 197, 202, 203, 207, 278n. 12, 281n. 38

George III (king), 109, 265n. 48
Gibbons, Luke, 63, 150–1, 226n. 15, 244n. 2, 265n. 45
Gilpin, William, 173–4
global, 24, 173, 174, 179, 192, 194, 196, 205, 223, 227n. 7, 242n. 10
glossaries, 31, 44–9, 241n. 88
  Gaelic/English, 4, 21, 29, 44–6, 49
  for Highlands, 71
  Latin/English, 46, 69
  for trade, 68
Golden, James, 263n. 26, 270n. 91
Goux, Jean-Joseph, 240n. 87
Graff, Harvey, 252n. 89, 259n. 51
grammar, 9–16
  of books and schools, 8–14, 36, 63, 64, 67, 173, 179, 181
  case, 10, 181–3
  egalitarian aspirations, 247n. 30
  eighteenth century, 10, 273n. 29
  imperial, 16, 21, 29, 32, 47, 61, 68, 85, 194, 250n. 69
  Johnson and, 65, 80, 245n. 12
  masculine authority of, 14
  rote rules of, 80
  rules, corruptive role of, 80, 145
  tables, 173, 181
  transformational, 223
Gramsci, Antonio, 34, 235n. 25
Grant, Anne, 255n. 6
Grant, Damien, 109, 232n. 50, 254n. 3
Grant, John, 165, 268n. 73
Greenblatt, Stephen J., 252n. 90
Greene, Donald, 257n. 28
Grose, Francis, 258n. 44
Grossberg, Lawrence, 242n. 102, 271n. 7
Grub Street, 112
Guillory, John, 25, 26, 226n. 19, 229n. 31

Habermas, Jurgen, 139–40, 225nn. 9, 13, 247n. 33, 260n. 6, 264n. 41
Hanes, Louise, 132, 133, 254n. 3
Harris, James, 11, 12, 14–15, 79–80, 179
Harris, Roy, 12, 41, 226n. 21, 228n. 26, 238nn. 66, 67, 239n. 82, 240n. 87
Harvie, Christopher, 276n. 49
Havelock, Eric, 238n. 66
Haywood, Ian, 185, 276n. 44
Hebrew, 174, 192
Hechter, Michael, 16–17, 20, 224n. 4, 230nn. 36, 37, 38, 233n. 5
Hedrick, Elizabeth, 244nn. 7, 13, 248n. 44, 249n. 49
hegemony, 34
Helgerson, Richard, 244n. 1

Index

Henley, John, 229n. 33, 273n. 29
Highlanders
  ambivalence towards, 37
  in British imperial army, 176, 272n. 17
  child, figure of, 194–5
  caricatures of, 37–8
  emigration, 62
  and Gaelic language, 176
  scholars, 37, 193–5
  subduing, and Lowland rhetoric lectures, 153
Highlands
  administrative infrastructure, dismantling, 34
  ancient inhabitants of, 193
  clans, British attempts to destroy, 52
  as colonial and national space, 37, 230n. 36
  commercial activity in, 47, 170–1, 237n. 51
  economic status, 231n. 44, 237n. 51, 270n. 89
  English instruction in, 10, 19, 29–49, 72, 176
  linguistic domination of, 3, 33, 72, 224n. 6
  missionaries in, 12, 37
  pedagogical practices, 239n. 83
  resistance, 49–62
  and standard English, 19
historiography, 7, 175, 185–96, 270n. 4
Hogg, James, 1
Holly, Grant, 280n. 31
home rule, in Scotland, 2
Horgan, A. D., 244n. 12
Horkheimer, Max, 181, 226n. 23, 240n. 86
Hottentots, 102, 194, 254n. 101
Houston, R. A., 238n. 68, 239n. 73, 240n. 87
Hudson, Nicholas, 142, 260n. 4, 267n. 63
Huet, Marie-Helene, 101, 253n. 96
Hume, David, 80, 86, 96, 139, 148, 249n. 50
Hutcheson, Francis, 148

Identity
  Anglo/British, 29, 31, 104–6, 115, 118, 134, 137
  British, 2, 23, 138, 139
  and colonialism, 237n. 50
  communal, 244n. 1
  cultural, 2, 32, 34, 50, 60, 63, 174
  formation, negative, 38, 236n. 49, 258n. 42
  linguistic, 50, 173, 198, 221, 223
  multiple, 1, 6, 7
  and national language, 2–3, 7, 23, 31, 34, 50, 221, 223
  reciprocal formation, 2, 3, 5, 222–3
  and social transition and tensions, 176, 203, 272n. 18
illiteracy
  among laboring classes, 98
  and disorderly behavior, 42
  see also literacy
imitation, 4, 23, 60, 116, 123, 126, 150, 152, 163, 208, 217, 218, 219, 220, 221, 265n. 43, 281n. 45
impartial spectator, 6, 149–50
imperial grammar, 14, 16, 20, 29, 32, 60, 61, 75, 76, 79, 84, 86, 87–93, 173, 186, 194, 222, 259n. 69
  alternative views of, 86
  and cultural nationalism, 76
  and standard English, 68
  transparency of, 85, 212
  vs. oral language, 159
imperial lexicographies, 68–71
imperialism, 2, 5, 8, 14, 15, 29–30, 38, 65, 185, 223, 281n. 45
  British, second-wave of, 9, 176
  and cultural nationalism, 76, 174
  and English language, 66
  and Gaelic–English glossary, 49
  Johnson on, 72
  and Johnson's *Dictionary*, 65
  and language theory in England, 10–13, 46, 64, 65, 66, 68–76, 96, 98, 246n. 17, 248nn. 39, 41
  and linguistic transparency, 212
  and national literary culture, 29, 55–6
  and resurgent national identity, 29, 30
  Scotland as training ground for, 3
  see also nationalism
improvement, 15, 33–5, 38, 138, 139, 140, 155, 170, 171, 172, 216n. 3, 219, 229n. 32, 233n. 89
India
  educational policies in, 39
  improvements in, 237n. 54
  linguistic homogenization in, 224n. 6
Industrial schools, 38–9
Innes, Thomas, 188
instruction of literacy, 31, 41, *also see* pedagogy
internal colonialism, 3, 16–20, 37, 38, 230nn. 36, 37
Ireland, 2, 16, 17, 42, 55, 226n. 14, 250n. 70, 253n. 95
  English instruction in, 233n. 8
Irish
  nineteenth-century caricatures, 226n. 14
  references, in Johnson's *Dictionary*, 250n. 70
  used as synonym for Scots Gaelic, 233n. 1
Irish/Scots language differences, 180
irony, 67, 212–14, 220–1, 281n. 45, 282n. 46

Jack, R. D. S., 257n. 34
Jacobite poetry, 4, 31, 50, 56, 253n. 95

Jacobitism, 7, 29, 31, 34, 36, 39, 47, 50, 60, 65, 114, 141, 226n. 17
  defeat of, and English vernacular, 65
  see also Culloden, Battle of
Jameson, Fredric, 202, 278n. 14, 280n. 30
Johnson, Claudia, 217, 279n. 22, 281n. 34
Johnson, J., *New Royal and Universal English Dictionary*, 110
Johnson, Samuel, 6, 16, 23, 43, 244n. 5
  assistants, 96
  attitude towards Scots, 90–2, 172
  authority, cultural, 133, 216, 245n. 7
  on Blair's sermons, 96–7
  and charity schools, 252n. 89
  and colonial imagery used to describe his *Dictionary* work, 89–90
  on commerce, 166–7
  Dictionary of the English Language (see specific sub-headings under *Dictionary*...)
  and *Female Quixote*, 199
  on feminization of language, 82, 206, 249n. 54
  and French, 246n. 16
  on Gaelic literacy, 43, 172
  on grammar, 65, 80, 245n. 12
  on imperialism, 72
  Journey to the Western Islands of Scotland, 158–9, 248n. 41
  and Latin, 84, 99, 100
  on linguistic stability, 216
  and Locke, 73–4, 245n. 13
  on metaphor, 73–6, 93, 248n. 45, 268n. 67
  as outsider, 252n. 85
  on *Poems of Ossian*, 164, 177
  rhetoric of inclusion/exclusion, 67, 90–2
  on Shakespeare's language, 94–5
  and Shaw, 173, 177, 178, 179, 180, 273nn. 26, 27
  and Smollett, 104, 106, 108–9, 115, 133, 134
  Vinerian lectures, 86, 87
Jones, Charles, 8–9
Jones, Rowland, 193, 277n. 60

Kahn, Madeleine, 278n. 5
Kay, Billy, 251n. 74
Kelly, Gary, 277n. 2, 280n. 25, 281nn. 45, 46
Kenrick, William, 113
Kernan, Alvin, 244n. 6
Kidd, Colin, 175, 188–9, 231n. 48, 255n. 5, 270n. 2, 274n. 30, 276n. 53
Kirk Session Minutes, analysis, 42
Knowlson, James, 226n. 24
Kolb, Gwin, 244n. 7, 253n. 100
Kramnick, Isaac, 246n. 21
Kramnick, Jonathan, 253n. 99, 259n. 54

Kroll, Richard, 239n. 83

labor, division of, 58, 170
Land, Stephen, 146, 226n. 21, 228n. 27, 240n. 84, 263n. 29
Lane, A. Archibald, 65
language
  academy, 71
  advanced, 152–65
  aesthetic understanding of, 144, 162, 171, 263n. 30
  civilizing nature of, 40, 98
  conceptions of
    eighteenth century, 10, 46, 226n. 21, 229n. 33
    Enlightenment models, 81, 240n. 86
    seventeenth century, 240n. 84
    see also theories of language
  cultural aspects of, 6, 55, 63, 81, 141, 173
  customary usage, 20, 64, 84–7, 180
  of equivalence, 181, 183
  of feeling, 143–52
  figurative, 72–6, 162, 163
  Gaelic glossaries, 4, 21, 29, 44–6, 49
  gender aspects, 12, 13, 14, 16, 191, 199
    feminization, 190, 191, 205–7, 249n. 54
    and Johnson, 77–84, 199
    maleness of, 157, 260n. 3
    masculine, 81, 142, 157, 161
    metaphor as female, 228n. 28
    mistakes by women, 109, 130, 206–9
    and multiculturalism, 176
    regulation of language, 77–84
    reproductive qualities of gendered female, 77–84, 100–1
    and translation, 101
    use by uneducated women, 109, 130
    women as linguistic authorities, 81
  gestural, 15
  and national identity, 1, 2, 5, 6, 14, 15, 64, 84–7, 141, 144, 148, 152, 187, 198
  oral, 59, 158, 159
  originary, 52–3, 152–65, 192–6
  peripheral/periphery, 104, 131–7, 178, 201
    dialects, 201
  picture theory of, 146
  plain, 12, 16, 46, 123, 151, 152, 162, 163, 201, 202, 207, 212, 213, 216, 221, 240n. 85
    see also plain language
  polite, 6, 79–84, 136, 201, 202, 214, 260n. 3, 261n. 16
  and effeminacy, 157
  etiquette, 201
  language of feeling, 143–52
  naturalness of, 140

and women, 80–1, 199, 205–6
political aspects
  alienation of colonial subjects, 88
  assimilation, 4–5, 29–47
  associated with political authority, 59
  and empire, 46
  foreign impacts on, 89–90
  as hierarchizing force, 42
  and the Highlands, 10, 19, 29–49, 72
  imposition on Scotland, 1, 19–20
  and the Lowlands, 3–4, 22, 138
  national affinities, 146
  and national identity, 2–3, 4–5, 7, 23, 31, 50, 187, 221
  standardized, and state power, 229n. 31
  printed, *see* printed language
  public/private character, 59, 123–4
  regional differences in, 66
  regulation of, 77–9
  rules, 10, 145
  scatological, 22, 126–7
  seventeenth-century theories of, 11
  spelling standardization, 179
  spoken, and accent, 114
  standard, *see* standard English
  sublime, 143, 157, 162, 163
  synchronic/diachronic poles, 69, 187–8
  theories of, *see* theories of language
  universal, 10, 15, 40–1, 81, 227n. 24
  vernacular, 63–5, 147, 202
  see also doubled language; dialects; Gaelic; Scots Gaelic; standard English
language academy, need for, 71
language communities, 67, 128–9
Lascelles, Mary, 215, 281n. 37
Latin, 5, 10, 11, 12, 13, 37, 45–6, 65, 69, 72, 84, 93, 99, 100, 124
  abilities in Scotland, 236n. 42
  grammar, and Gaelic, 179, 181, 183
  influence on Johnson's *Dictionary*, 65, 93, 99, 100, 246n. 20
Latin/English dictionaries/glossaries, 46, 69
law, *see* common law; natural law
Lectures on Rhetoric and Belles Lettres (Blair), 22, 143–71
Lectures on Rhetoric and Belles Lettres (Smith), 22, 143–71
Lenin, V. I., 24, 232n. 53
Lenman, Bruce, 234n. 22, 260n. 1
Leonard, Sterling, 110, 111, 145, 228n. 25, 229n. 34, 248n. 39, 256n. 21, 261n. 12, 263n. 26
Levine, Joseph, 246n. 20, 270n. 4, 274n. 30, 275n. 42
Lewis, C. S., 215–16, 281n. 37

Lhuyd, Edward, 174, 189, 271n. 10
liberation, and literacy, 41, 68, 247n. 30
limit case, 4
Linguacide, 42
linguistic(s)
  assimilation, *see* assimilation
  Cartesian, 8–11, 223, 227n. 22
  of community, 19, 97, 116, 128
  conversion, 63, 97
  custom, 84–103
  dialectic, 20–4, 185–96
  differences, 102, 106, 154, 202
  dualism, 1, 18, 198
  dystopias, 129, 221
  identity, 50, 63, 64, 198, 223
    reciprocal formation, 2, 222–3
  model, in Smollett, 122–31
  patrimony, 63, 75, 88, 250n. 66
  pedagogy, 130, 239n. 83
    see also pedagogy
  propriety, 111, 208
  relativism, 183, 275n. 41
    see also relativism
  standardization, 32, 108, 110, 121
  value, and commerce, 246n. 17
    see also imperialism
literacy, 21, 41–4, 72, 238n. 66, 274n. 31
  and capitalism, 49
  and colonialism, 29, 60, 96–7, 248n. 41
  and commerce, 240n. 87
  disciplining powers of, 41
  English, 42–4
  Gaelic, 43–62
  and imperial administration, 41, 42
  instruction, 31, 41–9, 61, 243n. 118, 247n. 30
  and liberation, 41, 247n. 30
  novel role in, 122
  and oral language, 42, 158, 274n. 31
  spread of, 149, 238n. 66
  universal, 129
  volatility of, 32, 40, 44, 48–9, 55, 56
  women's, 130
  see also illiteracy; reading; writing; language
Literacy cultures, 29, 51–9, 62
Literary traditions, Gaelic, 28–9
literature, college, 141
Lloyd, David, 24, 175, 232n. 52, 237n. 50, 272n. 15
local, 18, 19, 23, 173, 174, 179, 192, 194, 196, 205, 223, 271n. 7
Locke, John, 245n. 13, 248n. 44
London, print culture in, 106–15
Longinus, 161
Lowlands
  clubs, 140, 151, 161

Lowlands (*cont.*)
    consolidation with English, 134–5, 138–9
    elite of, 3, 33–4, 138–43
    English mastery, importance of, 138
    moral leadership movements, 35
    national membership, 107
    peripheral nature of, 152–3
    as province, 117
    rush to imitate English, 141, 153
    Scots language of, 3, 8–9, 105–16
        see also Scots language
    SSPCK membership, 34
    and standard English, 3–4, 22, 110, 138–9
Lowth, Robert, 64, 244nn. 10, 11
luxury, 118
Lynch, Deidre, 231n. 49, 244n. 7, 256n. 25, 279n. 20, 280n. 27
Lynn, Steven, 244n. 7

Mac Aulay, Donald, 51, 233n. 2, 242n. 103
Mac Mhaighstir Alasdair, Alasdair, *see* MacDonald, Alexander
MacDiarmid, Hugh, 61, 243n. 123
MacDonald, Alexander, 233n. 7, 238n. 62, 275n. 34
    in 1715 rebellion, 41, 50
    activist stance, 54
    and bardic tradition, 58
    changes allegiance, 50
    classical allusions, 55
    critical interpretations, 29–31, 58
    education, 37
    and Gaelic, 10, 31, 44–7, 82, 190, 242n. 104
    Jacobite poetry, 50, 56, 57
    on a national language, 103
    poetry, 29, 50–61, 243n. 122, *see also* Jacobite poetry
    print vernacular, importance of, 49–50
    royal tutor, 51
    and standard English, 29
    on universal structure of language, 40–1
Mackenzie, Henry, 156
MacMhuirich family, 37
Macnicol, Donald, 177, 273n. 23
MacPherson, D., 194–5, 277n. 61
MacPherson, James, 18, 53, 134, 164, 195, 242nn. 106, 110, 265n. 49
    whiggism of, 270n. 2
    see also Ossian controversy; Poems of Ossian
Macpherson, John, 190, 193, 272n. 14
Makars, 236n. 44
malapropisms, 127
Malcolme, David, 189–90, 242n. 104, 276n. 55
Manning, Susan, 224n. 1
manuscript, 50, 54, 239n. 73, 241n. 92

market, cultural, 20, 23, 175
Markley, Robert, 240n. 84
Martin, Benjamin, *Lingua Britannica Reformata*, 73
Martin, Martin, 54, 257n. 31
Martz, Louis, 108–9, 256n. 17, 257n. 31
Marx, Karl, 250n. 65, 269n. 87
masculine language, 6, 14, 81, 142, 157
masculinity, 58, 105
Mason, George, 102, 253n. 98
Mayer, Robert, 258n. 36
McClintock, Anne, 225n. 12, 271n. 12
McCracken-Flesher, Caroline, 224n. 1
McCrone, David, 271n. 11
McElroy, Jarvis, 265n. 46
McGuirk, Carol, 267nn. 58, 60
McIntosh, Carey, 247n. 26, 258n. 39, 261nn. 12, 14
McLuhan, Marshall, 64, 244n. 6
Meek, Donald, 37, 48, 236n. 46, 237n. 54, 241n. 92
metaphors, 52
    Johnson on, 73–6, 93, 166, 248n. 45, 268n. 67
    Locke on, 228n. 28
    in national language, 162
middle-class, in England, 98, 105, 199, 202, 278n. 12
Mignola, Walter, 248n. 39
Miller, Karl, 224n. 1
Miller, Thomas, 149–50, 225n. 10, 226n. 15, 260n. 4, 261nn. 13, 14
Mills, Frederick, 234n. 23
mimicry, 3, 4, 40, 56, 57, 150, 178
    in Austen, 216–19
    in catechisms, 57
    colonial, 9, 56
    linguistic, 112
missionaries, in the Highlands, 12, 33–8
missionary societies, 37, 234n. 23, 236n. 46
Mitchell, Hugh, 244n. 11
Mitchison, Rosalind, 230n. 36, 234n. 21
models of language, *see* theories of language
modernity, 189
modernization, 1, 19, 153, 155–6, 175, 185, 186
Monboddo, Lord, 139, 248n. 43
Mooneyham, Laura, 278n. 7
Moreau, Noelle Bisseret, 128
Mother's Catechism, 43
Mugglestone, Lynda, 20, 135, 231n. 47, 251n. 76, 259n. 46, 262n. 23, 272n. 18, 279n. 21
Mukherjee, Meenakshi, 281n. 42
Mullan, John, 263n. 30
multiculturalism, 23, 174, 175, 176, 186, 196
Murphy, Peter, 155, 241n. 90, 270n. 89

Murray, David, 239n. 81
Murray, James, 97, 222
Murray, Laura, 61, 243n. 121
myth of origins, 102–3, 157–71, 195

Nairn, Tom, 19, 32, 169, 201, 230nn. 39, 41, 232n. 55, 234n. 14, 260n. 1, 269n. 86, 278n. 11
Nares, Robert, 132
national culture, 85
　and ancestral heritage, 185
　cross national experience, 204
　gender exclusions, 129
　impact of empire, 46
　legitimizing of, 3
　plurality of, 125
national hierarchy, 97
national identity, 3, 52, 198, 232n. 50, 236n. 49
　and feminized language, 206
　and language, 2–3, 7, 23, 31, 50–1, 141, 144, 148, 152, 201–4, 222
　and print technology, 2, 5, 64, 244n. 6
　Tory-influenced, 117–18
national language, 2, 14, 61, 103, 122, 135
　corrupting influences on, 165–71
　figurative, 72–6
　gendering of, 77–84, 135, 157, 199
　see also language; standard English
nationalism, 3, 4, 5, 24, 25, 66, 94, 128, 129, 137, 185–96, 203, 223, 232n. 52, 281n. 45
　bardic, 54, 55
　Celtic, 232n. 57
　and colonialism, 4–5
　cultural, 24–7, 51, 81, 141, 155, 232n. 57, 244n. 1
　and ideology, 204
　and imperialism, 2–5, 8, 14, 15, 185–6, 190, 194–5, 222–3, 225n. 131
　and language, 4–5, 6, 14–16
　linguistic, 147, 199, 204
　myth, 185, 204
　and native language, 198–9
　and print, 5, 64, 244n. 6
　resistant, 25, 60
　rhetoric of, 88, 134
　spatial imagery, 116–21
　strategies of, 29–30
　and transnationalism, 23
native, 67, 108, 111, 113, 114, 135
Native Americans, *see* North America
native language, 6, 10, 18, 22, 71, 88, 89, 90, 94, 102, 144, 147–8, 220, 221
natural language, 14, 22, 24, 141, 152, 163, 206, 210
natural law, 245n. 9

nature, 219–20
　and culture, 142, 262n. 19
　Enlightenment's view of, 77
　and Scottish writing, 142, 261n. 11
Nelme, L. D., *An Essay Towards the Investigation of Origin and Elements of Language and Letters*, 164
neoclassical, 179, 184, 274n. 30, 275n. 42
neologisms, 133
new rhetoric, 22, 141
New Royal and Universal English Dictionary (Johnson), 110
new science, 46
New Vocabulary, A, 46
Newman, Gerald, 225n. 11
newspapers, and commerce, 247n. 33
Niranjana, Tejaswini, 46, 49, 239n. 82, 242n. 97
nobody (figure of), 21, 63, 67, 95–7, 99, 133, 203, 204, 206, 222, 244n. 3
North America
　cultural/linguistic differences, 238n. 59
　glossaries, 71
　Native Americans and Scots-Gaelic speakers, 37, 39, 40, 186–7, 236n. 46, 238n. 59, 243n. 121
North Briton, 110, 256n. 23
novels, 104, 105, 116, 122, 129
　educational role, 25, 122, 207, 212
　epistolary, 121–31, 202, 258n. 39
　language in, 199–200
　see also fiction
Noyes, Gertrude, 78, 244n. 7, 247n. 31
Nussbaum, Felicity, 225n. 12, 231n. 49, 256n. 25, 259n. 47

obsolete words, in Johnson's *Dictionary*, 93
Ong, Walter, 238n. 66, 279n. 18
oral language, 59, 104, 106, 113, 126, 127, 130, 134, 159, 161, 183, 274n. 31
　and literacy, 42, 158, 238n. 68, 267n. 63
orality, 1, 6, 72, 127, 159, 160–1, 274n. 31, 279n. 18
oratory, 81, 142, 161
　feminization through, 142, 260n. 3
Orientalists, 190
originary language, 52–3, 152–65, 188, 189, 192–6
　see also myth of origins
Ossian, 23, 53, 134, 177, 178, 184, 195, 242n. 110, 265n. 49, 273nn. 24, 26
Oxford English Dictionary, 9, 10, 14, 97, 181, 222, 251n. 80

Page, Norman, 204, 215, 216, 278n. 7, 281nn. 35, 41

"panoptical time," 194
Parker, Patricia, 81, 82, 84, 249n. 53
parliament, Scottish, 2
Parry, Benita, 232n. 54
particular, 6, 14–16, 38, 63, 84, 85, 92–4, 99, 102, 103, 112, 114, 125, 127, 134, 136, 148, 154, 155, 159, 163, 173, 175, 178, 186, 192, 203, 204, 222, 279n. 16
partitioned subject, 21, 178
past, appeals to, 2, 15, 25–6, 31, 50, 52, 54, 66, 102–3, 157–71, 173, 175, 185–96, 222, 242n. 104, 244n. 21, 271n. 5
paternalism, and feudalism, 203
Paxman, David, 226n. 24, 249n. 60, 271n. 6
pedagogy, 10, 13, 26, 33–44, 51, 64, 97–8, 130, 140, 176, 194, 197, 198, 212, 215–16, 219, 221
  linguistic, 130, 239n. 83
  national, 13–14
Pennant, Thomas, *A Tour in Scotland MDCCLXIX*, 174
Perfed, William, 66
performance, 21, 30, 34, 129, 152, 215–19, 265n. 47, 281n. 36
periphery, 3, 4, 7, 17, 18, 19, 20, 22, 24, 32, 53, 106, 107, 115–22, 125–7, 133–4, 137, 141, 152, 178, 205, 212, 220, 234n. 15, 271n. 12
  writers of, 220, 222
personal pronouns, in Gaelic, 184
Peyton, V. J., 168–9, 269n. 85
Phillips, Edward, 247n. 35
Phillips, K. C., 280n. 26
Phillipson, N. T., 230n. 36, 234n. 21, 260n. 1
philology, 10, 23, 71, 85, 176, 186, 188, 189, 192–6, 222, 227n. 23, 272n. 19, 273n. 28
philosophic words, 72
Piggot, Stuart, 187, 276n. 48
Pinkerton, John, 165, 268n. 68, 269n. 74
Pittock, Murray, 29, 31, 55, 60, 226n. 17, 233n. 6, 243n. 120
plaid, wearing made illegal, 52
plain style, 12, 16, 46, 123, 151, 152, 162, 163, 201, 202, 207, 212, 213, 216, 221, 240n. 85
  see also language, plain
Pocock, J. G. A., 249n. 61
polite language, *see* language: polite
polyglot dictionaries, 68
Poovey, Mary, 205, 279n. 16, 281n. 34
Pope, Alexander, 71, 184
pornography, eighteenth-century, 127
Porter, Roy, 262n. 17
Port-Royal Grammar, 10
postal network, in Britain, 122, 258n. 38
Potkay, Adam, 142, 149, 162, 232n. 51, 261n. 14, 265n. 42, 268n. 70

Poussa, Patricia, 250n. 68
Pratt, Mary Louise, 19, 31, 57, 128, 221, 231n. 46, 233n. 10, 259n. 49
Preston, Thomas, 131, 259n. 55
Prickett, Stephen, 254n. 102
Pride and Prejudice, see Austen
primitive signification, 72–6
primitivism, 153–4, 156
print, 3, 5, 16, 21, 22, 64, 93, 145, 149, 154, 166, 225n. 13
  and national consciousness, 2, 5, 64, 244n. 6
print culture, 48, 58, 105–15, 154
print and Scots Gaelic identity, 41, 47–9
print technology, as standardizing factor, 2, 64, 123
printed language
  Anglo-British imposition of, 42
  authoritative, 71
  as commodity, 166
  distinct from popular, 93–4
  intranational simultaneity, 145
  Lowland Scots role in standardizing, 5, 105, 206
  see also writing
private sphere, 5, 58–9, 60, 62, 67, 94, 140, 151–2, 161, 201–3, 211
prose, Gaelic, 48
Protestant succession, 234n. 15
Protestantism, 32, 33, 41, 42, 44, 235n. 29
public sphere, 58, 139–40, 152, 225n. 9, 252n. 88, 264n. 41
Pudendorf, Samuel von Freiherr, David, 277n. 2

Quintilian, 81, 143, 262n. 21
quotations, in Johnson's *Dictionary*, 76

Ramsay, Allan, 255n. 9, 265n. 46
Ray, John, *Collection of English Words not Generally Used*, 92, 251n. 75
readerships, 48, 76, 97–8, 106, 107, 221
reading, reformatory powers of, 42, 207, 279n. 23
Reddick, Alan, 90, 244nn. 4, 7
Reed, Joel, 248n. 39
region, 5, 18, 19, 20, 48, 63, 66, 84, 100, 106, 135, *see also* local
regional differences, in English, 66
Reid, Thomas, 145
Reinert, Thomas, 251n. 81, 252n. 83
relativism, linguistic and cultural, 25, 179, 183, 195, 199, 270n. 4, 275n. 41
Renaissance, dictionaries in, 68
Renan, Ernest, 88, 250n. 67

Index

resistance, 3, 5, 17, 21, 24, 25, 27, 30, 31, 32, 35–6, 37, 51–62, 99–103, 114, 128, 194, 196, 198, 205, 230n. 41, 252n. 92, 253nn. 99, 100
Resurrection of the Ancient Scottish Language, The (MacDonald), 4, 29, 52–3, 59
rhetoric
 aristocracy and, 202
 Augustan tradition, 216
 classical, 145, 202
 new, 141
 Smith and Blair's lectures on, 143–52
 studies, 22
Richards, Shaun, 238n. 59
Richardson, Charles, 254n. 103
Richardson, Samuel, 199
Richetti, John, 254n. 4, 259n. 47
Robertson, John, 268n. 71
Robertson, William, 38, 139, 236n. 48
Romanticism, 179, 263n. 26, 265n. 50, 267n. 63, 274n. 30
Rosenblum, Michael, 108–9, 254n. 4, 256n. 16, 259n. 47
Ross, Christina, 252n. 86
Ross, Ian, 235n. 36, 264n. 39
Ross, Marlon, 269n. 87
Rothstein, Eric, 256n. 20
Rousseau, Jean-Jacques, 159, 160, 266n. 51, 269n. 75
Royal Society, 46

Said, Edward, 71, 190, 205, 226n. 23, 236n. 49, 248n. 38, 272n. 19
Sales, Roger, 207, 277n. 2
Salvaggio, Ruth, 77, 248n. 47, 249n. 48
Saxon language roots, 91, 102, 191
scatological language, 22, 126–7
Schellenberg, Betty, 116, 257n. 30
Scherwatzky, Steven, 248n. 40
schizophrenia, cultural, 4, 5, 6, 55–6
 see also, doubledness, identity
Schmitt, Cannon, 258n. 42
schools, 13–14, 32–49, 98, 252n. 89
Schultz, Karla, 280n. 30
Schwarzschild, Edward, 257n. 35
science, new, 46
scientists, in Enlightenment, 78
Scotland
 Church of, 58–9
 Lowlands not colonial space, 3
 English as native tongue, 148
 epistolary tour of, 117
 home rule in, 2
 legal/political past, 188–9
 national character, 156

Scoto-phobia, 3–4, 102, 105, 108, 136
Scots Gaelic, 6, 18
 Bible, 48
 changes in eighteenth century, 43–9, 134
 and culture, 2, 18, 195
 differences from Irish, 180
 equated with ignorance and barbarism, 29, 234n. 24
 gendered, 59, 173
 grammar, 172–96
 Johnson's opinion of, 90–1, 248n. 41, 251n. 73
 learning, 241n. 90
 nonsensical attributions, 100
 oral, 179–80, 183
 peripheral dialect, 104, 116
 revaluation of, 154–5, 172–96
 varieties of, 2
 vernacular, 48, 49–50
 and Welsh, 134, 135
 women poets, 199
 see also Gaelic
Scots language, 2, 6, 90–3, 147, 154, 155, 161, 168, 197, 264n. 36, 271n. 5
 Robert Fergusson's, 99
 and Johnson, 90–3
 polyvocal nature of, 134
 see also Gaelic; Scots Gaelic
Scots Magazine, 138–9
Scots nationalism, 29–31, 61, 99, 169, 188–9, 222
Scott, Walter, 13, 255n. 12
Scotticisms, 90–3, 96, 97, 108, 124, 126, 155, 172, 245n. 11, 251n. 73, 269n. 81, 271n. 5
Scottish accents, 1, 106, 108, 113, 115, 132, 138–9
Scottish Enlightenment, 38, 188, 206, 236n. 46
Scottish parliament, 2
 disbanding of, 33–4
scripture, teaching of, 43, 47–8, 176, 187, 188
Sekora, John, 118, 257n. 33
Select Society for promoting the Reading and Speaking of the English language in Scotland, 139
Sense and Sensibility, see Austen
sentiment, 5, 114, 123, 140, 147, 150, 155, 164, 187, 188, 191, 209, 214, 216, 219, 220, 221, 222, 280n. 30
 theories of, 222n. 30, 225n. 43, 263n. 30
sexuality, female, 127
Shaftesbury, Earl of, 148
Shakespeare, William
 Johnson and, 94–5, 98, 132, 245n. 12, 259n. 56

Shaw, William, 23, 172, 177, 178, *182*, 270n. 1, 271n. 5, 273n. 21
   and British nostalgia, 186
   and Celtomania, 5, 23, 173–4
   English assimilation, 18
   Johnson affiliation, 173, 177–9, 180, 273nn. 26, 27
   language of equivalence use, 181, 183
   on oral Gaelic, 5, 10, 16, 23
   on Ossian poems, 177, 178
Shell, Marc, 240n. 87
Sher, Richard, 179, 273nn. 22, 27
Sherbo, Arthur, 246n. 23, 252n. 91, 254n. 3
Sheridan, Thomas, 138–9, 142, 146, 163, 260n. 3, 262n. 18, 263n. 27
Shields, David, 260n. 6
Short Introduction to English Grammar (Lowth), 64
Siebert, Donald T., 244n. 7
Simpson, David, 278n. 11
Simpson, Kenneth, 224n. 7, 232n. 50, 254n. 4, 266n. 53
Sims, John, 253n. 97
Sinclair, Sir John, 270n. 3
Siskin, Clifford, 228n. 29, 260n. 3
slang, *see* cant
Sledd, James H., 244n. 7, 253n. 100
Smith, Adam, 5, 22, 88, 139, 143–71, 250n. 64, 254n. 102, 261n. 9, 262n. 20, 269n. 83
   impartial spectator, 218–19
   moral philosophy, 150
   and polite language, 5, 140, 143–6, 157, 201
   on translation, 167–8
   Wealth of Nations, 166–7, 170
Smith, Anthony, 25
Smith, G. Gregory, 224nn. 1, 7
Smith, John, 187, 190, 276n. 51
Smith, Olivia, 84, 229n. 36, 236n. 49, 247n. 29, 252n. 85
Smollett, Tobias, 3–4, 21–2, 104–37, 255n. 7
   Anglo-British identity, 104–7, 254n. 1
   and the British Academy movement, 108
   critical traditions, 110–11
   cultural authority, 109, 117
   hybridized English, 136–7
   Jacobite sympathies, 113–14, 255n. 12, 257n. 28
   and Johnson, 108–9
   linguistic model, 116–31
   on luxury, 118
   politics, 257n. 28
   representations of women in novels, 105, 126–30
   Scottish identity of, 111, 115, 257n. 31
   and standard English, 105–10, 122–7, 232n. 50

Smout, T. C., 234n. 16, 238n. 63
Snyder, Edward, 175, 272n. 13
sociability, 138–51, 187, 201
Society for Propagating Christian Knowledge, 98, 130
Society in Scotland for the Propagation of Christian Knowledge, 20–1
   caricatures of Highlanders, 38
   Enlightenment vision of, 36, 39, 41
   failure, 234n. 20
   formation of, 33
   and gender roles, 58–9
   industrial schools, 39
   literacy instruction, 42–3
   as missionary society, 37, 234n. 23
   resistance to, 36
   role in emigration, 62
   teaching of scripture, 187, 188
Sorensen, Knud, 216, 281n. 35
Southam, B. C., 280nn. 24, 26
Spanish vernacular grammars, 248n. 39
space
   representations of, 63, 95, 102, 115–23, 172, 173, 197, 201
   transcending of, 11, 12, 15, 16, 20, 41, 42, 64, 66, 72, 86–7, 116, 126, 134, 159–60, 176, 178, 194, 203, 204, 220, 276n. 46
spatial differences, 16–18, 22, 102
SPCK, *see* Society for Propagating Christian Knowledge
Spectator, The, 84, 102, 151
Spector, Robert, 108, 255n. 13
Spivak, Gayatri, 238n. 66
Sprat, Thomas, 46, 240n. 84
Spurr, David, 236n. 49
SSPCK, *see* Society in Scotland for the Propagation of Christian Knowledge
stadial history, 39, 153, 236n. 46, 265n. 49
standard English, 3–5, 19–20, 22, 29, 63–5, 88, 108, 128, 133–4, 154, 198, 222, 247n. 27
   accentless, 128
   aestheticized, 149, 162
   beautiful elements, lack of, 163
   and commerce, 169
   elimination of Scots terms, 108
   hybrid, 136–7
   identity of language, 17
   and MacDonald, 29
   naturalness of Lowlanders, 141
   and Smollett, 105–10, 122–7, 232n. 50
   and spatial hierarchies, 115
   and universal grammar, 222
   see also imperialism; language
standardization, linguistic, 32, 45–9, 108
standardized Gaelic, 31, 32, 47–9

Starnes, Dewitt, 78, 244n. 7, 247n. 31
State, 5, 19, 34, 37, 59, 64, 81, 185, 188, 194, 221, 234n. 21
  and language, 64, 67, 84–7
Stein, Peter, 244n. 9
Steiner, George, 211, 221, 242n. 97, 278n. 7
Sterne, Laurence, 184
Stevenson, Robert Louis, 1, 6, 56–7, 224n. 2, 226n. 14, 243nn. 115, 116
Stewart, Maaja, 279n. 16
Stewart, Susan, 88, 184, 250n. 65, 254n. 104
Stillman, Robert E., 226n. 22
Stokes, Myra, 203, 206, 208, 279n. 19
Stone, Lawrence and Jean Fawtier, 278n. 12
strategic essentialism, 243n. 124, 278n. 3
Strauss, Dietrich, 266n. 55
Street, Brian, 44, 239n. 80
Struever, Nancy, 147, 263n. 33, 264n. 40, 278n. 13
Strunk, William Jr., 25, 232n. 56
Stuart, Charles Edward (The Young Pretender), 50, 51
Stuart, John, *see* Bute, 3rd Earl of
Stuart, John (son of James), 241n. 91
Stuart, Sir James, 47, 48, 236n. 46
style, concept of, 202–3
sublime, 142, 146, 173
sublime language, 143, 157, 162, 163
Suleri, Sara, 32, 234n. 13
Summers, David, 149, 264n. 35
Sussman, Charlotte, 119, 254n. 4
Sutherland, Kathryn, 262n. 25
Swift, Jonathan, 66, 71, 246n. 22

Table Alphabeticall, A (Cawdrey), 69, *70*
taste, 4, 109, 112, 132, 137, 141, 150, 151, 263n. 26
Tatler, The, 151
"Tears of Scotland, The" (Smollett), 113–14
Temple, Kathryn, 274n. 31
theories of language 5, 10–14, 21, 22, 23, 24, 64, 65, 84, 140, 142, 146–8, 163, 197, 222, 229nn. 33–35, 240nn. 84, 86, 245n. 13, 254n. 101, 267nn. 62, 63, 273nn. 28, 29
  and colonialism and imperialism, 11, 14, 15, 16, 32, 46–7, 66, 68–71, 88, 167, 179–83, 187–88, 222, 239n. 83, 245n. 13, 254n. 104
  national 2, 15, 16, 64–6, 80–7, 106, 122, 142, 145–8, 183, 187–8, 194, 197, 222, 275n. 41
  and translation 47, 167, 169, 239n. 82
  and transnationalism, 16, 33
  see also universal grammar
Thom, Martin, 250n. 67, 265n. 50
Thomsen, Inger Sigrun, 280n. 32, 281n. 35
Thomson, Derick, 29, 31, 55, 233nn. 3, 6, 236n. 45, 239n. 73, 242nn. 112, 113
time
  transcending of, 11, 12, 15, 16, 41, 42, 64, 66, 72, 86–7, 88, 126, 134, 159–60, 172, 187, 194, 203–4, 220, 281n. 45
  see also past
Tooke, John Horne, 102, 164, 253n. 97, 254nn. 102, 103
Tour Thro' the Whole Island of Great Britain (Defoe), 117, 118
tourism, 115–22
  domestic, 207
  of the Highlands, 174
trade
  free, 168
  and national integration, 117
  see also commerce
transcoding, 27, 30–1, 49, 221
transformational grammar, 223
translation, 10, 12, 23, 28, 29, 30, 32, 40, 44–9, 57–8, 65, 66, 68–72, 82, 86, 90, 95, 101, 106, 108, 112, 133, 165, 170, 183–4, 191–6, 211, 223, 224n. 6, 270n. 89, 275n. 32
  ballad, 175
  metaphorics of, 58
  New Testament, 47
  Ossian poems, 178
  Smith on, 167–8
  and Smollet, 105
translation model, 211, 212, 239n. 82
transliteration, 44, 47
transnationalism, 16, 19, 20, 23, 26, 27, 47, 49, 147–8, 175, 195
transvestism, narrative, 57–8, 198, 242n. 97
travel, 115–22, 174
Trevor-Roper, Hugh, 230n. 40
Trumpener, Katie, 26, 53, 175, 225n. 12, 232n. 57, 242n. 105, 253nn. 92, 95, 272nn. 16, 20
Tytler, H. W., 101

uncanny, 40, 211
Underwood, Gary, 132
universal, 5, 6, 10–12, 15, 16, 20, 23, 26, 40, 41, 47, 53, 60, 64, 103, 128, 147, 148, 149, 154, 173, 176, 179–81, 186, 195, 222, 233n. 89, 270n. 4, 271n. 6, 274n. 29
universal grammar, 7–13, 15, 23, 65, 80, 179, 185, 192, 223, 227nn. 22, 23, 24, 245n. 11, 273n. 29
universal history, 153, 265n. 49
universal reason, 81
universalization, 38, 39, 48, 107, 184, 192
usage, 67, 81, 82–7

Varney, Andrew, 256n. 20

ventriloquism, 215–16
vernacular, English, 6, 16, 22, 63, 64, 66, 71, 99, 100, 202, 228n. 30
  Scots, 99, 154–6
  Scots Galic, 48, 49–50
  see also dialects
verisimilar fiction, 96
Vickers, Brian, 240n. 84
Vinerian lectures, 86, 87
Visawanathan, Gauri, 224n. 6, 237n. 54, 239n. 80
voice, 113–15, 136
Volosinov, V. N., 8, 10, 69, 71, 247n. 36
vulgar/vulgarisms, 13, 84, 92, 93, 94, 97, 119, 127, 150, 166, 201, 214

Wales, 2, 42, 224n. 6, 226n. 14
Wallace, Robert, 36, 236n. 41
Wallerstein, Immanuel, 17
Warburton, William, 77
Warner, Michael, 225n. 13
Warton, Thomas, 101, 246n. 24
Watson, George, 276n. 45
Wechselblatt, Martin, 67, 87, 244n. 7, 245n. 14, 248n. 40, 249n. 62
Weinbrot, Howard, 174, 244n. 7, 271n. 9, 276n. 54
Welsh, 132–5
Whig history, 226n. 17
Whiggism, *see* Celtic Whigs
White, Allon, 85, 249n. 56, 252n. 87
White, E. B., 232n. 56
  The Elements of Style, 25
White, Hayden, 236n. 49
Whorf, Benjamin Lee, 275n. 41
Wilkes, John, 110
Williams, Nick, 258n. 45
Williams, Raymond, 71, 247nn. 27, 37, 252n. 85, 277n. 2
Willinsky, John, 97, 251n. 80
Willison, Jo, 42, 239n. 72
Wilson, Kathleen, 130, 225n. 12, 230n. 41, 247n. 30, 259n. 52
Wimsatt, W. K., 72, 248n. 42, 251n. 77
Withers, Philip, 121, 239n. 75, 258n. 37
Withrington, D. J., 35, 235n. 30
Womack, Peter, 38, 229n. 32, 230n. 38, 236n. 47, 237n. 51, 271n. 8, 272n. 17, 276n. 47
women
  alienation from legitimate language, 206
  bourgeois, 204, 205, 206, 212
  and cant, 206–7
  cultural prerogatives of, 80–2
  doubled position of, 205, 206
  and gender exclusions, 129
  and gossip, in Austen's novels, 203
  and grotesque language, in Smollett, 127
  as guardians of proper language, 80–1, 205–6, 267n. 61, 279n. 21
  as linguistic outsiders, 126, 133
  mistake-ridden language, 127–30
  and national vernacular, 202
  poets, 199
  and polite language, 199, 260n. 3
  position resembles Scots, 205, 206
  and public sphere, 199
  readers, 13, 97, 207, 282n. 46
  speakers, 127
  uneducated, use of language, 109, 127, 135, 206
  as unpersons after marriage, 206
  writers, 199, 205, 215
Wood, Ellen Meiksin, 227n. 24, 278n. 11
word, alien, 69, 71
word lists, *see* glossaries
words
  in glossary 44–9
  and ideas, 146
  native *vs.* foreign, 144–5
Works of the Caledonian Bards (Clark), 23, 187, 190–1
Wright, Patrick, 185, 188, 275n. 43
writing *vs.* speech, 66, 160, 179–80

Yadav, Alok, 24, 232n. 54, 234n. 24, 243n. 124, 250nn. 68, 70
Young, Robert, 191, 226n. 23, 243n. 115, 272n. 18, 277n. 18, 277n. 57
Young Pretender, The, 50, 51
Youngson, A. J., 231n. 44, 272n. 17

Zemka, Sue, 41, 224n. 6, 238n. 64, 239n. 71, 240n. 85
Zenzinger, Peter, 255n. 9, 266n. 56